Selected Plays

A Note on the Translations

This collection includes a new translation of *The Dance of Death* (I). All other translations have previously appeared as follows:

August Strindberg, *The Ghost Sonata* and *The Pelican*, in *The Chamber Plays*, trans. Evert Sprinchorn (New York: E. P. Dutton, 1962); paperback 2d revised edition (Minneapolis: University of Minnesota Press, 1981).

August Strindberg, *To Damascus* (I) and *Crimes and Crimes*, trans. Evert Sprinchorn, in *The Genius of the Scandinavian Theater* (New York: The New American Library, 1964).

A Note on Stage Directions

The stage directions in these translations follow the nineteenth-century Scandinavian custom of indicating left and right from the point of view of the audience, not the actor.

Selected Plays

VOLUME 2
The Post-Inferno Period

August Strindberg

Translated and Introduced by Evert Sprinchorn

University of Minnesota Press □ Minneapolis

Copyright © 1986 by the University of Minnesota
All rights reserved. No part of this publication may be reproduced, stored in a retrieval system, or transmitted, in any form or by any means, electronic, mechanical, photocopying, recording, or otherwise, without the prior written permission of the publisher.

Published by the University of Minnesota Press
2037 University Avenue Southeast, Minneapolis MN 55414.
Published simultaneously in Canada
by Fitzhenry & Whiteside Limited, Markham.
Printed in the United States of America.

All rights whatsoever in these plays are strictly reserved. Inquiries about performances or readings should be directed to Samuel French, 25 West 45th Street, New York, NY, 10036.

Library of Congress Cataloging-in-Publication Data

Strindberg, August, 1849-1912.
  Selected plays.

  Contents: v. 1. The pre-Inferno period—v. 2. The post-Inferno period.
  1. Strindberg, August, 1849-1912—Translations, English. I. Sprinchorn, Evert. II. Title.
  PT9811.A3S635 1986   839.7'26   85-30224
  ISBN 0-8166-1339-7 (pbk. : v. 2)
  ISBN 0-8166-1338-9 (pbk. : v. 1)

The University of Minnesota
is an equal-opportunity
educator and employer.

> With two actors I could create a little world; and with three, move it.
>
> August Strindberg

Contents

To Damascus (I)	381
Crimes and Crimes	481
The Dance of Death (I)	559
A Dream Play	641
The Ghost Sonata	733
The Pelican	785
Strindberg's Plays	835
Selected Readings	839

Plays contained in Volume I: *Master Olof, The Father, Miss Julie, Creditors, The Stronger,* and *Playing with Fire.*

Introduction to *To Damascus*

Much of the best work that Strindberg produced from 1886 to 1892 was part of what he called an "artistic-psychological" series (letter of 22 December 1887), in which he hoped to furnish "clues to the pathology of the soul" obtained by means of "all the resources of modern psychology." (*A Madman's Defense*, 1887-88.) Although he consulted medical books, scientific tomes, and learned journals, his chief source for these clues was his own life, especially married life. The psychological battle of brains that fascinated him was more often than not the battle of the sexes. When his first marriage came to an end, so did the artistic-psychological series. *Playing with Fire* and its companion piece, *The Bond*, both written in 1892, concluded the series by connecting its origin with its termination. Whereas the first play harks back to the time when he initially met the woman who was to become his wife, *The Bond* depicts the bitter and painful legal battles that took place at the time of their divorce.

In 1892, separated from his wife and children, and slighted by Swedish publishers and theater producers, Strindberg left his native country to begin a new life and another career. For the next five years he lived the life of a drifter, obeying the whim of the moment, yielding to impulse, moving erratically from Germany to Austria to France, changing his mailing address more often than the season changed, and living almost entirely off the generosity of friends and supporters. In 1893 he married an Austrian journalist, much younger than himself, but that union lasted only a few years.

He wrote no plays during this period. All his creative energies went into scientific pursuits and painting. Instead of continuing his studies in psychology, he investigated the physical world. He performed countless experiments in his makeshift, portable laboratory, attempting to demonstrate that the so-called chemical elements were not elemental and that the atom was not the basic building block of the physical universe. Flying in the face of orthodox scientific thinking, he dreamed of achieving a transmutation of the elements, that old alchemical dream. The experiments failed of course, the only tangible result being damage to his hands for which he had to be treated at a hospital in Paris. Ironically, his stay in the hospital occurred just when he was gaining some fame among Parisian intellectuals as a dramatist and essayist.

His lack of success in the laboratory did not deter him from formulating a new conception of the cosmos, radically different from the one he had entertained in the 1880s when he had proclaimed himself a Darwinist, a naturalist, and an atheist. Then life had appeared to him as a struggle for survival, a brutish struggle, even if brains had replaced brawn, with no other purpose than the improvement of the species. In his naturalistic plays he had made it clear that Darwinian evolution, scientific determinism, and moral indifference were inseparable from one another. In *Creditors*, Tekla's polyandrous nature was no more to be condemned than Gustav's thirst for revenge.

Nevertheless, an ethical question kept asserting itself. In his preface to *Miss Julie* he had written that "the naturalists have banished guilt along with God, but the consequences of an act — punishment, imprisonment, or the fear of it — cannot be banished." The idea of punishment, the need to adjust the punishment to the crime, seemed to introduce a moral element into the naturalistic scheme. Moreover, Strindberg could never quite subjugate the religious yearnings that had been inculcated on him when he was a child. Even as an atheist, he had a nostalgia for God. "I sometimes wish I still had God and heaven with me," he wrote in 1886 (letter to Frölander, 18 February).

When his travels during those years of apparent drifting are charted, they can be seen as leading to a definite goal. He had embarked on a journey to find what had been lost in the atheistic eighties. His endless treks, his frustrating alchemical research, his experimental painting freed his mind and opened up the unconscious, and there he found what he had been looking for. He might have taken to heart the words of Novalis: "We dream of traveling through the world. But isn't the world within us? We little know the depths of our own minds. The mysterious road goes inwards."

In *The Father*, and in some of his other writings, Strindberg had ventured into the dark continent of the human soul, usually following but sometimes leading the clinical psychologists who were investigating the causes of neurosis and hysteria. In the 1890s he embarked on a solitary expedition that would take him into the interior of the dark continent, guided by dreams, impulses, and free-floating ideas. At almost the same time, Sigmund Freud set out on a similar journey, hoping to reveal those powerful mental processes that are hidden from consciousness.

In *To Damascus*, written in 1898, Strindberg represented his own discoveries in dramatic form by projecting his inner life on the outer, thus giving a shape and form to the intangible unconscious world. His restless wanderings became the physical counterpart of his spiritual struggles. In the course of his journey his whole life had been turned around, and the structure of the play represents this turnabout, the late scenes repeating the early scenes in reverse order. More difficult was the problem of putting onstage the peculiar topography of the unconscious. Strindberg resorted to symbols, colors, literary allusions, myths, legends, and all the resources of the theater. A table and two chairs would not suffice for this new supranaturalistic drama. He needed total theater in which a visual or aural effect could be more suggestive than words. In the second of the seaside scenes, the three unrigged masts of a foundered ship are an obvious reminder of Golgotha. But these crosses bear no thieves and no savior. Their emptiness becomes a vivid symbol of the hero's quest for a moral order that lies beyond Christianity and vicarious atonement. Here the significance of the symbol is obvious and underscored in the accompanying dialogue. Elsewhere the symbol is unexplained, the legend obscure, the allusion personal.

Although the story line of *To Damascus* is extremely simple, the inner action is extraordinarily complex. Everything that happens is seen from the protagonist's point of view as he tries to make sense of what is happening to him inwardly. The first step in this process is the fragmentation of his personality. The opening scene of the play shows this occurring step by step as the hero begins his descent into the unconscious. All the characters he meets have an existence in their social world; but the protagonist gives them specific roles to play that accord with fragments of his personality. The Doctor, for instance, represents the hero's conscience; and The Beggar, the skeptical ego of the artist who lives from hand to mouth.

To objectify the subjective, and to give a sense of the confusion in the hero's mind while simultaneously intimating that in all this confusion there is coherence and meaning, Strindberg used analogies, parallels, and extended metaphors. The hero's journey or pilgrimage provides the basic parallel, serving to remind the viewer of Saul's conversion on the way to Damascus. The hero's descent into his unconscious is also a descent into a hell of anguish and torment; hence the first nine scenes suggest the nine circles of Dante's inferno. At various times in the play the hero is compared to Cain, Lucifer, Jesus, and other figures of legend and myth. In design and form, *To Damascus* is a collage of myths and metaphors, allegories and allusions. Although Strindberg knew of the symbolic techniques employed in medieval religious drama and of its use of correspondences to link the spiritual realm to the physical and heaven to earth, *Damascus* puts all the elements together in an entirely new way, no different in principle from what artists like Picasso and Braque were to do a decade later and what Joyce was to achieve in that intricate construct he called *Ulysses*. Literary critics and historians have been slow to realize the truth of Maurice Valency's 1963 description of *Damascus*: "a quasi-medieval work that was to furnish the blueprint for the most advanced drama of the twentieth century, and perhaps for the Joycean novel as well; . . . astonishing as it may be, such seems to be the case."

It is likely that painters provided the inspiration for some of Strindberg's new literary and dramatic techniques. An innovative painter himself, he was aware of the new directions being taken by the Postimpressionists. He admired the allegorical canvases of Puvis de Chavannes, who was coming back into favor at this time. He was familiar with the paintings of the still virtually unknown Gauguin and closely acquainted with Edvard Munch, who was creating in oils, etchings, and lithographs indelible images of his inner torment. Gauguin had painted symbolic self-portraits in which he depicted himself as Christ in the Garden of Gethsemane and as Adam with halo, apple, and snake. Strindberg transferred to the stage the allegorical quality of Puvis, the ironic allusiveness of Gauguin, and the subjectivism of Munch, along with the conventional and overt symbolism of the Pre-Raphaelite painters. His development from *Miss Julie* to *To Damascus*, from naturalism to what he termed supernaturalism, closely paralleled the path from impressionism to neo-impressionism and symbolism taken by the experimental artists.

Because the subjective aspects of the chief character completely dominate the drama, *To Damascus* is usually seen as a precursor of expressionistic theater (which indeed it is), rather than as a symbolist drama.

Unfortunately, this association with the heaviness, somberness, and unpent emotionalism of expressionistic drama has led to a basic misunderstanding of the play. In spirit, *Damascus* is much closer to Joyce's novel. Like *Ulysses*, Strindberg's play is a kind of comedy. In both novel and play the intellect of the hero-author coolly analyzes what his troubled soul is suffering. The sudden shifts in tone, the unexpected parallels and correspondences, the juxtaposition of old myths and new ideas produce a distancing effect, allowing the readers or viewers to enjoy the cleverness of the author at the same time that they understand the deep emotion lying beneath the glittering surface. Even the resolution is brought about by means of a pun.

Staging *To Damascus*, Part I, as a portentous drama of madness is a common and lamentable mistake. The proper tone for the play is suggested in the first scene when The Stranger remarks that he does not know if he is joking or serious. One of those closest to Strindberg at the time *To Damascus* was written found that the key to the man lay in his peculiar and enigmatic smile, "half skeptical and self-mocking, half resigned and melancholy." Strindberg's humor is much like Hamlet's, and in the long run there is nothing that wears better. What keeps *To Damascus* fresh and satisfying, no matter how often it is read, is that strange Strindbergian mixture of humor and melancholy, of tragic anguish and comic frustration. And if it is not there when the play is staged, something very essential to the spirit of the whole will be lacking.

When it was produced for the first time, in 1900, Strindberg saw to it that the young actress who had enchanted him as Puck in *A Midsummer Night's Dream* was cast as The Lady. He fell in love with her, and she later became his third wife. On the day of the opening of the play, he sent her the following note along with some red roses.

> Dear Miss Harriet Bosse,
> Since I shan't put in an appearance at the theater tonight I want to thank you now for what I saw at the dress rehearsal. It was great and beautiful, although I thought the part should have been given in a lighter tone, with some touches of roguishness, with less reserve and more buoyance.
> A little bit of Puck—that was my first bit of advice to you, and will be my last!
> A smile or two in the midst of misery indicates there is still hope, and after all the situation turns out not to be hopeless.
> Anyway, good luck to you on your journey over the stones and thistles. It's a rough road. I can only strew it with a few flowers.
> August Strindberg

To Damascus

(Till Damaskus)

Part I

CHARACTERS

THE STRANGER
THE LADY
THE BEGGAR
THE DOCTOR
THE SISTER
THE OLD MAN
THE MOTHER
THE ABBESS
THE CONFESSOR
MINOR CHARACTERS and PHANTOMS

SCENES*

ACT I: On the Street Corner
At the Doctor's Home

ACT II: In the Hotel Room
By the Sea
On the Road
In the Ravine
In the Kitchen

ACT III: In the Rose Room
The Asylum
The Rose Room
The Kitchen

ACT IV: In the Ravine
On the Road
By the Sea
In the Hotel Room

ACT V: At the Doctor's Home
The Street Corner

Time: 1898

---

* The act divisions given here were not followed when the play was first staged in 1900 at the Dramatic Theater in Stockholm. Strindberg wanted only one intermission—after the Asylum scene—and no curtains, except to mark the intermission and the end of the play. Grandinson, the director, went along with the idea of a single intermission but shifted it to the end of the first Rose Room scene. And, probably because of difficulties in making some of the scene changes, he also brought the curtain down briefly at the end of the first scene, at the end of the second Kitchen scene, and at the end of the second Hotel Room scene, thus providing a five-act division but different from the one given in the printed version of the play.

ACT I

On the Street Corner

A street corner in a small mid-European town. A bench under a tree. One can see the side portal of a small Gothic church. A post office, and a café with sidewalk tables. The post office and the café are closed.

The sound of a funeral march (Mendelssohn's "Songs without Words," Opus 62, No. 3) is heard drawing nearer and then fading away.

The Stranger is standing at the curb and seems to be wondering which way to go. The clock in a church tower strikes, first four strokes in a high tone, sounding the quarter, then three strokes in a lower tone.

The Lady enters. Greets The Stranger. She starts to go past him, but stops.

THE STRANGER: Ah, there you are. I knew you would come.

THE LADY: Then you did call for me. I might have guessed. I could feel it. —Why are you standing here on the street corner?

THE STRANGER: Have to stand somewhere while I'm waiting.

THE LADY: Waiting for what?

THE STRANGER: If only I knew. For forty years I've been waiting for something. Luck, I believe it's called. Or at least the end of bad luck. —There it comes again. That terrible music! Listen to it. Don't go, please don't go, I beg you. When you leave me, I'm all alone and frightened.

THE LADY: Now just a minute! Yesterday was the first time we met. It's true we talked for four hours—the two of us—and I admit you aroused my sympathy. But you shouldn't take advantage of it like this.

THE STRANGER: It's true, I shouldn't. But I implore you:

don't leave me all alone. I'm in a strange town—without a single true friend. And my few acquaintances are worse than strangers to me—more like enemies, I'd say.

THE LADY: Enemies wherever you go, lonesome all the time. Why on earth did you leave your wife and children?

THE STRANGER: I wish I knew. Above all, I wish I knew why I exist, why I'm standing here, which way I should turn, what I should do. —Do you believe that there are some people damned from the start?

THE LADY: No, I don't believe that.

THE STRANGER: Take a look at me.

THE LADY: Haven't you ever been happy?

THE STRANGER: No. Whatever I thought was happiness turned out to be a mirage to lure me into more misery. And whenever the golden fruit fell into my hands, it turned out to be poisoned or rotten inside.

THE LADY: What's your religion?—if you don't mind my asking.

THE STRANGER: Simple. When things get too tough, I'll go my way.

THE LADY: Go where?

THE STRANGER: Into the great nothingness. The fact that I have—death here within my grasp gives me an absolutely incredible sense of power.

THE LADY: My God! Playing with death!

THE STRANGER: Playing with life, you might say. I was a writer, a creator of fictions. In spite of my congenital melancholy, I have never been able to take anything really seriously, not even my own great sorrows. And there are moments when I doubt that life is any more real than my novels.

> *The funeral procession is heard, the choir chanting "De profundis."* *

---

* Psalm 130.

Here they come again. Why must they go parading around the streets like that?

THE LADY: Is that who you're afraid of?

THE STRANGER: Not afraid; just edgy. Makes me feel things are bewitched. . . . It's not death I'm afraid of, but being alone. In my loneliness I meet someone. I don't know whether it's myself or someone else. All I know is that in the midst of my loneliness I'm not alone. The air thickens, congeals. Certain presences begin to take shape, invisible but tangible, and possessing a life of their own.

THE LADY: How fascinating!

THE STRANGER: Yes. For some time now everything has struck me as remarkable. Before all I saw was objects and movements, forms and colors. Now I see meanings and connections. Life, which was all nonsense before, now begins to make a kind of sense. Where I formerly saw only chance and chaos I now see plan and purpose. —That's why, when I met you yesterday, I straightway got the notion that you were sent here either to save me or destroy me.

THE LADY: Silly! Why should I want to destroy you?

THE STRANGER: We each of us have our purpose in life—that was yours.

THE LADY: I haven't the faintest idea—. Now really, how could I? You know, I've never met a person like you, never in my whole life. Just to look at you makes me want to cry. . . . What's on your conscience? Something that hasn't been found out, something you haven't been punished for?

THE STRANGER: A good question. I'm sure I haven't more sins on my conscience than many who go around carefree and happy. —Oh yes, one: I couldn't abide being made a fool of—by Life, I mean.

THE LADY: It's impossible to live without being deceived or cheated to some extent.

THE STRANGER: Seems to be a law—one that I'd like to get

around. . . . Maybe there's some other secret in my life that I'm not aware of. . . . You know, there's a story in my family that I'm a changeling.

THE LADY: A what?

THE STRANGER: A changeling. A child whom the elves substituted for the human child that was born.

THE LADY: Do you believe that?

THE STRANGER: No, although I must admit it has something to be said for it—as a symbol, you understand. When I was a child, I cried all the time and felt as if I didn't belong anywhere. Hated my parents as much as they hated me. Couldn't stand orders, conventions, laws. I longed for the forest and the sea.

THE LADY: Have you ever had—visions?

THE STRANGER: Never! But I have often sensed that two different spirits were in control of my destiny. The one gives me everything I ask for while the other stands beside him and wipes filth on it, so that when the gift is handed to me, I don't even want to touch it. No, it's really true, I've had all I wished for in life—and have found it all worthless.

THE LADY: You've had everything and you're still not satisfied!

THE STRANGER: That's what I call damnation—God-damnation!

THE LADY: Don't. I don't like you taking the Lord's name in vain. —Why haven't you wished for something beyond this life, far beyond, where the dirt of life doesn't exist?

THE STRANGER: Because I doubted there was anything beyond this existence.

THE LADY: What about the elves?

THE STRANGER: A fairy tale. —Don't you think we might sit down here on the bench?

THE LADY: All right. But first tell me honestly what it is you're waiting for.

THE STRANGER: Honestly, I'm waiting for the post office to open. There's a letter in poste-restante waiting there for me. It's been forwarded and forwarded without catching up to me.

They sit down.

Now what about you? Tell me something about yourself?

The Lady crochets.

THE LADY: There's nothing to tell.

THE STRANGER: It's strange, but I like to think of you as impersonal and nameless. I don't even know your name. I'd like to christen you myself. What shall I call you? . . . I have it! I shall call you Eve. (*Making a gesture to the wings.*) A fanfare, if you please! (*The funeral march is heard.*) Oh, no, not again! That funeral march. —Now let me assign you an age, since I don't know how old you are either. . . . From here on you shall be thirty-four, and consequently born in 1864. —As for your character and disposition, since I don't know that either, I shall endow you with a very kind nature—your voice reminds me so much of my poor dead mother's. By mother I mean of course the abstract conception of mother, pronounced "mom." You see, my mother never fondled me in her lap or dandled me on her knee. I remember only how she whipped me. Reared and raised in hate, I was. Hate! Give as good as you get. Blow for blow! An eye for an eye! You see this scar on my forehead? I got that from an ax swung by my dear brother—whose front tooth I knocked out with a stone. My father threw me out of my sister's wedding—so I didn't bother going to *his* funeral. I was born, as they say, outside the bonds of matrimony, while the family was involved in bankruptcy proceedings and with everybody dressed in mourning after the suicide of my uncle. That's my family! The fruit doesn't fall far from the tree. I figure that altogether I have escaped by the skin of my teeth fourteen years punishment at hard labor and so I have every reason to be grateful to, if not exactly contented with—the elves.

THE LADY: I love to hear you talk, really I do. But please leave the elves out of it. That really bothers me, it really does.

THE STRANGER: Well, I really don't believe in them. However, that doesn't prevent them from cropping up all the time. Aren't elves unblessed souls who have never been redeemed? There you have my case. Bewitched! There was a time when I thought my redemption was at hand. Through a woman. Seventh heaven. What a delusion! It was the beginning of the seventh hell.

THE LADY: How you talk! Perhaps you are a lost soul now, but you don't have to be.

THE STRANGER: You mean peals of church bells and drops of holy water will lull me into peace? . . . I've tried that. It only made matters worse. Made me feel like the devil when he sees the sign of the cross. —Let's talk about you now.

THE LADY: Why bother? . . . Have you ever been accused of wasting your talents?

THE STRANGER: Of course. What haven't I been accused of? No one in my town was hated as much as I was, no one shunned as much. Left the house alone, came back home alone. If I went into a restaurant, everybody moved five yards away from me. When I wanted to rent rooms, they were always taken. Priests denounced me to their congregations, teachers to their classes, and parents to their children. And once the church council tried to take my children from me. That's when I forgot myself and raised my hand against—heaven.

THE LADY: Why did they hate you?

THE STRANGER: Ask them! —Oh, I know. You see I couldn't bear to see people suffer. So I told them to free themselves and promised I would help them. I said to the poor: don't let the rich suck you dry! And to the women: don't let the men oppress you! And I said—and this was the worst—I said to the children: don't obey your parents when they're unjust. The consequences? Utterly incomprehensible. They all ganged up on me—rich *and* poor, men *and* women, parents *and* children. And on top of that came illness and poverty, beggary and dishonor, divorce and lawsuits, exile, loneliness, and now finally—. Do you think I'm mad?

THE LADY: No, I don't think that.

THE STRANGER: You must be the only one. And all the dearer to me for that.

THE LADY (*rising*): Now I really have to leave . . .

THE STRANGER: You too? You see.

THE LADY: But you can't stay here.

THE STRANGER: Where would you suggest I go?

THE LADY: Home to your work.

THE STRANGER: I'm no worker, I'm a writer.

THE LADY: I don't want to hurt your feelings, but you said yourself that writing is a gift. It can be taken back. Don't forfeit it.

THE STRANGER: Where are you going?

THE LADY: On an errand . . .

THE STRANGER: Are you religious?

THE LADY: No, I'm nothing at all.

THE STRANGER: Good! Then you can become something. Oh, how I wish I were your blind old father, whom you would lead about the streets while he sang for pennies. But the unfortunate thing is that I can't grow old. Same way with the elves' children. They don't grow up, they just grow a big head, and they cry and cry. . . . I wish I were somebody's dog. I could follow him around, never be alone. A scrap of food once in a while, a kick now and then, petted once a day, beaten twice—

THE LADY: Now I really have to go. Goodbye.

THE STRANGER (*absentmindedly*): Goodbye. (*He remains sitting on the bench. Takes off his hat and wipes his forehead. Then he begins to draw in the sand with his cane.*)

> *The Beggar enters. Very strange looking. He is grubbing about in the gutter.*

THE STRANGER: What do beggars hope to find in gutters?

THE BEGGAR: Is that any of your business? Besides, I'm not a beggar. Have I begged you for anything?

THE STRANGER: Sorry, I beg your pardon. Appearances can be so deceptive.

THE BEGGAR: I can assure you of that. For instance, can you guess who I am?

THE STRANGER: No, I neither can nor care to. I'm not interested.

THE BEGGAR: One doesn't know that in advance. Interest comes afterward, when it's too late. *Virtus post nummos!**

THE STRANGER: A bum speaking the language of the Romans! What next?

THE BEGGAR: You see! You are interested. *Omne tulit punctum qui miscuit utile dulce.*** My dear sir, you see before you a man who has succeeded in everything he's tried his hand at, for the very good reason that he hasn't ever done anything. I should call myself Polycrates – he of the golden ring. I've had everything I've wanted from life. However, since I never really wanted anything, it was all too easy, and bored by my success, I threw away the ring –. Now that I'm getting on in years, I regret my action and spend my time looking for it in the gutters. And since the search gets to be rather monotonous at times, I am not above picking up – in place of the golden ring, you understand – a few discarded cigar butts.

THE STRANGER: I can't make out whether you're ironic or incoherent.

THE BEGGAR: My problem, too.

THE STRANGER: Now do you know who I am?

---

* *Quaerenda pecunia primum, virtus post nommos.* First seek money; virtue or reputation is secondary.
** He who mixes entertainment with instruction wins complete approval. – Horace.

THE BEGGAR: Haven't the faintest idea. And I'm not interested.

THE STRANGER: Interest usually comes afterward—. How do you like that? You've got me mouthing your words. It's like picking up old butts. Disgusting!

THE BEGGAR (*tipping his hat*): And you wouldn't care to share a butt with me?

THE STRANGER: That scar on your forehead?! —How—?

THE BEGGAR: This? Oh, I got that from a close relative.

THE STRANGER: What are you trying to do? Scare me? Are you real? Let me touch you. (*He feels The Beggar's arm.*) Yes, you are. —Listen, would you be good enough to accept a small gift on condition that you look for Polycrates' ring in some other part of town? (*Hands him a coin.*) *Post nummos virtus.* —There I go again, chewing old—. Get out, get out!

THE BEGGAR: All right, I'm going. I'm going. Good sir! You've given me altogether too much. Here, let me give you back three-fourths of it. Then we can consider it a token of friendship.

THE STRANGER: Friendship! Who said we're friends?

THE BEGGAR: Well, at least I'm yours. And when you're *alone* in this world, you can't be too particular.

THE STRANGER: You're pushing your luck, old boy! Take my advice—Scram!

THE BEGGAR: Thank you, good sir! But the next time we see each other, I'll have some advice for you. See you around. (*Leaves.*)

THE STRANGER (*sits down and writes in the sand with his cane*): Sunday afternoon! Long, dull, gray, quiet Sunday afternoon. The families have eaten their sauerkraut and roast beef with boiled potatoes. The old ones are napping and the young men are playing chess and smoking cigarettes. The servants are off at vespers, and the stores are all closed. God, what a mortally dull afternoon, day of rest, when the soul itself nods off, when there's no more chance of seeing a familiar face than there is of getting a drink—.

The Lady returns. She now has a flower in her bosom.

THE STRANGER: Extraordinary! I can't say two words without having to eat them.

THE LADY: Still sitting here?

THE STRANGER: If I sit here writing in the sand or something else, seems to make no difference—as long as I write in the sand.

THE LADY: What are you writing? Let me see.

THE STRANGER: I believe it says: Eve, 1864. —No, don't step on it.

THE LADY: Why? What will happen?

THE STRANGER: Bad luck, for you—and for me.

THE LADY: You're sure?

THE STRANGER: Positive. Just as certain as I am that the Christmas rose you're wearing on your breast is a mandragora. It stands for evil and slander—as a symbol. As a medicine it is known as the hellebore and was formerly used to cure madness. Will you give it to me?

THE LADY (*hesitating*): As medicine—?

THE STRANGER: —Have you read my books?

THE LADY: You know I have. I can thank you for my independent spirit and my belief in justice and human dignity.

THE STRANGER: Then you haven't read my latest ones.

THE LADY: No. And if they're not like the first ones, I want nothing to do with them.

THE STRANGER: Good! Then you must swear, here and now, never to open another book of mine.

THE LADY: Let me think about it. . . . All right, I swear.

THE STRANGER: Don't forget now. And don't let me catch you breaking your promise. Remember what happened to Bluebeard's wife when curiosity tempted her to open the forbidden room.

THE LADY: You're behaving more and more like Bluebeard yourself. Or haven't you noticed? You're oblivious to the fact that I'm a married woman . . . that my husband is a doctor . . . that he admires your work so much that he would welcome you with open arms . . . if you were to come home with me.

THE STRANGER: I've done my best to forget all that. I've wiped it completely out of mind. It doesn't exist for me.

THE LADY: In that case, how about coming home with me this afternoon?

THE STRANGER: No. How about coming with me?

THE LADY: Where?

THE STRANGER: Out into the big wide world, no place in particular. Haven't got a home—live out of my suitcase. And as for money, I have some now and then, but not very often. It's the one thing that life obstinately refused to give me, perhaps because I haven't wished for it hard enough.

THE LADY: Hmmmm.

THE STRANGER: What are you thinking?

THE LADY: I'm astonished that I'm not insulted by your proposition. Are you joking?

THE STRANGER: Joking or serious, what's the difference? —Listen. . . . The organ's playing. Divine service is over. The bars will soon be open.

THE LADY: I'll bet you drink a lot, don't you?

THE STRANGER: Inordinately! Wine makes my soul shed its skin and soar out into space, to see things nobody ever imagined and hear things never heard before.

THE LADY: What about the morning after?

THE STRANGER: I suffer the exquisite pangs of conscience. All my tensions are relieved by feelings of guilt and remorse. I revel in my body's pain while my soul floats like a cloud around my head. It's like being suspended between life and death, when the soul tries out its wings and could fly away if it wanted to.

THE LADY: Come into the church with me. Only for a moment. No sermons, I promise you, only the beautiful music of vespers.

THE STRANGER: No, not into the church. Depresses me. Reminds me that I don't belong there, that I'm a lost soul, with about as much chance of getting in as I have of becoming a child again. And that happens only when you're in your dotage – or out of your mind.

THE LADY: You've already found that out, have you?

THE STRANGER: Oh, I've come a long ways. I can see myself lying chopped up in Medea's kettle, slowly boiling and bubbling away. Either I end up in the soap factory, or else I rise up rejuvenated from my own juices. It all depends on Medea's skill.

THE LADY: That sounds oracular. Shall we see if you can become a child again?

THE STRANGER: That would mean beginning at the cradle – and with the right one in it!

THE LADY: Exactly. –Now you wait for me right here while I go into St. Elizabeth's chapel. I'm glad the café isn't open. If it were, I'd beg you, "Please, pretty please, don't drink."

> She leaves. The Stranger sits down again and writes in the sand. Six Pallbearers and some Mourners enter, dressed in brown. One of the Pallbearers is carrying a flag with the insignia of the carpenters' union on it, decorated with brown crepe. Another is carrying a huge broadax decorated with spruce branches. A third, a small cushion with a judge's gavel on it. They stop in front of the café and wait.

THE STRANGER: Excuse me, whose funeral? (*Pointing to the ax.*) A lumberjack?

FIRST PALLBEARER (*points to the flag*): Close. A carpenter. (*He makes a sawing sound.*)

THE STRANGER (*imitates the sound*): A real carpenter or the insect?

SECOND PALLBEARER: The kind that bores into wood. (*He makes a ticking sound.*)

THE STRANGER: That's a beetle.

SECOND PALLBEARER: Yes. What do you call it?

THE STRANGER (*to himself*): Death-watch beetle. I won't say it. (*To the Second Pallbearer.*) Goldsmith beetle. Right?

SECOND PALLBEARER: No. The kind that bores into walls and sits there ticking when somebody's about to die. (*A ticking is heard, coming from nowhere.*)

THE STRANGER: What the hell's going on? Trying to scare me? Are the dead performing miracles? Won't work. I don't scare easily, and I don't believe in miracles. —All the same, I do find it eerie that you mourners are dressed in brown. Why not black, which is inexpensive, practical, and appropriate?

THIRD PALLBEARER: We are in black. So it seems to our simple minds. But if you, good sir, would have it brown, then so be it.

THE STRANGER: I find you all very peculiar, and that's a fact. I trust that my disquiet is part of my hangover. That Moselle wine! —Sir, that stuff on the ax—it looks like—. What is it?

FIRST PALLBEARER: The vine of the grape.

THE STRANGER: The grape, of course! I knew it couldn't be spruce. Looks exactly like spruce. —Ah, thank heavens, they're opening the bar! About time.

> *The Café Proprietor comes out to take orders. The Pallbearers and The Stranger sit down. During the following dialogue they give their orders and are served. The Stranger orders Moselle wine, and a bottle is brought to his table.*

THE STRANGER: He must have been a merry old soul, the man you buried. Here you are getting drunk immediately after the sobering occasion.

FIRST PALLBEARER: A good-for-nothing. Refused to take life seriously.

THE STRANGER: And probably drank too much?

SECOND PALLBEARER: Afraid so.

THIRD PALLBEARER: Didn't mind letting others care for his wife and children. A real bum.

THE STRANGER: Not very considerate of him, I'm sure. No doubt that accounts for the beautiful and moving funeral oration. —I say, would you mind not leaning on my table? You're spilling the wine.

FIRST PALLBEARER: Listen, mister, I paid just as much to drink here as you.

THE STRANGER: There is still a big difference between you and me.

The Pallbearers murmur ominously.

The Beggar enters.

THE STRANGER: Him again! Now he's cadging drinks.

THE BEGGAR (*sits down and strikes the table with his fist*): Waiter!

The Proprietor comes out. Looks disdainfully at The Beggar.

THE BEGGAR: Bottle of wine. Moselle.

The Proprietor goes into the café and comes out with a poster in his hand.

PROPRIETOR: I'm sorry but I'll have to ask you to leave. I can't serve you. You're wanted by the revenue service. For income tax evasion. Here's the wanted list—your name, age, and description.

THE BEGGAR: *Omnia serviliter pro dominatione.** I'm a man of

---

* "He played in every way the slave to secure the master's place." A reference to Otho's currying favor with the Roman soldiers in hope of becoming emperor. Tacitus, *Histories* I, 36.

independent means, with a Ph.D. I don't believe in paying taxes to a government I don't believe in. Now—if you don't mind—a bottle of Moselle!

THE PROPRIETOR: Moselle! That's very funny. You want something for nothing? You'll get a free ride to the police station and the workhouse.

THE STRANGER: Couldn't you settle this somewhere else? You're disturbing your customers.

THE PROPRIETOR: We'll settle this in a minute. And you can be a witness that I'm handling this fair and square.

THE STRANGER: I find this whole business extremely painful. Just because a man doesn't pay his taxes—(*Coughs self-consciously.*) —doesn't mean he hasn't a right to some of life's small pleasures.

THE PROPRIETOR: Listen to him! Friend of panhandlers and deadbeats! I got you pegged.

THE STRANGER: Now just a minute! I happen to be a respected and well-known—

The Proprietor and the Pallbearers laugh.

THE PROPRIETOR: Suspected, more likely!

More laughter.

Wait—wait. . . . This description—thirty-eight years old, brown hair, moustache, blue eyes—no occupation—no known source of income—married but has deserted his wife and abandoned his children—known for his subversive political views— gives the impression of not being in full possession of his faculties. —Well, I'll be—

THE STRANGER (*stands up, overwhelmed, his face ashen*): What's going on? What is this?

THE PROPRIETOR: Damned if it doesn't check out point for point.

THE BEGGAR: Could it be him and not me?

THE PROPRIETOR: Sure looks like it. That makes you two of a kind in my book, and you can trot out of here arm in arm.

THE BEGGAR (*to The Stranger*): Come on. We better move along.

THE STRANGER: We?! This is a frame-up!

> *The church bells begin to ring. The sun comes out and lights up the stained-glass rose window over the portal, which now opens to reveal the interior of the church. An organ is heard and a choir singing "Ave Maris Stella."*

THE LADY (*emerging from the church*): Where are you? What's the matter? Why did you call for me again? You're like a child on apron strings.

THE STRANGER: I'm scared, don't you see? Something's happening that I can't explain—something unnatural.

THE LADY: I thought you said you weren't afraid of anything, not even death.

THE STRANGER: I'm not—not of death—but this other thing—the unknown . . .

THE LADY: All right. There, there. Give me your hand like a good boy. You're sick. I'll take you to the doctor. My doctor. Come!

THE STRANGER: I just might take you up on that. —Tell me, is this carnival time or are they always dressed like that?

THE LADY: I don't see anything strange.

THE STRANGER: But that beggar—he's disgusting! Do I really look like him?

THE LADY: You will if you go on drinking. —Now you go in and pick up your letter at the post office, and then come on home with me.

THE STRANGER: No, no post office for me. Anyway there'll be nothing but court orders and legal papers in that letter.

THE LADY: But suppose there isn't—?

THE STRANGER: There'll be some other kind of bad news.

THE LADY: All right, have it your way. But you can't escape destiny. Right now I feel as if some higher power were sitting in judgment over us, about to hand down a verdict.

THE STRANGER: You too! Just now I heard the gavel rap, the chairs being pushed back from the bench, the clerks sent out. . . . How agonizing. . . . No, I won't go with you.

THE LADY: What are you doing to me? . . . In the chapel I couldn't pray. The light went out on the altar and a cold wind blew across my face just when I heard you call for me.

THE STRANGER: I didn't call. I only longed for you . . .

THE LADY: You're not the helpless child you pretend to be. You're unbelievably strong. I'm afraid of you.

THE STRANGER: When I'm alone I'm like a paralytic. But as soon as I leech on to someone, strength comes flowing back into me. Right now I want to feel strong again. I'll go with you.

THE LADY: Good! You can be my hero and liberate me from the werewolf.

THE STRANGER: You've got a werewolf?

THE LADY: I've got a husband.

THE STRANGER: Great! I'm your man! Battling dragons, freeing princesses, slaying werewolves—that's living!

THE LADY: Well, then come, my liberator! (*She draws her veil down over her face, kisses him quickly on the mouth, and rushes out.*)

> *The Stranger stands for a moment stupefied.*
>
> *A high chord of women's voices, almost a shriek, is heard from within the church. The lighted rose window suddenly darkens. The tree over the bench trembles. The Pallbearers rise from their places and look upward at the sky as if they see something strange and terrifying.*
>
> *The Stranger hurries out after The Lady.*

* * *

At the Doctor's Home

A yard enclosed by the three wings of a one-story wooden house with a tiled roof. Rather small windows in all three wings. To the right, a veranda or porch enclosing the glass doors to the house. To the left, by the windows, a rambler rosebush, and some beehives on a stand. In the middle of the yard, a very high woodpile shaped like a gourd or an Oriental cupola. Beside it, a water pump. Above the middle wing rises the top of a huge walnut tree. In the right corner, a gate to the garden.

Near the pump is a big turtle.* To the right are steps down to a wine cellar. An icebox and a garbage can. Below the porch are a lawn table and some chairs.

The Doctor's Sister comes down from the porch with a telegram in her hand.

THE SISTER: Well, my dear brother, I think lightning is about to strike you.

THE DOCTOR: That's nothing new, my dear sister.

THE SISTER: This time it's different. It's Ingeborg. She's on her way home—and she's bringing someone with her. Guess who.

THE DOCTOR: Who? . . . I don't have to guess, I know. I've felt for a long time it was going to happen. Even wished for it. I've always admired him, learned a lot from his books, wanted to meet him. And now he's here. Well, well. Where on earth did Ingeborg dig him up?

THE SISTER: In the city, I'd guess. The literary salons.

THE DOCTOR: I've often wondered if he could possibly be one of my school chums who had that name. I hope not. There was something ominous about that young boy. And by this time all the fatal tendencies in him would have developed enormously.

---

* The Oriental shape of the woodpile and the presence of the turtle, living in a virtual state of Nirvana, are meant to suggest the peace and resignation of Buddhism.

THE SISTER: Don't let him come here. Go away. Say you have guests.

THE DOCTOR: No use. You can't escape fate.

THE SISTER: How odd. Nothing intimidates you, but you crawl on your belly before a chimera you call fate.

THE DOCTOR: Experience has taught me not to waste time and energy struggling against the inevitable.

THE SISTER: Why do you let your wife run around compromising herself and you?

THE DOCTOR: It all seems so simple to you. I let her do what she wants because after we'd been engaged I released her from all promises. I pictured to her a life of freedom in contrast to the virtual imprisonment she had known before. Besides, I couldn't love her if she only did what I told her. I didn't want a slave for a wife.

THE SISTER: So you invite your enemy into your home.

THE DOCTOR: All right, all right!

THE SISTER: You let her drag home the very man who'll destroy you. Oh, how I detest that man!

THE DOCTOR: I know. His last book is just as disgusting as the others. It also gives signs of mental disturbance.

THE SISTER: Then why don't they put him away?

THE DOCTOR: A lot of people think they should. But I can't find any evidence that he's actually gone over the edge.

THE SISTER: Naturally! You're half-crazy too. And you spend half your time with a wife who's completely out of her mind.

THE DOCTOR: I can't deny that maniacs have always attracted me. They're not boring. They've got originality (*A steamboat whistle is heard.*) —What's that? Someone's screaming!

THE SISTER: Your nerves *are* on edge. It's only a steamboat whistle. . . . Last warning: get away while you still have a chance.

THE DOCTOR: I might give it some thought if I weren't nailed to the spot. . . . From where I stand I can see his portrait in my study. . . . And the sunshine casts a shadow that distorts his face. He looks like – huh! My God, do you see what he looks like?

THE SISTER: He looks like the devil himself. – Run!

THE DOCTOR: I can't.

THE SISTER: You might at least defend yourself.

THE DOCTOR: That's what I used to do. But this time it's like a storm approaching. How many times haven't I wanted to stand my ground but couldn't. This time is different. The ground's a magnet and I'm a piece of metal. . . . If the worst comes, I can always say it wasn't my doing. . . . They're coming through the front door.

THE SISTER: I didn't hear anything.

THE DOCTOR: Yes, but I hear. I hear. And now I can see them, too. It is he, my childhood friend. . . . He got into trouble in school – some kind of prank. I got the blame and was punished. He got the nickname Caesar, I don't know why.

THE SISTER: And this man is –

THE DOCTOR: Yes. *C'est la vie.* . . . Caesar!

THE LADY (*entering*): Hello, my dear! I've brought someone with me. Very sweet and charming.

THE DOCTOR: So I hear. Bring him in. I'd like to meet him.

THE LADY: He's in the guest room freshening up.

THE DOCTOR: Are you pleased with your conquest?

THE LADY: I believe he's the most unhappy man I've ever met.

THE DOCTOR: That's extravagant.

THE LADY: Yes, I guess so. Everybody's unhappy nowadays.

THE DOCTOR: Isn't that the truth! (*To his Sister.*) Maybe you could show him the way.

The Sister leaves.

THE DOCTOR: Did you have an interesting trip?

THE LADY: Yes. I met an awful lot of strange people. . . . Have you had many patients?

THE DOCTOR: No. This morning there was no one in the waiting room. My practice seems to be going downhill.

THE LADY (*kindly*): You poor dear. . . . Shouldn't that wood be taken inside pretty soon? It'll rot there.

THE DOCTOR (*without sounding reproachful*): Yes, of course it should. And the bees should be killed and the fruit in the orchard picked. But I just don't feel up to anything.

THE LADY: You're tired, my dear.

THE DOCTOR: Tired of everything.

THE LADY (*without bitterness*): And you've got a poor wife who's no help to you.

THE DOCTOR (*gently*): You shouldn't say that. I'm not thinking it.

THE LADY (*facing the porch*): Now!

> *The Stranger, dressed more youthfully than in the first scene, enters from the porch, trying to appear confident and self-assured. He seems to recognize The Doctor, loses his composure momentarily, but regains it.*

THE DOCTOR: Hello. I hope you'll make yourself at home here.

THE STRANGER: Thank you, Doctor.

THE DOCTOR: You've brought good weather with you. We certainly need it here. It's been raining for six weeks.

THE STRANGER: Not seven? Rain on the Day of Seven Sleepers* means seven weeks of rain. But now that I think of it, we haven't come to that yet. Stupid of me . . .

---

* July 27.

THE DOCTOR: If you're accustomed to the pleasures of the city, I'm afraid our simple life here will seem rather tiresome.

THE STRANGER: Not at all . . . I'm as much at home in one place as another. . . . I don't have any reason for asking, but I can't help it. Haven't we met each other before—when we were boys?

THE DOCTOR: Never.

> *The Lady has sat down at the table and begun to crochet.*

THE STRANGER: Are you sure?

THE DOCTOR: Quite sure. I've followed your career from the beginning with the greatest interest, as my wife has no doubt told you. If we had met before, I would certainly have remembered it—your name, at least. . . . Well, now you see how a country doctor lives.

THE STRANGER: If you could imagine how a freedom-fighter—so-called—lives, you wouldn't envy him at all.

THE DOCTOR: I think I can guess. I know how people love their chains. Maybe things are supposed to be that way, since that's the way things are.

THE STRANGER (*listening to something offstage*): Strange. Who's playing the piano next door?

THE DOCTOR: Can't imagine. Do you know, Ingeborg?

THE LADY: No, I don't.

THE STRANGER: Mendelssohn's "Funeral March" still persecuting me. I don't know if it's something in my ear or . . .

THE DOCTOR: Have you had auditory hallucinations before?

THE STRANGER: Not hallucinations, but there are little recurring events, real ones, that seem to haunt me. . . . Don't you hear someone playing?

THE DOCTOR *and* THE LADY: Why, I think someone is—

THE LADY: And it is Mendelssohn.

THE DOCTOR: Mendelssohn *is* very popular nowadays.

THE STRANGER: I know that. But why do they have to play him just here, just now? (*He gets up.*)

THE DOCTOR: If it will make you feel any better, I'll ask my sister . . . (*He goes in by way of the porch.*)

THE STRANGER (*to The Lady*): I can't breathe here. I won't be able to sleep a night in this house. He actually looks like a werewolf. When he's around, you turn into a pillar of salt. This whole place reeks of murder, it's haunted. I'm getting out the first chance I get.

THE DOCTOR (*coming out*): Well, you were right. The girl who works at the post office was playing the piano.

THE STRANGER (*agitated and nervous*): Good. That explains that. . . . Rather a unique place you have here, Doctor. Everything is so—unusual. That woodpile, for instance—

THE DOCTOR: Yes, lightning has knocked it down twice.

THE STRANGER: How awful. And you still keep it there?

THE DOCTOR: For just that reason. That's why I built it two yards higher this summer. Tempting fate, you see. Also because it provides more shade that way. Like Jonah's gourd.* Looks like Jonah's gourd, doesn't it? Come autumn and away it goes into the woodshed.

THE STRANGER (*looking around*): And here you have Christmas roses. Where did you get them? And blooming in the summertime? . . . Everything is backward.

THE DOCTOR: Oh, those. Well, you see, I have a mental patient staying here—

THE STRANGER: Here in the house?

THE DOCTOR: Oh, he's harmless, quiet and tranquil. The only thing that gets him excited is the lack of plan and purpose in nature. He thinks it's stupid that the Christmas roses have to

* See Jonah 4:6.

freeze in the snow, so he brings them into the cellar and sets them out again in the spring.

THE STRANGER: A madman in the house. . . . How very disquieting.

THE DOCTOR: No need to worry. He's very peaceable, I assure you.

THE STRANGER: I wonder what drove him insane?

THE DOCTOR: Who can say? It's a mental disease; there's nothing physically wrong.

THE STRANGER: And is he . . . here . . . free and loose?

THE DOCTOR: The madman? Oh, he wanders about the garden, putting nature to rights. If his presence bothers you, I'll lock him up in the cellar.

THE STRANGER: Why not put the poor devils out of their misery?

THE DOCTOR: One never knows whether they are ripe and ready.

THE STRANGER: For what?

THE DOCTOR: For what comes next.

THE STRANGER: Nothing comes next.

Pause

THE DOCTOR: Who knows?

THE STRANGER: I know it feels horrible here in this yard. Got any cadavers here?

THE DOCTOR (*at the icebox*): As a matter of fact, I do. I've got a few stumps on ice here, which I'm sending on to the medical school. (*Draws out a leg and an arm.*) Look at these.

THE STRANGER: My God, I must be in Bluebeard's castle.

THE DOCTOR (*sharply*): What's that supposed to mean?

(*Glances piercingly at his wife.*) Do you think I murder my wives? Hm?

THE STRANGER: Hardly. It's obvious you don't. —But you do have ghosts in the house, I'll bet.

THE DOCTOR: Do we! Talk to my wife. Ask her. (*He has withdrawn behind the woodpile so that he cannot be seen by The Lady and The Stranger.*)

THE LADY: You can speak up, if you want to. He's quite deaf. But watch it—he can read lips.

THE STRANGER: I know. . . . I've never spent a more painful half hour in all my life. We stand around talking like idiots because no one has the courage to say what's really on his mind. A moment ago I was in such agony I almost slit my wrists just to cool off a little. Right now I feel more like lighting a bomb under him and telling him the plain truth. Let's tell him right to his face that we're running off together, that we've had enough of his games.

THE LADY: I hate you when you talk like this. You can at least behave decently under all circumstances.

THE STRANGER: My, aren't you the proper little lady!

The Doctor reappears, visible to the two, who continue their conversation.

THE STRANGER: Well, make up your mind. Are you coming with me now, before it gets dark?

THE LADY: I . . .

THE STRANGER: Why did you kiss me yesterday? Why?

THE LADY: Please . . .

THE STRANGER: Be funny if he's taking in every word of this. I wouldn't trust him.

THE DOCTOR: Now what should we do to amuse our guest?

THE LADY: I'm sure he doesn't expect much in the way of amusement. His life hasn't exactly been one long party.

The Doctor blows a whistle. The Madman appears in the garden. He is wearing a strange costume and has a laurel wreath on his head.

THE DOCTOR: Caesar! Come here!

THE STRANGER (*very uncomfortable*): Is his name Caesar?

THE DOCTOR: It's only a nickname I gave him in memory of an old school chum of mine . . .

THE STRANGER (*on edge*): What?

THE DOCTOR: Yes, a strange case. He framed me and I got all the blame.

THE LADY (*to The Stranger*): Can you imagine a child being so wicked?

The Stranger is in agony. The Madman approaches.

THE DOCTOR: Come in, Caesar, and make your bow to the great author.

THE MADMAN: Is he the great man?

THE LADY (*to The Doctor*): Why did you have to call him in here when you can see how it upsets our guest?

THE DOCTOR: Caesar will be on his best behavior, won't he? Otherwise he'll get a whipping.

THE MADMAN: He may be Caesar, but he isn't great. He doesn't know which came first, the chicken or the egg. But I do.

THE STRANGER (*to The Lady*): I'm going. I've had enough. You've lured me into an ambush. —Well, what am I supposed to think? Next minute he'll amuse me by releasing the beast.

THE LADY: You've got to have absolute faith in me, no matter how it looks. —And don't talk so loud.

THE STRANGER: I tell you, he won't leave us alone for a moment, that monster werewolf of yours—. Not for a second.

THE DOCTOR (*looking at his watch*): You must excuse me. I

have a call to make. Take about an hour. I hope you don't mind waiting.

THE STRANGER: I'm used to waiting – for what never comes.

THE DOCTOR (*to The Madman*): Caesar, you rascal, come here! I'm going to lock you in the cellar. (*He leaves with The Madman.*)

THE STRANGER (*to The Lady*): What's going on? Who's persecuting me? You tell me your husband is sympathetic toward me. I believe you, but he can't open his mouth without torturing me. Every word he spoke stabbed me like a needle. – God, there's that funeral march again! I can really hear it! . . . And there's the Christmas rose again. . . . Why does everything have to keep coming back again and again? Corpses and beggars and fools and madmen and whole lives and childhood memories. . . . You've got to get out of here, you've got to! It's sheer hell! Let me take you away from all this!

THE LADY: Why do you think I brought you here? You see, now no one can say you simply stole another man's wife. You're rescuing me. – But I have to know one thing: can I rely on you?

THE STRANGER: You mean how I feel about you?

THE LADY: Let's not talk about feelings. We took them for granted from the start. They'll last as long as they last.

THE STRANGER: You mean my finances? I've got a lot of money coming to me. All I have to do is write or send a wire –

THE LADY: That's good enough for me. – Well, that's it, then. (*She puts away her crocheting.*) Go out through the garden and follow the lilac bushes until you come to the wooden gate at the back. Open it and you'll be on the highway. I'll meet you in the next town.

THE STRANGER (*hesitates*): Slipping out through back doors isn't exactly to my taste. I'd rather have it out with him right here in the middle of the yard –

THE LADY (*with a gesture*): Hurry!

THE STRANGER: No. You come with me.

THE LADY: All right. . . . I will. I'll even go first. (*She turns around and throws a kiss in the direction of the porch.*) My poor little werewolf!

ACT II

In the Hotel Room

Enter The Stranger, The Porter, and The Lady.

THE STRANGER (*with an overnight bag in his hand*): You mean to say this is the only room available?

THE PORTER: Right.

THE STRANGER: But I can't stay in this one.

THE LADY: He says there isn't any other. And every hotel in town is filled.

THE STRANGER (*to The Porter*): That'll be all.

The Lady sinks down exhausted in a chair without taking off her hat or coat.

THE STRANGER: Should I order something?

THE LADY: Yes: a cup of hemlock would do nicely.

THE STRANGER: I feel the same way. Kicked out of one hotel after another because we don't have a marriage license — wanted by the police for questioning because we don't have the right papers — and on top of all that we had to end up in this hotel of all hotels, the last one on earth for me. And in this room of all rooms — number eight. . . . Someone is setting me up. Someone.

THE LADY: Not number eight! I don't believe it.

THE STRANGER: You mean, you *too*? Here in this room!

THE LADY: Have you —?

THE STRANGER: Yes.

THE LADY: Let's get out of here. The street, the woods — anywhere.

THE STRANGER: I'd love to. But I'm just as tired as you are. Hounded from place to place—I feel I'm being hunted down by someone.* I knew we'd end up here, even though I fought against it and headed away from here. Who can fight against trains that are late, trains that break down, missed connections? We had to end up here, in this very room. The devil's behind it. But this isn't the last round between him and me.

THE LADY: I'm beginning to think we'll never have another moment of peace as long as we live.

THE STRANGER: Just look! Nothing's changed. There's that perpetually withering Christmas rose. And there, there's another. (*Pointing to a picture on the wall.*) And there hangs the Hotel Breuer in Montreux. I stayed there once, too.

THE LADY: Have you been to the post office?

THE STRANGER: I was waiting for that. As a matter of fact, I have. And in return for my five letters and three telegrams I got one telegram informing me that my publisher will be out of town for two weeks.

THE LADY: Then we're done for!

THE STRANGER: As good as.

THE LADY: In five minutes they'll be here to look at our passports. And then the manager will come and ask us to leave.

THE STRANGER: After that there's only one way out . . .

THE LADY: Two.

THE STRANGER: Forget it. The second one's impossible.

THE LADY: What's that?

THE STRANGER: Going to your parents.

THE LADY: You're already reading my mind.

THE STRANGER: We can't have any secrets from each other anymore.

---

* In the original the reference is to the Wild Hunt of Germanic folklore. Also at the end of Act II, p. 439.

THE LADY: The end of the honeymoon.

THE STRANGER: Maybe . . .

THE LADY: Send just one more telegram!

THE STRANGER: I know I should, but I can't budge from this spot. I no longer believe that anything I do can possibly have any effect whatsoever. —Someone has paralyzed me.

THE LADY: Me too. . . . We promised each other never to talk about the past, and all we do is drag it along just the same. Look at the wallpaper. He's lurking among the flowers.

THE STRANGER: Yes, I see him. Everywhere I look I see him. Repeated hundreds of times. . . . But I see someone else in the tablecloth pattern. . . . It's supernatural. It must be an illusion. . . . All I need now is to hear my funeral march and then everything will be just perfect. (*He listens.*) There it is!

THE LADY: I don't hear anything.

THE STRANGER: Really? I must be well on my way.

THE LADY: Shall we go home? My home?

THE STRANGER: The last and the worst possible way out. Coming home like tramps, like beggars. Anything but that.

THE LADY: But certainly it—. No, you're right. It's too much. Bringing shame and disgrace—and hurting my parents. We'd see each other humiliated. We'd never respect each other again.

THE STRANGER: I think I'd rather die. . . . Still I feel it's inevitable. I'm beginning to long for it. If it's got to happen, let's get it over with as soon as possible.

THE LADY (*takes out her crocheting*): Maybe so, but I have no desire to be humiliated in front of you. There must be some other way. . . . Suppose . . . suppose we got married. That could be managed quick enough. My marriage was annulled in the country where I got married. . . . All we have to do is take a little trip and get married by the same priest who married—. But I guess that would be humiliating for you.

THE STRANGER: It's right in style with everything else. This honeymoon is turning out to be a pilgrimage. Or running the gauntlet.

TO DAMASCUS [ACT II]

THE LADY: That's the truth. In five minutes the manager will be here to tell us to leave. There's only one way to put an end to all these humiliations. We've got to make up our minds to swallow the last bitter pill. Sh! I hear footsteps . . .

THE STRANGER: That's it then. But I'm ready this time—ready for anything. If I can't fight those I can't see, at least I can show them how much punishment I can take. —Pawn your jewels, and I'll redeem them as soon as my publisher gets back—that is, if he doesn't die in a train wreck or drown in his bathtub. —I've always wanted respect, so it's the first thing I have to sacrifice.

THE LADY: All right, we're agreed. Don't you think we better leave on our own before we get thrown out? My God, he *is* coming! The manager!

THE STRANGER: Off we go. Running the gauntlet between bellboys and waiters and doormen and room clerks. —Red with shame, white with rage. Wild animals can hide in their holes, but we're forced to parade our shame. —You might at least put down your veil.

THE LADY: Isn't it great?—the life of a liberated woman!

THE STRANGER: And here's the great liberator!

They leave.

* * *

By the Sea

A cabin on a cliff overlooking the seashore. Outside the cabin are a table and some chairs. The Stranger and The Lady, dressed in light-colored clothes, appear younger-looking than in the previous scene. The Lady is crocheting.

THE STRANGER: Three days of peace and happiness at the side of my wife—and now I feel uneasy again.

THE LADY: What are you afraid of?

THE STRANGER: That it won't last.

THE LADY: Why not?

THE STRANGER: I don't know. I just feel that it has to end—abruptly, terribly. There's something false in the very brightness of the sun and the stillness of the air. I just feel that happiness cannot be part of my life.

THE LADY: But it's all settled. My parents are resigned, my husband has been friendly and understanding in his letters—

THE STRANGER: What difference does all that make? Fate is spinning its web. Once again I can hear the gavel rap, the chairs being pushed back from the bench. Sentence has been pronounced. But I think it was pronounced even before I was born. Even in my childhood I began serving my sentence. . . . There isn't one single moment in my life I can look back on with joy.

THE LADY: Darling, you've had everything you wished for in life.

THE STRANGER: Everything I wished for, yes. Unfortunately, I forgot to wish for gold.

THE LADY: Back to that again.

THE STRANGER: Do you blame me?

THE LADY: Oh, be quiet.

THE STRANGER: What are you always crocheting? You sit there like one of the three Fates, drawing the threads between your fingers. . . . But I like it. The most beautiful sight I know of is a woman bent over her work or her child. What are you crocheting?

THE LADY: Nothing at all. Just crocheting . . .

THE STRANGER: It looks like a net of nerves and knots to catch your thoughts. I bet your brain looks like that inside.

THE LADY: If only I had half the thoughts you say I have! But I haven't any at all.

THE STRANGER: That's probably why I like to have you near me. It's why you're so good for me, so perfect I can't imagine life without you. . . . Now the clouds are gone and the sky is clear and the air is soft as baby's breath. Feel, feel! Now I'm filled with life. In moments like this I really live. I can feel myself swell up, thin out, and stretch out to infinity. I'm everywhere now, in the sea which is my blood, in the hills which are my bones, in the trees, in the flowers. My head reaches as high as the heavens and I look out over the whole universe, which is all me, and I feel all the strength and power of the creator in me, for he and I are one. I want to take it all in my hands and knead it into something more nearly perfect, more enduring, more beautiful. I want to see it all created anew and every created being happy – born without pain, living without sorrow, dying in silent contentment. Eve, come die with me now, Eve, this very instant, for in the next, all the pain will be back with us again.

THE LADY: No, I'm not ready to die yet.

THE STRANGER: Why not?

THE LADY: I keep thinking there's still something I have to do. Perhaps I haven't suffered enough yet . . .

THE STRANGER: Is that the reason for living?

THE LADY: It seems like it. – Let me ask you a favor.

THE STRANGER: Name it.

THE LADY: Please don't blaspheme against heaven the way you did just now. And don't compare yourself to the Creator. You remind me of Caesar back home.

THE STRANGER (*suddenly on edge*): Of Caesar! How can you know –? Tell me –

THE LADY: Did I say something wrong? I didn't mean to. It was stupid of me to say "back home." It just slipped out. Forgive me.

THE STRANGER: Why compare me to Caesar? Blaspheming – was that all?

THE LADY: Yes, of course, that's all.

THE STRANGER: I believe you. I know you don't want to hurt me. And yet you do hurt me, you like everyone else I come in contact with. Why, why?

THE LADY: Because you're too sensitive.

THE STRANGER: Now you're on that again. You mean I'm trying to hide something? You mean that makes me touchy?

THE LADY: God knows I didn't mean anything of the sort. —Here we go again, arguing, and suspecting each other. It's like an evil spirit between us. We've got to drive it out before it's too late.

THE STRANGER: Well, why accuse me of blasphemy? I'm simply quoting a very old saying, "Lo, we are gods!"

THE LADY: If that's true, why can't you get yourself out of this mess—get both of us out?

THE STRANGER: You think I can't? Give me time. You've only seen the beginning.

THE LADY: If the end is going to be anything like the beginning, heaven help us!

THE STRANGER: I know what you're afraid of. I had intended holding back my little surprise, but I won't torture you any longer. (*He pulls out a registered letter, unopened.*) Look what I've got!

THE LADY: The money!

THE STRANGER: Came this morning! "The smiting angel can do nought!"*

THE LADY: Don't! He can!

THE STRANGER: How?

THE LADY: "A haughty spirit goeth before a fall."

THE STRANGER: It isn't the haughtiness, it's the spirit the gods can't stand! (*Waving the letter.*) This was my Achilles' heel. I've been able to endure everything except this deadly poverty, which always hit me where it hurts.

THE LADY: If you don't mind my asking, just how much did you get?

* From Luther's "Ein' feste Burg." In the original Swedish, Strindberg paraphrases a line from a Swedish hymn.

THE STRANGER: I don't know. I haven't opened the letter yet. I have a pretty good idea how much I'm supposed to get. Let's take a look. (*Opens the letter.*) What's this? No money! It's a royalty statement showing I've got nothing coming. Something's wrong. It's crazy.

THE LADY: I'm beginning to think you're right.

THE STRANGER: That I'm damned and cursed, you mean? Didn't I tell you? So I take this little curse between my two fingers and throw it back at the magnanimous donor—(*He throws the letter up in the air.*)—followed by my curses.

THE LADY: Please! You scare me when you carry on like this.

THE STRANGER: Good! I'd rather see you scared than laughing at me. I won't be laughed at. —Now watch this! I've hurled the challenge. Now you're going to see a real wrestling match. A championship fight between giants! (*He bares his chest and throws a challenging glance upward.*) Come on out and fight. I'm ready and waiting! Strike me with thy lightning—if thou darest. Make me tremble with thy thunder—if thou canst!

THE LADY: No, no, don't!

THE STRANGER: Yes, yes! —Who are you who dare to wake me from my dream of love? To snatch the cup from my lips and the woman from my arms? What's the matter, are you jealous, you gods or devils? Little bourgeois gods, that's what you are— who parry the thrust of the sword with needle jabs from behind, who refuse to meet on the dueling ground but answer the challenge with an unpaid bill—the delivery boy's way of embarrassing the master before his servants. No lunge, no stoccado—just spit and whine. Well, you Powers, Principalities, Dominions, I spit on you!

THE LADY: May heaven never punish you.

THE STRANGER: Pooh! The heavens remain blue and still, the sea stays blue and silent. . . . Sh! an idea is beginning to ferment in my brain. I can hear a poem coming on. . . . The rhythm—that comes first. This time it's like hoofbeats, with spurs jangling and swords clanging. And there's a flapping sound like sails being lashed by the wind. . . . No, they're flags . . . flags . . .

THE LADY: It's the wind in the trees.

THE STRANGER: Shh. . . . They're riding over a bridge, a wooden trestle over a dry river bed—flinty stones echoing the hooves. . . . Wait . . . wait. . . . Now I hear voices saying the rosary—men and women together. . . . The Hail Mary. . . . But now I see—do you know where?—in your crocheting—a huge kitchen—white—the walls are whitewashed. Three small deep-niched windows with latticework, and flowers. In the left corner, a stove. To the right, a table with pine benches. And over the table in the corner, a black crucifix, and below it a lamp burning. In the ceiling, soot-blackened beams. On the walls, mistletoe hanging, dried mistletoe.

THE LADY (*frightened*): Where do you see this? Where?

THE STRANGER: In your crocheting.

THE LADY: Do you see any people?

THE STRANGER: I see an old man, a very old man, sitting at the kitchen table . . . bent over a hunting bag . . . but his hands are clasped together in prayer. . . . And an elderly woman is kneeling on the floor. . . . And now I can hear—coming from outside, from the porch, maybe—the Hail Mary. . . . The two people inside look as if they were made of wax. . . . And there's a veil over everything. . . . No, it's not a poem, not my imagination. (*Awakens.*) —What was it?

THE LADY: It was real, all real. That was the kitchen in my parents' home. And you've never seen it. The old man was my grandfather—a forester. And the woman was my mother, praying—for us. It's six o'clock now—that's when the workers are in from the fields and saying their rosaries in the shade . . .

THE STRANGER: I don't know that I like this. Am I getting to be clairvoyant, too? . . . But it was so restful there. A beautiful room, snow-white, with mistletoe and flowers. —Why were they praying for us, I wonder?

THE LADY: Yes, I wonder, too. Have we done anything wrong?

THE STRANGER: Who knows what's wrong?

THE LADY: I've read that wrong simply doesn't exist, but still . . . I wonder. . . . I want so terribly much to be with my mother. Not my father. He abandoned me just as he deserted my mother.

THE STRANGER: Why did he leave your mother?

THE LADY: Who knows why people do things like that? The children least of all. —Please, please, let's go home. I want so much to go home.

THE STRANGER: One more lion's den, one more snake pit? Why not? For your sake I'll go home with you. But not like a prodigal son, no, you'll see me go through fire and water for your sake.

THE LADY: How do you know?

THE STRANGER: A hunch.

THE LADY: Then you must have guessed by now that it's a rough road. My parents live in the mountains. You can't even get a wagon up those trails.

THE STRANGER: It's like a fairy tale. It's like something I must have read or dreamed . . .

THE LADY: Maybe. Yet everything you'll see will be perfectly natural, though perhaps a little out of the ordinary—but then even the people aren't ordinary. . . . Are you ready to come with me?

THE STRANGER: Completely ready—come what may!

THE LADY (*kisses him on the forehead and makes the sign of the cross, simply, shyly*): Come.

* * *

On the Road

A landscape with rolling hills. On a bluff to the right stands a chapel. A road lined with fruit trees winds its way into the distance. Between the trees are shrines, calvaries, and Alpine crosses marking the scenes of accidents. In the foreground is a road sign with a notice: "Vagrancy forbidden in this district."

The Stranger and The Lady.

THE LADY: You poor man, you're exhausted.

THE STRANGER: Won't deny it. But to be hungry because I've run out of money—that's humiliating. I never thought that would happen to me.

THE LADY: I guess we had better be ready for anything and everything. I think the gods are frowning on us. Look, my shoe has split wide open. Oh, I could just cry when I think we have to come home looking like tramps.

THE STRANGER (*pointing to the sign*): "Vagrancy forbidden in this district." Why the devil does that sign have to be right there in big, black letters?

THE LADY: It's always been there, as long as I can remember. . . . Just think, I haven't been here since I was a child. I thought the road was so short then. Those hills weren't so high, and the trees were smaller, and I could hear birds singing—or so it seemed.

THE STRANGER: The birds sang for you all the year round then. What a child you are. Now they sing only in the springtime and it's already autumn. In those days you danced your way along this endless calvary, picking flowers at the foot of the cross.

Far in the distance a hunting horn is heard.

What's that?

THE LADY: I know that sound. It's Grandfather's hunting horn. He's coming in from the hills. . . . What a good, kind, wonderful old man! Let's hurry. We can reach home before it gets dark if we hurry.

THE STRANGER: How far do we have to go?

THE LADY: Not far. Only over the hill and across the river.

THE STRANGER: Is that the river I hear?

THE LADY: Yes. I was born and brought up near that big rushing river. I was eighteen before I crossed over to this side to find out what was shimmering on the horizon. . . . Now I know.

THE STRANGER: You're crying.

THE LADY: Good kind Grandfather. . . . When I was getting into the boat he said to me, "There lies the world, my child. When you've seen enough of it, come back to your hills. The hills will cover you and hide you." . . . Well, I've seen enough. . . . Enough.

THE STRANGER: We'd better move on. It's a long road, and night is falling.

They pick up their coats and move on.

* * *

In the Ravine

The narrow entrance to a ravine between pine-covered cliffs.

In the foreground, a shed. Leaning against the door is a broom with a goat's horn hanging from its handle.

To the left, a blacksmith shop with the door open, emitting a red glow. To the right, a water mill.

In the background, the ravine, with a millstream spanned by a footbridge. The jags in the cliffs form huge profiles.

At the rise of the curtain The Blacksmith is standing in the doorway of his shop, and The Miller's Wife in the doorway of the mill. When The Lady enters, they gesture to each other and disappear through their respective doors. The clothes of The Lady and The Stranger are torn.

The Lady enters and approaches the blacksmith shop.

THE STRANGER (*entering*): It looks like they're hiding from us.

THE LADY: I can't believe it.

THE STRANGER: What a strange landscape! Everything has been deliberately arranged to give me the willies. What's that broom doing there and that ointment horn? They've probably always been there, but I still can't help thinking of witches. . . . Why is the shop black and the mill white? Because one's covered with soot and the other with flour. Simple enough. All the same, when I saw that blacksmith standing in the red glow of his fire directly opposite that white miller girl, I couldn't help thinking of an old poem.* . . . Look at those giants up there. . . . It's insufferable! Look, you can see that werewolf of yours up there. I may have rescued you from him, but that's his profile up there all the same. . . . Look at it.

THE LADY: Yes, yes, I can see it. It's only the cliff.

THE STRANGER: I know it's only the cliff, but still it's *him*.

THE LADY: I don't have to tell you *why* we see him.

THE STRANGER: You're thinking of . . . conscience, which rears its ugly head when you're tired and hungry but goes away when you're full and rested. . . . Isn't it like being damned to have to make our way like beggars? —Look, even our clothes are ripped and torn after climbing the mountains and hiking through thorn bushes. . . . I tell you, someone's fighting against me.

THE LADY: Well, you challenged him!

THE STRANGER: I wanted a fair fight with clean weapons— not with unpaid bills and empty pockets. But if that's the way it's going to be, here's my last cent. Old Nix the water sprite is welcome to it—if he exists. (*He throws a coin into the stream.*)

* In the Icelandic poem *The Song of the Sun* (Sólarljóð), a product of a Christian visionary, the world mill stands at the entrance to the kingdom of the damned. The grain it grinds to powder are the giants.

THE LADY: Now look what you've done! We needed that to pay for the ferry across the river. Now as soon as we walk into the house, we'll have to talk about money.

THE STRANGER: What else do we ever talk about?

THE LADY: Maybe that's because you've never had anything but contempt for it.

THE STRANGER: As for everything else.

THE LADY: Everything isn't contemptible. Some things are good.

THE STRANGER: Name one!

THE LADY: You just come with me. You'll see . . .

THE STRANGER: All right, I'm coming—. (*He hesitates as he is about to pass by the blacksmith shop.*)

THE LADY (*who has gone ahead*): Are you afraid of the fire?

THE STRANGER: No, but—

> *The hunting horn is heard in the distance. He hurries past the shop after her.*

* * *

In the Kitchen

> *A large kitchen with whitewashed walls in a mountain cabin. Three windows in the right corner, two of them in the rear and one in the right wall. The windows are small and set in deep niches with flower pots. The beamed ceiling is black with soot. In the left corner, a built-in brick stove and oven with copper, bronze, iron, and pewter utensils, and wooden mugs and buckets. In the right corner, a crucifix with a votive candle. Beneath it, a rectangular table with benches along the wall.*
>
> *Mistletoe is hanging here and there. A door in the rear. Through it can be seen a poorhouse, and through the windows at the back, a church.*

Near the stove is bedding for the dogs and a table for the poor.

At the table under the crucifix sits The Old Man with his hands clasped and his hunting bag in front of him.

He is in his eighties, powerfully built, with white hair and a full beard, and dressed like a forester.

The Mother is kneeling in the center of the floor; gray-haired, going on fifty, dressed in black and white.

From outside the voices of men, women, and children can be heard clearly reciting the last words of the Hail Mary: "Holy Mary, Mother of God, pray for us sinners now and at the hour of our death. Amen."

THE OLD MAN *and* THE MOTHER: Amen.

THE MOTHER: You know what I heard today? They saw two vagrants down by the river. Their clothes were torn and dirty. Soaked to their skins from the water—. And when they were supposed to pay the ferryman, they didn't have a cent on them. Now they're sitting in the ferryhouse, drying out their clothes.

THE OLD MAN: Good! Let them sit there.

THE MOTHER: Be not forgetful to entertain beggars; they might be angels in disguise.

THE OLD MAN: True. —All right, let them come here.

THE MOTHER: I'll put some food out on the table for the poor folk, if that won't bother you.

THE OLD MAN: No, of course not.

THE MOTHER: Shall I set out some cider?

THE OLD MAN: Yes, let them have some cider. . . . You might also build a fire in the stove. They'll be cold and wet.

THE MOTHER: There isn't much time to get a fire going—but—well, if you wish it, Father.

THE OLD MAN (*looking out the window*): Yes, please.

THE MOTHER: What are you looking at?

THE OLD MAN: I'm looking at the rising river and wondering, as I've wondered for seventy-five years, when shall I ever reach the sea?

THE MOTHER: Feeling sad, Father?

THE OLD MAN: . . . *et introibo ad alterem Dei; ad Deum qui lactificat juventutem.** . . . Yes, I'm depressed. . . . *Deus, Deus meus; quare tristis es anima mea, et quare conturbas me?***

THE MOTHER: *Spera in Deo*—***

> *A Maid enters, signals to The Mother, who goes over to her. They whisper. The Maid leaves.*

THE OLD MAN: I heard that. . . . My God, how much am I supposed to endure?

THE MOTHER: You don't have to meet them. You can go up to your room.

THE OLD MAN: No, I shall take it as a kind of penance. Why do they come here like tramps?

THE MOTHER: They must have got lost or run into some bad luck. . . . You don't suppose—?

THE OLD MAN: But she's bringing her—her—lover with her. Shameless.

THE MOTHER: You know what a strange girl Ingeborg is. No matter what she does she gets away with it. Even makes it seem right and proper. Have you ever seen her blush because she did something indecent or look hurt because somebody rebuked her? I never have. It's not that she's impudent or shameless—quite the contrary. She's just innocent. Part of her charm.

---

* I will go unto the altar of God, to God, who giveth joy to my youth.
** O God, my God. Why art thou sad, O my soul, and why dost thou trouble me?
*** Hope in God. —This and the previous two Latin quotations are from Psalms 42 and 43.

THE OLD MAN: It's amazing how you can't get mad at her. She has no sense of responsibility. You can't insult her. It's as if she didn't have a self of her own—or as if she were two different persons, one doing bad all the time and the other always giving absolution. . . . But as for that man—! I've never detested anyone from afar as much as I detest him. He sees evil everywhere, yet there's no man I've heard more evil about than him.

THE MOTHER: True. Possibly Ingeborg has some role to play in that man's life—and he in hers. Maybe they're going to torment each other to redemption.

THE OLD MAN: Even if that were true, I have no desire to be an accomplice in an affair that seems shameless to me. . . . That man—under my roof! But I suppose I have to stand for it—like everything else. God knows, I've deserved it.

THE MOTHER: In God's name, then.

The Lady and The Stranger enter.

THE MOTHER: Come in. Welcome to you both.

THE LADY: Thank you, Mother.

She goes over to The Old Man. He rises and regards The Stranger carefully.

THE LADY: God bless you, Grandfather. . . . This is my husband. . . . Aren't you going to shake hands?

THE OLD MAN: Let me take a look at him first. (*He goes over to The Stranger, lays his hands on his shoulders, and looks him in the eye.*) Young man, what are your intentions in coming to this house?

THE STRANGER (*forthrightly*): None but to keep my wife company, and only because she insisted.

THE OLD MAN: If that's true, you're welcome here. I have a long and stormy life behind me, and I've finally found some peace and solitude. I beg you not to disturb it.

THE STRANGER: I didn't come to ask for any favors, and I'll leave without asking for any.

THE OLD MAN: I don't like that answer, young man. We all need each other. Perhaps even I need you. One never knows.

THE LADY: Grandfather, please!

THE OLD MAN: Yes, yes, my child. . . . Well, I won't wish you happiness—it doesn't exist. However, I will wish you the strength to bear your fate. . . . I'll leave you for a while with your mother. She'll take care of you. (*He leaves.*)

THE LADY (*to The Mother*): Have you set that table for us, Mother?

THE MOTHER: The table for the poor? Of course not. How could you think that? We thought you were somebody else.

THE LADY: I suppose we do look awful after getting lost in the mountains. And if Grandfather hadn't signaled with his hunting horn, I don't know what we'd—

THE MOTHER: Grandfather? Why, he gave up hunting long ago.

THE LADY: It must have been somebody else's horn. —But just look at me! I better go up to the Rose Room and get everything fixed up.

THE MOTHER: You just run along. I'll be up soon . . .

> *The Lady wants to say something but cannot find the words. She leaves.*

THE STRANGER (*to The Mother*): I've seen this room before.

THE MOTHER: And I've seen you before. In a way, I've been expecting you.

THE STRANGER: As one expects an accident?

THE MOTHER: Why do you say that?

THE STRANGER: I'm a walking catastrophe. Devastation wherever I go. But since I have to go somewhere, and since I can't change my fate, I feel no compunction . . .

THE MOTHER: Just like my daughter—no misgivings and no conscience.

THE STRANGER: Really? I'm surprised to hear you say that.

THE MOTHER: Why? You think I meant something bad? I don't go around saying bad things against my own child. I made the comparison only because I thought you knew what she was like.

THE STRANGER: I haven't noticed the characteristics you mention in Eve . . .

THE MOTHER: Why do you call Ingeborg Eve?

THE STRANGER: I gave her a name of my own choosing to make her mine. I intend to re-create her according to my tastes and desires—

THE MOTHER: In your image! (*She smiles.*) I've heard how the black magicians up in the hills carve a figure of the one they want to bewitch, and baptize it with the name of the person they want to destroy. That's how you're planning to use your self-made Eve to destroy her whole sex.

THE STRANGER (*stares astonished at The Mother*): I'll be damned! What a devil you are! Forgive me—you are my mother-in-law. You are also religious. How can you nourish such thoughts?

THE MOTHER: They are yours.

THE STRANGER: This is getting to be interesting. I thought I was going to enjoy an idyll of peace and quiet in the forest, and I end up in a witch's kitchen.

THE MOTHER: Not quite. However, you apparently forget, or perhaps didn't know, that I was shamefully disgraced by my husband who deserted me and that you're a man who ignominiously deserted his wife.

THE STRANGER: Frank enough. Now I know just where I stand.

THE MOTHER: Now I want to know where I stand. Can you support two families?

THE STRANGER: If everything goes well, yes.

THE MOTHER: Everything doesn't. Not in this world. And money can be lost.

THE STRANGER: My talent is my capital. I can't lose that.

THE MOTHER: Really? Don't tell me you haven't seen the greatest talents dry up . . . gradually over the years, or suddenly overnight?

THE STRANGER: I've never met anyone with such a knack for shaking a man's faith in himself.

THE MOTHER: You're bloated with over-confidence. That last book of yours must have knocked a few pounds off.

THE STRANGER: You read that too?

THE MOTHER: Yes. I know all your secrets. So don't play any games with me and we'll get along just fine. —One more thing— a trifle, but it casts an embarrassing shadow on this house: why didn't you pay the ferryman?*

THE STRANGER: Money is my Achilles' heel. I threw away my last cent. —Can't one talk of anything besides money in this house?

THE MOTHER: Yes. But in this house it's customary to think of one's obligations first and pleasures afterward. —You mean you came here on foot because you didn't have any money?

THE STRANGER: I'm afraid that's right.

THE MOTHER (*smiling*): And you have had nothing to eat?

THE STRANGER: No . . .

THE MOTHER: Why—you're just like a little boy, happy-go-lucky, careless—

THE STRANGER: I've had my share of rough times—never anything quite like this, though.

---

* Charon, who ferried the dead across the Acheron, demanded a fare of one obolus. The Acheron, river of woe, was one of several rivers in the realm of Hades.

THE MOTHER: I almost feel sorry for you. You look so miserable. I'd laugh if I didn't know you'd soon be crying—and others with you. . . . Now that you've won her be sure you hold on to her. She loves you. If you leave her, you'll never smile again, I promise you, or even remember what it was like to be happy.

THE STRANGER: A threat?

THE MOTHER: No, a warning. . . . Go and have your supper.

THE STRANGER (*indicating the table for the poor*): At that table?

THE MOTHER: A very poor joke, but it might come true. Wouldn't be the first time.

THE STRANGER: I'm sure. I'm ready to believe anything can happen. It can't get much worse.

THE MOTHER: That's what you think. Wait and see.

THE STRANGER (*depressed*): It wouldn't surprise me. (*Leaves.*)

The Mother is alone for a moment. Then The Old Man enters.

THE OLD MAN: Well, that was no angel in disguise.

THE MOTHER: At least not an angel of light.

THE OLD MAN: Careful. The people around here are awfully superstitious. I heard them talking when I was down at the river. One fellow said that his horse shied at him. Another fellow said his dogs acted up so much he had to tie them up. The ferryman said he was certain the boat got lighter when he stepped on board. Superstitious nonsense, of course—but well—

THE MOTHER: Well what?

THE OLD MAN: Oh, nothing. . . . I saw a magpie fly through the window to their room, a closed window—right through the windowpane. I guess my eyes are failing me.

THE MOTHER: Probably that's it. But why do we sometimes see right and sometimes not . . . ?

THE OLD MAN: Just being in the same room with that atheist makes me sick. I get a pain, right here in my chest, if he so much as looks at me.

THE MOTHER: We've got to get him out of here. . . . You know, I don't think he's going to enjoy himself here.

THE OLD MAN: Exactly what I was thinking. He won't be around long. Did I tell you I got a letter tonight warning me about that man? The process servers are after him.

THE MOTHER: The process servers in this house!

THE OLD MAN: For his unpaid bills. —But we mustn't forget: he's our guest. The laws of hospitality have to be respected, even for tramps, even for our enemies. Leave him alone for a few days, let him catch his breath. He's being hunted down. You can see he's in the clutches of Providence now. He's going through the mill. First the grinder, then the sifter.*

THE MOTHER: I've already felt an irresistible call to act as the agent of Providence . . .

THE OLD MAN: Careful you don't get your revenge and your calling mixed up.

THE MOTHER: I won't—if it's possible.

THE OLD MAN: Good night . . .

THE MOTHER: Do you think Ingeborg has read his latest book?

THE OLD MAN: Have no idea. Probably not. How could she have become devoted to a man with ideas like that?

THE MOTHER: Exactly. She hasn't read it. But she will. . . . She will . . .

---

* The mills of the gods grind slowly, but they grind exceedingly fine. —Sextus Empiricus.

ACT III

In the Rose Room

A simply furnished, cozy room in the forester's lodge. The walls have been calcimined with a rose-red solution. The curtains are thin, rose-red muslin. Flowers are standing in the rather small lattice windows. To the right, a desk and a bookcase. To the left, a sofa, with rose-red drapes above it arranged to form a baldachin. Chairs and tables in Old German style.*

A door in the rear. Outside, a landscape and the poorhouse, a dark, dismal building, its black windows curtainless. The sun is shining brightly.

The Lady is sitting on the sofa, crocheting. The Mother is standing, holding in her hand a book with red covers.

THE MOTHER: Don't tell me you won't read your own husband's books.

THE LADY: Not that one. I promised him I wouldn't.

THE MOTHER: I should think you'd want to find out everything you could about him. You're placing your whole future in his hands.

THE LADY: What good would that do? We're perfectly happy.

THE MOTHER: You don't ask much of life, do you?

THE LADY: Why should I? You don't get what you ask for anyway.

THE MOTHER: I don't know whether you were born with all the wisdom of the world or if you're as innocent as an idiot.

THE LADY: I don't know either.

* In *Inferno* Strindberg remarks that the old torture chamber in Stockholm was known as the Rose Chamber.

THE MOTHER: As long as the sun is shining and you've got something to eat, you're happy.

THE LADY: Yes. And if the sun isn't shining, I don't complain.

THE MOTHER: To change the subject—do you know the process servers are after your husband because of his debts?

THE LADY: Yes, I know. It's always that way with writers.

THE MOTHER: Honestly, can you tell me whether he's crazy or cunning or what?

THE LADY: No, don't you see—well, he's neither one nor the other. He's different, that's all. And what makes it boring sometimes is that there's nothing I can tell him that he hasn't heard before. So we don't talk very much. But he's happy when I'm around, and I'm happy when he's near.

THE MOTHER: I see. Well, that means you've already reached the still waters right above the falls. It won't be long now. —Maybe you'd have something to talk about if you read the things he's written.

THE LADY: Maybe. If you want to, you can leave it here. I don't care.

THE MOTHER: No, take it and hide it. Won't he be surprised when you start quoting from his masterpiece.

THE LADY (*hiding the book in her bag*): He's coming! I think he can feel from far off when somebody's been talking about him.

THE MOTHER: What a shame he can't feel when others suffer because of him—from far off. (*She leaves.*)

> *The Lady is alone for a moment. Reads at random in the book. Appears shocked. Hides the book in her bag.**

THE STRANGER (*entering*): I can tell your mother's been here. Naturally you talked about me. Her nasty words are still ricocheting from wall to wall—still slashing the air and blackening

---

* The book is *Le Plaidoyer d'un fou* (A Madman's Defense), Strindberg's frank and detailed account of his first marriage.

the sunbeams—I can even make out the impression her body left on the air in this room—and she left a little memento behind her, the fetid smell of a crushed snake.

THE LADY: My, you're really on edge today, aren't you?

THE STRANGER: I'm strung as tightly as a violin and someone's rasping out a duck call on my nerves with a horsehair bow. Onk! Onk! —You know what a duck call is, don't you? . . . There's someone here, someone stronger than I am—someone searching me out with huge searchlights wherever I go. —I wonder, do they practice witchcraft in these parts?

THE LADY: Don't turn your back to the sun. Look out at the countryside, and you'll calm down.

THE STRANGER: No, I can't bear to look at that poorhouse. It must have been built there just for me. And there's a crazy old woman always standing there, beckoning me.

THE LADY: What's the matter with you? Do you feel you're being treated badly here?

THE STRANGER: In one way, no. I'm stuffed with delicacies, as if I were being fattened for the kill. But nothing tastes good to me because I know they hate to give it to me. I can feel the hate here, like the cold blast from an ice cellar. I can feel a cold wind everywhere, even though it's deathly still and unbearably hot. And always I hear that damned mill grinding away . . .

THE LADY: It's not grinding now.

THE STRANGER: Oh, but it is. Grinding . . . grinding . . .

THE LADY: Now listen, darling, no one here hates you. Maybe they feel sorry for you, that's all.

THE STRANGER: And something else—why do the people cross themselves when they see me coming down the road?

THE LADY: Because they've just finished reciting their prayers to themselves—that's all. . . . I hear you got a very unpleasant letter this morning.

THE STRANGER: Made my hair stand on end. I wanted to spit

fate right in the eye. Imagine, I've got money coming to me, but I can't put my hands on it, and now I'm being dragged into court—by my children's guardians, for not paying the alimony. Have you ever heard of such a humiliating situation? And I'm not to blame. I know what's right, I want to do the right thing, but I'm not allowed to. Is that my fault? No, but the shame is mine. The whole thing's unnatural. The devil's behind it.

THE LADY: But why?

THE STRANGER: Who the hell knows why? Why are we put here on earth poor ignorant creatures, ignorant of laws, customs, conventions, which in our ignorance we break and then get spanked for? Why do we grow up with our heads filled with noble dreams that we struggle to make come true? And why are we always forced down into all the filth we try to rise above? Why? Why?

> *The Lady has been reading in the book, unnoticed by The Stranger.*

THE LADY (*indifferently*): Must be some reason, even if we can't figure it out.

THE STRANGER: If the idea is to teach humility, as they say it is, then it's a damned poor way, because it only makes me more arrogant, more proud. . . . Eve—

THE LADY: Don't call me that!

THE STRANGER (*stung*): Why not?

THE LADY: I don't like it, any more than you like being called Caesar.

THE STRANGER: Back to that again.

THE LADY: Back to what again?

THE STRANGER: You had some ulterior motive for using that name. It didn't just—

THE LADY: Caesar? No, I didn't. But I see that I'm about to be enlightened.

THE STRANGER: Exactly. I want the honor of dying by my

own hand. —I am Caesar, the schoolboy who played a schoolboy trick for which someone else was punished. That someone was your husband—the werewolf. You see how fate amuses itself by weaving the strands together forever and ever. What a noble pastime!

> *The Lady is about to say something, but hesitates and remains silent.*

THE STRANGER: Well, say something.

THE LADY: I can't.

THE STRANGER: Come on. Can't you say he became a werewolf because of me—because I caused him to lose his faith in the justice of heaven when he was unfairly punished for what someone else had done? Say it, so I can tell you my conscience made me suffer ten times as much as he did, and that I came out of that religious crisis so cleansed in spirit that I never again did a thing like that.

THE LADY: It isn't that. It isn't that.

THE STRANGER: Then what is it? . . . I see. You no longer have any respect for me.

THE LADY: No, it isn't that either.

THE STRANGER: What then? You want me to writhe in shame in front of you? Then it really would be all over between us.

THE LADY: No. No.

THE STRANGER: Eve—

THE LADY: Don't call me that! You make me think awful things . . .

THE STRANGER: You've broken your promise. You've read my book.

THE LADY: Yes.

THE STRANGER: That was pretty mean.

THE LADY: My intentions were good. I thought that—

THE STRANGER: Good intentions! The road to hell. —Well, that does it. Blown to pieces! And I provided the powder myself. . . . It's great! Everything has to come back, repeat itself, everything—little schoolboy tricks and big manly crimes. That we reap as we sow, fair enough. But if only someday I could see a good deed get its reward. —Never get to see that. Shame on that angel who records every fault, big and small. There isn't a person living who would do that. And people forgive, but the gods never do.

THE LADY: Don't say that. Don't. Say you can forgive.

THE STRANGER: I'm not small-minded, you know that. But what have I to forgive you?

THE LADY: I don't know that I dare to tell you . . .

THE STRANGER: You might as well. Maybe that will make us even.

THE LADY: Well . . . he and I used to read the curse from Deuteronomy over you—the person who had ruined his life.

THE STRANGER: What sort of curse is that?

THE LADY: It's from the fifth book of Moses. The priests recite it in chorus when Lent begins.

THE STRANGER: I don't recall it. But what difference does it make?—one curse more or less.

THE LADY: It matters because in my family there's a tradition that whoever we curse will be struck down.

THE STRANGER: Well, I don't believe in it. —Although I haven't the slightest doubt that evil emanates from this house. May it redound on their heads! That's my prayer. . . . (*Reverting to earlier thoughts.*) According to the custom of the country, there's nothing for me to do now but blow my brains out—which I can't do since I still have some obligations to fulfill. How do you like that! I can't even be allowed to die—which means I've lost the last remnant of what I called my religion. That's really ingenious. I've heard that men can wrestle with God, and not without success, but even Job couldn't fight with Satan. . . . (*Pause.*) Maybe we should talk a little bit about you.

THE LADY: Not now, but perhaps soon. . . . After reading your terrible book—I've only glanced at it here and there, but that's enough—I feel as if I've eaten of the tree of knowledge. My eyes have been opened, and I know the difference between good and evil. I didn't before. Now I see what an evil man you really are, and I know why you wanted to call me Eve. But if she brought sin with her, another mother brought redemption. If the first brought corruption to life, the second brought life with a blessing. So you can't use me to destroy my whole sex. I think I may have an altogether different purpose in your life. We'll see.

THE STRANGER: So you've eaten of the fruit of the tree of knowledge, have you? —Goodbye.

THE LADY: Are you leaving?

THE STRANGER: Of course. You can't expect me to stay here.

THE LADY: Don't go!

THE STRANGER: I have to. I'm up to my neck in trouble. I have to clear it up. I'll go and say goodbye to the old folks and then come back to you. —I'll be back in a moment. (*He leaves.*)

THE LADY (*stands petrified for a moment. Then she goes to the door and looks out*): Oh, no! He's gone! He's gone! (*She sinks to her knees.*)

* * *

The Asylum

The refectory in an old cloister. It resembles a simple, whitewashed church with rounded Romanesque arches, but the walls are marked with damp stains forming strange figures.

A dining table with bowls on it. At the end of the table, a lectern. In the rear, a door to the chapel. Lighted candles on the table. On the left wall, a painting of Michael slaying the dragon.

At a long dining table to the left, The Stranger is sitting alone, dressed in a white hospital gown, with a bowl in front of him. At the table to the right are sitting the

TO DAMASCUS [ACT III]

Pallbearers in brown from the first act; The Beggar; a Woman in Mourning with Two Children; another Woman who resembles The Lady but is not she, and who is crocheting instead of eating; a Man who resembles The Doctor but is not he; The Madman's Double; Doubles of The Father and The Mother; The Brother's Double; The Parents of the "prodigal son," * and others. All are dressed in white but over their white gowns they are wearing gauze costumes in various colors. Their faces are waxen and deathly white. Their whole appearance and all their gestures are ghostlike.

As the curtain rises, all are finishing the Lord's Prayer, except The Stranger.

The Stranger gets up and goes over to The Abbess, who is standing at the serving table.

THE STRANGER: Mother, may I speak to you a moment?

THE ABBESS (*in the black-and-white habit of the Augustinians*): Yes, my son.

They go downstage.

THE STRANGER: First I want to know where I am.

THE ABBESS: In the cloister of "The Helping Hand." You were seen in the mountains above the ravine, with a cross you had torn down from a calvary, and you were using it to challenge someone you imagined you could see in the clouds. You had a fever, and you fell over the cliff. That's where you were found, uninjured but delirious, and then you were brought here to the hospital and put to bed. Since then you've been raving deliriously, and complaining of a pain in your thigh, although we haven't been able to find an injury.

THE STRANGER: What was I raving about?

* The parents of the "prodigal son" are The Old Man and The Mother, who had regarded The Stranger as their own son. Strindberg looked upon his wife's parents as his own.

THE ABBESS: You had the usual feverish dreams that sick people have. You reproached yourself with everything imaginable, and you kept seeing before you all your "victims," as you called them.

THE STRANGER: Anything else?

THE ABBESS: Your thoughts revolved mainly around money, and you kept insisting on paying for your treatment here in the hospital. I tried to calm you by assuring you that we don't accept payment here. This is a house of charity.

THE STRANGER: I don't want charity. I don't need charity.

THE ABBESS: It's true that it's more blessed to give than to receive, but it takes a certain nobility of soul to receive and be grateful.

THE STRANGER: I don't need to receive anything, and I ask for nothing. You can't force me to be grateful.

THE ABBESS: As you wish.

THE STRANGER: Can you tell me why none of these people will sit at the same table with me? They get up and move away . . .

THE ABBESS: Perhaps they're afraid of you.

THE STRANGER: Afraid? Why?

THE ABBESS: Well you do look rather . . .

THE STRANGER: I look! What about them? How do they look? Are they for real?

THE ABBESS: If you mean do they exist, yes, they are terribly real. If they appear strange to you, it may be because you still have the fever—or because of something else.

THE STRANGER: But I seem to recognize them, all of them. And I see them as if they were in a mirror. . . . They're only pretending to eat. Is this some kind of a charade? . . . That couple sitting over there, they look like my parents—fleetingly. . . . I've never been afraid of anything before, because life never meant anything to me. But now I'm growing more and more frightened.

TO DAMASCUS [ACT III]   449

THE ABBESS: If you don't believe that they are actual persons, we can call the confessor over and he can introduce them to us. (*She signals to The Confessor, who comes over.*)

THE CONFESSOR (*in a Dominican habit, black and white*): Yes, Sister?

THE ABBESS: Could you tell our patient here who those people are sitting at that table?

THE CONFESSOR: Of course. That's easily done.

THE STRANGER: Before you do that—haven't we met before?

THE CONFESSOR: Yes, I sat at your bedside while you were sick with fever, and, at your request, I heard your confession.

THE STRANGER: My confession!

THE CONFESSOR: Yes. I could not give you absolution, however, since I felt that your confession consisted of nothing but the ravings of a fevered mind.

THE STRANGER: What do you mean?

THE CONFESSOR: Why, there was scarcely a crime or a sin that you did not take upon yourself—and, moreover, deeds of such depravity that it is customary to submit to the strongest penance before asking for absolution. Since you have now regained your senses, I feel I should ask if there are any grounds for these self-accusations.

The Abbess withdraws.

THE STRANGER: What right do you have to ask that?

THE CONFESSOR: None at all, that's true. —But I forgot—you wanted to know about these people in whose company you find yourself. I believe it's fair to say that they are not the most fortunate of human beings. There, for example, we have a lunatic called Caesar.* He lost his mind reading the works of a certain

---

* At the end of 1888 Strindberg was corresponding with Nietzsche when the German philosopher went mad. Strindberg feared that the same fate might befall him. One of Nietzsche's letters was signed "Caesar."

450   TO DAMASCUS [ACT III]

author who was more notorious than praiseworthy. And then we have a beggar who won't admit he's a beggar because he's gone to the university, learned Latin, and doesn't believe in taxes. Next there's the doctor—or the werewolf, as he's called—whose story is too familiar to need repeating. And then a mother and a father who grieved themselves to death over a wicked and depraved son who raised his hand against them. That he did not follow his father's remains to the cemetery, and that he, while intoxicated, profaned his mother's grave, are deeds that need not concern us. And there sits his poor sister whom he drove out into the winter snow—with the best of intentions, or so he insisted. There sits a deserted wife with two uncared-for children, and there sits another wife, crocheting. All in all, nothing but old acquaintances. Go and say hello to them.

During the latter part of this speech, The Stranger has turned his back to the company. He now goes and sits at the table to the left, keeping his back to the others. When he lifts his head, he sees the picture of Michaël and lowers his eyes.

The Confessor goes forward and stands behind The Stranger. At the same time a Catholic requiem is heard from within the chapel. The Confessor speaks softly to The Stranger, while the music continues quietly.

THE CONFESSOR:

*Quantus tremor est futurus
Quando judex est venturus
Cuncta stricte discussurus,
Tuba mirum spargens sonum
Per sepulchra regionum
Coget omnes ante thronum.
Mors stupebit et natura,
Cum resurget creatura
Liber scriptus proferetur
In quo totum continetur
Unde mundus judicetur.
Judex ergo cum sedebit*

TO DAMASCUS [ACT III] 451

Quidquid latet apparebit
*Nil inultum remanebit.**

He goes to the lectern at the table to the right. Opens the breviary. The music ceases.

THE CONFESSOR: We shall now continue the lesson. "But if thou wilt not harken unto the voice of the Lord thy God, to observe all his commandments and his statutes, all these curses shall come upon thee, and overtake thee. Cursed shalt thou be in the city, and cursed shalt thou be in the field. Cursed shall be thy basket and thy store. Cursed shalt thou be when thou comes in, and cursed shalt thou be when thou goest out."

THE COMPANY (*with subdued voices*): Cursed shalt thou be!

THE CONFESSOR: "The Lord shall send upon thee curses, vexation, and rebuke, in all that thou settest thine hand for to do, until thou be destroyed, and until thou perish quickly; because of the wickedness of thy doings, whereby thou hast forsaken me."

THE COMPANY (*loud*): Cursed shalt thou be!

THE CONFESSOR: "The Lord shall cause thee to be smitten before thine enemies; thou shalt go out one way against them, and flee seven ways before them; and shalt be removed into all the kingdoms of the earth. And thy carcass shall be meat unto all the fowls of the air, and unto the beasts of the earth, and no man shall fray them away.

"The Lord will smite thee with the botch of Egypt, and with the

---

* From the *Dies Irae*, a *sequentia* peculiar to the requiem Mass, "What trembling there will be/ When the Judge comes/ To make stringent examination of all things./ The trumpet scattering awesome sound/ Through the tombs of the earth's regions/ Will herd all men before His throne./ Death and nature will stand aghast/ When creation rises again./ The written Book will be brought forth/ In which everything is contained/ From which the world will be judged./ Thus when the Judge is seated,/ There will emerge manifest anything that lies hidden;/ Nothing will be left unpunished."

scab and with the itch, and with a fever, and with an inflammation, and with an extreme burning, and with madness and blindness and astonishment of heart; and thou shalt grope at noonday as the blind gropeth in darkness, and thou shalt not prosper in thy ways: and thou shalt be only oppressed and spoiled evermore, and no man shall save thee. Thou shalt betroth a wife, and another man shall lie with her: thou shalt build an house, and thou shalt not dwell therein: thou shalt plant a vineyard, and shalt not gather the grapes thereof. Thy sons and thy daughters shall be given unto another people, and thine eyes shall look, and fail with longing for them all the day long: and there shall be no might in thine hand. And among these nations shalt thou find no ease, neither shall the sole of thy foot have rest: but the Lord shall give thee there a trembling heart, and failing of eyes, and sorrow of mind. And thy life shall hang on a thread before thee; and thou shalt fear day and night, and shalt have no assurance of thy life. In the morning thou shalt say, Would God it were even! and at even thou shalt say, Would God it were morning! And because thou servedst not the Lord thy God in the abundance of all things, therefore shalt thou serve Him in hunger and in thirst, and in nakedness and in want of all things, which the Lord shall send against thee. And he shall put a yoke of iron upon thy neck, until he have destroyed thee."*

THE COMPANY: Amen!

> *The Confessor has read the curse fast and loud, without directing himself to The Stranger. The others, except for The Lady who is crocheting, have listened and joined in the curses, but without appearing to notice The*

---

* The curse is from Deuteronomy, Chapter 28. Though a Catholic version would be more appropriate to a reading in this cloister, I have used the King James version because it follows Strindberg's text more closely. However, I have had to make some changes even in the King James version, most notably in the last lines where it reads: "Therefore shalt thou serve thine enemies. . . . " Strindberg himself did not reproduce the text of any of the three or four Swedish Bibles that I have been able to consult.

Stranger. Throughout the reading he has sat with his back to the others, lost in thought.

THE STRANGER: What was that?

THE CONFESSOR: That was the curse from Deuteronomy.

THE STRANGER: So that's what it was. But as I remember, it also offered a blessing.

THE CONFESSOR: Yes—to those who keep His commandments.

THE STRANGER: Ah, yes, of course. —I can't deny that for a moment I was quite shaken. The question is: am I being exposed to temptation that must be resisted or given warnings that must be obeyed? . . . Anyway, one thing is certain: I've still got my fever, and I'm going to see a real doctor.

THE CONFESSOR: Yes, but be sure he's the real one.

THE STRANGER: Of course, of course.

THE CONFESSOR: The one who cures those "exquisite pangs of conscience."

THE ABBESS: And if you should ever have need of charity, you know where you can find it, don't you?

THE STRANGER: No, I don't.

THE ABBESS (*softly*): Then let me tell you. In a rose-red room near a great rushing river.

THE STRANGER: In a rose-red room. . . . That's true. . . . How long have I been lying sick here?

THE ABBESS: Exactly three months today.

THE STRANGER: A fourth of a year! (*Sighs.*) Have I been asleep the whole time? Or where have I been (*Looks out the windows.*) Why, it's already fall. The trees are bare, and the clouds are blue with cold. . . . It's coming back to me. . . . Do you hear a millwheel turning? A hunting horn echoing in the hills? A forest murmuring . . . a river roaring . . . and a woman crying? Yes, you're right. That's the only place I'll find charity. —Goodbye. (*He leaves hastily.*)

THE CONFESSOR (*to The Abbess*): A mad fool! Mad fool!

* * *

The Rose Room

The curtains have been removed. The windows are like black holes gaping into the darkness outside. The furniture is covered with brown sheets and pushed together in the center of the room. The flowers are gone. A large black stove is lit. The Mother stands ironing white curtains by the light of a single lamp.

A knocking is heard at the door.

THE MOTHER: Come in.

THE STRANGER (*entering*): Hello. —Where's my wife?

THE MOTHER: So it's you. —Where have you been?

THE STRANGER: In hell—I think. . . . Where's my wife?

THE MOTHER: Which one?

THE STRANGER: That's good.

THE MOTHER: Don't you think the question has its point?

THE STRANGER: Absolutely. Everything has its point— except my existence.

THE MOTHER: There may be a reason for that. But the fact that you've noticed it is a point in your favor. —Now where have you been?

THE STRANGER: I don't know whether it was a poorhouse or a madhouse or just a plain ordinary hospital. I prefer to take it all as a bad feverish dream. I've been sick—lost my memory—I still can't believe that three months have gone by. . . . But where's my wife?

THE MOTHER: I should be asking you that. When you left her, she left here—to look for you. But whether or not she got tired of looking, I don't know.

THE STRANGER: It looks ghastly here. . . . Where's the old man?

THE MOTHER: Gone. And where he's gone he has no more sorrows.

THE STRANGER: Dead?

THE MOTHER: Yes, he's dead.

THE STRANGER: You say that as if you're trying to add him to the list of my "victims."

THE MOTHER: Would I be wrong?

THE STRANGER: He could take care of himself, and he was capable of nourishing a good healthy hatred.

THE MOTHER: You're wrong. He could only hate what was evil—in himself and others.

THE STRANGER: All right, I was wrong—as usual.

Pause.

THE MOTHER: What did you expect to find here?

THE STRANGER: Charity.

THE MOTHER: Really. —How was it at the hospital? Sit down and tell me about it.

THE STRANGER (*sitting down*): I don't care to recall it. Besides, I don't know if it actually was a hospital.

THE MOTHER: Strange. What happened after you left here?

THE STRANGER: I fell somewhere up in the mountains, hurt my thigh, and fainted. —None of your sarcasm now, or I won't tell you the rest.

THE MOTHER: I'll be sweet as sugar.

THE STRANGER: I wake up one day. I'm in a bed with steel rails, painted red. And three men are pulling on a rope that runs through two pulleys. And every time they pull, I feel myself grow two yards longer. And—

THE MOTHER: You were in traction, and they were trying to set your hip.

THE STRANGER: That could be. I never thought of that. But

later—oh . . . I lay there and saw—like a panorama—my whole life unroll before me, from childhood through youth and all the way up to . . . and when the roll ended, it began all over again. . . . And all the time I could hear a millwheel turning and the millstone grinding. . . . And I can still hear it . . . I can even hear it now.

THE MOTHER: Those couldn't have been very pretty pictures you saw.

THE STRANGER: No, they weren't. . . . I finally came to the conclusion that I was a louse.

THE MOTHER: Why use that expression?

THE STRANGER: You'd prefer me to call myself wicked, depraved, unprincipled, wouldn't you? But that sounds like bragging. Furthermore, it has the ring of certainty about it and I'm still not certain—about anything.

THE MOTHER: Still skeptical?

THE STRANGER: Afraid so, about a lot of things. One thing does seem clearer to me, however.

THE MOTHER: Yes?

THE STRANGER: That there are things . . . forces . . . powers . . . that I . . . didn't believe existed.

THE MOTHER: Haven't you also noticed that neither you nor anyone else has charge of your unusual destiny?

THE STRANGER: That's what I mean.

THE MOTHER: You're making progress.

THE STRANGER: That isn't all that's happened. I'm bankrupt. I can't write. And on top of that, I can't sleep at night.

THE MOTHER: Can't sleep?

THE STRANGER: Nightmares—I guess that's the word for them. . . . But last and worst is that I don't dare to die because I'm no longer certain that our misery ends when our end comes.

THE MOTHER: Oh?

THE STRANGER: That's not all. What's even worse is that I have become so disgusted with myself that I want to crawl out of my skin. I don't see much chance of that, however. If I were a Christian, I couldn't obey even the first Commandment—love thy neighbor as thyself—because that would mean hating my neighbor—which is exactly what I do. It really must be true that I'm a rotten heel. I've always suspected it, of course, but since I didn't want to be made a fool of, I kept a close eye on all the others. When I saw that they weren't any better than I, I became furious when they tried to act superior.

THE MOTHER: Don't you see that you've misunderstood everything by thinking of it as an affair just between you and the others, when it's really a matter between you and Him?

THE STRANGER: Who?

THE MOTHER: The Invisible One who has been working out your destiny.

THE STRANGER: I'd love to meet him face to face!

THE MOTHER: You'd die!

THE STRANGER: Oh, no, I wouldn't!

THE MOTHER: What is it that makes you so infernally rebellious? If you can't bend like the rest of us, you'll be snapped in half like a dry twig.

THE STRANGER: I don't know what it is that makes me as defiant as Satan himself. I can shake and tremble before an unpaid bill, but if I were to climb Mount Sinai and confront the Almighty Himself, I wouldn't even shield my eyes.

THE MOTHER: Holy Mary Mother of God! Talk like that, you must be the Devil's brood!

THE STRANGER: Seems to be the general opinion around here. I thought that those who were in league with Old Nick were showered with honors, goods, gold—especially gold. Now how can you suspect me?

THE MOTHER: Because you are a curse on my house.

THE STRANGER: Then I shall leave your house—

THE MOTHER: In the middle of the night? No. . . . Where do you intend to go?

THE STRANGER: I'm going to look for the only person I don't hate.

THE MOTHER: What makes you think she'll want to see you?

THE STRANGER: I'm certain she will.

THE MOTHER: I'm not!

THE STRANGER: Well, I am!

THE MOTHER: I'll change that. You'll see.

THE STRANGER: You can't do a thing about it.

THE MOTHER: Oh, yes, I can.

THE STRANGER: Like hell you can!

THE MOTHER: We seem to have used up the sugar. We'd better stop. . . . Do you mind sleeping in the attic?

THE STRANGER: Doesn't matter where, I won't sleep anyway.

THE MOTHER: All right. . . . Pleasant dreams—whether or not you think I mean it.

THE STRANGER: There aren't any rats in the attic, are there? I'm not afraid of ghosts, but I don't like rats.

THE MOTHER: Not afraid of ghosts? That's a relief. No one has ever slept through the night up there—whatever the reason may be.

THE STRANGER (*lingers a moment. Then says*): You know, you're the meanest person I've ever met in my life. Must be because you're religious.

THE MOTHER: Good night.

* * *

The Kitchen

It is dark, but the moon throws on the floor shifting shadows of the window lattices as storm clouds draw by.

TO DAMASCUS [ACT III] 459

Under the crucifix in the corner to the right, where The Old Man used to sit, a horn, a gun, and a hunting bag are hanging on the wall. A stuffed hawk or similar bird of prey stands on the table. The windows are open and the curtains are fluttering, and the rags and cloths, the aprons and towels that are hanging to dry on the line in front of the stove are flapping in the wind. One can hear the soughing of the wind, the roar of a distant waterfall, and now and then the sound of pounding on a wooden floor.

THE STRANGER (*enters, half-dressed, a lamp in his hand*): Is anyone here? . . . No one. (*Moves forward with the light, which lessens somewhat the play of the shadows.*) What's that moving on the floor? . . . Is anyone here? (*He goes toward the table, but when he catches sight of the bird he stops, petrified.*) Jesus Christ!

THE MOTHER (*enters, dressed, a lamp in her hand*): You still up?

THE STRANGER: Yes. I couldn't sleep.

THE MOTHER (*gently*): Why not, my son?

THE STRANGER: I heard footsteps over my room.

THE MOTHER: That's impossible. There's no attic above your room.

THE STRANGER: I know. That's what bothered me. — What's that crawling on the floor like snakes?

THE MOTHER: That's the moonlight.

THE STRANGER: Of course, the moonlight. And that's a stuffed bird. And those are old rags. Everything is so simple and natural — and that's exactly what bothers me. . . . Who was that knocking in the middle of the night? Is somebody locked out?

THE MOTHER: No, it's a horse stamping in his stall.

THE STRANGER: I've never heard of a horse stamping like that.

THE MOTHER: Some horses have nightmares.

THE STRANGER: Odd. What are nightmares?

THE MOTHER: Who knows?

THE STRANGER: Do you mind if I sit down for a moment?

THE MOTHER: Yes, sit down. Let's have a serious talk. I was mean and cruel to you last night. Please forgive me. You understand, it's just because I am so awfully mean that I make use of religion in the same way I'd make use of a hair shirt and a stone floor. . . . As for nightmares, not to offend you by asking, I'll give you my own opinion of what they are. They're my bad conscience. I don't know if it's myself or someone else who is punishing me, and I don't assume I have the right to find out. That's how I see it. . . . Now suppose you tell me what happened in your room.

THE STRANGER: I—I really don't know. I didn't actually see anything, but when I walked into the room, I felt there was someone there. Looked around with the lamp, but didn't see anyone. So I went to bed. Then it began—someone walking with heavy steps right over my head. . . . Do you believe in spooks and ghosts?

THE MOTHER: No, I don't. It's against my religion. But I do believe that our sense of right and wrong has the power to create its own form of punishment.

THE STRANGER: Yes. . . . Well, anyhow, after a short while, I felt an ice-cold current of air aimed at my chest—probing around until it found my heart—and then that grew cold—and I had to get out of bed . . .

THE MOTHER: And then?

THE STRANGER: Then I had to stand there in the middle of the room and watch the whole panorama of my life roll by—everything—everything. . . . There's nothing worse, nothing.

THE MOTHER: I know what it's like. I've been through it too. There's no name for that illness, and there's only one cure.

THE STRANGER: What's that?

THE MOTHER: You know what. You know what children have to do when they've been bad.

THE STRANGER: No, what do they have to do?

THE MOTHER: First, say they're sorry and ask to be forgiven—

THE STRANGER: And next?

THE MOTHER: Try to make things right.

THE STRANGER: Isn't it enough that you suffer as you deserve to suffer?

THE MOTHER: That's vengeance, that's all that is.

THE STRANGER: Of course, what else?

THE MOTHER: If you've ruined someone's life, can you make it good again? Can you undo a bad deed? Undo what's done?

THE STRANGER: No, that's true. —But I was forced to do what I did, forced to take, because nobody would acknowledge that I was right. Why blame me? Blame the one who forced me—and shame on him. —Ohh! (*His hand clutching his chest.*)* Ohh! He's here, here in this room—and he's tearing my heart from my chest. Ohh!

THE MOTHER: Bend down!

THE STRANGER: I cannot!

THE MOTHER: On your knees!

THE STRANGER: I will not!

THE MOTHER: Christ have mercy on you! The Lord have mercy on you! (*To The Stranger.*) On your knees before Him who was crucified! Only He can undo the past.

THE STRANGER: No, not before Him! No, not Him! And if I'm forced to, I'll take it back—later!

THE MOTHER: Kneel—kneel, my son!

THE STRANGER: I cannot kneel—I cannot. —Help me. Almighty God!

Pause.

---

* An attack of angina pectoris.

THE MOTHER (*quickly mumbles a prayer. Then says*): Is it better now?

THE STRANGER (*recovering*): Yes. . . . Do you know what that was? It wasn't death. It was annihilation.

THE MOTHER: Annihilation of the divine. What we call the death of the spirit.

THE STRANGER (*earnestly, without irony*): Is that what you're getting at? . . . I think I'm beginning to understand.

THE MOTHER: My son: you have left Jerusalem and you are on the way to Damascus. Go there. The same way you came here. And plant a cross at each station, but stop at the seventh. You don't have fourteen, as He had.

THE STRANGER: You're talking in riddles.

THE MOTHER: Let me put it this way. Travel. Look up those you have something to say to. And first of all, your wife.

THE STRANGER: Where?

THE MOTHER: Seek and ye shall find. And on your way don't forget one person in particular – the werewolf, as you call him.

THE STRANGER: Oh, no. Never!

THE MOTHER: I understand that's what you said when circumstances were forcing you this way. But, as I told you, I knew you would come. I was waiting for you.

THE STRANGER: Why?

THE MOTHER: No logical reason.

THE STRANGER: Just as I saw this kitchen in a – what shall I call it – a rapture of some sort . . .

THE MOTHER: That's why I regret having tried to separate you and Ingeborg. You were meant to meet each other. – Anyway, you better go and look for her. If you find her, good – if you don't, maybe that was meant to happen too. – The dawn is breaking. It's morning, and the night is over.

THE STRANGER: And what a night!

THE MOTHER: You won't forget it!

THE STRANGER: Not all of it, that's certain.

THE MOTHER (*looks out of the window. As if to herself*): Son of the morning, why art thou fallen from heaven?*

Pause.

THE STRANGER: Have you noticed how—just before the sun goes up—a shiver runs through you? Are we children of darkness that we tremble before the light?

THE MOTHER: Don't you ever get tired of asking questions?

THE STRANGER: Never. I long for the light, you see.

THE MOTHER: Then go and look for it. And peace be with you.

---

* See Isaiah 14:12: "How art thou fallen from heaven, O Lucifer, son of the morning." Lucifer is the planet Venus when it appears as the morning star.

ACT IV

In the Ravine

Same landscape as before, but now it is autumn, and the trees are bare.

The mill is working, and there is hammering in the blacksmith shop.

The Blacksmith stands in his doorway at the left; The Miller's Wife in the doorway at the right.

The Lady is dressed in mourning, with a jacket and a patent leather hat (derby style).

The Stranger wears a Bavarian Alps outfit: lodenjoppe (shooting jacket), knickers, climbing shoes, alpenstock, and a green hat with a feather in it. Over this outfit he is wearing a brown ulster (Kaiser-mantel) with a hood.

THE LADY (*enters, in traveling clothes, tired and woebegone*): Did you by any chance see a man wearing a brown coat pass by here recently?

The Blacksmith and The Miller's Wife shake their heads.

THE LADY: Could you put me up for the night?

The Blacksmith and The Miller's Wife shake their heads sternly.

THE LADY (*to The Blacksmith*): Do you mind if I stand here in the doorway and warm myself for a moment?

The Blacksmith pushes her away.

THE LADY: Thanks. God help you! (*She leaves and is seen on the footbridge before she disappears from sight.*)

TO DAMASCUS [ACT IV] 465

THE STRANGER (*enters, in traveling clothes*): Did you by any chance see a lady wearing a jacket cross the stream here?

The Blacksmith and The Miller's Wife shake their heads.

THE STRANGER: Could you let me have a loaf of bread? I've got money to pay for it.

The Miller's Wife spurns the money.

THE STRANGER: No charity?

The echo in the distance mimics his voice, "Charity!" The Blacksmith and The Miller's Wife break out in long, loud laughter, which is picked up and repeated by the echo.

THE STRANGER: This is more like it. Eye for eye, tooth for tooth! That always helped to relieve my conscience. (*He goes into the ravine.*)

* * *

On the Road

Same landscape as before, but now it is autumn.

The Beggar is sitting at one of the shrines. Beside him are a lime twig and a birdcage with a starling in it.*

THE STRANGER (*enters, dressed as in the previous scene*): Did you see a lady wearing a jacket go by here? I suppose a beggar sees everybody who passes by.

THE BEGGAR: I've seen five hundred passers-by pass by. But

---

* The birdcage may be intended to associate The Beggar with the bird-catcher Papageno in Mozart's *The Magic Flute*. (Suggested by Barry Jacobs.)

would you mind not calling me a beggar? Seriously. I've got a job.

THE STRANGER: Oh, it's you. I didn't recognize you.

THE BEGGAR: *Ille ego qui quondam*—*

THE STRANGER: What kind of work do you do?

THE BEGGAR: I've got a bird here that whistles and talks.

THE STRANGER: I see: the bird does the work.

THE BEGGAR: Yes, I've got myself well set up.

THE STRANGER: Do you catch birds too?

THE BEGGAR: Oh, the lime twig? Not at all. That's only for appearance's sake.

THE STRANGER: You're only interested in appearances?

THE BEGGAR: Yes. What else is there to interest one? What's inside—nothing but muck.

THE STRANGER: And that's your philosophy in a nutshell?

THE BEGGAR: The whole of my metaphysical system. It may indeed appear to some to be antiquated; however—

THE STRANGER: Come now, let's have at least one serious word from you. Tell me something about your past.

THE BEGGAR: Usch! What good does it do to muck around in garbage? A waste of time. Push ahead, eyes front, keep moving. —Don't think I always feel like joking. Not on your life! It's only when I meet you. You're damned comical, you know.

THE STRANGER: How can you laugh? You've wasted your whole life.

THE BEGGAR: Now that's hitting home. —Listen, if you can't laugh at the whole mess, not even when it's someone else's, you'd

* I, the man who once—. From the *Aeneid*, the false opening. Aptly alluded to here because Virgil is speaking of his transformation from bucolic to martial poet. The Beggar is participating in The Stranger's transformation.

better cash in your chips. —Let me give you some advice. Follow these wheel tracks in the muck here; you'll come down to the sea; that's where the road ends. Sit down there and take a rest and you'll get a new slant on things. Up here there are too many bad omens, religious relics, unhappy memories, which keep your thoughts from flying off to the rose room. You just follow the trail, just follow the trail. And if it gets too dusty, lift up your wings and give a few flaps.

Talking about wings reminds me: a little bird once told me about Polycrates and his ring. Now he got all the good things in the world and didn't know what to do with them. So he spread the word in the east and in the west about the empty universe he had helped to create out of the universal void. I wouldn't insist it was you, except I'm so dead certain I'd take my dying oath on it. I once asked you if you knew who I was, and you said it didn't interest you. I offered you my friendship in return, which you refused with a curt little "Get out!" Fortunately I'm not one to take such things to heart. So I'm giving you a piece of good advice, something to ruminate on: follow the trail.

THE STRANGER (*avoiding him*): No, you're not going to trick me again.

THE BEGGAR: Good sir, you always think the worst, so you always end up with the worst. Just for once: why don't you try to think the best?

THE STRANGER: I want to. I do want to. But if I'm always tricked and cheated, I've got a right to—

THE BEGGAR: No. You've never got that right!

THE STRANGER (*as if to himself*): Who reads me like an open book? Turns my soul inside out? Who is persecuting me? Wherefore persecutest thou me?

THE BEGGAR: Wherefore persecutest thou me? Saul!

> With a gesture of terror, The Stranger leaves. Chords from the funeral march are heard as before.

THE LADY (*enters*): Has a man wearing a brown coat gone by here?

THE BEGGAR: Yes, just now. A poor devil limping on his way.

THE LADY: The man I'm looking for doesn't limp.

THE BEGGAR: Neither does this fellow, actually. But he seems to have contracted trouble in his thigh, which made him a little unsteady. Don't mind me: I'm just being mean. —Look in the dust of the road.

THE LADY: Where?

THE BEGGAR (*pointing*): There. You see the wheel tracks? And beside it the imprint of a thick shoe made by a heavy tread.

THE LADY (*looking carefully at the tracks*): That's him. Yes, they are heavy steps. . . . Do you think I can catch up with him?

THE BEGGAR: Follow the trail!

THE LADY (*takes his hand and kisses it*): Thank you, my friend. (*She goes.*)

* * *

By the Sea

The same landscape as before, but now it is winter. The sea is blue-black. Clouds like giant heads tower up on the horizon. In the distance are the three white, unrigged masts of a foundered ship, resembling three white crosses. The table and the bench under the tree are still there, but the chairs are gone.

Snow on the ground.

Now and then the clang of a bell buoy is heard.

The Stranger enters from the left. Stands for a moment looking out over the sea; then exits to the right, behind the cabin.

The Lady enters from the left and appears to be following the footprints of The Stranger in the snow. Goes out to the right in front *of the cabin.*

The Stranger reenters from the right, crosses left, discovers The Lady's footprints. Stands and looks back to the right.

The Lady reenters, runs into his arms, but suddenly falls back a step.

THE LADY: Are you pushing me away?

THE STRANGER: No. There seems to be something between us.

THE LADY: I suppose there is. What a reunion!

THE STRANGER: It's gotten very cold as you can see. Winter.

THE LADY: I can feel the cold streaming out from you.

THE STRANGER: I was caked in ice up in the mountains.

THE LADY: Will spring ever come again?

THE STRANGER: Not for us. We've been driven out of the Garden of Eden. All we can do is pick our way over the stones and thorns. And after we've cut our feet and pricked our hands, we'll pour salt in our wounds—each other's. And the mill will be grinding and grinding and never, never stop, for there's never a lack of water.

THE LADY: I'm afraid you're right . . .

THE STRANGER: But I refuse to submit to the inevitable. I won't have us lacerating ourselves. I'll carve myself up as an offering to the gods. I'll say I'm the one that's to blame. It was I who told you to break out of your prison, it was I who enticed you to come with me. You can lay all the blame on me for what we've done and for what came of it.

THE LADY: You couldn't bear it.

THE STRANGER: I think I could. There are moments when I feel that I bear within me all the sin and sorrow, all the scandal and shame of the whole world. There are moments when I think that we commit crimes and do wrong because the wrongdoing in and by itself is a punishment imposed on us. . . . Not so long ago, I lay sick with a fever. And among other things—so much happened—I dreamed I saw a crucifix without anyone crucified on it. And when I asked the Dominican—there was a Dominican there too—when I asked him what it meant he said, "You won't have Him suffering for you; consequently, you yourself must suffer." And that's why people have become so sensitive to their suffering—in a way they weren't in the old days.

THE LADY: And that's why our consciences crush us: there's no one to help carry them.

THE STRANGER: You've come around to that, eh?

THE LADY: Not quite—but I'm on my way.

THE STRANGER: Put your hand in mine and let's move on from here together.

THE LADY: Where to?

THE STRANGER: Back, the same way we came. Are you tired?

THE LADY: Not any longer.

THE STRANGER: I fell down exhausted time and again. But then I met a strange beggar—you probably remember him, the one they say looks like me. And he asked me, by way of an experiment, to believe that his intentions were good. So I believed—as an experiment—and . . .

THE LADY: And—?

THE STRANGER: Everything went well for me! . . . And since then I've found the strength to push ahead.

THE LADY: Then let's push ahead!

THE STRANGER (*facing the sea*): All right, but it's getting dark and the clouds are piling up . . .

THE LADY: Don't look at the clouds . . .

THE STRANGER: Down below—what's that?

THE LADY: A shipwreck, that's all.

THE STRANGER (*whispers*): Three crosses. . . . What new Golgotha lies ahead of us?

THE LADY: They're white. That means something good.

THE STRANGER: Can anything good happen to us again?

THE LADY: Why not? Give it time.

THE STRANGER: Come on, let's go.

* * *

In the Hotel Room

Same as before. The Lady is sitting beside The Stranger, crocheting.

THE LADY: Say something.

THE STRANGER: What? Since we entered this room everything I say is dull and boring.

THE LADY: Why did you have to keep on going until we came to this awful room?

THE STRANGER: I don't know. It was what I wanted least of all. That's why I had this ache to come here – to be tormented.

THE LADY: And have you been tormented . . . ?

THE STRANGER: Yes. All the joy's gone out of life. I'm deaf to music and blind to beauty. All day long I hear that mill grinding and all I see is that great panorama of mine, only now it's expanded into a vast cosmorama. . . . And at night . . .

THE LADY: I heard you cry out in your sleep. What was it?

THE STRANGER: A dream I had . . .

THE LADY: A genuine dream – or –

THE STRANGER: Of terrifying reality. A dream with a curse on it. Because – because I have an irresistible urge to talk about it – and to you of all people. Which I mustn't, because that would be opening the door to the forbidden room.

THE LADY: The past?

THE STRANGER: Yes.

THE LADY (*without insinuation*): There's certain to be something crazy locked up in secret rooms . . .

THE STRANGER: Yes, isn't there.

Pause.

THE LADY: Well, tell me.

THE STRANGER: I'm afraid I can't stop myself. . . . Here goes: I dreamed I saw – your – former husband – married – to my former wife – so that my children now had him for a father . . .

THE LADY: Nobody but you could dream up a thing like that.

THE STRANGER: But suppose – suppose it's true. . . . And I saw him beat them – (*Rises.*) – and when, as a matter of course, I strangled him, I –. No, I can't go on with it. . . . All the same, I can't rest until I'm absolutely certain. And to be certain, I'll have to go to him in his own home.

THE LADY: So that's where we're heading!

THE STRANGER: To the edge of the abyss. And the guardrail is gone. I've got to take the plunge. I've got to see him.

THE LADY: But suppose he won't see you?

THE STRANGER: I'll apply as a patient. I'll tell him about my sickness.

THE LADY (*frightened*): I wouldn't do that if I were you.

THE STRANGER: I know what you're hinting. He'll find an excuse for locking me up. . . . I'm willing to risk it. I have a crazy desire to risk everything – freedom, life, comfort, happiness. What I need is an emotional blow so great it will shock me to the depths of my being, and what rises to the surface will be the real me. I need some torture that will redress the balance in our relationship. I don't want to be in debt any longer. So down into the snake pit, and the sooner the better.

THE LADY: Couldn't I go with you . . . ?

THE STRANGER: Why? My torments will do for both of us.

THE LADY: Then I can really call you my liberator, and the curse I pronounced over you would turn into a blessing. – Have you noticed that it's spring again?

THE STRANGER: I can tell by that Christmas rose. It's beginning to wither.

THE LADY: Don't you feel spring in the air?

THE STRANGER: Yes. I can feel the ice in my chest thawing . . .

THE LADY: Maybe the werewolf can cure you completely.

THE STRANGER: We shall see. We shall see. Perhaps he isn't so awful.

THE LADY: He's certainly not as cruel as you are.

THE STRANGER: Still—my dream. Suppose . . .

THE LADY: Suppose it was only a stupid dream. . . . Look, all my yarn is gone! That's the end of my silly crocheting. How terribly dirty it is!

THE STRANGER: You can always wash it.

THE LADY: Or dye it.

THE STRANGER: Rose-red.

THE LADY: Never.

THE STRANGER: It looks like a rolled manuscript.

THE LADY: With our story on it.

THE STRANGER: Written in blood and tears and the dust of the road.

THE LADY: Yes. End of story. Except for the last chapter. That's yours.

THE STRANGER: And we'll meet at the seventh station. Where we began.

ACT V

At the Doctor's

The set is very much as in Act I. The woodpile, however, is only half as big. Near the porch is a workbench with surgical instruments on it, scalpels, forceps, and so on.

The Doctor is polishing these instruments.

THE SISTER (*coming from the porch*): There's a patient to see you.

THE DOCTOR: Who is it?

THE SISTER: I didn't get to see him, but here's his card.

THE DOCTOR (*reading the card*): You know . . . this really beats everything.

THE SISTER: Is it he?

THE DOCTOR: It's he. Of all the brazen nerve. I don't despise courage but this direct approach smacks of contempt. It's like a challenge flung in my face. Well, show him in.

THE SISTER: Are you serious?

THE DOCTOR: Absolutely. However, if you feel like it, you can let him have a few of your blunt, well-chosen words.

THE SISTER: I'd already made up my mind to.

THE DOCTOR: Good for you. You rough him up a little and I'll polish him off.

THE SISTER: Don't worry. I'll tell him everything your soft heart keeps you from saying.

THE DOCTOR: Keep my heart out of it. —And get out of here before I lose my temper. —And close the door!

The Sister goes.

THE DOCTOR: Caesar, what are you doing over there by the garbage cans again?

The Madman enters.

Tell me, Caesar: if your worst enemy comes to you and puts his head in your lap, what do you do?

THE MADMAN: I cut off his head!

THE DOCTOR: Now, now, that's not what I taught you.

THE MADMAN: No, you said you should heap coals of fire on it. But I think that would be a pity.

THE DOCTOR: So do I. It's too cruel and cunning. . . . Don't you think it would be better to take just a little revenge so that he could stand up like a man and feel himself quits?

THE MADMAN: If you already know what to do, why ask me?

THE DOCTOR: Shut up, I'm not talking to you. . . . All right, we'll lop off his head and then — then we'll see!

THE MADMAN: Depending on how he behaves himself.

THE DOCTOR: Precisely. How he behaves himself. . . . Not a word out of you now. And get away from here.

THE STRANGER (*enters from the porch. He appears ill-at-ease and disturbed, but there is also an air of resignation about him*): Doctor, I . . .

THE DOCTOR: Yes?

THE STRANGER: I suppose you're surprised to see me here?

THE DOCTOR (*seriously*): I had long ago stopped being surprised by anything. I see I shall have to make a new beginning.

THE STRANGER: May I talk to you confidentially?

THE DOCTOR: Yes, about anything that may be considered proper between two civilized people. Are you ill?

THE STRANGER (*hesitating*): Yes.

THE DOCTOR: Why come to me?

THE STRANGER: You should be able to guess.

THE DOCTOR: I don't want to. . . . What's your trouble?

THE STRANGER (*faltering*): Insomnia.

THE DOCTOR: That's not an illness, that's a symptom. Have you been to see a doctor before?

THE STRANGER: I've been sick in bed . . . in an institution . . . with a fever. . . . But it was a most unusual fever.

THE DOCTOR: What was so unusual about it?

THE STRANGER: Let me ask you something. Is it possible to be up and about and still be delirious?

THE DOCTOR: Yes, if you're crazy—not otherwise.

The Stranger gets up and then sits down again.

THE DOCTOR: What was the name of the hospital?

THE STRANGER: It was called "The Helping Hand."

THE DOCTOR: There's no hospital with that name.

THE STRANGER: What is it—a cloister?

THE DOCTOR: It's a lunatic asylum.

The Stranger gets up, nervous.

THE DOCTOR (*gets up and calls*): Sister! Close the front door, will you? And the wooden gate in the back yard! (*To The Stranger.*) Please sit down, sit down. —I was just making certain the doors are closed. Too many tramps hanging around here.

THE STRANGER (*calming himself*): Doctor, tell me honestly: do you think I'm insane?

THE DOCTOR: As you know, it's not customary to give an honest answer to that question, and anyone who asks it usually doesn't believe what he's told. Therefore it doesn't make the slightest difference what my opinion is. On the other hand, if you yourself actually feel that your soul is sick, you'd better consult a spiritual healer.

THE STRANGER: Couldn't you take on that position just for a moment?

THE DOCTOR: No, I'm not qualified.

THE STRANGER: But if—

THE DOCTOR (*interrupting*): Besides, I haven't the time. We're preparing for a wedding here in the garden.

THE STRANGER: My dream . . .

THE DOCTOR: What's the matter? I thought it would ease your mind to hear that I had managed to console myself, as it's called. I thought it would make you happy, downright happy. That's usually the case. But instead you seem to feel even worse. . . . There's something beneath this. Let me probe around a bit. . . . Now why does it distress you so much if I marry a widow . . . ?

THE STRANGER: With two children?

THE DOCTOR: Ah, ha, let me see. . . . Ah! I understand. What a hell of an idea! Really worthy of you. You know, if there were a hell, you'd be commander-in-chief. Your ability to devise new tortures far surpasses my wildest creations. And yet they call me a werewolf.

THE STRANGER: It may be that—

THE DOCTOR (*interrupting*): For a long time I hated you, as you probably know, because an inexcusable act of yours furnished me with an undeserved reputation. But as I grew older and more understanding, I realized that although the punishment I received then was unjust, I had nevertheless deserved it for other pranks of mine that had never been discovered; and furthermore that you were a child with enough conscience to punish yourself. So that matter needn't bother you either. Is that what you came here to clear up?

THE STRANGER: Yes.

THE DOCTOR: Will you be satisfied if I say you are free to go?

The Stranger looks questioningly.

Or did you think I intended to lock you up? Or hack you to pieces with my instruments? Kill you, perhaps? "Why not kill the poor devils?"

The Stranger looks at his watch.

THE DOCTOR: You can still make the boat.

THE STRANGER: May I shake your hand?

THE DOCTOR: No, I can't shake hands with you. I can't bring myself to it. Besides, what good will it do for me to forgive you if you haven't the strength to forgive yourself? . . . There are some things that can be helped only by being undone. There's no help for this.

THE STRANGER: "The Helping Hand."

THE DOCTOR: Not so bad, after all, was it? — You challenged fate and you lost. No shame in a battle well fought. I did too, but as you can see, I've been dickering with my woodpile and got him to come down a bit. I want the thunder to stay out of my house, and I no longer play with lightning.

THE STRANGER: One station more — and then I'm home.

THE DOCTOR: Never home, my dear sir! — Goodbye.

THE STRANGER: Goodbye.

* * *

The Street Corner

Same as the first act. The Stranger is sitting on the bench under the tree, writing in the sand.

THE LADY (*entering*): What are you doing?

THE STRANGER: Writing in the sand. Still at it.

THE LADY: Same old song. Don't you hear any new ones?

THE STRANGER (*pointing to the church*): Yes, but from in there . . .

THE LADY: And there's still no music in your life?

THE STRANGER (*pointing to the church*): Yes, but it's coming from there. . . . There is someone I've wronged without knowing it.

THE LADY: And I thought our journey would be about over when we finally got back here.

THE STRANGER: Back where we began—on the street between the bar, the church—and the post office. The post office! P-O-S-T.* Wait a minute. Didn't I leave a registered letter there without bothering to claim it?

THE LADY: Yes, you said it was only bad news.

THE STRANGER: Or legal papers. (*Striking his forehead.*) Ooh, that's what it is.

THE LADY: Now, you go in there and tell yourself it's good news.

THE STRANGER (*ironically*): Good!

THE LADY: Pretend! Convince yourself!

THE STRANGER (*heading for the post office*): All right, I'll try.

> *The Lady waits, walking up and down the sidewalk. The Stranger comes out from the post office with a letter in his hand.*

THE LADY: Well?

THE STRANGER: Am I ashamed! It was the money. It was there the whole time.

THE LADY: You see! . . . All our trials and tribulations, all our tears—all in vain.

---

* The Stranger thinks of the Latin phrase *Post nummos virtus* from Act I, scene 1. (Suggested by Barry Jacobs.)

THE STRANGER: Not in vain! It may look like dirty playing, but it really isn't. I wronged someone, the Unseen One, when I suspected that—

THE LADY: Sh, sh. No more of that. No accusations.

THE STRANGER: Right. It was my own stupidity—or meanness. . . . I didn't want to be made a fool of by life—and so I was! . . . But what about those elves—?

THE LADY: They made the switch. . . . Let's go.

THE STRANGER: Yes, let's go and hide ourselves in the mountain where we can be alone with our misery.

THE LADY: Yes, the mountains hide and cover.* But first I have to light a candle for my good Saint Elizabeth.

The Stranger shakes his head.

THE LADY: Come. Please.

THE STRANGER: Oh, well, I can always pass through. But as for staying there—definitely not.

THE LADY: How do you know? . . . Come on. . . . You'll get to hear some new songs in there.**

THE STRANGER (*following her toward the church door*): Maybe. Maybe.

THE LADY: Come!

* See Revelation 6:16
** See Revelation 5:9 and 14:3; and frequently in Psalms.

Introduction to
Crimes and Crimes

Strindberg had a hard time deciding what to call this play. *Intoxication* was one title; *Guilty?—Not Guilty?* another. The second is taken from an essay in Søren Kierkegaard's book *Stages on Life's Way*. There are three of these stages for Kierkegaard: the aesthetic, the ethical, and the religious; and Kierkegaard explains them by studying man's relation to woman in each of the three stages. For the aesthete, the relation is purely erotic; for the ethical man, the relation brings with it the obligations of marriage and of family; for the religious man, it means suffering and a questioning of God's purpose. Intoxicated by success, the hero of *Crimes and Crimes* slips from the ethical to the aesthetic stage, and then, accused of a crime he did not commit, comes to realize through his suffering that there is yet another stage that lies beyond his understanding.

Strindberg begins his play somberly in a Parisian cemetery to indicate the seriousness of his theme. After that, however, *Crimes and Crimes* becomes a play of sexual passion, adultery, and a mysterious death—the sort of play that would appeal to the average theatergoer. The characters are artists and lovers; the action moves from bohemian hangouts to glamorous restaurants; and the story has a great deal of suspense.

Strindberg knew the people he was writing about. He always associated with bohemians, even married them. In Berlin he was the center of a heavy-drinking group of poets and painters that included Edvard Munch. In Paris the still unappreciated Paul Gauguin was an acquaintance. A prominent member of the Berlin group was the Polish writer Stanislaw Przybyszewski, whose obsessions were sex and Nietzsche. Przybyszewski abandoned his common-law wife and two children to marry a Norwegian girl who was Munch's friend and model and, for a time, Strindberg's mistress. In 1896 the discarded wife killed herself and the children. Przybyszewski was detained by the police at first, suspected of having murdered them, and released after questioning. For the plot of *Crimes and Crimes*, Strindberg combined this actual event with an imaginary one. Alone in Paris, he had at times wished that his daughter Kerstin by his second wife might fall ill so that he would be summoned home to wife and child. Once he had thought it, he felt as guilty as if he had actually committed some crime. His first wife, Siri, had borne him a child with the same name, Kerstin, who had died in infancy shortly after he and Siri had hastily married to legitimize the baby's birth.* Was there in all this a complicated pattern drawn surreptitiously in the mind? Our consciences do punish us, not only for what we do but for what we think. There are crimes, and there are crimes. Some can be dealt with in the courts of law; some must be brought to a higher court, the court of individual conscience that has a place somewhere in Kierkegaard's third stage. Although Strindberg's hero never reaches those heights, he does come to understand that they exist, even if they are not for him.

Once again, as in *To Damascus*, Strindberg sought to give concrete dramatic form to intangible ideas. And once again he experimented with new techniques, even though he was presumably writing for the conventional theater. Parallel scenes make up the structure of the play, but Strindberg handles them like musical themes. *Crimes and Crimes* is a play in the form of a sonata. Scene by scene it corresponds to the structure of Beethoven's "Tempest" Sonata, opus 31, no. 2. A passage from that sonata, specified in the script, becomes a leading motif, the aural symbol of the hero's troubled conscience.

The musical shape of the play never constricts the dramatic flow. As a matter of fact, the repetition of scenes and themes lightens the tone, obvious patterns and repetitions being a characteristic of comedy. The atmosphere of the *belle époque* in Paris is as enchanting as an impressionist painting, and the emotionally overheated world of artists and writers has always been good theater. Offsetting these appealing qualities is the moralizing tendency of the play, which is likely to irritate those who find comedy and homily an unappealing mixture. Like Maurice in the play, they want the theater and the church to remain separate institutions, one for Saturday, one for Sunday.

* Gunnar Ollén, *Strindbergs dramatik*, 4th ed., Stockholm, 1982, p. 271.

Crimes and Crimes
or
Intoxication
(Brott och Brott)

A Comedy

CHARACTERS

MAURICE, playwright
JEANNE, his mistress
MARION, their five-year old daughter
ADOLPHE, artist
HENRIETTE, his mistress
EMILE, workingman, Jeanne's brother
MADAME CATHERINE
THE ABBÉ
MINOR CHARACTERS

SCENES

Cemetery

Crêmerie
Auberge des Adrets
Bois de Boulogne
Crêmerie
Auberge des Adrets
Luxembourg Gardens
Crêmerie

Paris. The 1890s

ACT I

Scene I

The upper allee of cypresses in the Montparnasse Cemetery in Paris. At the back can be seen burial chapels and stone crosses with the inscription "O Crux! Ave Spes Unica!"; also the ivy-covered ruin of a mill.

A Woman in Mourning, tastefully dressed in black, is kneeling and murmuring prayers at a grave covered with flowers.

Jeanne is walking up and down as if she were waiting for someone.

Marion is playing with withered flowers that she picks up from a heap of rubbish on the path.

The Abbe is walking far down the allee, reading his breviary.

THE CARETAKER (*enters. To Jeanne*): Look here, this ain't no playground!

JEANNE (*meekly*): I'm just waiting for someone. I'm sure he'll be here soon.

THE CARETAKER: Maybe so. But you can't touch the flowers.

JEANNE (*to Marion*): Throw the flowers away, darling.

THE ABBÉ (*approaches and is greeted by The Caretaker*): Can't the child play with flowers that have been thrown away?

THE CARETAKER: I'm sorry. We got orders. No touching the flowers. [They say there's a lot of arsenic in the ground here—

from all the bodies.]* Don't know if it's true, but I got my orders.

THE ABBÉ (*to Marion*): In that case there's nothing to do but follow orders. —What's your name, little girl?

MARION: Marion.

THE ABBÉ: And what is your daddy's name? (*Marion bites her finger and is silent.*) Forgive me, madam; I didn't mean to be inquisitive. I was just trying to calm the child.

The Caretaker has left.

JEANNE: I know that, Father. I wish you could calm me, too. I'm all upset. I've walked and waited here for two whole hours.

THE ABBÉ: Two hours—for some man! How people torment each other! "O Crux! Ave Spes Unica!"

JEANNE: Yes, what does it mean? It's written all over here.

THE ABBÉ: It means: "Hail the cross! Our only hope!"

JEANNE: Is it the only one?

THE ABBÉ: Our only certain one.

JEANNE: Pretty soon I'll believe you're right, Father.

THE ABBÉ: May I ask why?

---

* The sentence within brackets is not in Strindberg's text. There was at this time concern about the prevalence of arsenic in burial grounds. The toxicologist M. J. B. Orfila had written about it, and Strindberg knew Orfila's chemical writings. In his poetic essay "In the Cemetery," Strindberg writes, "I had been warned that my frequent visits [to the cemetery] might be harmful because of the mephitic fumes that infused the air there. I had in fact noticed a certain taste of verdigris that remained in my mouth even two hours after my return home." The idea that the flowers in a cemetery might be dangerous was much more common in Strindberg's time than it is in ours. In one of his earlier works, *Old Stockholm* (1880–82), he quotes an old saying, "Children who pick flowers on graves will get maggots in their fingers."

JEANNE: You've already guessed. He has kept us waiting for two hours in a cemetery. That's the end of the affair, I suppose.

THE ABBÉ: And when he's left you once and for all, what then?

JEANNE: We'll throw ourselves into the river.

THE ABBÉ: Oh, no, no!

JEANNE: Oh, yes, yes.

MARION: I want to go home, Mama. I'm hungry.

JEANNE: Now, my dearest, just be patient a little while longer and we'll soon go.

THE ABBÉ: "Woe unto them that call evil good and good evil."

JEANNE: What is that woman doing over there at the grave?

THE ABBÉ: She seems to be communing with the dead.

JEANNE: But you can't, can you?

THE ABBÉ: She seems to be able to.

JEANNE: You mean that the misery doesn't end when the end comes?

THE ABBÉ: Don't you know that?

JEANNE: How can one know that?

THE ABBÉ: Hmm! . . . I see. . . . Well, my good woman, the next time you need to be enlightened on this point, look me up in the Chapel of Our Lady in Saint-Germain. —Ah, here comes the man I think you're waiting for.

JEANNE (*embarrassed*): No, that isn't him, but it's someone I know . . .

THE ABBÉ (*to Marion*): Goodbye, my little Marion! God bless you! (*Kisses the child. Leaves.*) Remember: in Saint-Germain-des-Pres!

EMILE: Hello, Sis! What are you doing here?

JEANNE: I'm waiting for Maurice.

EMILE: You'll have a long wait. I saw him on the Boul' Mich

having lunch with a bunch of his pals an hour ago. — Hello there, Marion! (*Kisses the child.*)

JEANNE: I suppose he was surrounded by women?

EMILE: Of course! Oh, that doesn't mean anything, Jeanne. After all, he's a playwright, with a new play opening tonight. They were probably some of the actresses.

JEANNE: Did he recognize you?

EMILE: No. He doesn't know me from Adam. No reason why he should. I'm an ordinary workingman — and I don't care to be treated condescendingly.

JEANNE: What if he leaves us without a penny?

EMILE: In that case I'll have to introduce myself to him. You don't expect that. He really loves you. And after all, he would never leave his little girl.

JEANNE: I don't know what to think. I just know that something's going to happen to me, something terrible!

EMILE: Hasn't he promised to marry you?

JEANNE: No, not promised, just acted like he would.

EMILE: Acted—! Oh, fine, fine! Remember what I told you in the beginning: don't get your hopes up; that kind doesn't marry our kind.

JEANNE: It has happened.

EMILE: Sure. — But face up to it: you wouldn't be happy in his world. You wouldn't even understand what they were talking about. Sometimes I eat at his restaurant — out in the back, of course — and I can't understand a single word they're saying.

JEANNE: You eat there?

EMILE: Yeah, in the kitchen.

JEANNE: Really? He's never invited me there.

EMILE: Well, you can give him credit for that. It means he's got some respect for the mother of his little Marion. A lot of very strange women there, I tell you.

JEANNE: Oh?

EMILE: Not that he ever bothers with them. No sir, he's all right!

JEANNE: I know. But if the right woman came along, she'd know how to drive him crazy.

EMILE (*smiling*): The things you say, Jeanne! —Listen, do you need some money?

JEANNE: No, not money.

EMILE: Things can't be too bad, then. —Look! Down there! There he comes. And here I go. Goodbye, Marion!

JEANNE: Is it really him? Yes, it is!

EMILE: Now don't you go driving him crazy, Jeanne—with your jealousy! (*Leaves.*)

JEANNE: Don't be silly!

Maurice enters.

MARION (*rushes to meet him and is swept up in his arms*): Papa! Papa!

MAURICE: Hello, hello, my darling little girl! (*Greets Jeanne.*) Jeanne! Can you ever forgive me for keeping you waiting so long? Can you?

JEANNE: Of course I can.

MAURICE: Well, say it as if you meant it!

Maurice goes up to her. Jeanne kisses him on the cheek.

MAURICE: Sorry, I couldn't hear.

Jeanne kisses him on the mouth.

Now I heard you! That's more like it! —Well, this is it. My fate hangs in the balance. Tonight is opening night. Either it's a big hit—or a huge flop. SRO or "Closes Saturday!"

JEANNE: I'll pray for you and it'll be a hit!

MAURICE: Good girl. Might help; it certainly can't hurt. —Look down there. See that haze? That's Paris! Today Paris doesn't know who Maurice is, but in twenty-four hours she will! That haze, which has wrapped me in obscurity for thirty years, will disperse. I'll blow it away, I'll suddenly appear, emerge like Aladdin's genie. I'll be somebody. My enemies—that means everybody who wishes they could do what I've done—will writhe with envy, and that will be my pleasure, seeing them suffer what I've had to suffer.

JEANNE: Please don't say such things! Please.

MAURICE: Why not? It's the simple truth.

JEANNE: Maybe, but don't say it anyway! —What about afterward?

MAURICE: Afterward we'll be in clover. You and Marion will bear the name of the great and famous playwright: Maurice Gérard!

JEANNE: Then you do love me?

MAURICE: Of course. I love you both, both just as much—but perhaps Marion just a little bit more.

JEANNE: I'm glad. You might get tired of me, but never of her! I know that.

MAURICE: Don't you have any faith in me?

JEANNE: I don't know. . . . I'm afraid of something, afraid that something terrible will happen . . .

MAURICE: You're just tired and depressed after waiting so long. Please forgive me, Jeanne. What is there to be afraid of?

JEANNE: The unexpected. Something you can feel, without having reasons . . .

MAURICE: I can't feel anything but success—and for very good reasons: the infallible instinct of the professional theater crowd, their knowledge of what the public wants—not to mention their intimate friendship with the critics! So now you just calm yourself and—

JEANNE: I can't. I just can't! You see, there was an abbé here just now who was very kind to us. I'd lost faith—in you—in everything—waiting so long for you. You'd sort of—well, not wiped it out exactly—but smeared it over, like you soap windows. But the old man rubbed the soap away and the light fell through the window, and I could see through it. —I'll pray for you tonight in the Chapel of Our Lady in Saint-Germain.

MAURICE: You're giving me the willies! Now I'm the one who's scared.

JEANNE: They say the fear of the Lord is the beginning of wisdom.

MAURICE: "God"? What's that? Who's he?

JEANNE: He gave you joy when you were a child and strength when you became a man. Now He will help us through the terrible times that lie ahead.

MAURICE: What lies ahead? You talk about the strangest things. Things I never even think about.

JEANNE: I don't know; I can't say. I haven't dreamed anything, haven't seen, haven't heard anything; but during the last two terrible hours I've suffered so much heartache I'm prepared for the worst.

MARION: I want to go home, Mama. I'm hungry.

MAURICE: Of course you shall go home, my darling child. (*Hugs her.*)

MARION (*whimpering*): Oh! You're hurting me, Papa.

JEANNE: We have to go home for dinner. Goodbye, Maurice. Good luck!

MAURICE (*to Marion*): Where did I hurt you, my sweetest, dearest little girl? You know that I only want to do good to you!

MARION: Then come home with us! Please! Please!

MAURICE (*to Jeanne*): You know, when I hear her say that, I feel I should do what she says. But then I hear the voice of reason calling me. I've got obligations. . . . Goodbye, my little girl! (*Kisses Marion, who puts her arms around his neck.*)

JEANNE: When do I see you again?

MAURICE: We'll meet tomorrow, darling! Never to part!

JEANNE (*embraces him*): Never, never, never to part! (*She makes the sign of the cross on his forehead.*) God go with you!

MAURICE (*moved in spite of himself*): My darling, dearest Jeanne!

> *Jeanne and Marion walk toward the right; Maurice toward the left. At the same moment they turn toward each other and throw kisses at each other.*

(*Coming back.*) Jeanne! I'm so ashamed! I'm always forgetting you, and you're the last person in the world to speak up. Here's the ticket for tonight.

JEANNE: Thanks, dear, but—you should be where you belong tonight, alone, and I should be where I belong—with Marion.

MAURICE: Dear Jeanne, who's as wise as she is good. I'll swear there's not another woman in the world who would give up a night on the town to do her guy a favor. It's my night to shine. Tonight I take on the world. The battlefield is no place for women and children. And you knew!

JEANNE: Maurice—don't make too much of a simple woman like me. I mean, I don't want to disappoint you, ever. —Oh, look! I'm just as forgetful as you are. I bought these for you—a tie and a pair of gloves. Maybe you could wear them tonight—for me. I'm so proud.

MAURICE (*kissing her hand*): Thank you, my darling girl!

JEANNE: Oh! And Maurice! Don't forget like you always do—to go to the barber. I want you to look so handsome. I want everybody to admire you—

MAURICE: You haven't a grain of jealousy in you, have you?

JEANNE: It's an ugly word.

MAURICE: You know, right now I could forget all about tonight's triumph—yes, it will be a triumph for me, I'm sure—

JEANNE: Sh! Sh! Don't—

MAURICE: —and come home with you!

JEANNE: Exactly what you mustn't do! —Go on now. Destiny calls.

MAURICE: All right. Goodbye. And let come what may!

JEANNE (*alone with Marion*): O Crux! Ave Spes Unica!

Scene 2

> *The Crêmerie, a small restaurant with regular customers.*
>
> *To the right, a buffet with a large goldfish bowl, vegetables, fruits, canned preserves, etc. Farther back right is the entrance door. At the rear the door to the kitchen, where the workingmen eat. Through the kitchen the back door to the garden can be seen. In the rear to the left is a raised counter and cupboard and shelves with all sorts of bottles. To the right, a long marble-topped table runs along the wall, and parallel to it in the middle of the floor stands another such table. Wicker chairs at the table. The walls are covered with oil paintings, given by artists in payment of their bills.*
>
> *Madame Catherine is sitting at the counter. Maurice is leaning against the counter, his hat on, smoking a cigarette.*

MADAME CATHERINE: Your big night, eh, Maurice?

MAURICE: That's right. In a few hours, it will all be over.

MADAME CATHERINE: Are you nervous?

MAURICE: Cool as a cucumber.

MADAME CATHERINE: I wish you the best of luck, anyway. You deserve it, Maurice, after the rough time you've had.

MAURICE: Thanks, Catherine. You've been very kind to me. Without your help I would have gone down the drain by this time.

MADAME CATHERINE: We won't talk about that now. I help anyone who isn't lazy and who's serious. I just don't like to be taken advantage of. Are you coming back here after the play is over and having a drink with your old friends? You won't forget us?

MAURICE: Forget you! Of course not. It was my idea, wasn't it?

Henriette enters from the right. Maurice turns about; tips his hat; stares at Henriette, who looks him over carefully.

HENRIETTE (*to Madame Catherine*): Have you seen Adolphe?

MADAME CATHERINE: No, Madame! Expect he'll be here soon. Won't you sit down?

HENRIETTE: No thanks. I prefer to wait outside. (*She leaves.*)

MAURICE: Who in blue blazes was that?!

MADAME CATHERINE: That was Adolphe's—friend . . .

MAURICE: Ah, ha, so that's her!

MADAME CATHERINE: Haven't you seen her before?

MAURICE: No. He's been hiding her from me, afraid I'd steal her.

MADAME CATHERINE: Ha ha! —Good-looking, isn't she?

MAURICE: Good-looking? Let me see. . . . Funny, I can't tell you. I didn't even see her. It was as if she flew into my arms instantaneously; came so close to me that I couldn't focus my eyes on her. But she left her impression in the air. I can still see her as she stood there. (*He walks over to the door and makes a gesture as if he were putting his arm around someone's waist.*) Ow! (*Shakes his finger as if he'd been stuck with a needle.*) Why, she's got pins in the waist of her dress. A real stinger! Dangerous!

MADAME CATHERINE (*smiles*): You're crazy! You and your women!

MAURICE: Crazy, crazy! But you know what, Madame Catherine! I'm leaving before she comes again. Otherwise . . . well, who the hell knows? —Scary!

MADAME CATHERINE: Afraid?

MAURICE: Yes, not only for my sake—for others.

MADAME CATHERINE: Well, then, get out, get out!

MAURICE: You saw, didn't you? She didn't walk through the door: she vanished, and a little whirlwind sprang up which pulled me after her. —Go ahead and laugh! —But why is that palm tree on the sideboard still shaking? What a diabolic woman!

MADAME CATHERINE: Leave, man, leave, before you're really hooked.

MAURICE: I want to leave but I can't. . . . Do you believe in fate, Catherine?

MADAME CATHERINE: No, I don't. I believe in God and his goodness, and that He'll help us against the powers of darkness, that is, if we ask for His help in the right way.

MAURICE: Ah ha, you see? Powers of darkness! That's it! —And isn't that what I hear out in the hall right now?

MADAME CATHERINE: It certainly is. She's pacing back and forth, swishing her skirts. When you tear a sheet into rags, it sounds like that. Go! Get out! Out! Through the kitchen!

Maurice dashes for the kitchen door but bumps into Emile.

EMILE: Beg your pardon! I'm sorry!

Emile withdraws to the kitchen. Adolphe enters, followed by Henriette.

ADOLPHE: Why, if it isn't Maurice! Hello, how are you? Henriette, I want you to meet my oldest and dearest friend. Henriette—Maurice.

MAURICE (*stiffly formal*): How do you do?

HENRIETTE: We've met before.

ADOLPHE: Really? When? If I may ask.

MAURICE: Just a moment ago! Right in here.

ADOLPHE: Oh! —Well, you can't leave now. Not until we've had a little chat.

MAURICE (*after getting a warning signal from Madame Catherine*): I'd love to, but I don't have the time.

ADOLPHE: Take time! We won't stay long.

HENRIETTE: I won't bother you, if you men want to talk business. None of my affair.

MAURICE: Our sort of affairs have nothing to do with business! Won't do to talk about them.

HENRIETTE: Then we'll talk about something else! (*Takes his hat and hangs it up.*) Now why don't you be nice to me and give me a chance to get to know the great playwright!

> *Madame Catherine makes another warning gesture at Maurice, who takes no notice.*

ADOLPHE: That's right, Henriette; reel him in before he gets away!

> *They sit down at a table.*

HENRIETTE (*to Maurice*): You're lucky to have Adolphe for a friend, Maurice. He never talks of anybody but you. I feel I'm playing second fiddle.

ADOLPHE: Oh, cut it out! Look who's talking. She's never given me a moment's peace because of you, Maurice. She's read everything you've written. She wants to know who influenced you, what books you read. She's asked me how you looked, how old you were, what you like and what you don't like. I've had you for company morning, noon, and night. It's as if the three of us were living together.

MAURICE: Why, you dear sweet thing, why didn't you come here and take a look at the phenomenon for yourself? One look and your curiosity would have been satisfied.

HENRIETTE: Adolphe didn't want me to. (*Adolphe looks embarrassed.*) Not that he was jealous . . .

MAURICE: Why should he be jealous? He knows I've got a girl.

HENRIETTE: Maybe he felt he couldn't rely on your always having the same girl.

MAURICE: Can't imagine why. My heart is notorious for its constancy.

ADOLPHE: But that wasn't the reason —

HENRIETTE (*interrupting him*): Perhaps you haven't had to stand the acid test.

ADOLPHE: Now how do you —

HENRIETTE (*interrupting*): — There's never been a faithful man since this evil little world began.

MAURICE: Well, time there was one!

HENRIETTE: Where?

MAURICE: Here!

Henriette laughs.

ADOLPHE: You know, this sounds just like —

HENRIETTE (*interrupting again and continuing to talk directly to Maurice*): Do you think I'd trust my dear Adolphe for more than a season?

MAURICE: It's not for me to question your lack of faith in people, but I'd stake my life on Adolphe's faithfulness.

HENRIETTE: No need to. I was talking through my hat. I take it all back. Not because I'm trying to be as high-minded as you, mind you, but because Adolphe really *is* faithful. . . . It's become a habit with me — seeing only the bad side; I can't stop it, in spite of my best resolutions. But I'm sure if I were to see a lot more of you two, you'd bring out the best in me. Forgive me, Adolphe, will you? (*She puts her hand to his cheek.*)

ADOLPHE: You're always saying such bad things, and always doing the right thing. As for what's really going on in that head of yours—I haven't the faintest idea.

HENRIETTE: Who knows what goes on in our heads?

MAURICE: Yes, imagine being held responsible for our thoughts. Life would be impossible.

HENRIETTE: Don't tell me you have evil thoughts?

MAURICE: Of course I do. And in my dreams I commit the grimmest crimes . . .

HENRIETTE: In dreams, oh, well—! Do you know that I—no, I'm ashamed to talk about it—

MAURICE: Oh, come on! Come on!

HENRIETTE: Last night I dreamed that I was quite calmly dissecting the muscles in Adolphe's chest—sculptress that I am—and Adolphe, like the sweet man he is, didn't put up any resistance at all. He even helped me through some troublesome spots, since he knows more anatomy than I do.

MAURICE: Was he dead?

HENRIETTE: No, he was alive.

MAURICE: How disgusting! You must have waked up screaming.

HENRIETTE: No. That's what amazes me. I'm really quite sensitive to the suffering of others. Isn't that true, Adolphe?

ADOLPHE: Absolutely! I might even say extremely sensitive, especially to animals.

MAURICE: I'm just the opposite—quite insensitive to my own sufferings as well as to others' . . . !

ADOLPHE: Now he's telling lies against himself. Isn't he, Catherine?

MADAME CATHERINE: Maurice wouldn't say boo to a goose. He was on the verge of calling in the police because I didn't change the water for the goldfish often enough – the ones over there on the sideboard. . . . Look at the dears. It's as if they understood what I was saying . . .

MAURICE: Isn't this wonderful! Here we sit whitewashing ourselves to look like angels, and yet, by and large, each one of us is ready to stab someone discreetly in the back to win glory, gold, or a woman. . . . Did I hear you say you were a sculptor, Mademoiselle?

HENRIETTE: In a way. Good enough to make a bust. And as for making one of you, which I've long dreamed of doing, I think I'm more than good enough.

MAURICE: Help yourself! At least that's one dream that we can make come true. Want to start?

HENRIETTE: No. I don't want to begin to study you until after tonight, after you've become a success. You won't be the real you until that happens.

MAURICE: So sure of my success?

HENRIETTE: It's written all over you. You're going to be the conquering hero tonight. I'm sure you feel it yourself . . .

MAURICE: Why?

HENRIETTE: Because I feel it! This morning I was down in the dumps, now Henriette's herself again.

Adolphe looks somber, lost in thought.

MAURICE (*embarrassed*): Listen . . . I've got an extra ticket – but only one. Here, Adolphe, you can do what you want to with it.

ADOLPHE: Thanks, Maurice. I relinquish it to Henriette.

HENRIETTE: No, I can't let you do that.

ADOLPHE: Why not? Besides, I never go to the theater. Always too hot and stuffy there.

HENRIETTE: At least you'll come and take me home when the show's over?

ADOLPHE: If you insist. Otherwise there's Maurice. . . . He'll be coming back here. We'll be having a party for him.

MAURICE: Oh, come on, Adolphe, you can certainly take the trouble to come and meet us. I beg you! Look, I'm on my knees! All right. Don't wait outside the theater. Meet us at the Auberge des Adrets. You could wait for us there. How about it? Agreed?

ADOLPHE: Not so fast, not so fast! You're a genius at settling questions to your own advantage without giving a guy a chance to think about them.

MAURICE: What is there to think about? Are you going to pick up your girl or aren't you?

ADOLPHE: You don't seem to realize what insignificant little acts can lead to. But I've got my hunches.

HENRIETTE: Sh-sh-sh! Can't be spooky in broad daylight! Whether he comes or not, we can always find our way back.

ADOLPHE (*has gotten up from his chair*): I've really got to go— I've got a model coming. "Goodbye. —Best of luck to you, Maurice! Tomorrow you'll be in another world! Goodbye, Henriette!

HENRIETTE: Are you really going?

ADOLPHE: Have to!

MAURICE: All right. Goodbye. See you soon!

Adolphe leaves, nodding goodbye to Madame Catherine as he goes out.

HENRIETTE: Well, we finally got to meet each other!

MAURICE: What's so extraordinary about that?

HENRIETTE: I guess it had to happen, since Adolphe did everything he could to prevent it.

MAURICE: Did he?

HENRIETTE: Don't tell me you didn't notice!

MAURICE: Yes, I noticed. Why do you have to mention it?

HENRIETTE: Just because.

MAURICE: But I don't have to mention that only a moment ago I was about to run off through the kitchen to avoid meeting you and that I was prevented by someone closing the door in my face.

HENRIETTE: Then why do you?

MAURICE: I don't know.

Madame Catherine knocks over some glasses and bottles.

Take it easy, Catherine. There's no danger.

HENRIETTE: Is that supposed to be a signal—or a warning?

MAURICE: Probably a bit of both.

HENRIETTE: What am I—a locomotive? Do I need signalmen to keep the track clear?

MAURICE: And switchmen! Switches are the dangerous places!

HENRIETTE: You can be nasty, can't you?

MADAME CATHERINE: Maurice isn't at all nasty. Up to now he's been as kind and loyal to those close to him as anyone could possibly be—especially those he's obligated to.

MAURICE: Oh, quiet, quiet!

HENRIETTE (*to Maurice*): The old cat is sharpening her claws . . .

MAURICE: We can walk down to the boulevard, if you want to.

HENRIETTE: Good idea! This is no place for me. I can feel her hatred clawing at me . . . (*Leaves.*)

MAURICE (*walking after her*): Goodbye, Catherine.

MADAME CATHERINE: Just a second! May I tell you something? Maurice!

MAURICE (*stopping reluctantly*): What is it?

MADAME CATHERINE: Don't do it! Don't do it!

MAURICE: Do what?

MADAME CATHERINE: Just don't do it!

MAURICE: Fear not! She's not my kind of girl. But I find her interesting in a way.

MADAME CATHERINE: You're too sure of yourself! That's bad.

MAURICE: No, that's good. —So long! (*Leaves.*)

ACT II

Scene 1

The Auberge des Adrets, on the Boulevard St. Martin, a café decorated in a flamboyantly theatrical, baroque style. Tables and armchairs here and there in nooks and corners. The walls are hung with weapons and armor; the wainscot shelves are lined with glasses and flagons, etc.

Maurice in tails and Henriette in evening gown are sitting at a table with a bottle of champagne and three filled champagne glasses. They are sitting facing each other, each with a glass. The third glass stands at the upstage side of the table, where a third empty armchair seems to be awaiting the missing third party.

MAURICE (*laying his watch on the table*): If he's not here in five minutes, he won't come at all. —In the meantime, what about drinking with his ghost? (*Clinking his glass against the third glass.*)

HENRIETTE (*doing the same*): Your health, Adolphe!

MAURICE: He won't come!

HENRIETTE: He will!

MAURICE: Won't!

HENRIETTE: Will!

MAURICE: What a night, what a wonderful day! I still can't believe it. A new life has begun for me! The producer thinks I'll make a hundred thousand francs out of this play. . . . You know how much that is? I'm buying a villa outside the city—and I'll still have eighty thousand left! I won't be able to take this all in until tomorrow, because right now I'm tired, tired, dead tired. (*Sinking down in his chair.*) Have you ever been really and truly happy?

HENRIETTE: Never! — How does it feel?

MAURICE: I can't begin to describe it! Can't find the words. I keep thinking how mortified and envious my enemies must be. . . . Awful, isn't it? But it's the truth.

HENRIETTE: Is that what success means — getting even?

MAURICE: Doesn't the conquering hero count bodies to measure the extent of his victory?

HENRIETTE: Are you that bloodthirsty?

MAURICE: Not really. But when you've been walked on year after year, it feels just great to get their heels off your chest and to breathe deeply again!

HENRIETTE: Don't you think it's strange that you're sitting here alone with me, an insignificant girl whom you don't know, on a night like this, when you should be showing yourself as the man of the hour before all the people on the boulevards, in all the night spots . . .

MAURICE: I suppose it is a little peculiar, but I like it here. Your company is all I need.

HENRIETTE: You're not happy, are you?

MAURICE: No, I feel rather sad. In fact, I feel like crying.

HENRIETTE: Why? What's the matter?

MAURICE: All this good luck. It all seems sour or on the verge of turning — into bad luck.

HENRIETTE: So sad, so melancholy! What more do you want?

MAURICE: The one thing that makes life worth living . . .

HENRIETTE: You don't love her any longer?

MAURICE: No, not in the way I think of love. She hasn't read my play, you know. Doesn't even want to. (*He sighs.*) Oh, she's good-hearted, self-sacrificing, sensitive, but to go out on the town with me, making a night of it like this — she'd think that was sinful. You know, I once treated her to a bottle of champagne.

Instead of enjoying it, she picked up the wine list to see how much it cost. And when she saw the price, she cried! She cried because little Marion needed new clothes! —Beautiful, isn't it? Even touching. But I don't get any fun out of it! And I want to get some fun out of life before it all disappears down the drain! All my life I've had to do without. But now, now—a new life begins for me!

The clock strikes twelve.

A new day. A whole new era.

HENRIETTE: Adolphe won't come.

MAURICE: No, now he won't. And now it's too late to go down to the Crêmerie.

HENRIETTE: They're waiting for you there.

MAURICE: Let them wait! They made me promise, and now I take back my promise. —Do you wish you were there?

HENRIETTE: No, not in the least!

MAURICE: Will you stay with me then?

HENRIETTE: With pleasure! If you can put up with me!

MAURICE: Would I ask you otherwise? —It's strange, but what good is the laurel crown of victory if you can't lay it at the feet of some woman. Everything is worthless if you don't have a woman . . .

HENRIETTE: Don't tell me you have to be without a woman! You?

MAURICE: Look at me!

HENRIETTE: Don't you know that a man at the peak of fame and fortune is irresistible?

MAURICE: How should I know? I haven't been in a position to find out.

HENRIETTE: You are strange! At this moment you're the most

envied man in Paris, and you sit here brooding, with a bad conscience, just because you ignored an invitation to drink a cup of chicory coffee with an old lady in that dump she runs . . .

MAURICE: Yes, my conscience does plague me. Even this far away I can tell they are hurt, can feel their righteous indignation, their animosity. They were my friends when I was nobody. Good old Catherine had first claim on my night of success. The party would have meant a lot to them. Cast a ray of hope over those who are still trying to make it. Now I've betrayed them. I can hear what they're saying. "He'll come. Good guy. Doesn't forget his friends. Doesn't go back on his word. He'll come, take my word." —Now they'll have to eat their words.

> *During this speech someone in the next room has begun to play Beethoven's Sonata No. 17 in D minor, Opus 31, No. 2 — the finale allegretto — at first very softly, then faster and faster, passionately, stormily, and finally with complete abandon.*

Who can be playing at this time of night?

HENRIETTE: Must be some night owl like us. . . . You know, you didn't present the case correctly. Remember that Adolphe promised to come and pick us up. We waited, and *he* didn't keep *his* promise. So you should have a clear conscience . . .

MAURICE: Do you really think so? . . . I believe you as long as you go on talking, but as soon as you stop, the millstones of my conscience begin to grind again. —What have you got in that package?

HENRIETTE: Oh, it's only a laurel wreath. I wanted to send it up to you on the stage, but I didn't get a chance. Let me give it to you now. If your head is hot, the laurel will cool it — so they say. (*She stands up and puts the laurel wreath on his head; kisses him on the forehead.*) Hail the conquering hero!

MAURICE: No, don't do that.

HENRIETTE (*on her knees*): Hail to the king!

MAURICE (*standing up*): No, please! It gives me the creeps!

HENRIETTE: You scaredy-cat! Maurice, the coward! Afraid of success! Who ran off with your self-confidence, little man?

MAURICE: Little man! Yes, you're right. I'm no giant hurling lightning bolts and rolling thunder balls. I'm the dwarf who guards the treasure, who forges his sword silently, deep within the mountain. So you think I shy from the victor's laurel? You think I fear that ghost there, staring at me with the green eyes of jealousy and monitoring my passions—passions of whose force you know nothing! —Vanish, ghost! (*He sweeps the third champagne glass to the floor.*) You have no place here! You stayed away and you lost your rights—if you ever had any! You stayed away from the battlefield because you knew you were beaten. As I crush this glass under my feet, so shall I grind into dust that image of yourself which you have built in a little temple that shall be yours no longer!

HENRIETTE: Bravo! That's more like it! Bravo!

MAURICE: There! I've sacrificed my best friend, my most devoted supporter, on your altar, Astarte! Are you satisfied?

HENRIETTE: Astarte! I love that! From now on I'm Astarte! —I think you really do love me, Maurice.

MAURICE: Of course I love you! —Ah, daughter of destruction, lady of pain! You like the smell of blood. You rouse my fighting spirit! Where did you come from? Where will you lead me? I must have loved you even before I saw you. When they talked about you, I trembled. When I glimpsed you in the doorway, I felt you physically. When you left, I still held you in my arms. I tried to get away from you, but someone stopped me. We were driven together, like wild game by the baying hounds. Who's guilty in all this? Your friend, my friend, our pander.

HENRIETTE: Guilty or not guilty—what's that got to do with it? And what's guilt? Adolphe is guilty, guilty of not having brought us together sooner. He committed the crime, robbing us—of two weeks of bliss that he had no right to. I'm jealous of him on your account. I hate him because he betrayed you with me. I want to wipe him from the living, erase even the thought of him, render him unborn, unmade, nonexistent.

MAURICE: Right! We'll drive his ghost into the wild woods,

bury our memories of him, and let the days we spend with each other pile up like rocks on top of him. (*Raising his glass.*) Our fate is sealed! Woe betide us! What's next, Astarte?

HENRIETTE: A new life! Remember? — What have you got in that package?

MAURICE: Package? I've forgotten.

HENRIETTE (*opens the package and takes out a tie and a pair of gloves*): My God, what an awful tie! Must have come from the five-and-dime!

MAURICE (*snatching the things from her*): Don't touch them!

HENRIETTE: From her?

MAURICE: Yes, from her.

HENRIETTE: Give them to me!

MAURICE: No! She's better than we are. Better than everyone!

HENRIETTE: No, not better. Just sillier and stingier! A ninny who cries because somebody drinks champagne . . .

MAURICE: Because her child didn't have enough clothes! She's good. Good.

HENRIETTE: My, aren't you the bourgeois one! I thought you were an artist. You're not — but I am and when I do your bust I'll carve MIDDLE CLASS on your brow — and skip the laurel crown! What's her name? Jeanne?

MAURICE: Yes. How did you know?

HENRIETTE: All housemaids are called Jeanne.

MAURICE: Henriette!

> *Henriette takes the tie and the gloves and throws them in the fireplace.*

(*Weakly.*) The Goddess Astarte! You want to see that woman sacrificed to you too? All right. You can have her. But if you demand an innocent child I'm through with you.

HENRIETTE: What draws you to me? Tell me.

MAURICE: If I knew, I could break the spell. I think it must be the bad qualities you possess and that I lack. I think it must be the evil in you, which attracts me with all the irresistible charm of the new and different . . .

HENRIETTE: Have you ever committed a crime?

MAURICE: No, not a real one. Have you?

HENRIETTE: Yes.

MAURICE: You have? What did it feel like?

HENRIETTE: Better than doing a good deed. That only makes you the same as the others. It felt greater than doing something heroic, because that only raises you above the crowd; they give you an award for that. But the crime I committed carried me away, transported me to the other side of life, beyond society, beyond my fellow human beings. Since that moment I've only lived a half life, a dream life, and that's why reality can never have any claim on me.

MAURICE: What did you do?

HENRIETTE: I won't tell you. Fraidy-cat!

MAURICE: Can't you ever be found out?

HENRIETTE: Never! But that doesn't prevent me from thinking about those five stones in the Place de Roquette where the guillotine used to stand. And I never cut cards, because I'm sure to turn up the five of diamonds . . . *

MAURICE: That kind of crime? Not—?

HENRIETTE: Yes, it was!

MAURICE: That's terrifying. —And fascinating! Doesn't your conscience bother you?

HENRIETTE: Never. Let's change the subject, if you don't mind.

---

* The guillotine was set up outside the Roquette prison in the center of five stones forming a design like that on the five of diamonds.

MAURICE: What shall we talk about? Love?

HENRIETTE: One doesn't talk about love until it's over!

MAURICE: Were you in love with Adolphe?

HENRIETTE: I don't know. His good heart had the same appeal as a beautiful, long-lost childhood memory. But when I looked at him carefully, there was so much about him I didn't like. I had to spend a lot of time changing, rubbing out and filling in, to make a decent picture of him. When I heard him talking, I couldn't help noticing how much he had learned from you, how he had misunderstood it and misapplied it. Now just imagine, when I got to see the original, how pitiful the copy seemed to be! — That was why he was afraid that you and I would meet. And when it happened, he understood immediately that his time was up.

MAURICE: Poor Adolphe!

HENRIETTE: I feel sorry for him too. I know how he suffers.

MAURICE: Quiet. . . . Someone's coming!

HENRIETTE: My God, suppose it's him!

MAURICE: That would be unbearable!

HENRIETTE: No, it isn't him. Suppose it had been. You're a playwright. Let's see you rehearse the scene.

MAURICE: All right. He'd be a little mad at you — at first — because he made a mistake about the café — looked for us in the wrong place — then his irritation would give way to pleasure at seeing us — seeing that *we* hadn't deceived him. And in the joy of discovering that he had unjustly suspected us, he would come to love and cherish us both. He would be delighted that we two had become such fast friends. It had always been his fondest dream — I can hear him making a long speech at this point — his fondest dream that we three might form a triumvirate to set the world a great example of a friendship that makes no demands. "Yes, I trust you, Maurice, not only because you are my friend, but because I know your heart lies elsewhere!"

HENRIETTE: Wonderful! Right on the nose! You must have

been in this situation before. You know, Adolphe is one of those men who believes that three's company and two's a crowd. He can never have any fun with his girl unless there's a friend along.

MAURICE: So I was called in to amuse you. —Sh! . . . There *is* somebody out there! —It's him!

HENRIETTE: No, it isn't. Don't you know this is the witching hour? That's when you hear things—and see things sometimes. Staying up all night has the same sort of magic as crime. Puts you over and above the laws of nature.

MAURICE: There's a horrifying punishment for that. . . . I've got goose pimples. I don't know whether I'm frozen or frightened.

HENRIETTE (*takes her long coat with the fur collar and wraps it around him*): Put something on. This will warm you.

MAURICE: Oh, that's wonderful! It's as if I had crawled inside your skin, as if my body, pulverized from lack of sleep, was being recast in your mold. I can actually feel how I'm being reshaped. I'm getting a new soul, new ideas. And here, where your breasts have formed a bulge, a new life begins to swell up.

> During the whole of this scene, the pianist in the next room has been practicing the Beethoven Sonata, sometimes pianissimo, sometimes madly fortissimo. Occasionally there has been silence; occasionally only bars 96-107 of the finale have been heard.

What a strange bird, practicing the piano in the middle of the night! . . . I've had enough! Do you know what? —We'll drive out to the Bois de Boulogne and have breakfast in the pavilion and watch the sun come up over the water.

HENRIETTE: Wonderful.

MAURICE: But first I have to send a message home to have the morning reviews sent out to the pavilion. —Henriette, what the hell! Let's invite Adolphe!

HENRIETTE: That's really crazy, but why not? Even an ass can help pull the triumphal chariot! Let him come!

They stand up.

MAURICE (*taking off the coat*): I'll go ring.

HENRIETTE: Wait a second! (*She throws herself into his arms.*)

Scene 2

A large, handsome room in a restaurant in the Bois de Boulogne. Carpets, mirrors, chaise longues, and divans. At the rear, French windows looking out on the lakes. In the foreground a table is spread with flower arrangements, bowls of fruit, decanters of wine, plates of oysters, varieties of wineglasses, and two lighted candelabra. To the right, a low table with newspapers and telegrams piled on it.

Maurice and Henriette are sitting at opposite sides of this table.

The sun is rising.

MAURICE: There isn't a shadow of a doubt. The newspapers say it's a hit; the telegrams congratulate me. A new life is beginning, and this is our wedding night because you were the only one to share my hopes and triumphs. You handed me the laurel crown of victory. I feel as if everything came to me from you!

HENRIETTE: What a wonderful night! Have we only dreamed it, or have we actually lived it?

MAURICE (*standing up*): And what a morning on top of such a night! It seems like the first day of creation, with the rising sun lighting up the newborn world. The earth is being created for the first time. Look! —It's breaking free of those clouds of placenta drifting off into space. There lies the Garden of Eden basking in the rosy light of a dawning day. And here stand the first two human beings. . . . You know, I'm so happy I feel like crying when I think that all of mankind is not just as happy as I am. . . . Do you hear that rustling and murmuring in the distance, like ocean waves washing stony beaches, like the soughing wind in the woods? Do you know what that is? That's Paris, Paris whispering my name! Do you see the columns of smoke rising to the sky, thousands upon thousands of them? That's from the fires on my altars—and if it isn't, it should be, because I want it to be. All the telegraph keys in Europe are tapping out my name at this very moment. The Orient Express is carrying the news to the Far East toward the rising sun, while ocean steamers are carrying it to the far, far West! —The world is mine, and that's why it's beautiful! Oh, how I wish I had wings for us both, to get away from here and fly far, far away, before someone spoils my happiness, before envy and jealousy wake me from my dream— because it probably is just a dream!

HENRIETTE (*offering her hand*): Feel! and you'll know you're not dreaming!

MAURICE: No, it isn't a dream, but once upon a time it was! You know, when I was a poor young man who walked down there in the woods and looked up to this pavilion, it seemed to me like a castle in a fairy tale, and I'd dream that being up in this room with its balcony and its thick curtains would be absolute bliss! And to sit here with the woman I love and watch the sun rise while the candelabra were still burning—that was the wildest dream of my youth. Now it's come true; I have nothing more to live for! —Do you want to die now, with me?

HENRIETTE: No! You crazy fool, now I want to begin to live!

MAURICE (*standing up*): To live? Living is suffering. —And now comes reality! I can hear him running up the steps, panting with anxiety, his heart pounding with the fear that he has lost his most precious possession. I'll bet you Adolphe is under this roof right now. And in one minute he'll be standing in the middle of this room.

HENRIETTE (*tense*): It was a stupid trick to invite him here. I'm sorry we did. —Anyhow, it will give us a chance to see how much you know about psychology—see how right you were.

MAURICE: When you're dealing with emotions, there's always room for error.

The Headwaiter enters to deliver a card to Maurice.

Show the gentleman in. (*To Henriette.*) We're going to regret this, I'm sure!

HENRIETTE: Bit late for that. —Quiet!

Adolphe enters, haggard, pale, and hollow-eyed.

MAURICE (*trying to appear casual*): Well, well, Adolphe! Where were you hiding out last night?

ADOLPHE: I looked for you at the Hôtel des Arrêts. I waited for an hour.

MAURICE: That was the wrong place. We waited for you at the Auberge des Adrets for two hours. And we're still waiting for you, as you can see.

ADOLPHE (*relieved*): Thank God.

HENRIETTE: Good morning! Adolphe, you must be jinxed! You've got to stop tormenting yourself for no good reason. I'll bet you're thinking that we tried to avoid you. You know we sent for you, but you still look as though you weren't wanted.

ADOLPHE: I'm sorry. Forgive me. I've had a horrible night.

They sit down. Embarrassed silence.

HENRIETTE (*to Adolphe*): Well, aren't you going to congratulate Maurice on his great success?

ADOLPHE: Oh, my God, of course! —The play is a great hit. Everyone says so—even those who envy you. The world is at your feet, Maurice. I feel such a nothing next to you.

MAURICE: Oh, nonsense! —Henriette, give Adolphe a glass of wine.

ADOLPHE: No thanks, not for me. Nothing at all, thank you.

HENRIETTE (*to Adolphe*): What's the matter with you? Are you sick?

ADOLPHE: No, but I think I'm coming down with something.

HENRIETTE: Your eyes . . .

ADOLPHE: What about them?

MAURICE: How did things go at the Crêmerie last night? I suppose they're mad at me?

ADOLPHE: No one's mad at you. But everyone was in such a gloom, I couldn't bear it. They're not mad at you, you understand, they're sympathetic and considerate. When you didn't show up, they understood. Madame Catherine herself defended you and proposed a toast to you. We all rejoiced in your success as if it had been our own.

HENRIETTE: Such good, kind people! Aren't you lucky to have such wonderful friends, Maurice!

MAURICE: Yes, better than I deserve.

HENRIETTE: Everybody has exactly the friends he deserves. Everybody likes you, Maurice. . . . Don't you feel how the air caresses you today? It's filled with the good wishes of a thousand souls . . .

Maurice stands up to conceal his emotion.

ADOLPHE: —a thousand souls thanking you for making them feel better. Everyone was writing such pessimistic stuff, saying people were bad, life hopeless, without meaning. Then you came along with your play. Made everybody feel good. Felt like lifting up their heads. Things aren't so bad, after all, they're thinking. And thinking like that actually makes them better, you know.

Henriette tries to hide her feelings.

ADOLPHE: I feel I'm intruding. I'll stay just a moment longer. I just want to warm myself in your sunshine, Maurice. Then I'll go.

MAURICE: Why do you want to go? You just got here.

ADOLPHE: Why? Because I've seen what I never really needed to see. I can tell what's going on. (*Silence.*) Sending for me was very considerate of you. Better, more straightforward than hiding it from me. Hurts less than being deceived. You see, I do think the best of people, Maurice. That's something you've taught me.

(*Silence.*) But there's something I think I should tell you, Maurice. Just a while ago I passed through the Church of Saint-Germain, and I saw a woman and a child there. I don't wish that you could have seen them—what's done can't be undone—but if you gave them a thought or a good word before you set them adrift in this big city, you might enjoy your success with complete peace of mind. That's all I wanted to say. Goodbye.

HENRIETTE: Why do you have to go?

ADOLPHE: You don't really want me to answer that!

HENRIETTE: No, I guess not.

ADOLPHE: Goodbye. (*Leaves.*)

MAURICE: "And lo, they knew that they were naked."

HENRIETTE: A bit different from the scene we were expecting, wasn't it? . . . He's too good for us.

MAURICE: I'm beginning to think everybody is.

HENRIETTE: Look. . . . The sun has gone behind the clouds, and the woods have lost their rosy hue.

MAURICE: So I see. And the blue water has turned black. Come on, let's leave. Let's fly south, where the skies are always blue and the trees are always green.

HENRIETTE: Yes, let's! —But without goodbyes to anyone!

MAURICE: No, *with* goodbyes!

HENRIETTE: You said we were going to fly. You offered me wings—but you've got lead weights on your feet. —I'm not jealous, but I know that if you go to say goodbye and find yourself with two pairs of arms around your neck, you'll never be able to break that stranglehold.

MAURICE: I'm sure you're right—except that it would take only *one* pair of arms to hold me fast.

HENRIETTE: The child? It's the child, not the woman. Right?

MAURICE: That's right. The child.

HENRIETTE: The child! Another woman's child! And for that

I have to suffer! Why does that child have to stand in my way when I want to get ahead, when I've got to get ahead?

MAURICE: Yes, why? Better if it had never existed!

HENRIETTE (*walking up and down in great agitation*): Absolutely! But it does exist! Like a rock in the road, an immovable rock that's bound to upset the wagon.

MAURICE: You mean the triumphal chariot! —You can drive the ass till it drops, but the rock remains. Damn it, damn it! (*Silence.*)

HENRIETTE: What are we going to do? Must be something.

MAURICE: There is! We'll get married. Then *our* child will make us forget the other child.

HENRIETTE: The one will kill the other!

MAURICE: Kill! What a word to use!

HENRIETTE (*suddenly soft, pleading*): Your child will kill our love!

MAURICE: Never! Don't you see, our love will kill everything that stands in its way, but it cannot be killed!

HENRIETTE (*cuts a deck of cards, which is lying on the mantelpiece*): You see! The five of diamonds! The guillotine! —Is it really possible that everything is all worked out in advance? That our thoughts are led like water through pipes, and that there's nothing we can do about it? No, I don't want it to end that way! I don't want to end there! . . . You know, it's the guillotine for me, if my crime is discovered.

MAURICE: Tell me about it. No better time than this.

HENRIETTE: No, I'd regret it later. And you'd loathe me. —No, no, no. . . . Have you ever heard that a person could be hated to death? No? Well, I tell you my father was seared with the hatred of my mother and my brothers and sisters, and he melted away like wax in the fire. (*Gesture of aversion.*) No, no. Let's talk about something else. —For God's sake, let's get away from here! The air is poisoned. Tomorrow the laurel will be withered, the triumph forgotten; within a week another conquering hero will be the public idol. We've got to get away! But first, Maurice, darling, you'll go and embrace your child and arrange for its immediate future. As for the mother of the girl, I don't see any reason why you should have to meet her.

MAURICE: Thank you, Henriette! You really have a good heart. You usually keep it under wraps. But I love you twice as much when you show it.

HENRIETTE: Afterward you'll go to the Crêmerie and say goodbye to the old lady and all your old friends! Be sure you settle all your affairs! Once we leave here, I don't want you brooding over what you should have done.

MAURICE: I'll clear up everything. And tonight we'll meet at the train station.

HENRIETTE: Right! We'll be on our way—south, toward the sea and the sun!

ACT III

Scene 1

The Crêmerie.

The gas lamps are lit. Madame Catherine is sitting at the buffet; Adolphe at one of the tables.

MADAME CATHERINE: My dear Adolphe, that's life! You young folks expect too much, and then you sit around and cry if you don't get it.

ADOLPHE: No, that's not how it is. I'm not reproaching anybody. I still like them both as much as ever. There's just one thing that really hurts me. You see, I felt so close to Maurice—so close that there was nothing I'd have denied him if it would have made him happy. But I've lost him. That's what hurts—more than the loss of her. I've lost them both. Makes me feel twice as lonesome. . . . There's still something else that bothers me. Can't put my finger on it.

MADAME CATHERINE: Don't sit there brooding. Get to work, amuse yourself. . . . Don't you ever go to church, Adolphe?

ADOLPHE: What on earth would I do there?

MADAME CATHERINE: There's a lot to look at—and there's the music. Be a change for you, anyway.

ADOLPHE: Perhaps. But this sheep doesn't belong to that fold: I'm not devout. And besides, Madame Catherine, you know that faith is a gift, and nobody's given it to me, not so far.

MADAME CATHERINE: All right, Adolphe, no use forcing things. —Now what's this I've been hearing today? I hear you sold a painting in London for a lot of money and got a medal for first prize? Is it true?

ADOLPHE: Yes, it's true.

MADAME CATHERINE: Well, of all the—! And you never said a word about it?

ADOLPHE: I'm afraid of success. —Besides, it doesn't mean a thing at this moment. It's like seeing a ghost. You know what they say: you mustn't tell anyone you've seen it because you're just asking for more trouble.

MADAME CATHERINE: Well, Adolphe, I've always said you were an odd duck!

ADOLPHE: You don't understand, Catherine. I've seen how bad luck goes hand in hand with the good. When things are going against you, you find out who your friends are. They stick by you. When things go well, everybody sticks by you. You don't know who your friends are. . . . You asked me if I ever went to church. I didn't give you a straight answer. You see, this morning, I did go into the Church of Saint-Germain—without really knowing why. I felt I was looking for someone whom I might thank for my good luck. But I didn't find anyone. . . . So instead I put a gold coin in the poor box—and that's all that came of my visit to the church. I don't call that much of a change.

MADAME CATHERINE: At least you did something—and it was good of you to think of the poor when luck came your way.

ADOLPHE: It was neither good nor bad; I did it because I couldn't help myself. —But something else happened to me in church. I saw Maurice's girlfriend Jeanne and their child there. Crushed beneath his triumphal chariot! They looked as if they'd lost everything in the world.

MADAME CATHERINE: I just don't understand how you kids have arranged things with your consciences. I can't figure it out! How could a good, conscientious, sensitive man like Maurice abandon his girl and his child without a moment's hesitation? Explain that, if you can.

ADOLPHE: I can't. I don't think he understands it himself. I met them this morning and everything seemed so perfectly natural to them. They couldn't imagine things could be any other way. They looked as if they'd just done their good deed for the day, or fulfilled a sacred duty. Catherine, there are some things we can't explain, so how can we judge them? Besides, you saw how the whole thing happened. Maurice felt the danger in the air; I sensed it. I tried to keep them from meeting; Maurice wanted to run away; but it was all no use. It was as if an invisible being had woven the plot and driven them into each other's arms. I suppose I should disqualify myself in this case, but I don't hesitate for a moment to pronounce the verdict: not guilty.

MADAME CATHERINE: Well, Adolphe, to be as forgiving as you are, that's true religion!

ADOLPHE: Goodness me! Catherine, you don't suppose I'm religious without knowing it!

MADAME CATHERINE: Still, letting oneself be driven to sin—or letting oneself be tempted—that's a sign of weakness—or corruption. If you feel you can't resist, you should pray for help, and then it comes. But he didn't. He was too stuck-up. —Who's this coming? Well, if it isn't the abbé!

ADOLPHE: What's he doing here?

The Abbé enters.

THE ABBÉ: Good evening, Madame. Good evening, young fellow.

MADAME CATHERINE: Can I be of any help, Father?

THE ABBÉ: I'm looking for Monsieur Gérard. Have you seen him today?

MADAME CATHERINE: No, I haven't. They're doing his play at one of the theaters; he's probably busy up there.

THE ABBÉ: I have some . . . some bad news for him—bad in more respects than one.

MADAME CATHERINE: May I ask what sort of news?

THE ABBÉ: Yes, of course; it's no secret. His daughter—the one born out of wedlock—to Jeanne—she's dead.

MADAME CATHERINE: Dead?

ADOLPHE: Marion dead!

THE ABBÉ: Yes. She passed away suddenly this morning without any apparent symptoms of earlier illness.

MADAME CATHERINE: Oh God! Mysterious are Thy ways.

THE ABBÉ: The mother's grief and distress make Maurice's presence imperative. We must try to find him. —Let me ask you one question—in strictest confidence, of course. Did Maurice love his child, or was he indifferent toward her?

MADAME CATHERINE: Love his little Marion! Father, all of us here know how dearly he loved her.

ADOLPHE: There's absolutely no doubt about that, Father.

THE ABBÉ: I'm certainly glad to hear that. Makes things clear in my mind, at least.

MADAME CATHERINE: Was there any doubt?

THE ABBÉ: Yes, unfortunately. There's an ugly rumor circulating in this part of town that he deserted his child and the mother to run away with another woman. Within the last few hours this rumor has turned into a direct accusation, and the people are furious. They're calling him a murderer. They are even threatening his life.

MADAME CATHERINE: My God, what on earth is going on? What is all this?

THE ABBÉ: Let me assure you. I am completely convinced that he is innocent. And the mother is just as certain as I am. But appearances are so much against him, I'm afraid he'll find it difficult to clear himself with the police.

ADOLPHE: Is this a police case?

THE ABBÉ: Yes, the police had to step in for his own good. To protect him against the anger of the people. The police inspector's probably on his way here right now.

MADAME CATHERINE (*to Adolphe*): Do you see what happens when you can't tell good from evil, and start flirting with sin? God punishes, that's what!

ADOLPHE: Then he's less merciful than people are.

THE ABBÉ: You seem to know a lot about this.

ADOLPHE: Not a lot, but I've got eyes.

THE ABBÉ: But do you understand what you see?

ADOLPHE: Perhaps not yet.

THE ABBÉ: Let's look at the matter more closely —. Oh, here's the inspector.

The Inspector enters.

THE INSPECTOR: Gentlemen, Madame Catherine. I'm sorry to disturb you. I have to ask you some questions concerning Monsieur Gérard, who, as I suppose you already know, is the victim of a hideous rumor, which, by the bye, I don't for a moment believe.

MADAME CATHERINE: No one here believes it either!

THE INSPECTOR: Good, that strengthens my opinion. Still, for his sake, I want to be certain he gets a proper hearing.

THE ABBÉ: Fair enough. I'm sure he'll get justice, even though it won't be easy.

THE INSPECTOR: Appearances are all against him; that's the trouble. I've seen innocent people die on the scaffold before they had a chance to prove they were innocent. Now here's the evidence against him. (*He consults his notebook.*) The little girl Marion, left alone by her mother, was secretly visited by her father, who seems to have gone to some trouble to find out exactly when the child would be alone. Just fifteen minutes after the father left, the mother came home and found the child dead. That looks bad for the accused man. On the other hand, the autopsy has revealed no signs of violence and no traces of poison. Good! But the doctors point out that there are some newly discovered poisons that do not leave any traces! Now, all this is circumstantial — and all quite likely due to coincidence. I'm accustomed to that in my business! Regrettably, there is more incriminating evidence. — Last night Maurice was seen at the

Auberge des Adrets with an unidentified lady. Their conversation, according to the waiter's testimony, dealt with crime. Words like Place de Roquette and guillotine were spoken—a rather strange subject for conversation between two lovers of good breeding and respectable position! . . . But let that pass. We all know that people who stay up all night drinking are quite likely to dig up some of the bad stuff that lies in the depths of their souls, however respectable they may be. —More damaging is the testimony of the headwaiter who served them a champagne breakfast in the Bois de Boulogne this morning. He testifies to having heard them wish for the death of a child. The man is reported to have said, "Better if it never existed." To which the woman replied, "Absolutely. But it does exist." And later in the conversation someone said, "The one will kill the other," to which the reply was: "Kill. That's no word to use," and "Our love will kill anything that stands in its way"! And also: "The five of diamonds" . . . "the guillotine" . . . "Place de Roquette." —Now as you can see, all this builds quite a case against the man. —As does one more final fact: the trip out of the country that the two of them have planned for tonight. There you have the hard facts.

MADAME CATHERINE: I never heard anything so horrible. I don't know what to believe.

THE ABBÉ: There's something unearthly about this. God help him!

ADOLPHE: Caught in a net of circumstances!

MADAME CATHERINE: He had no business there in the first place.

ADOLPHE: Are you beginning to lose faith in him?

MADAME CATHERINE: I don't know what to think. —People are angels one minute and devils the next.

THE INSPECTOR: It's all very odd. We'll just have to wait until we hear his explanation. We can't judge him unheard. Good evening, gentlemen—Madame Catherine. (*Exits.*)

THE ABBÉ: Something unearthly about this, truly!

ADOLPHE: I'd say it's demons at work, out to destroy man.

THE ABBÉ: No, it's either punishment for unknown transgressions—or it's a frightening testing of the soul.

Jeanne enters, in mourning.

JEANNE: Good evening. —Excuse me for asking, but has Maurice been here?

MADAME CATHERINE: No, Madame, but he might come at any moment. . . . I guess that means you haven't seen him since . . .

JEANNE: Not since yesterday morning . . .

MADAME CATHERINE: I can't tell you how sorry I am. You poor dear!

JEANNE: Thank you, Madame. (*To The Abbé.*) —Oh, Father?

THE ABBÉ: My child. I thought I might be of some help. And by a stroke of luck I had a chance to talk to the inspector here.

JEANNE: The inspector! I'm sure he suspects Maurice too, doesn't he?

THE ABBÉ: No, he doesn't. None of us does. It's just that appearances are against him—alarmingly, I must admit.

JEANNE: You mean the conversation the waiter overheard. That doesn't mean a thing. I've heard that sort of talk when Maurice has had a little to drink. He's always carrying on about crime and punishment. Besides, it seems to me that his woman friend said the worst things. Oh, how I'd like to meet her face to face and tell her what I think of her.

ADOLPHE: My dear Jeanne, that woman may have wronged you, but I know she never really meant to. She has no evil intentions, I assure you. Has no intentions at all, as a matter of fact. Just follows the inclinations of her heart. I know her. She's a good woman, and she's got nothing to be ashamed of.

JEANNE: All right, Adolphe. If you say so. That means that I have no one to blame for what happened except myself. I was a fool and that's why I'm being punished now. (*She's cries.*)

THE ABBÉ: Come now, don't be so hard on yourself. I know

you well enough, and I know how seriously you took the responsibilities of being a mother. The fact that there was no time to give either religious or legal sanction to the birth of the child was not your fault. No, there is more here than meets the eye.

ADOLPHE: What?

THE ABBÉ: I wish I knew.

Henriette enters, dressed for traveling.

ADOLPHE (*rises resolutely and approaches Henriette*): Henriette?

HENRIETTE: Hello, Adolphe. Where's Maurice?

ADOLPHE: Do you know what—. Or maybe you don't know?

HENRIETTE: I know the whole story. Forgive me, Madame Catherine, but I'm going out of town, I just had to stop by for a moment. (*To Adolphe, but indicating Jeanne.*) Who is that? —Ah!

Henriette and Jeanne stare at each other. Emile can be seen in the kitchen doorway.

HENRIETTE (*to Jeanne*): There must be something I can say, without sounding crude or cynical. But if I simply tell you that I sympathize as deeply with you in your great sorrow as anyone closer to you does, you must believe me. . . . You must. I deserve your pity even if not your forbearance. (*Holds out her hand toward Jeanne.*)

JEANNE (*staring at her*): I believe you, at least for the moment. (*She takes Henriette's hand.*)

HENRIETTE (*kissing Jeanne's hand*): Thank you!

JEANNE (*pulling her hand back*): Don't! I don't deserve it! I don't!

THE ABBÉ: Excuse me, but since we are all together here and, at least for the moment, in a conciliatory mood, I wonder if Mademoiselle Henriette might not clear up some of the doubt and confusion surrounding the main point of the accusation against Maurice. Could you tell us, as between friends, what you meant when you spoke of killing, of crime, and of the Place de Roquette? We know truly that these words could have had absolutely nothing to do with the death of the little child, but it would relieve us to hear exactly what you were talking about. Won't you tell us?

HENRIETTE (*after a pause*): I can't! I can't tell you!

ADOLPHE: Henriette! What do you mean, you can't tell us? You can't leave us in the dark!

HENRIETTE: I can't tell you. Don't ask me to!

THE ABBÉ: Didn't I say there was something unearthly about this?

HENRIETTE: I knew all along this moment had to come. It had to! (*To Jeanne.*) I swear to you that I am without guilt in the death of your child. Isn't that enough?

JEANNE: Enough for us, perhaps. But what about justice?

HENRIETTE: Justice? If you only knew how right you are!

THE ABBÉ (*to Henriette*): And if you only understood the import of your words!

HENRIETTE: Do you understand them better than I?

THE ABBÉ: I think I do.

Henriette studies The Abbé.

Don't worry. Even if I guess your secret, I won't reveal it. Besides, legal justice is not my concern. But divine grace is.

Maurice, dressed for traveling, enters in a great hurry. Without noticing the rest of the people, who are in the foreground, Maurice goes directly to the counter where Madame Catherine is sitting.

MAURICE: Catherine, don't be mad at me because I didn't show up. Look, I've come here just to beg your forgiveness before I leave. I'm heading south tonight at eight o'clock.

Madame Catherine is stunned, silent.

You are mad at me! (*Looks around.*) What's going on? —Is this a dream, or isn't it? —I can see it's real, but you all look like figures in a wax museum. . . . Jeanne standing like a statue, dressed in black . . . and Henriette looking like a corpse. . . . What does it mean?

General silence.

No one answers—that means it's something terrible!

Silence.

MAURICE: Come on now, answer! —Adolphe, my friend, what is it? —And—(*Indicating Emile.*)—and there's a detective!

ADOLPHE (*coming forward*): Don't you know?

MAURICE: Know what? Tell me!

ADOLPHE: Marion is dead!

MAURICE: Marion . . . dead?!

ADOLPHE: Yes, this morning.

MAURICE (*to Jeanne*): That's why you're in black. Oh, Jeanne, Jeanne, who did this to us? Who?

JEANNE: God took her from us.

MAURICE: But I saw her in the pink of health this very morning! She couldn't just die! Somebody—somebody did this. (*Seeking out Henriette with his eyes.*)

ADOLPHE: Don't look for the guilty party here. No one here did it. But, unfortunately, the police have got leads pointing to the one person who should be above suspicion.

MAURICE: Meaning who?

ADOLPHE: Who do you suppose? Your careless talk last night —and this morning—puts you in a bad light, to say the least!

MAURICE: You mean they were listening to us? —Let me think . . . what were we talking about? . . . Oh! My God!

ADOLPHE: All you have to do is explain why you said those things. We'll believe you!

MAURICE: I can't! I won't! Go ahead and put me in jail, I don't care! Marion is dead . . . dead. . . . And I've killed her!

General commotion.

ADOLPHE: Think what you're saying, Maurice. Don't talk like that!

MAURICE: Like what?

ADOLPHE: You said you killed Marion.

MAURICE: Does anybody really believe that I'm a murderer? —That I could kill my own child? Catherine, you know me. Do you—?

MADAME CATHERINE: I don't know what to believe now. "Out of the abundance of the heart the mouth speaketh."

MAURICE: You don't believe me . . .

ADOLPHE: All you have to do is explain. —Explain what you meant when you said that your "love kills everything that stands in its way."

MAURICE: I see. You know that too! —Maybe Henriette will explain that?

HENRIETTE: You know I can't!

THE ABBÉ: Well, if you don't put your cards on the table, we can't help you. A moment ago I would have sworn you were innocent. Now I wonder.

MAURICE: Jeanne, what you have to say means more than all the rest put together.

JEANNE (*coldly*): Just answer me one thing: when you were having that orgy in that hotel, you swore you wanted someone dead. Who?

MAURICE: Did I? Well, maybe! Yes, yes, I know I'm guilty — but just as much not guilty! Let me out of here. I can never forgive myself.

HENRIETTE (*to Adolphe*): Go with him. He may do something stupid!

ADOLPHE: Why me?

HENRIETTE: Who else?

ADOLPHE (*without bitterness*): You're closer to him. — Wait, there's a carriage stopping outside.

MADAME CATHERINE: It's the inspector! — I've seen a lot in my time, but I've never seen fame and fortune vanish so quickly.

MAURICE (*to Henriette*): From the triumphal chariot to the police wagon!

JEANNE (*simply*): Pulled by an ass — who was that?

ADOLPHE: Me, of course.

The Inspector enters with a summons in his hand.

THE INSPECTOR: Summons to Police Headquarters — at once, tonight — for Maurice Gérard . . . and Henriette Mauclerc. . . . Are you both here?

MAURICE *and* HENRIETTE: Yes!

MAURICE: Are we being arrested?

THE INSPECTOR: No, not yet. You're just being called in for questioning.

MAURICE: And then what?

THE INSPECTOR: Who knows?

Maurice and Henriette go toward the door.

MAURICE: Goodbye, everybody.

Everyone is deeply moved. The Inspector, Maurice, and Henriette leave.

EMILE (*comes in and approaches Jeanne*): Come, Sis, I'll go home with you.

JEANNE: Emile, what do you think of all this?

EMILE: He's innocent!

THE ABBÉ: Too simple. As I see it, it's despicable to break one's promise—and unforgivable when a woman and a child are involved.

EMILE: I'd be inclined to feel the same way, since it's my own sister. But I can't throw any stones. I once made the same kind of mistake myself.

THE ABBÉ: Ah, yes. Well, that doesn't apply to me. Nevertheless, I won't cast the first stone. No need to, as I see it. Actions have a way of judging themselves: the consequences constitute the punishment.

JEANNE: Pray for him! For both of them!

THE ABBÉ: No, I'm not going to do that. It's impertinent to want to change God's mind. And, I tell you, there's certainly something unearthly about all this.

Scene 2

The Auberge des Adrets. Adolphe and Henriette are sitting at the same table at which Maurice and Henriette sat in Act II. Adolphe has a cup of coffee in front of him; Henriette, nothing.

ADOLPHE: You really think he'll come here?

HENRIETTE: I'm absolutely certain. The police released him this noon for lack of evidence. He didn't want to show himself on the streets until after dark.

ADOLPHE: I can imagine how he feels! —You know, since yesterday life has become a horrible nightmare for me, too.

HENRIETTE: What do you think it is for me? I'm afraid to live; I hardly dare to breathe; I'm even afraid to think. Spies everywhere, overhearing me. They even read my thoughts.

ADOLPHE: Yes. So it was here you were sitting that night I couldn't find you!

HENRIETTE: Oh, don't talk about it! I could die of shame when I think of it. Adolphe, you're made of different stuff than Maurice and me—better stuff. . . . (*Adolphe shushes her.*) But you are! What on earth induced me to stay with him? I was lazy, I was tired—he was drunk with success, he enraptured me—I don't know, I can't explain it. Yet, if you had come here, it would never have happened, I know that. —Anyway, today you're on top, and he's at the bottom. A nobody—worse! Yesterday he had one hundred thousand francs; today he doesn't have a sou to his name. They've closed his play. He'll never clear himself with the public after this scandal. Leaving the mother of his child—for another woman! He might just as well have murdered the child. They say he did, anyway. They've got it all figured out: the child died of sorrow, which, in their minds, makes Maurice responsible for her death.

ADOLPHE: Henriette, you know I'm on your side. But I want you above suspicion. Why can't you tell me what you were talking about? It was a party, a happy occasion—why talk about death and executions? It couldn't have been just chance.

HENRIETTE: No, chance had nothing to do with it. We couldn't help ourselves. I don't want to talk about it. Probably because I don't deserve to seem clean or above suspicion in your eyes. Because I'm not.

ADOLPHE: Above suspicion—or clean?

HENRIETTE: Oh, let's change the subject. —Don't you suppose that there are a lot of unpunished criminals walking around? Maybe our closest friends?

ADOLPHE (*fidgeting*): I don't know. What do you mean?

HENRIETTE: Don't you think that everyone at some point in his life has done something he could be punished for if the law knew about it?

ADOLPHE: I'm sure of it. But nothing goes unpunished; conscience takes care of it. (*Stands up and unbuttons his coat.*) And— something else—no one is truly good who hasn't made some bad mistakes. (*Breathes heavily.*) To be able to forgive, you've got to have felt the need to be forgiven. . . . I once had a friend, we called him "Wonder Man" because he never said a bad word about anybody, was ready to forgive everybody and everything, took every insult with a wonderful complacency. He baffled us. Finally, much later in life, he gave me his secret in a nutshell: "I'm full of remorse," he said, "I'm atoning." (*Sits down.*)

Henriette is silent. Looks at him wonderingly.

(*As if to himself.*) Some crimes you can't find in the lawbooks; they're the worst ones because we've got to punish them ourselves, and we're harder on ourselves than any judge or jury could be.

HENRIETTE (*after a pause*): What happened to your friend? Did he stop atoning?

ADOLPHE: He tormented himself for years. Eventually that gave him peace of mind. But life could never hold any joy for him. He could never take a compliment in the right spirit, never felt he was worthy of recognition, didn't dare accept awards. In a word, he could never forgive himself.

HENRIETTE: Never? What had he done?

ADOLPHE: He wanted his father dead. And when his father suddenly died, the son imagined he had murdered him. Such ideas were considered a sign of illness, of course, so they put him away—in an institution. And after a while he came out "sound as a bell"—as they put it. But the guilt feelings were still there, and he went right on punishing himself.

HENRIETTE: You said "imagined." Are you sure he didn't kill his father—by wishing him dead?

ADOLPHE: You mean in some mysterious way?

HENRIETTE: Maybe. Don't you believe that hate can kill? I'm certain that my mother and my family hated Father to death. He had an awful way of being systematically opposed to everything we wanted to do, every inclination we might have, every wish we cherished. And if it was more than just a wish—a desperate, heartfelt need we couldn't live without—he tried to cut it out of our systems. That only made the resistance against him grow. It collected in batteries generating hatred, and the current finally grew so strong he was blasted by it—shriveled—lost all interest— finally wished he were dead.

ADOLPHE: Your conscience never bothered you?

HENRIETTE: No! I don't know what conscience is.

ADOLPHE: Really? You'll soon find out. (*Silence.*) How do you suppose Maurice will look when he walks in here? What do you think he'll say?

HENRIETTE: That's funny. Yesterday morning when we were waiting for you, we tried to guess the same thing about you.

ADOLPHE: And—?

HENRIETTE: We got it all wrong.

ADOLPHE: Tell me, why did you send for me?

HENRIETTE: Wickedness. Arrogance. Sheer cruelty!

ADOLPHE: I don't understand. You confess your sins, but you don't regret them.

HENRIETTE: That's because I don't feel completely responsible for them. They're like dirt on things you handle every day. Some of it's bound to stick on you, but you wash it off at night. Do you really think people are as good as you say they are?

ADOLPHE: I think they're a little bit better than most people think—and a little worse.

HENRIETTE: You're being evasive.

ADOLPHE: No, I'm not. —Will you be evasive if I ask you something? Do you still love Maurice?

HENRIETTE: I won't know until I see him. Right now I don't feel any longing for him. I think I could survive without him.

ADOLPHE: That's probably true. But the fact is your life is now bound up with his. —Quiet!

HENRIETTE: Strange how everything comes again, everything

repeats itself. Exactly the same situation, the same words, as yesterday when we were waiting for you . . .

Maurice enters, white as a corpse, hollow-eyed, unshaven.

MAURICE: Here I am, my friends—if it really is me. I've spent one night in jail, and now I don't know who I am. (*Looks carefully at Henriette and Adolphe.*)

ADOLPHE: Sit down and pull yourself together.

MAURICE (*to Henriette*): Maybe you don't want me around?

ADOLPHE: Cut it out. Why be bitter against us?

MAURICE: In these twenty-four hours I've grown so hateful and suspicious I can't stand to have anyone around. Besides, who wants to keep a murderer company!

HENRIETTE: But you've been cleared!

MAURICE (*producing a newspaper*): By the police, sure, but not by the public. Take a look at the murderer Maurice Gérard, former playwright, and his mistress Henriette Mauclerc, former—

HENRIETTE: They've got my picture! Oh, my God! When my mother sees this—and my family—oh, God!

MAURICE: I even look like a murderer. And they're dropping hints that my play is a plagiarism. What's left of the conquering hero of yesterday? Not one shred. And in my place in all the advertisements stands my enemy and rival Octave, raking in my hundred thousand francs. "Oh, Solon! Solon!"* There's justice for you! And success! Adolphe, you don't know how lucky you are that you haven't been lucky.

HENRIETTE: Evidently you don't know that Adolphe was a great success in London. He walked off with first prize. Got a gold medal for his painting.

* See the story of Croesus and Solon in Herodotus's *History* I, chap. 30.

MAURICE (*frowning*): No, I didn't know that. Is it true, Adolphe?

ADOLPHE: It's true enough. But the medal—I sent it back.

HENRIETTE (*pointing it up*): Sent it back! I didn't know that! Maybe you can't accept recognition either—like your friend?

ADOLPHE: My friend—? (*Embarrassed.*) Oh, yes; yes, of course.

MAURICE: Well, Adolphe, your success gladdens me—but it puts a lot of distance between us.

ADOLPHE: I understand. Good fortune or bad, doesn't make any difference. We'll each be alone. My success hurts your feelings. It's a great life!

MAURICE: You shouldn't complain! What about me! It's as if a black veil had been put over my eyes. Everything's there, but nothing's the same. I was in this very room, this very spot, yesterday, but now it's all different. I recognize you—and you—but you're wearing different faces. I sit here fumbling for the right words, and I can't find them. I ought to be defending myself, but I can't. I was better off in jail. At least there weren't any curiosity seekers staring at me. Look at Maurice the murderer! And his loving mistress! But you don't love me anymore, Henriette. And you don't mean a damn thing to me! Today you're ugly—coarse, empty, disgusting.

> *Two Plainclothes Men have quietly seated themselves at one of the rear tables.*

ADOLPHE: Take it easy, Maurice! You're free. You've been cleared of all suspicion. It will be in all the evening papers. There won't be any more accusations; your play will go on again. Listen, if worse comes to worse, you can write a new one. Get away from Paris for a year; let things die down. They loved you because you looked at the bright side. Said people were good and decent. They'll soon be saying the same about you.

MAURICE: Ha! People! Ha!

ADOLPHE: You don't really believe it, do you—that people are good?

MAURICE: Did I ever? It was only a passing mood, a new angle, a courtesy paid to the great beast, the people. I was admired, considered better than the average. And I'm rotten. Imagine what the others are like!

ADOLPHE: I'm going out to buy the evening papers. One of each. After you've read them, we'll see what you have to say.

MAURICE (*turning to the rear*): Two detectives! —You see, they let me go just to keep me under surveillance. They're waiting for me to spout off at the mouth and give myself away!

ADOLPHE: They're not detectives. You're imagining things! I know who they are. (*Starts to leave.*)

MAURICE: Don't leave us alone, Adolphe. I'm afraid Henriette and I might start letting down our hair.

ADOLPHE: Take it easy, Maurice. Don't think of the past, think of your future. Henriette, keep him calm and cool. Be back in a jiffy! (*Leaves.*)

HENRIETTE: Now what's your opinion—about being guilty —or not guilty?

MAURICE: Well, I haven't killed anyone, like some people I know. I was drunk and shooting off at the mouth. You're the one with a crime on your head. It's come back to haunt you, and you've tried to foist it off on me.

HENRIETTE: I like that! Of all the nerve! You cursed your own child—wished she didn't exist—and wanted to run away without saying goodbye. That was you! Who told you to go to Marion and to put in an appearance at Madame Catherine's? Me!

MAURICE: You're right, of course. I'm sorry. You were more thoughtful than I was. It's all my fault. Forgive me. —But still it isn't. I'm not to blame for what's happened. I feel I've been framed, set up. Guilty—not guilty. Not guilty—guilty? It's driving me crazy. —Look at them, sitting there, taking it all in. —And not even a waiter who wants to bother with us. I'm going out to tell them I want a cup of tea. Can I get you something?

HENRIETTE: Nothing, thanks.

Maurice goes out.

FIRST DETECTIVE (*coming over to Henriette*): Hey, Toots! Mind showing me your identification papers?

HENRIETTE: Who the hell do you think you're talking to?!

FIRST DETECTIVE: Watch your tongue, girlie! I'm talking to you!

HENRIETTE: What do you want?

FIRST DETECTIVE: I'm with the vice squad. Yesterday you were here with one guy and today you're here with another. That looks like soliciting to me, and that puts you under my jurisdiction. And they don't serve unescorted ladies here! So out you go. Come on!

HENRIETTE: My escort's coming right back . . .

FIRST DETECTIVE: What escort? He ain't even here.

HENRIETTE: Oh, God! Please—you don't understand. . . . My mother . . . my family! . . . I'm a respectable girl, I tell you.

FIRST DETECTIVE: That's what they all say. Listen, I know you from the papers. You got your picture in them. Now come on!

HENRIETTE: Where? Where are you taking me?

FIRST DETECTIVE: Where do you think? Down to headquarters. We'll give you a little card that authorizes you to get free and compulsory medical checkups!

HENRIETTE: Oh, my God! You're not serious! You can't be!

FIRST DETECTIVE (*grabbing Henriette by the arm*): Does this feel like I'm joking?

HENRIETTE: Oh, God, help me! (*On her knees.*) —Let me go! —Maurice! Help me!

FIRST DETECTIVE: Shut your damn mouth! What a crazy bitch!

Maurice comes in, followed by The Waiter.

THE WAITER: I'm telling you we don't want your sort in this place. Pay your check and get out! And take your floozy with you!

MAURICE (*completely crushed; looks through his billfold*): Henriette, pay for me and let's get out of here. I don't have a cent on me!

THE WAITER: What do you know! I ain't seen that before. The dame paying for her fancy-man.

HENRIETTE (*looking through her purse*): My God! I don't have any money either! Where's Adolphe? Why doesn't he come?

FIRST DETECTIVE: What a couple of crumbs! All right, start unloading. Find something you can leave as security. Tarts like her got lotsa rings on their fingers.

MAURICE: I can't believe this is happening! How could we—

HENRIETTE (*taking a ring off her finger and handing it to The Waiter*): The abbé was right; it's unearthly!

MAURICE: The devil's at work, if you ask me. —Look, if we go now, you know what Adolphe's going to think?—that we deceived him and ran off together.

HENRIETTE: That's right in style with everything else, isn't it? I'm ready to throw myself into the river. How about you?

MAURICE (*taking her by the hand and walking out with her*): End it all? Sure. Why not?

ACT IV

Scene 1

The Luxembourg Gardens. Near the statue of Adam and Eve. The wind is blowing in the trees and whipping up leaves, dried grass, and bits of paper on the ground.

Maurice and Henriette are sitting on a bench.

HENRIETTE: You don't want to die?

MAURICE: I'm not up to it. Can't face that cold grave. With just a sheet on top of me and a little sawdust under. No thanks! Besides, I've got some unfinished business this side of the grave — if I could figure out what it is.

HENRIETTE: I know what you're getting at.

MAURICE: What?

HENRIETTE: Revenge. It's obvious when you think about it. Jeanne and her brother deliberately sent those detectives to embarrass us. It was too perfect. Only a woman could think up that kind of revenge.

MAURICE: My thoughts exactly. — Only you don't go far enough. These past few days have given me some insight. That's what suffering does for you. Think about this: that waiter at the Auberge des Adrets and the *maître d'* at the Pavilion — why weren't they called to testify at the hearing?

HENRIETTE: My God! You're right! I never thought of that. They had no evidence to give because they never overheard anything!

MAURICE: But how could the inspector know exactly what we said?

HENRIETTE: He didn't. He guessed. Deduced it. He saw it was a case of sexual jealousy, and one case is like another.

MAURICE: No, I've got it! Our behavior gave it away. He saw it was a case of a woman and two men. He said we called Adolphe an ass. What else do you call the deceived man? Idiot, usually—right? But we had mentioned a wagon, the triumphal chariot, so it couldn't be "idiot"; it had to be "ass." Simple deduction.

HENRIETTE: What fools they made of us! And we let them get away with it!

MAURICE: That's what we get for blaming ourselves—thinking they're good and we're bad. No more of that! Take that inspector—there's a real bastard for you—there's somebody behind him. There has to be.

HENRIETTE: You mean the abbé, playing private detective.

MAURICE: Exactly! An abbé! He gets to hear confessions. It all fits in! Adolphe himself said he'd been to the Church of Saint-Germain in the morning. What was an atheist like him doing in church? He blabbed, of course, moaned about losing his girl. All the abbé had to do was make up a list of leading questions to give to the inspector.

HENRIETTE: You don't trust Adolphe?

MAURICE: I don't trust anybody, not anymore!

HENRIETTE: Not even Adolphe!

MAURICE: Least of all! How can I? I took his mistress from him.

HENRIETTE: Well, since you started this, I could tell you more. You heard him say that he refused the gold medal he won in London. You know why?

MAURICE: No.

HENRIETTE: Because he treats himself like dirt. Thinks he's unworthy. He once took a penitential vow never to accept any honors.

MAURICE: You're joking! I don't get it. What's he done that's so awful?

HENRIETTE: Some crime not punishable under the law. He virtually admitted it, pretending he was telling me about someone else.

MAURICE: Him too! "The Wonder Man!"—always so sweet and forgiving.

HENRIETTE: That's what I've been telling you. We're not worse than the others. But the devils are on our backs, riding us to hell. It's not fair!

MAURICE: Adolphe, too! I can't get over it. Makes you lose all faith in people. —Listen, if he was capable of one crime, why not others? Maybe he was the one who sicced the police on you yesterday. Come to think of it, didn't he slip away when he saw our pictures in the papers? And he lied when he said those guys weren't detectives! I tell you, a deceived lover is capable of anything—anything!

HENRIETTE: He couldn't be that low. It's impossible!

MAURICE: Why not? Face up to it—he's a bastard. . . . What did you talk about yesterday before I came?

HENRIETTE: He said only good things about you.

MAURICE: You're lying!

HENRIETTE (*controls herself; changes tone*): Listen . . . there's still somebody left whom you haven't cast your suspicions on, and I wonder why. Have you considered Madame Catherine? She's been very shifty—until finally she said straight out that she thought you were capable of anything.

MAURICE: She did, she did! Shows you what she's really like. Anybody who thinks somebody is a bastard for no good reason is a bastard himself! Take my word for it.

Henriette looks at him.

Silence.

HENRIETTE: Anybody who thinks somebody is a bastard is a bastard himself.

MAURICE: What are you getting at?

HENRIETTE: What I just said!

MAURICE: Are you implying that I—?

HENRIETTE: That's exactly what I'm implying! Tell me: did you meet anyone besides Marion that morning you went to say goodbye?

MAURICE: Why ask that?

HENRIETTE: One guess!

MAURICE: Well, since you seem to know, yes, I also met Jeanne.

HENRIETTE: Why did you lie to me?

MAURICE: I wanted to spare you.

HENRIETTE: You expect me to believe that, after you've lied to me! Oh, no, dear Maurice; now I believe you did do it. You killed her.

MAURICE: Wait a minute! Wait a minute! I've been blind. These thoughts—sneaking up on me, even though I fought against them. Now I see. It's remarkable that what lies right under your nose is the last thing you see. What you don't want to believe, you don't believe. —Tell me, where were you yesterday morning after we separated in the woods?

HENRIETTE (*uneasily*): I don't understand . . .

MAURICE: Either one of two places: either you were with Adolphe, which you couldn't have been because he was at his art class, or else you were—with Marion!

HENRIETTE: You did kill her, didn't you?

MAURICE: No, you did! You did. You were the only one who would gain anything if the child disappeared—if the rock was removed from the road, as you so aptly phrased it!

HENRIETTE: You said that; I didn't!

MAURICE: The one who stands to gain: that's the legal principle.

HENRIETTE: Oh, Maurice! We're running around in circles, like slaves on a treadmill whipping each other. Let's stop before we drive each other crazy.

MAURICE: You already are!

HENRIETTE: We can't go on like this, Maurice. Let's break it off, before we go insane.

MAURICE: All right. Let's.

HENRIETTE (*standing up*): Goodbye then.

> *Two Plainsclothes men can be seen at the rear. Henriette turns around and goes back to Maurice.*

Those two men again!

MAURICE: The dark angels who want to drive us out of the garden.

HENRIETTE: And who force us to come together—like metals being welded.

MAURICE: Welded, yes. Or do you mean wedded? Should we? Build a little nest; shut our doors on the world; find some kind of peace?

HENRIETTE: Lock ourselves in a torture chamber? The community property would be two skeletons in the closet. You'd torture me by bringing up Adolphe's name; I'd torture you by reminding you of Jeanne—and Marion.

MAURICE: Don't. Don't mention her. You know she's being buried today—perhaps at this very hour.

HENRIETTE: Why aren't you at the funeral?

MAURICE: Jeanne and the police both warned me off. My presence, they said, might inflame the crowd.

HENRIETTE: Besides everything else, you're a coward.

MAURICE: When it comes to failings, I lack for none. What did you ever see in me?

HENRIETTE: A couple of days ago you were a different person, worth loving.

MAURICE: And now I'm in the gutter.

HENRIETTE: No. But you're decking yourself with borrowed vices.

MAURICE: Borrowed? From whom? You?

HENRIETTE: You might say. Because when you appear to be getting worse, right away I feel a little bit better.

MAURICE: Like lovers transmitting diseases to each other.

HENRIETTE: On top of everything else you're coarse – vulgar.

MAURICE: You don't have to tell me. I don't feel I'm the same person since that night in jail. They locked up one guy and let out another – through the gates that separate us from society. Right now I feel like the enemy of all mankind. I'd like to set fire to the whole earth and dry up the seven seas. Nothing less than a *Götterdämmerung* can wipe out my shame.

HENRIETTE: I got a letter from my mother today. She's a widow. Father was a major. She had a proper upbringing, very genteel, and she's got old-fashioned ideas about honor and marriage and such things. Do you want to read it? – No, of course you don't. Do you know that I've become virtually an outcast? Nobody – I mean people with reputations – wants to be seen in my company. And if I walk around alone, the police will harass me. Don't you see? We have to get married.

MAURICE: We disgust each other, so we have to marry each other! Sounds like hell on earth. One thing, Henriette; if we're going to spend the rest of our lives together, you've got to tell me your secret – to even the odds and make a fair game of it.

HENRIETTE: All right. . . . I had a girlfriend, who got herself into trouble. You know, the usual story. I wanted to help her because her whole future was at stake. So. . . . But I bungled the job, and she . . . didn't survive.

MAURICE: You were foolish. You shouldn't have gotten involved. But you were trying to do the right thing; I can see that.

HENRIETTE: That's what you say now. But the next time you get mad at me, you'll use it against me.

MAURICE: No, I won't. The trouble is that it weakens my trust in you. And I'll be afraid to have you around. The girl's lover is still around, isn't he? – and knows what you did?

HENRIETTE: He went along with it!

MAURICE: That's what bothers me. Suppose his conscience should start gnawing at him? It happens, you know. Suppose he can't stand it and tells the whole story to the police.

HENRIETTE: You think I haven't thought about that? Those thoughts are always there, right behind me. That's why I live as fast as I can. I don't want to stop and let those thoughts catch up with me.

MAURICE: But you want to bring them into our marriage — as part of the community property. That's a bit much, isn't it?

HENRIETTE: It wasn't a bit much when I shared the shame and dishonor of Maurice the murderer!

MAURICE: For God's sake, let's get off this merry-go-round.

HENRIETTE: You're not getting off yet. Oh, no! Not until I've stripped you naked. You're not going to go around thinking yourself better than I am. Oh, no, you're not!

MAURICE: You want to fight. All right, if that's what you want!

HENRIETTE: A fight to the finish!

A roll of drums is heard in the distance.

MAURICE: They're closing the garden. . . . "Cursed is the ground for thy sake; . . . thorns and thistles shall it bring forth to thee."

HENRIETTE: "And the Lord said unto the woman . . . "

A CARETAKER (*in uniform. Politely*): Sorry, Madam, Monsieur; we have to close the garden.

Scene 2

The Crêmerie. Madame Catherine at the counter, making entries in her ledger. Adolphe and Henriette at a table.

ADOLPHE (*relaxed and friendly*): I swear to you for the last time: I did not sneak away from you. I thought you had gone off and deserted me. You've got to believe me.

HENRIETTE: But why did you tell us they weren't detectives?

ADOLPHE: I really didn't think they were. I was only trying to reassure you.

HENRIETTE: All right; if you say so, I believe you. But, then, you've got to believe me now. I've got these deep suspicions, and I can't harbor them any longer.

ADOLPHE: Very well.

HENRIETTE: And you mustn't tell me I'm seeing things or imagining them.

ADOLPHE: It sounds like you're afraid you are.

HENRIETTE: Nothing of the sort. But I know how skeptical you are. Anyway, you mustn't tell anybody. Promise?

ADOLPHE: Promise.

HENRIETTE: It's just too horrible! . . . I'm half certain that Maurice is guilty. Really. I've got evidence.

ADOLPHE: What!

HENRIETTE: Let me finish; then you can judge for yourself. —When Maurice said goodbye to me in the woods, he told me he wanted to see Marion alone, while her mother was out. But now we know that he met Marion's mother. In other words, he was lying to me!

ADOLPHE: Possibly. Maybe he had a good reason. Doesn't make him a murderer.

HENRIETTE: Don't you understand? Don't you see?

ADOLPHE: See what?

HENRIETTE: You don't want to see! —All right. There's nothing for me to do but tell the police. Then we'll see if he can come up with an alibi.

ADOLPHE: Henriette, you've got to listen to me. You've got to hear the truth, even if it hurts. You're pushing each other over the edge. I'm not joking. You both feel—to some extent—guilty. And that makes you—him and you both—suspect each other of anything and everything. . . . Tell me if I'm wrong: he suspects you of having killed Marion. Doesn't he?

HENRIETTE: He's that crazy, yes!

ADOLPHE: His suspicions are crazy but yours aren't?

HENRIETTE: Show me where I'm wrong. Prove my suspicions aren't justified.

ADOLPHE: That's easy. The coroner revised his report. They found that Marion died of some sort of disease—with an odd name I've forgotten.

HENRIETTE: Am I supposed to believe that?

ADOLPHE: It's in today's papers—the coroner's report.

HENRIETTE: I don't believe it! It could have been faked!

ADOLPHE: Cut it out, Henriette! Calm down. You're driving yourself crazy. And be careful about making reckless accusations. You might land in jail. Easy does it. (*He places his hand on her head.*) Do you hate Maurice?

HENRIETTE: Immeasurably!

ADOLPHE: If love can turn to hate, it must have been cankered to begin with.

HENRIETTE (*calming down*): What am I going to do? Tell me. You're the only one who understands me.

ADOLPHE: You don't want my sermons.

HENRIETTE: Is that all you've got to offer?

ADOLPHE: That's all. But they have helped me.

HENRIETTE: All right. Get up in your pulpit.

ADOLPHE: To start with, you've got to turn your hatred against yourself. Lance your own boils. And cut out the core.

HENRIETTE: You'll have to explain that.

ADOLPHE: First of all, leave Maurice. If you're apart from each other, you can't feed on each other's guilt. Give up your career as an artist. You only took it up because you wanted to get away from home—so you could lead a carefree existence. An artist's life! Well, you see how carefree it's been. Go home to your mother.

HENRIETTE: Never!

ADOLPHE: All right. Go somewhere else then.

HENRIETTE: You know a lot about these things, don't you? And I can guess why. I know why you refused to accept the gold medal.

ADOLPHE: You saw through that little story of mine?

HENRIETTE (*nods*): What did you do to find peace of mind?

ADOLPHE: Just what I told you to do. I admitted my guilt, took on the burden of it, felt remorse, decided to change my life, and settled down to a life of penance.

HENRIETTE: How can I feel remorse if I don't have a conscience? Is remorse a matter of grace, like faith?

ADOLPHE: Isn't everything? But it doesn't come unless you apply yourself. . . . So apply yourself.

Henriette is silent.

Don't wait too long. There's a time limit on applications. If you're late, you'll be turned out, and then there's no turning back.

HENRIETTE (*after a moment's silence*): Conscience—is it the fear of being punished?

ADOLPHE: No. It's the disgust our better half feels for the misdeeds of our worse half.

HENRIETTE: Then I must have a conscience, too?

ADOLPHE: Of course you have. But—

HENRIETTE: Tell me, Adolphe: are you what's called religious?

ADOLPHE: Not a bit.

HENRIETTE: It's all so strange. . . . What is religion, anyway?

ADOLPHE: I haven't the faintest idea. I don't think anyone has. Sometimes it strikes me that it's a punishment, because the only ones who get religion are the ones who suffer from a bad conscience.

HENRIETTE: A punishment. Yes. . . . Now I know what I have to do. —Goodbye, Adolphe.

ADOLPHE: You're leaving?

HENRIETTE: Yes, I'm leaving. Going where you said. —Goodbye, dear Adolphe. —Goodbye, Catherine.

MADAME CATHERINE: Are you off in such a hurry?

HENRIETTE: Yes.

ADOLPHE: Do you want me to go with you?

HENRIETTE: No. I want to go alone. That's the way I came in—one spring day—thinking I belonged where I didn't belong, and believing there was something called freedom, which doesn't exist! . . . Goodbye. (*Leaves.*)

MADAME CATHERINE: I hoped she'd never come here again. I wish she had never come here in the first place!

ADOLPHE: Who knows? Maybe she had some purpose to serve here. Anyway, she deserves sympathy, tons of it.

MADAME CATHERINE: Don't we all!

ADOLPHE: She's done less harm than we have, if you ask me.

MADAME CATHERINE: Possibly; but I doubt it.

ADOLPHE: You're always so hard and stern, Catherine. Why? Haven't you ever done anything wrong?

MADAME CATHERINE: Of course I have, I'm a poor sinner like everybody else. But if you've fallen through the ice once, you've got a right—I'd say a duty—to warn the others: "Danger!" Doesn't mean you're stern or heartless. Didn't I say to Maurice the instant that woman walked in here: danger, stay away! But he didn't listen. He went right ahead, like a stubborn, naughty child. And people who behave that way should get a spanking.

ADOLPHE: Hasn't he had his spanking?

MADAME CATHERINE: Apparently he didn't get spanked hard enough. He's still mad at the world.

ADOLPHE: A spanking! That's what most people think is the answer to a very involved matter.

MADAME CATHERINE: Bosh! You sit around cudgeling your brains, philosophizing about your wicked ways, and in the meantime, the police have solved the problem. Now leave me alone. I'm trying to add.

ADOLPHE: Here comes Maurice!

MADAME CATHERINE: Yes, God have mercy on him!

MAURICE (*comes in, flushed and excited; sits down with Adolphe*): Hello! Hello!

> *Madame Catherine nods and continues to add her accounts.*

ADOLPHE: Are you all right?

MAURICE: I am now. Because the pieces are beginning to fall into place!

ADOLPHE (*handing Maurice a newspaper, which he does not take*): So you've seen the paper?

MAURICE: No, I've had enough of papers—nothing but libels.

ADOLPHE: Better read it before you say anything more.

MAURICE: Forget it! Same old lies. I've got some real news for you! You want to know who committed the murder? I'll tell you who.

ADOLPHE: No one did. No one!

MAURICE: For fifteen minutes the child was left alone. And where was Henriette during that time? She was *there*! And she's the one who did it.

ADOLPHE: Oh, come off it, you're nuts.

MAURICE: Oh, no, I'm not! Henriette's nuts. She thinks I did it! She's threatened to turn me in to the police!

ADOLPHE: Henriette was just here and said exactly the same thing. You're both nuts! The doctors reexamined the evidence and found that Marion died from a well-known disease—only I can't remember the name of it.

MAURICE: I don't believe it!

ADOLPHE: That's what she said too. But the coroner's report is in the papers.

MAURICE: Coroner's report? . . . Ha! Probably faked to get somebody off the hook.

ADOLPHE: She said so, too. You're both sick. But at least I got through to her. She realized what was happening to her.

MAURICE: Where did she go?

ADOLPHE: To start over.

MAURICE (*hesitates; calms down*): Were you at the funeral?

ADOLPHE: Yes, I was there.

MAURICE: Well?

ADOLPHE: Jeanne has resigned herself to the situation. She has nothing against you.

MAURICE: She's a good woman.

ADOLPHE: Then why did you give her up?

MAURICE: I was in a crazy mood. Thought the world was my oyster. . . . And we were drinking champagne.

ADOLPHE: And Jeanne cried when you drank champagne.

MAURICE: Yes, now I see why. I've written to ask her to forgive me. . . . Do you think she will?

ADOLPHE: I believe so. She can't hate anyone.

MAURICE: Do you think she'll forgive me completely? Let me come back to her?

ADOLPHE: I don't know about that. After what you did to her, you can hardly expect her to trust herself with you again.

MAURICE: I still feel she keeps a corner of her heart for me. I know she'll come back.

ADOLPHE: That's pretty presumptuous. You suspected her and her decent, hardworking brother of taking revenge by sending the police to pick up Henriette as an unregistered prostitute! And now you think she'll take you back!

MAURICE: She wasn't taking revenge. She was only—. What I mean is—well, Emile's got a great sense of humor, I'll bet.

MADAME CATHERINE: You think he'd play a dirty trick like that? He may be only a workingman, but if only everyone was as decent and upstanding as he! He's a perfect gentleman: understanding, tactful—

EMILE (*entering*): Monsieur Gérard?

MAURICE: Yes, that's me.

EMILE: Pardon me, but I've got something to say to you in private.

MAURICE: You can say it here. We're all friends.

The Abbé enters and sits down.

EMILE (*glancing at The Abbé*): I still think it might be better if—

MAURICE: It doesn't matter. The abbé is also a friend of mine, even if we don't have the same views.

EMILE: I guess you know who I am. My sister has simply asked me to give you this package as her reply to your letter.

Maurice takes the package and opens it.

There's only one thing I've got to add. Since I seem to be my sister's guardian, and speaking for her and for myself, I acknowledge that Monsieur Gérard is freed from all obligations, now that the natural bond between you and her is no longer there.

MAURICE: No hard feelings?

EMILE: Why should there be hard feelings? On the other hand,

I'd very much like to hear you apologize, Monsieur Gérard, here in the presence of your friends, for believing that either I or my sister would be capable of such a low trick as sending the police to pick up Mademoiselle Henriette.

MAURICE: I withdraw those remarks. And I offer you my sincere apologies, if you'll be good enough to accept them.

EMILE: Accepted. Thanks. Good evening, everybody. (*Leaves.*)

ALL: Good evening.

MAURICE: The tie and the gloves that Jeanne gave me for the opening night of my play. I let Henriette throw them into the fire. . . . How did they get here? Everything is dug up again, everything comes back! . . . When she gave these to me at the cemetery, she said she wanted to see me looking my best. She wanted everyone to admire me. . . . But she stayed home alone. How it must have hurt her! How could it not? . . . I don't belong in the company of decent people. God! what have I done! Mocked the gift of a good heart, ridiculed the sacrifice made for my success. I threw this away. And for what! A laurel wreath that lies in a garbage can—a marble bust that belongs in the pillory. —Father, let me come to you.

THE ABBÉ: Welcome.

MAURICE: Give me comfort. Ease my heart.

THE ABBÉ: Do you expect me to contradict you and tell you that you have done nothing wrong?

MAURICE: Just say what is right.

THE ABBÉ: Since you ask, let me say I think your behavior has been every bit as disgusting as you've said it is.

MAURICE: What am I going to do? I can't go on like this.

THE ABBÉ: You know the answer to that as well as I do.

MAURICE: No. All I know is that I'm lost. My life is ruined; my career over before it got started; my honor and reputation forever destroyed.

THE ABBÉ: Ah! So that's why you turn your eyes to another and better world, which you now begin to believe in?

MAURICE: Yes, that's right.

THE ABBÉ: You've lived in the flesh, and now you want to live in the spirit. Are you quite certain that there is nothing in this world that can still tempt you?

MAURICE: Nothing! Fame is an illusion, gold is dry dust, and women are merely intoxicants. Let me hide myself behind your hallowed walls. Let me forget this terrible nightmare that lasted for two days and seemed like two eternities.

THE ABBÉ: Very well. But this is no place to arrange these matters. Let us meet in Saint-Germain tonight at nine o'clock. I happen to be preaching to the penitents of Saint-Lazare. This can be your first step on the long, hard road of penance.

MAURICE: Penance?

THE ABBÉ: Yes, I thought you wished to —

MAURICE: Oh, yes, yes . . . of course.

THE ABBÉ: There will be vigils from midnight until two.

MAURICE: That will be wonderful, glorious.

THE ABBÉ: Give me your hand. I don't want you looking back!

MAURICE (*standing up and offering his hand*): Here is my hand, and all my heart!

THE WAITRESS (*entering from the kitchen*): Telephone call for Monsieur Gérard!

MAURICE: From whom?

THE WAITRESS: From the theater.

Maurice tries to break away from The Abbé, but The Abbé holds him fast by the hand.

THE ABBÉ (*to The Waitress*): Did you ask what it's about?

THE WAITRESS: Yes. They wanted to know if Monsieur Gérard would be at the play tonight.

THE ABBÉ (*to Maurice, who is trying to get away*): Oh, no, I shan't let go!

MAURICE: Play? What are you talking about?

ADOLPHE: Well, you wouldn't read the papers!

MADAME CATHERINE and THE ABBÉ: You haven't read the paper!

MAURICE: I've had enough of lies and slanders! (*To The Waitress.*) Tell them I can't go to the theater tonight. Tell them I'm busy. Tell them I'm going to church!

The Waitress goes out to the kitchen.

ADOLPHE: Since you won't read the papers, I guess I'll have to give you the news. Now that you've been cleared, the theater is putting on your play again. And your literary friends have arranged to give you an ovation on the stage—a tribute to a great new talent!

MAURICE: You're joking! It can't be true!

ALL: It is true! It's no joke.

MAURICE (*after some moments of silence*): I don't deserve it.

THE ABBÉ: Good.

ADOLPHE: That's not all, Maurice!

MAURICE (*his face hidden in his hands*): Not all?

MADAME CATHERINE: A hundred thousand francs, Maurice! You see, they've come back too! And the villa outside the city! Everything comes back—except Henriette!

THE ABBÉ (*smiling*): Madame Catherine should take this matter a little more seriously.

MADAME CATHERINE: I can't, I can't. I can't keep a straight face any longer. (*She explodes into laughter, covering her mouth with her handkerchief.*)

ADOLPHE: Hey, Maurice! Eight o'clock at the theater!

THE ABBÉ: Nine o'clock at the church!

ADOLPHE: Maurice!

MADAME CATHERINE: Well, playwright? How are you going to end this?

> *Maurice puts his head on the table and wraps his arms over his head.*

ADOLPHE: Release him from his pledge, Father!

THE ABBÉ: No, indeed I shan't. It's not up to me to release him or bind him.

MAURICE (*standing up*): Very well. I'll go with you, Father.

THE ABBÉ: No, young man. I have nothing to give you except a good scolding and you can give yourself that. And you have other obligations—to yourself and to your public. The fact that you've learned your lesson so fast indicates to me that you have suffered as much as if it had lasted an eternity. And if Providence has given you absolution, what more can I do?

MAURICE: But why was I punished so severely? I was innocent.

THE ABBÉ: Severely? Two days! And you weren't innocent. We're also accountable for our words, our thoughts, our desires. And you murdered in your thoughts when some demon in you wished that your child were not alive.

MAURICE: You're right, of course. —But I stick to my decision. Tonight I meet you at the church to settle accounts with myself. Tomorrow—I go to the theater.

MADAME CATHERINE: Maurice, I think you've got it!

ADOLPHE: I know he's got it!

THE ABBÉ: Why, I believe he has!

Introduction to
The Dance of Death

Ambrose Bierce defined marriage as "a community consisting of a master, a mistress, and two slaves—making, in all, two." *The Dance of Death* is often interpreted to be about such a community, another version of the marital hell that Strindberg had depicted in *The Father*. It isn't. The sexual conflict is not fundamental in this play, and the strongest scenes do not reveal any bedroom secrets. Rather, the life of the senses is pitted against the life of the spirit. The title alludes to the medieval dance that pictured the omnipresence of death and reminded mortals that at any moment death might seize them and bring them to judgment.

Nor does *The Dance of Death* describe Strindberg's own marriage. The wife and husband in the play were modeled after Strindberg's sister Anna and her husband, Hugo Philp. Anna was musically gifted, but, like Alice in the play, her career and her love of music suffered because of her marriage to a man who had no artistic interests or inclinations. Hugo was a hardened materialist, unchanged in his outlook since his youth when he and Strindberg had been close friends. After Strindberg was blinded by the light on the road to Damascus and renounced the law of materialism, he put a great distance between himself and Hugo. He described his brother-in-law as "a black-hearted man, a despairing, anguished man, who believed in nothing but muscle power and malevolence—a cartload of topsoil, as he referred to himself" (*En blå bok*). Strindberg wrote *The Dance of Death* (Part One) in 1900, some months after Hugo, ill with diabetes, had suffered a heart attack. Like Curt in the play, Strindberg had stayed with him overnight on that occasion.

Written two years after *To Damascus*, *The Dance of Death* is another symbolic drama about a spiritual conversion. The round room, the setting sun, the churning sea, the pacing sentry, the telegraph apparatus, the grotesque dances, first Edgar's and later Alice's, are all elements in a spiritual drama in which Edgar comes so close to the line that divides the living from the dead, the body from the soul, that he catches a glimmering of what the life of the spirit is all about. Put more prosaically, his close brush with death makes him realize that he is more than a cartload of fertilizer in a Darwinian world and causes him to look at his fellow creatures with a more tolerant eye.

The five scenes of the play (Strindberg objected to act divisions, but costume and makeup changes made an intermission necessary) image a descent into a Swedenborgian hell, which is not a place but a state of mind in which physical needs and desires are dominant, and self-interest governs. After Edgar suffers a heart attack and learns that his wife is going to betray him, there occurs an influx of spirit, brought about by his anguish, and represented on stage in a remarkable actor's scene that is all pantomime.

The Dance of Death contains two magnificent roles: Edgar, a full-length portrait of domestic egomania, a parlor Napoleon; and Alice, his wife, the aborted actress, her career cut short by her marriage, who turns her home into a stage for her scenes of flamboyant rage, and who scarcely knows herself when she is acting and when she is not. Actors can, if they have the right temperaments, make comic mayhem of some of the scenes, and quite properly. Hell, not heaven, as the great poets have known is a place of laughter.

The Dance of Death is definitely not a tragedy. Although Strindberg is usually thought of as a gloomy writer, there is much more optimism in his work than in Beckett's, for instance. *Waiting for Godot*, a fashionably pessimistic play, has the same cyclical structure as Strindberg's play, the end linking up with the beginning. In *Godot*, nothing changes; everything will go on in the same ineffably boring way. In *The Dance of Death*, Edgar acquires a new outlook. He is wiser and more understanding than he was at the beginning.

Rilke understood. After seeing *The Dance of Death*, he said that "at first it seems so hopelessly obstinate to present humanity's disconsolation as its absolute condition, but when someone like this has power over even the most disconsolate, there hovers above the whole, unspoken, a concept of illimitable human greatness. And a desperate love."

The Dance of Death
(Dödsdansen)

Part One

CHARACTERS

EDGAR, captain in the Coast Artillery Corps
ALICE, his wife, formerly an actress
CURT, superintendent of the quarantine station
JENNY, a maid
AN OLD WOMAN
SENTRY

Scene: A military installation on an island in the Baltic Sea off the coast of Sweden.

Time: About 1900.

Scene: A round room, the interior of a fortress tower built of granite and situated on an island off the coast. At the rear, a wide, arched doorway with glass doors like French windows, through which can be seen an artillery emplacement, a large gun, the parapet, the shoreline, and the sea itself.

On each side of this doorway are windows with deep sills holding flowerpots and a birdcage. To the right of the doorway, an upright piano. Downstage of it, a small drop-leaf worktable with two armchairs on each side. Left of stage center is a flattop desk with telegraph apparatus on it. Farther downstage is a whatnot or étagère displaying portrait photographs. Near it, a chaise lounge. Against the wall, a sideboard.

A lamp hangs from the ceiling. Fastened to the wall near the piano are two large laurel wreaths with ribbons attached to them, and between the wreaths hangs the picture of a woman in theatrical costume.

By the doorway, a hat tree. Hanging on it, a military uniform, a sword, a belt, a helmet. Next to it, a secretary-bookcase with a hinged front. On its ledge, a candelabrum with six branches. Candlesticks on the desk, piano, and elsewhere.

On the wall to the left of the door, a mercury barometer.

[1]

It is a warm evening. The glass doors are wide open, and one can see the Sentry on duty guarding the artillery battery, pacing back and forth on the platform outside the doorway. He is wearing a helmet with crest. Now and then his saber, which he carries at a slant to his shoulder, glitters as it catches the red rays of the setting sun. The sea is dark and quiet.

Edgar is sitting in the armchair to the left of the worktable, thumbing and twirling the butt of a burned-out cigar. He is in fatigue dress, rather threadbare, and has on riding boots with spurs. He looks tired and bored.

Alice is sitting in the chair to the right, doing nothing. She looks tired but watchful.

EDGAR: How about playing something for me?

ALICE (*indifferently, not sharply*): Such as?

EDGAR: Something *you* like, my sweet.

ALICE: My repertoire is not to your taste.

EDGAR: Nor mine to yours.

ALICE (*avoiding a confrontation*): You want the doors left open?

EDGAR: Whatever you wish, my pet.

ALICE: All right, we'll leave them open. (*Pause.*) You're not smoking. Why not?

EDGAR: They don't seem to agree with me. Too strong.

ALICE (*almost kindly*): Get some milder ones. It's your only joy—so you say.

EDGAR: Joy? Where have I heard that word?

ALICE: Why ask me? It's as strange to me as it is to you. . . . Time for your whiskey, isn't it?

EDGAR: I'm going to hold off for a little while. . . . What's for supper?

ALICE: How should I know? Ask Christine.

EDGAR: About time for the mackerel to be running. It's autumn.

ALICE: Yes; autumn.

EDGAR: Autumn outside, autumn inside. However, even

though the autumn does bring with it the cold—outside and inside—a grilled mackerel, served with a slice of lemon, a glass of white Burgundy on the side, has something to be said for it.

ALICE: Food does make you eloquent.

EDGAR: Do we have any Burgundy left in the wine cellar?

ALICE: As I recall, we haven't for the last five years had a wine cellar.

EDGAR: You're so disorganized, Alice. Always have been. Well, we've got to stock up on provisions, for our silver wedding anniversary.

ALICE: You don't really intend to celebrate that!

EDGAR: Naturally!

ALICE: It would be more natural if we hid our misery—twenty-five years of it.

EDGAR: Dear, sweet Alice: miserable they may have been, but we've had our fun—now and then. Time is short and we've got to make the best of it. Time has an end.

ALICE: An end? If only there might be.

EDGAR: There is. An end. Period. Then you take what's left, put it in a wheelbarrow, and use it to fertilize the garden.

ALICE: There must be a simpler way to fertilize a garden.

EDGAR: That's the way it is. I didn't arrange it.

ALICE: Much ado about nothing. (*Pause.*) Has the mail come?

EDGAR: Yes.

ALICE: Did the butcher's bill come?

EDGAR: Yes.

ALICE: How much was it?

> *Edgar takes a sheet of paper from his pocket, puts his spectacles on his nose, and makes a stab at reading the bill. Then takes off his glasses.*

EDGAR: Read it yourself. I can't see anymore.

ALICE: What's the matter with your eyes?

EDGAR: Don't know.

ALICE: Age.

EDGAR: Nonsense! Me?

ALICE: Not me, certainly.

Edgar mutters.

ALICE (*looking at the bill*): Can you pay this?

EDGAR: Of course. (*Spitefully.*) But not today. Later.

ALICE: Later? —When you're placed on the retired list with a small pension? No good. Later, when you get sick again?

EDGAR: Sick? I've never been sick in my life. A little under the weather, maybe—once. I'll be around for another twenty years.

ALICE: Doctor doesn't think so.

EDGAR: That sawbones!

ALICE: He's a doctor. Who else knows about sickness?

EDGAR: I'm not sick. I've never had any sickness. And I'm not going to have any. I'm going to drop down dead—bam!—like a soldier in the field.

ALICE: Speaking of the doctor—you know he's giving a party tonight?

EDGAR (*riled*): What of it? . . . We're not invited because we don't associate with the doctor and his wife. And we don't associate with the doctor and his wife because we don't want to, and we don't want to because I despise them both! Scum!

ALICE: You call everybody scum.

EDGAR: Because everybody is scum.

ALICE: Except you.

EDGAR: Yes. Because I have conducted myself like a respectable human being no matter what happened. That's why I'm not scum. (*Pause.*)

ALICE: How about a game of cards?

EDGAR: Fire away.

ALICE (*takes a deck of cards from a drawer in the worktable and shuffles them*): You know the doctor gets the regimental band to play at his private parties.

EDGAR (*furious*): Because he pals around in town with the colonel. Playing footsie—that's all it takes!

ALICE (*dealing and turning up trumps*): Gerda was my good friend once. False friend, I found out.

EDGAR: You should have known better; you can't trust anybody. —What's trump?

ALICE: Put your glasses on.

EDGAR: Doesn't help. (*Impatiently.*) Well?—well?

ALICE: Spades is trump.

EDGAR (*disgruntled*): Spades?

ALICE (*leading a card*): Be that as it may, the fact is the wives of the new officers have blackballed us.

EDGAR (*playing a card and taking the trick*): So what! Who's going to notice? We never give any parties. I can be alone. Always have been.

ALICE: So can I. But what about the children? They're growing up without any friends.

EDGAR: They can make their own friends in town. —That one's mine. Do you have any trumps left?

ALICE: One. This one's mine.

EDGAR: Six and eight make fifteen.

ALICE: Fourteen. Fourteen.

EDGAR: Six and eight gives me fourteen. I've even forgotten how to add. And two makes sixteen. (*Yawns.*) Your deal.

ALICE: You're tired.

EDGAR (*dealing*): Not a bit.

ALICE (*listening to sounds in the distance*): You can hear the music all the way out here. (*Pause.*) You think Curt was invited?

EDGAR: Probably; he arrived this morning. Would have had all day to unpack his tuxedo. Even though he hasn't found time to call on us!

ALICE: Superintendent of the quarantine station. What do you know? Are they really going to have a quarantine station here?

EDGAR: Yes. Yes.

ALICE: Well, he's my cousin, in any case. He and I once bore the same name—

EDGAR: Hardly an honor—

ALICE: Listen, Edgar—(*Sharply.*) Leave my family alone, and I'll leave yours alone. Otherwise—

EDGAR: All right, all right! Don't let's start that again!

ALICE: Doesn't a superintendent of quarantine have to be a doctor?

EDGAR: No. It's only a civil service job—administration, bookkeeping. Anybody can do it. How do you think he got the job? He never amounted to anything.

ALICE: Poor Curt . . .

EDGAR: Poor! He cost me plenty. And leaving his wife and children like that! Disgraceful!

ALICE: Easy does it, Edgar.

EDGAR: I say disgraceful! . . . What the hell was he up to in America anyway? What? . . . I can't honestly say I long to see him. . . . But he was a decent chap, I'll give him that. At least you could have an intelligent argument with him.

ALICE: You mean he always gave in to you.

EDGAR (*haughtily*): Whether he gave in or not, he was still a person you could talk to. . . . On this island there isn't one damn person, not one, who understands what I'm talking about. It's a community of idiots.

ALICE: Odd, how Curt should come here just in time for our silver anniversary—whether or not we celebrate it.

EDGAR: What's so odd about that? —Oh, I see what you mean. Curt brought us together, didn't he? Or gave you away, as they say.

ALICE: Yes, he did.

EDGAR: Did he not! Just an idea he had. Hitching you and me together. Brilliant—wouldn't you say?

ALICE: Just popped into his head.

EDGAR: Yes, but we had to pay for it—not him.

ALICE: I might still be in the theater. All my old friends are stars now.

EDGAR (*standing up*): You see what I mean. . . . Now it's time for my whiskey. (*He goes to the cupboard and mixes himself a whiskey and water, which he drinks standing.*) What we need here is a footrail—to rest one's foot on. You could imagine yourself in Copenhagen, the American Bar.

ALICE: If all it takes to recall Copenhagen is a footrail, let's install one. Our happiest times, weren't they?

EDGAR (*pouring his drink down*): Yes. Remember Nimbs Restaurant? The *navarin aux pommes?* (*Smacks his lips.*)

ALICE: No, I remember the orchestra concerts at Tivoli.

EDGAR: That's what I like about you, Alice. All that culture.

ALICE: You ought to be happy that someone around here has some taste—

EDGAR: Oh, I am, I am.

ALICE: Everybody needs something to brag about—even you.

EDGAR (*drinking*): They must be dancing at the doctor's. I can hear the tubas. Oompah, oompah. Three-quarter time. Oompah, oompah.

ALICE: I can hear the melody. The "Alcazar Waltz." God, when was the last time I went waltzing?

EDGAR. You think you can still dance, Twinkle Toes?

ALICE: Ha!

EDGAR: Come off it! Your dancing days are over—like mine.

ALICE: I'm ten years younger than you.

EDGAR: That makes us exactly the same age. The lady is supposed to be ten years younger to even things up.

ALICE: How can you say that with a straight face? You're an old man. And I'm in the prime of life.

EDGAR: Of course you are. And you're so charming and gracious, sweet Alice—toward others. And how you lay it on.

ALICE: Should we light the lamp now?

EDGAR: Good idea!

ALICE: Then ring for Jenny.

Edgar goes slowly and stiffly to the desk and rings a bell. Jenny enters from the right.

EDGAR: Jenny, be a good girl and light the lamp for us. Hm?

ALICE (*sharply*): Light the lamp, he said. The ceiling lamp!

JENNY (*saucily*): Yes, ma'am! (*She lights the ceiling lamp, while Edgar watches her attentively. Then she starts to clean the lamp on the desk.*)

ALICE (*cuttingly*): Is that what you call wiping the chimney?

JENNY: Yes, I think so.

ALICE: Think so! What kind of answer is that?

EDGAR: Now, now. She's doing her best.

ALICE (*to Jenny*): Go! Get out! I'll light the lamp myself. I have to do everything around here.

JENNY: Yes, you may have to . . . (*She starts to leave.*)

ALICE (*standing up*): Go! Get out!

JENNY (*turning at the door*): I just wonder what you would say, ma'am, if I really did go.

> *Alice is silent. Jenny exits. Edgar crosses over and lights the lamp.*

ALICE (*uneasily*): You don't really think she'll give notice?

EDGAR: Wouldn't surprise me. We'd really be up the creek.

ALICE: It's all your fault. You spoil them.

EDGAR: That's not so. You can see for yourself they're always polite to me.

ALICE: Because you bow and scrape to them. You always do. You bow and scrape to everybody who's under you. You're a bully with the soul of a slave.

EDGAR: Is that so?

ALICE: Yes! You grovel before your own soldiers and your NCOs, but you think you're better than your equals and your superiors.

EDGAR: Ha!

ALICE: Typical tyrant! . . . Do you think she'll leave?

EDGAR: Unless you go out and apologize to her.

ALICE: Me?!

EDGAR: Well, not me. You'd say I was flirting with her.

ALICE: Oh, God! Suppose she goes! I'd have to do everything myself—all the cleaning—like the last time—and ruin my hands.

EDGAR: That wouldn't be the worst of it. If Jenny moves out, Christine will leave too, and we'd never get another servant to come out to this godforsaken island. You know how the pilot on the steamer deliberately warns off anybody who comes here looking for a job. And if he doesn't, my NCOs scare them off.

ALICE: Those damned NCOs—don't I know! I have to feed

them in my own kitchen because you haven't the guts to tell them to get out.

EDGAR: That's right. If I kicked them out of the kitchen, they wouldn't re-up for another hitch. And that, my pet, would be the end of the whole shebang. They'd put Long Tom in mothballs and close up the whole hardware shop.

ALICE: It would be the end. What would become of us?

EDGAR: Exactly. That's why the officers are thinking about petitioning the crown for commutation of rations.

ALICE: What?

EDGAR: Per diem payment instead of rations.

ALICE: For the officers?

EDGAR: No, for the noncoms of course.

ALICE (*laughs*): You've really lost your marbles!

EDGAR: That's more like it! That's what we need here—a good laugh.

ALICE: I've almost forgotten how to laugh.

EDGAR (*lighting a cigar*): Don't! Never forget how to laugh. Life's so tiresome.

ALICE: Fun it isn't, that's for sure. . . . Want to play another hand?

EDGAR: No, I've had enough.

Pause.

ALICE: You know, it gets my dander up, when I think about it, that my cousin, now that he's superintendent of the quarantine station, calls on our enemies first.

EDGAR: Who cares? Not worth talking about.

ALICE: Didn't you notice that in the list of arrivals in the newspaper he gave his occupation as "investor"? He must have inherited some money.

EDGAR: No kidding! A relative with money. That's a first in this family.

ALICE: In your family, maybe. Not in mine. We have a lot of rich relations.

EDGAR: If he's come into money, won't he be high-and-mighty! Need cutting down to size. Which means playing my cards very close to my chest.

The telegraph sounder begins to click.

ALICE: Who can that be?

EDGAR (*standing still*): Please, I'm trying to listen.

ALICE: Well, walk over to it.

EDGAR: Sh! I can hear . . . what they're saying. . . . It's the kids. (*He goes over to the telegraph apparatus and taps out a reply. Then the telegraph sounder sends a signal, and Edgar sends an answer.*)

ALICE: Well?

EDGAR: Hold your horses! (*Signs off.*) It was the kids. They called from the guardhouse in town. Judith wasn't feeling good and is staying home from school.

ALICE: Again! What else did they say?

EDGAR: Asked for money, of course.

ALICE: Why is Judith in such a hurry to get through school? If she graduated next year, it would be soon enough.

EDGAR: Try telling her that.

ALICE: She won't listen.

EDGAR: How often haven't I told her! But you know as well as I do that children do what they feel like.

ALICE: At least in this house.

Edgar yawns.

ALICE: Fine husband! Yawning in your wife's face.

EDGAR: What am I supposed to do? —Haven't you noticed that we say the same things to each other every day? Just now when you made your routine comment: "At least in this house," I would have given my routine reply: "It's not just *my* house." But since I've gone through that routine five hundred times, I decided to liven things up—to yawn instead. Which can be interpreted as meaning I'm too lazy to answer. Or it might mean: "Right you are, my pet." Or: "I've had enough."

ALICE: Aren't you in a lovely mood tonight!

EDGAR: Isn't it time for dinner?

ALICE: I suppose you know the doctor's supper party is being catered by the Grand Hotel.

EDGAR: No, I didn't. The Grand Hotel. At this time of year they've got woodcock on the menu. Makes my mouth water. Woodcock is the finest game bird of all—did you know that? But some people ruin the dear thing—they roast it in bacon fat. Barbarians!

ALICE: Disgusting! —Must you talk about food?

EDGAR: How about wine? I wonder what those barbarians are drinking with the woodcock.

ALICE: Should I play something for you?

EDGAR (*sitting at the desk*): The last resource! Sure, why not. —But please skip the funeral marches and your sad songs. I don't like propaganda with my music. I can always make out the message. "Listen to my sad song. I'm so unhappy." Miaow, miaow! "Listen to what a horrible husband I have." Baroom, baroom, baroom! "Oh, wouldn't it be lovely if he were dead!" Drum roll. Fanfare. And end with the "Alcazar Waltz." Da-da-da-da-dum-da-dum. And the Champagne Gallop." Darup, darup, darup! —Apropos champagne: there are two bottles left, if memory serves. Let's bring them up and pretend we have company. Hmm?

ALICE: No, let's *not* bring them up. They're mine. They were a present to *me*.

EDGAR: You're always so economical.

ALICE: And you're always so stingy. At least with your wife.

EDGAR: Well, it was only an idea. Now I don't know what to suggest. Maybe I should dance for you.

ALICE: No thanks. Your dancing days are over.

EDGAR: What you need is a woman in the house—someone you can talk to.

ALICE: Thank you. You need a man in the house.

EDGAR: Thank you. It's been tried, and to the mutual dissatisfaction of both parties. But it was fascinating to observe—like an experiment. —As soon as a stranger came into our house, we were happy. At the beginning.

ALICE: But not at the end.

EDGAR: Don't even think about it.

A knock is heard on the door at left.

ALICE: Who can be knocking this late in the day?

EDGAR: Jenny doesn't usually knock.

ALICE: Go and open the door. Don't stand shouting "Come in!" like you usually do. This isn't GHQ, you know.

EDGAR (*going to the door*): What have you got against GHQ?

Another knock.

ALICE: What are you waiting for? Open it.

Edgar opens the door and is handed a visiting card.

EDGAR: It's Christine. —Has Jenny gone?

Christine's answer cannot be heard.

(*To Alice.*) Jenny has gone.

ALICE: That makes me a housemaid again.

EDGAR: And me a hired hand.

ALICE: Can't you take one of the enlisted men and have him help out in the kitchen?

EDGAR: On permanent KP? These are not the good old days, Alice.

ALICE: The visiting card! Jenny wouldn't leave a visiting card when she's leaving. Whose is it?

EDGAR (*looks at the card through his spectacles, then hands it to Alice*): Read it. I can't see.

ALICE (*reading the card*): Curt! It's Curt! Hurry! Go out and fetch him in. Don't let him stand out there.

EDGAR (*as he goes out to the left*): Curt! Well, that's more like it!

Alice, perking up noticeably, arranges her hair.

* * *

Edgar enters from the left, with Curt.

EDGAR: Well, here he is: the man who abandons his friends! It's good to see you, you old son-of-a-gun! (*Embraces him.*)

ALICE (*going up to Curt*): Thank you. . . . It's been a long time.

EDGAR: Yes. Must be—let's see—fifteen years. And we've grown old.

ALICE: Oh, no. Curt hasn't changed. Still the same.

EDGAR: Sit down, sit down. —Now, first things first. What's on your roster? Are you invited out tonight?

CURT: Yes. I'm invited to the doctor's house not far from here. But I didn't promise I'd go.

ALICE: Good, then you can stay here where you belong—with your relations.

CURT: That does seem the most natural thing; but the doctor is my superior, and he might take it amiss.

EDGAR: Stuff and nonsense! I've never been afraid of my superiors.

CURT: It's not a question of being afraid; it's a question of tact —making things as pleasant as possible.

EDGAR: On this island, I'm the big shot. Stick with me, and no one will bother you.

ALICE: Oh, be quiet, Edgar. (*She takes Curt's hand.*) Big shots and superiors all aside, you're going to stay here with us. Why, it's only fit and proper, as they say.

CURT: All right, why not? You do make me feel welcome.

EDGAR: And why shouldn't you? We don't have any bones to pick . . . with each other . . .

> *Curt looks away, a little hurt.*

EDGAR: What's that supposed to mean? So you were a little careless. But you were young, and I've forgotten the whole thing. I'm not one to harbor grudges.

> *This turn of conversation has made Alice uneasy. All three seat themselves around the worktable.*

ALICE: So you've been out in the wide world?

CURT: Yes; and landed back here with you two.

EDGAR: Who you brought together in marriage twenty-five years ago.

CURT: It wasn't exactly like that, but never mind. It's great to see that you've stuck together for twenty-five years.

EDGAR: Oh, we've managed one way or another. Sometimes it's been touch and go, but, as you can see, we're still together. And Alice hasn't any cause to complain. Everything she could want; money pouring in. You didn't know I'm a famous author, now did you? Textbooks.

CURT: Yes, I remember when we went our separate ways you had written a book on firearms. Is it still used in the military schools?

EDGAR: Still used. Still number one—though they've tried to replace it with a poorer one. They use that one in *some* schools. Piece of junk!

Painful silence, broken by Curt.

CURT: I hear you've done some traveling, too. Gone abroad.

ALICE: Copenhagen. We've been there five times. Can you imagine?

EDGAR: Right. You see, when I took Alice out of the theater—

ALICE: *Took* me?!

EDGAR: Took, yes. A man takes a wife, and I took you!

ALICE: Brave, strong man, isn't he?

EDGAR: I never stopped hearing how I had cut short her brilliant career—hm, hm, hm—so to make it up to her, I had to promise to take her to Copenhagen. And I've kept my promise—faithfully. *Five* times we've gone there! Five. (*He holds up the five fingers of his left hand.*) Have you ever been to Copenhagen?

CURT (*smiles*): No; I've spent most of my time in America.

EDGAR: America? Must be an awful place. Nothing but bums and bushwhackers, I hear.

CURT (*frowning*): Well, it's not Copenhagen, admittedly.

ALICE (*trying to ease the tension*): Tell me—. Have you . . . ? Do you ever hear from your children?

CURT: No.

ALICE: You're a dear old friend, Curt, and I hope you won't mind my saying this, but wasn't it ill-considered to leave them like that?

CURT: I didn't leave them. The court took them from me and put them in the care of their mother.

EDGAR: Let's not talk about that now! It seems to me you are well out of that mess anyway.

CURT (*to Alice*): How are your children?

ALICE: Fine, thanks. They're attending school in the city. Nearly full-grown now.

EDGAR: A couple of able kids. The boy's got a brilliant mind. Brilliant! He'll be going to General Staff College.

ALICE: *If* they accept him.

EDGAR: Accept him? He's got the stuff the big brass is made of!

CURT: If I might change the subject: —the quarantine station that's being set up here for cholera, plague, what-have-you—the doctor will be my boss, as you know. Do you know him? What sort of man is he?

EDGAR: Man? He's no man. He's a dim-witted scoundrel, who'll stab you in the back.

CURT (*to Alice*): Doesn't sound too good, does it?

ALICE: Oh, it's not as bad as Edgar makes it sound. Although I have to admit we don't exactly get along.

EDGAR: A scoundrel, I tell you! That's what they all are: the customs inspector, the postmaster, the telephone operator, the druggist, the ship's pilot, the—the—what the hell do you call him?—the alderman—scoundrels one and all. And that's why I don't associate with them.

CURT: Have you locked horns with all of them?

EDGAR: Each and every one!

ALICE: Edgar's right, you know. It's impossible to associate with them.

EDGAR: This is the Devil's Island for tyrants and bullies. They were all shipped here.

ALICE (*sarcastically*): Didn't miss nary a one.

EDGAR (*taking it in stride*): Hm, hm, hm. That's supposed to be a dig at me. But I'm no tyrant. At least, not in my own house.

ALICE: Watch it, Edgar.

EDGAR (*to Curt*): Don't listen to her. I'm a very congenial husband. And the old lady is the best wife in the world.

ALICE: Curt, how about something to drink?

CURT: No, thanks, not now.

EDGAR: You're not on the wagon?

CURT: No, just not overdoing it.

EDGAR: Like the Americans, eh? The average, the common denominator?

CURT: Maybe.

EDGAR: Not my style. I want to go all the way; otherwise, forget it. A man should be able to hold his liquor.

CURT: To get back to your neighbors here on the island. My position is going to put me in contact with all of them. It won't be easy to steer clear of them. I mean, even if you don't want to get mixed up in other people's affairs, you can't help it.

ALICE: Don't fret, Curt. Mix with them if you have to. You'll always come back to us. This is where you have your real friends.

CURT: Isn't it awful to sit here surrounded by people you hate?

ALICE: It isn't fun, that's for sure.

EDGAR: It isn't at all awful. My whole life I've had nothing but enemies. I've thrived on them. As a matter of fact, they've helped me more than they've hurt me. And when I die I'll have the satisfaction of knowing I don't owe anybody a goddamn thing. Nobody ever gave me anything. Everything I own I had to fight for.

ALICE: True. Edgar's path hasn't been strewn with roses.

EDGAR: No. With thorns, with stones—sharp stones! And I did it with my own strength! Do you know what I mean?

CURT (*quietly, unassumingly*): Oh, yes. I know what you mean. And I came to see, ten years ago, how insufficient one's own strength is.

EDGAR: Ha! Then I feel sorry for you.

ALICE (*remonstrating*): Edgar!

EDGAR: No, I mean it! I really feel sorry for him—for anyone who doesn't rely on his own strength. Listen, it's perfectly true that when the machine breaks down, there's nothing left but what you can put in a wheelbarrow and haul out to manure the garden. But as long as the gears are turning, you've got to use them, use your hands and feet, keep slugging and kicking as long as the parts hold out! That's my philosophy.

CURT (*smiling*): I've always enjoyed hearing you talk, Edgar.

EDGAR: But you don't believe it's true.

CURT: No, I don't believe it's true.

EDGAR: Well, it is true, whether you like it or not.

> *During the last few minutes the wind has come up, and now one of the doors at the back swings open with a bang.*

EDGAR (*getting to his feet*): The wind's come up. I could feel it blowing up. (*He goes to shut the door. Taps the barometer.*)

ALICE (*to Curt*): You're staying for supper, aren't you?

CURT: Yes, if it's not a bother.

ALICE: No bother. It'll be something simple, I'm afraid. Our cook has moved.

CURT: That will be fine, I'm sure.

ALICE: Dear Curt; so easy to please. That's what I like about you.

EDGAR (*studying the barometer*): Fantastic how the barometer is falling. Look at it. I could feel it.

ALICE (*to Curt, softly*): Bad case of nerves. Worse tonight.

EDGAR: Shouldn't we be eating soon?

ALICE (*standing up*): I'm just about to take care of it. You two sit down and carry on with your philosophizing. (*To Curt, quietly.*) Don't contradict him; puts him in a bad mood. And for God's sake, don't ask why he never got to be a major.

> *Curt nods understandingly. Alice crosses to the right. Edgar sits down with Curt at the worktable.*

EDGAR: Whip up something special for us, honeybunch.

ALICE: Give me money, and you'll get something special, lambykins.

EDGAR: Money, always money.

> *Alice exits.*

* * *

EDGAR (*to Curt*): Money, money, money! I spend so much time doling out money, I'm beginning to think I'm a wallet with legs. Ever had that feeling?

CURT: I sure have. I thought I was a checkbook.

EDGAR (*laughing*): Oh, yes, you've been through the mill. Women, women! And, by God you latched on to a good one!

CURT (*patiently*): And that's water over the dam; let's forget it!

EDGAR: She was a pearl, wasn't she? Ha, a real gem! —Well, now, in my case, I can say that—in spite of everything—I got myself a good woman. She's solid, reliable—in spite of everything.

CURT (*smiles*): In spite of everything!

EDGAR: What's so funny?

CURT (*smiling*): In spite of everything! That's funny.

EDGAR: She's been a faithful wife, a fine mother—extraordinary. —But—(*He glances toward the door at right.*) she's got the temper of a she-devil. You know, there are moments when I've cursed you for hanging that albatross around my neck.

CURT (*amicably*): Don't blame me for that, Edgar, I never—

EDGAR: Yeah, yeah, yeah. A lot of talk. But you forget what's unpleasant to remember. Don't get your dander up. I'm used to giving orders and sounding off. You know what I'm like, you son-of-a-gun.

CURT: Yes; but the point is I did not foist Alice on you. Quite the contrary.

EDGAR (*not letting his flow of thought be interrupted*): Life is strange, don't you think?

CURT: You can say that again!

EDGAR: Getting to be old, I mean. Not much fun, but it's damned fascinating. Oh, I'm not saying I'm old; it's just that I'm *beginning* to get the feel of it. All one's friends die off. It gets lonesome.

CURT: You're lucky to have a wife to keep you company when you get older.

EDGAR: Lucky? Yes, I guess so. Even the children leave. . . . You know, you shouldn't have left yours.

CURT: But I tell you I didn't leave them. They were taken from me.

EDGAR: Now don't get sore just because I tell you—

CURT: But I keep telling you it wasn't like that.

EDGAR: Well, however it was, it's over and forgotten. Fact is, you're alone.

CURT: One gets used to everything, Edgar.

EDGAR: I wonder. Can you—I mean, can one get used to— being completely alone?

CURT: Look at me.

EDGAR: Yes. . . . What have you been doing these past fifteen years?

CURT: What a question! These fifteen years!

EDGAR: I hear you struck it rich.

CURT: I'm not rolling in the stuff.

EDGAR: Don't worry, I'm not putting the touch on you.

CURT: Edgar, if you need a loan . . .

EDGAR: Thank you very much, but I've got money in the bank —my own checking account. Listen—(*Casting a glance at the door at right.*) in this house we don't lack for anything. Can't. If I went broke, she'd pack up and leave.

CURT: I don't believe that.

EDGAR: It's a fact. You know what her SOP is? She doesn't ask for money any old day. She waits—waits until she knows I haven't got any, so she can yell at me, saying I can't support a family. She loves that!

CURT: I thought you said money was pouring in.

EDGAR: Of course. It just doesn't go very far.

CURT: Then it's not pouring in—not in the ordinary sense.

EDGAR: It's strange. Life. And so are we. Right?

The telegraph receiver has begun to click.

CURT: What's that?

EDGAR: Only a time check.

CURT: Don't you have a telephone here?

EDGAR: It's out in the kitchen. We use the telegraph so the telephone girls can't stick their nose in our business.

CURT: You must have a hell of a social life out here on the coast.

EDGAR: Stinks. But, then, life itself stinks. And you believe it goes on! Tell me, since you believe in a life after death, will there be peace in the life to come?

CURT: I'm sure there'll be storms and struggles even there.

EDGAR: Even there! If there is any *there*. I'd prefer annihilation.

CURT: What makes you think that annihilation occurs without pain and suffering?

EDGAR: Not for me. I'm going to drop down dead—bam! No pain, no suffering.

CURT: How do you know that?

EDGAR: I know what I know.

CURT: Sounds like you're not too happy with your life.

EDGAR (*sighs*): Happy? The day I die, I'll be happy.

CURT: That's something you don't know. (*Standing up.*) What on earth is going on in this house? What's happening? The place smells poisonous, like old peeling wallpaper. Just coming in here makes you sick. I'd walk out this instant if I hadn't promised Alice I'd stay. There must be corpses rotting under the floorboards. The air is so full of hate it's suffocating.

> *While Curt has been talking, Edgar has fallen into a semiconscious state, eyes open and staring.*

CURT: What's the matter with you? Edgar!

> *Edgar does not move. Curt shakes him by the shoulder.*

CURT: Edgar!

EDGAR (*coming to*): What did you say? (*Looking around.*) I thought it was Alice. . . . Oh, it's you. —Listen, I— (*He falls into a stupor again.*)

CURT: This is terrible! (*Curt goes to the door at right, opens it, and calls.*) Alice!

* * *

ALICE (*enters, wearing an apron*): What's the matter?

CURT: I don't know. Look at him!

ALICE (*calmly*): Oh, he gets those spells every once in a while. He just fades out. I'll play; that will make him come to.

CURT: No, don't do that! Don't—. Let me take care of this. . . . Can he hear? Can he see?

ALICE: Right now he can't hear, can't see.

CURT: You say that as if nothing has happened! Alice, what's going on here?

ALICE: Ask that one!

CURT: "That one?" God, Alice, that's your husband.

ALICE: A stranger to me, just as much a stranger as he was twenty-five years ago. I don't know anything about that man — except that —

CURT: Shhh! He can hear you.

ALICE: When he's like that, he can't hear a thing.

> *A bugle call is heard. Edgar starts, leaps to his feet, crosses to the hat tree, and puts on his saber and military cap.*

EDGAR: Excuse me! Got to check the guard posts. (*Exits through the rear doors.*)

* * *

CURT: Is he ill?

ALICE: I don't know.

CURT: Is he out of his mind?

ALICE: I don't know.

CURT: Has he been drinking?

ALICE: He talks liquor more than he drinks it.

CURT: Alice, now you sit down and you tell me what's going on. Calmly and truthfully.

ALICE (*sitting down*): You want the story of my life? How I've been sitting in this round tower for a lifetime, like a prisoner, guarded by a man I've always hated. A man I now hate so much that the day he dies I'll burst out laughing with joy.

CURT: Why haven't you left him?

ALICE: A good question. We separated twice while we were engaged, and since then we've thought of separating every day that passes. But we're welded together, I guess, and we can't free ourselves. Once we were separated—that is, we went our separate ways in the same house—for five years. Now nothing but death can separate us. And we know it. So we await death as a deliverance.

CURT: Why are you so alone, so isolated?

ALICE: Because he isolated me. Cut me off. Made my relatives leave the house. He *weeded* them out—that's what he called it. "Weeded" out my friends, everybody.

CURT: What about *his* relations? Did you "weed" them out?

ALICE: My God! I had to! They would have been the death of me. They took away my reputation, my self-respect. Would have taken my life, too. Finally I was reduced to keeping contact with people by means of that telegraph. The telephone was no good—those girls always listening in. I've taught myself how to use the telegraph, and he doesn't know it. —For God's sake, don't say a word about it, he'd kill me if he knew.

CURT: How awful, awful! —But why does he blame me for your marriage? You know how it was. Edgar was my friend when we were young. When he saw you, it was love at first sight. He came to me and asked me to be go-between. Right away I said no. My dear Alice, I can be honest with you. I knew how strong-willed you were, knew you had a cruel streak in you; I warned him. But when he became more insistent, I sent him around to your brother to let him plead his case.

ALICE: I'm sure that's how it was. Not that it makes any difference. He's told himself another story for so many years you can never make him believe anything else.

CURT: All right, let him blame me for everything, if that makes him feel any better.

ALICE: That's asking too much.

CURT: I'm used to it. What irks me is when he accuses me of abandoning my children. That's unfair.

ALICE: He's like that. He says whatever comes into his head; and what he says he believes. But he really likes you—you don't contradict him. Please try to bear with us. Maybe you came to us at this moment because you were meant to. . . . Sometimes I think we're the unhappiest couple on the face of the earth. (*She cries.*)

CURT: I've seen *one* marriage at close quarters. That was bad enough. But this is almost worse.

ALICE: You think so?

CURT: I do.

ALICE: Whose fault is it?

CURT: Alice, the moment you stop trying to find whose fault it is you'll feel a whole lot better. Try to accept it as a fact of life, or as a test.

ALICE: I can't. It's asking too much. (*Standing up.*) It's hopeless.

CURT: You poor fool. —Why do you hate each other like this? Do you know?

ALICE: No. It's a hate beyond reason. Without cause, without point or purpose. And also without end. It's crazy. You know why he's afraid to die? Because he's afraid I'd marry again.

CURT: Then he must love you.

ALICE: Probably. That doesn't prevent him from hating me.

CURT (*as if to himself*): That's love-hate, and it comes from the pit of hell. —Does he like it when you play for him?

ALICE: Oh, yes, but only ugly tunes. The uglier the better. Like that awful "Entrance of the Boyars," for instance. When he hears it, he becomes possessed and wants to dance.

CURT: He—dance?

ALICE: Oh, he can be a real card at times.

CURT: Maybe I shouldn't ask, but I can't help it. Your children—where are they?

ALICE: Two died. I guess you didn't know.

CURT: I'm sorry. You've had to bear that, too.

ALICE: What haven't I had to bear?

CURT: And the other two?

ALICE: Living in town. We couldn't have them here with us. He turned them against me.

CURT: And you, against him.

ALICE: Naturally. We formed factions, held caucuses, solicited votes, offered bribes. So, in order not to destroy them utterly, we sent them away. Children! They're supposed to make a marriage; they broke ours. The blessing became a curse. Sometimes I think we belong to a family with a curse on it.

CURT: Yes, after the Fall—it's true.

ALICE (*giving him a withering look; sharply*): Which fall?

CURT: The first. Adam and Eve.

ALICE: Oh. I thought you meant—something else.

Embarrassed silence.

ALICE (*clasping her hands together*): Curt, we're cousins, and you're my oldest friend. I know I haven't always behaved toward you as I should have, but, Lord knows, I've been punished. You've had your revenge.

CURT: What revenge? Nothing of the sort. Now just forget it!

ALICE: Do you remember that Sunday after you had gotten engaged? I had invited the two of you to dinner.

CURT: I say forget it!

ALICE: I have to say this—so you'll forgive me. When you arrived, we had gone and you had to go back.

CURT: So you had been invited out yourselves. There's nothing to talk about. Why are you so upset?

ALICE: There's more, Curt. Just now when I invited you to stay for supper, I thought there was something to eat in the kitchen. (*She hides her face in her hands.*) There isn't a scrap, not even a dry crust of bread. (*She sobs.*)

CURT: You poor darling! It's nothing to get upset about.

ALICE: Oh, no? Wait till he comes back, expecting dinner, and there's nothing. He'll explode. You've never seen him when he gets mad. Oh, God, the humiliation—!

CURT: Now you just let me take care of this. I'll go out and buy something.

ALICE: Buy? There's no place to buy anything on this island.

CURT: It makes no difference to me, you understand. But for his sake, and yours—there must be something. . . . We could—. We'll make a joke of the whole business when he comes in. Laugh about it. I'll say it's time for a drink, and I'll think of something while we're drinking. . . . You put him in a good mood, humor him, play something for him, some silly tune. Come here. Be sitting at the piano when he arrives.

ALICE: Look at my hands! Who can play the piano with hands like these? I have to scrub the pots and pans, wash the glasses, lay the fire, dust and mop—

CURT: I thought you had two servants.

ALICE: On paper an officer gets two servants. But they're always leaving us. Sometimes there's nobody. Nobody. Most of the time. —Oh, Curt, what am I going to do? —I mean, about supper? I wish the whole damn place would burn down.

CURT: Now, now, Alice.

ALICE: I wish the sea would rise and wash us all away.

CURT: Now, now. I won't hear such talk, Alice.

ALICE: What will he say? What will he do? —Curt, please, Curt, don't leave me!

CURT: No, Alice, I'm not going anyplace. I promise I won't leave.

ALICE: But you'll have to leave—sometime. . . . And then—!

CURT: Has he ever struck you?

ALICE: Me?! Course not! He knows I'd walk out on him. I've got some pride left.

From outside on the platform can be heard the Sentry's voice challenging someone: "Halt! Who goes there?" And Edgar's voice replying, "Friend."

CURT (*standing up*): Is that him?

ALICE (*frightened*): Yes, it's him.

Pause.

CURT: Now what do we do? What on earth do we do?

ALICE: I don't know. I don't know.

* * *

Edgar enters through the rear doors, in high spirits.

EDGAR: There! That's tended to. Made the rounds. Now I'm free. —Well, has she poured out her heart to you? Unburdened her soul? Isn't she the poor, unhappy one? Eh? Eh?

CURT: How's the weather out there?

EDGAR: Blowing up a storm. (*He opens one of the rear doors a trifle. Joshingly.*) Bluebeard and the maiden in the tower. And out there, the sentry, with saber unsheathed, guards the beautiful maiden. Then along come her brothers to rescue her. But the sentry is there, pacing. Look at him! Keeping time. A good sentry. Look at him. (*He hums and beats out a march rhythm in time with the sentry.*) Meli-tam-tam-ta, meli-talia-lie. Should we dance the sword dance? That will be something for Curt to see!

CURT: How about "The Entrance of the Boyars" instead?

EDGAR: Oh, ho, you know that, do you? —Alice, pretty Alice in her little apron, come and play for us. —Come, I said!

Alice goes reluctantly to the piano. As she passes Edgar, he pinches her arm.

EDGAR: And what little slanders have you been spreading about me?

ALICE: Me?

> *Curt averts his eyes.*
>
> *Alice plays "The Entrance of the Boyars." Edgar improvises a kind of Hungarian dance in the area behind the writing desk, clanging his spurs as he dances. Suddenly he falls to the floor, unnoticed by Curt and Alice. Alice plays the piece to its end.*

ALICE (*without turning around*): Once more?

> *Silence.*
>
> *Alice turns and sees Edgar lying unconscious, hidden from the audience by the desk.*

ALICE: God in heaven! (*She stands with her arms crossed over her breasts and sighs deeply, a sign of gratitude and release.*)

CURT (*turning around and hurrying to Edgar*): What is it? What's happened?

ALICE (*in the greatest possible suspense*): Is – he – dead?

CURT: I don't know! Help me!

ALICE (*not moving*): I can't. I can't touch him. . . . Is he dead?

CURT: No. He's still alive.

> *Alice sighs. Curt helps Edgar, who gets to his feet and is supported to a chair.*

EDGAR: What was that?

> *Silence.*

What was that?

CURT: You fell. Don't you know?

EDGAR: Fell?

CURT: Fell to the floor. How do you feel now?

EDGAR: Me? Feel? Nothing's the matter. Don't know what you're talking about. What are you gaping at?

CURT: You're ill.

EDGAR: Nonsense! Come, Alice, play—. Oh, it's coming again! (*His hand goes to his head.*)

ALICE: You see! You're sick.

EDGAR: Stop yelling! It's only a dizzy spell.

CURT: We've got to get a doctor. I'll telephone—

EDGAR: No, I don't want any doctor.

CURT: You have to have a doctor. If not for your sake, then for ours. We'll be held responsible.

EDGAR: I'll drive him out if he comes. I'll shoot him down! —Oh, it's coming again! (*Grabs his head.*)

Curt crosses to the door at right.

CURT: I'm telephoning! (*He exits.*)

* * *

Alice takes off her apron.

EDGAR: Will you get me a glass of water?

ALICE: I suppose I have to. (*She gives him a glass of water.*)

EDGAR: Aren't you a dear!

ALICE: Are you sick?

EDGAR: Forgive me for not being well.

ALICE: Can you take care of yourself?

EDGAR: It's obvious you won't.

ALICE: You can be sure of that.

EDGAR: This is it, Alice. The moment you've been waiting for, for so long.

ALICE: Yes. The moment you thought would never come.

EDGAR: Don't get mad at me.

*   *   *

Curt enters from the right.

CURT: Dreadful.

ALICE: What did he say?

CURT: He hung up. Just like that!

ALICE (*to Edgar*): You always treated him like dirt—you and your arrogance! What did you expect?

EDGAR: I'm feeling worse. Could you get a doctor from town?

ALICE: I'll have to use the telegraph. (*She goes to the telegraph apparatus on the desk.*)

EDGAR (*half-rising in astonishment*): Can—you—telegraph?

ALICE (*tapping out a message on the telegraph key*): Yes! Yes, I can telegraph.

EDGAR: You really can. All right: get to it. —What a deceitful woman! (*To Curt.*) Come and sit next to me.

Curt seats himself next to Edgar.

EDGAR: Hold my hand. . . . I'm sitting—and yet I'm falling. Can you imagine? Falling down something. . . . It's strange.

CURT: Have you had these attacks before?

EDGAR: Never.

CURT: While we're waiting for an answer from town, I'll walk over to the doctor's house and speak to him. He's attended you before, hasn't he?

EDGAR: Yes, he has.

CURT: He should know your medical history, then. (*He crosses left.*)

ALICE: We'll get an answer soon. —You're very kind, Curt. Come back as soon as you can.

CURT: As soon as I can. (*He leaves.*)

* * *

EDGAR: He's very kind—Curt. And so changed.

ALICE: And all for the better. I'm sorry for his sake that he should come to us right now, in all our misery.

EDGAR: Come to congratulate us! . . . I wonder how things really are with him. Did you notice that he didn't want to talk about himself?

ALICE: I noticed—but did anybody ask him?

EDGAR: His life. . . . Strange. . . . Our life. . . . I wonder if everybody's life is like this.

ALICE: Perhaps. The difference is that they don't talk about it.

EDGAR: Sometimes I've had this idea that misery seeks its own kind. I mean, those who are happy avoid those who are unhappy. That's why we never get to see anything but misery.

ALICE: Who do you know who's happy?

EDGAR: Let me think. . . . No. —Yes! The Edmarks.

ALICE: The Edmarks?! She was operated on last year. Still sick.

EDGAR: That's right. —Well, then I can't think of anybody. . . . What about the Krafts?

ALICE: Perfect example. Have you forgotten? The whole family lived in a paradise. Rich, respected, nice children, good marriages—everything perfect till the Krafts got to be fifty. Then their cousin killed a man, went to prison, dragged their name into all the papers. That was the end of paradise. The Kraft name in all the headlines. The Kraft murder case, remember? The old respected Krafts couldn't even show themselves in public. The children had to be taken out of school. My God, such happiness!

EDGAR: I wonder what sort of sickness I've got.

ALICE: What do you think it is?

EDGAR: Something to do with the heart. Or the head. It's as if my soul wanted to fly out and dissolve itself in a cloud of smoke.

ALICE: Do you feel like eating?

EDGAR: Yes, I could eat something. What are you cooking for supper?

ALICE (*agitated, she crosses the floor*): I'll ask Jenny.

EDGAR: Jenny? She left us.

ALICE: Yes, I know, I know. I forgot.

EDGAR: Ring for Christine. I want a fresh glass of water, anyway.

Alice rings.

ALICE: God, you don't suppose—? (*Rings again.*) She doesn't hear.

EDGAR: Go and look for her. If she's left too—God!

Alice goes to the door at left and opens it.

ALICE: Look. She's packed her suitcase. It's standing here in the hall.

EDGAR: Then she's left.

ALICE: What a hell! What a hell! (*She falls, sobbing, to her knees, and puts her head on a stool. Starts to sniffle.*)

EDGAR: Everything all at once. Even Curt had to show up to see us in this stinking mess. The only humiliation left is for Curt to walk in right now and see you like that and me like this.

ALICE: Don't worry, he won't. He's left us, too. You can bet on it. He won't be back.

EDGAR: Just like him!

ALICE: We're cursed, damned!

EDGAR: What's that supposed to mean?

ALICE: Don't you see how everybody avoids us? What's the matter with you!

EDGAR: Let them! I don't give a damn!

The telegraph sounder begins clicking.

EDGAR: There's the reply. —Shh! let me listen. . . . Everyone's busy. . . . Excuses. —Scum!

ALICE: You see! You didn't give a damn about doctors and now they don't give a damn about you. Didn't even pay their bills!

EDGAR: That's not true.

ALICE: Even when you could have, you didn't. You despised the doctors' work, just as you despise my work—everybody's work. They don't want to come. And the telephone is shut off because you despised that, too! Nothing means anything to you except your guns and cannons!

EDGAR: Don't stand there shooting your mouth off.

ALICE: You're getting yours, Edgar. Everything comes back. The big and the small.

EDGAR: Silly superstition! You talk like an old woman.

ALICE: You wait, you'll see. —Do you know we owe Christine six months' wages?

EDGAR: So what! She's stolen more than that from us.

ALICE: But I've had to borrow cash from her!

EDGAR: That's just like you!

ALICE: You ought to thank me! You know very well I had to borrow the money to pay for the children's travel home.

EDGAR: Didn't Curt time things perfectly! Scamp! And a coward to boot. Didn't have the guts to say he had had enough of us. Saw he was going to get a lousy meal here and skipped off to the doctor's party! Miserable wretch. They're all alike!

* * *

Curt enters hurriedly through the door at left.

CURT: Well, Edgar, old fellow, this is how it is. The doctor knows what the trouble is. It's your heart.

EDGAR: Heart?

CURT: For a long time now you've been suffering from arteriosclerosis and calcification around the heart.

EDGAR: Stony heart?

CURT: And—

EDGAR: Is it serious?

CURT: Well, it can be.

EDGAR: So it is serious.

CURT: Yes.

EDGAR: Fatal?

CURT: You simply have to be very careful. First, no cigars.

Edgar tosses his cigar away.

CURT: Second: no whiskey. . . . And next: off to bed.

EDGAR (*fear in his voice*): No. Not that. Not to bed. That's the end. Once in bed, you never get up again. I'll sleep on the sofa tonight. —What else did he say?

CURT: He was very kind and helpful, really. He'll come here right away, if you call for him.

EDGAR: Kind? Helpful? That hypocrite! I don't want to see his face! . . . Am I allowed to eat?

CURT: Not tonight. And for the next few days—only milk.

EDGAR: Milk! I can't stomach the stuff.

CURT: You'll have to learn.

EDGAR: No, I'm too old to learn. (*He clasps his hands to his head.*) Oh, it's coming again! (*He sits and stares unseeingly.*)

ALICE (*to Curt*): What *did* the doctor say?

CURT: That he *might* die.

ALICE: Hallelujah!

CURT: Take care, Alice. Take care. —Could you get a pillow and a blanket? I'll tuck him in on the sofa. I'll sit here on the chair and spend the night with him.

ALICE: What about me?

CURT: You go to bed. Your presence only seems to make his condition worse.

ALICE: All right. You're in charge. I know you mean the best for both of us. (*She crosses to the left.*)

CURT: "Both of you"—mind. I'm not going to get involved in your battles.

> *He takes the water carafe and goes out to the right, while Alice exits left.*

* * *

> *The sound of the wind outside is heard, louder. The doors at the rear blow open, and an Old Woman, sleazily dressed and unpleasant looking, peeps in.*

> *Edgar wakes up, pulls himself up, and looks around.*

EDGAR: They've left me—the bastards! (*He catches sight of the Old Woman and is suddenly frightened.*) Who are you? What do you want?

OLD WOMAN: I just wanted to close the door, mister.

EDGAR: Why? Why?

OLD WOMAN: Because it blew open, just as I was passing by.

EDGAR: You were going to rob us!

OLD WOMAN: Not much worth taking, is there? That's what Christine says.

EDGAR: Christine!

OLD WOMAN: Good night, sir. Sleep well. (*She closes the door and leaves.*)

* * *

Alice enters from the left, carrying pillows and a blanket.

EDGAR: Who was that at the door just now? There was someone, wasn't there?

ALICE: That was only Maia, from the old folks' home, on her way back.

EDGAR: Are you certain?

ALICE: Are you scared?

EDGAR: Scared? Never.

ALICE: Since you won't go to bed, you're going to sleep out here.

EDGAR (*goes to the chaise lounge and lies down*): This is where I want to lie. (*He attempts to take Alice's hand, but she pulls her hand away from him.*)

Curt enters with a carafe of water.

EDGAR: Curt, don't leave me!

CURT: I'm going to sit here with you the whole night, Edgar. Alice is going to say good night to you and go to bed.

EDGAR: Good night, Alice.

ALICE (*to Curt*): Good night, Curt.

CURT: Good night.

* * *

Curt takes a chair and places himself close to Edgar.

CURT: Don't you want to take off your boots?

EDGAR: No. A soldier wants to be armed and ready, always.

CURT: Are you expecting a battle?

EDGAR: Maybe. (*Raising himself up.*) Curt! You are the only person I've bared myself to. Promise me one thing. . . . If I die tonight . . . take care of my children.

CURT: Don't worry. I will.

EDGAR: Thank you, Curt. I know I can count on you.

CURT: Why is that? Why can you count on me?

EDGAR: We've never been friends, Curt; I don't believe in friendship. And our two families were born enemies, always fighting.

CURT: Yet you say you can count on me.

EDGAR: Yes. And I don't know why.

Silence.

Do you think I'm going to die?

CURT: Yes, you like everyone else. They're not going to make an exception of you.

EDGAR: So bitter, Curt?

CURT: Yes. — So afraid of dying, Edgar? The wheelbarrow, the manure for the garden?

EDGAR: What if — what if that wasn't the end?

CURT: Many people think it isn't.

EDGAR: And what comes after?

CURT: One surprise after another, I suppose.

EDGAR: But nothing is known for sure.

CURT: Exactly. That's the point. That's why one has to be ready for anything.

EDGAR: You're still not such a child, Curt, that you believe in hell?

CURT: And you don't believe in it? You're in the midst of it.

EDGAR: That's only a way of speaking, a metaphor.

CURT: You've described your hell so realistically that there's no way it can be a metaphor, poetic or otherwise.

Silence.

EDGAR: If you only knew the pain I'm suffering.

CURT: Physical?

EDGAR: No, not physical.

CURT: Then it must be spiritual. There's no third alternative.

Silence.

EDGAR (*raising himself up on his elbows*): I don't want to die!

CURT: A short while ago you wanted annihilation.

EDGAR: On condition it was painless.

CURT: But you see it isn't.

EDGAR: This? Is this annihilation?

CURT: The beginning of it.

EDGAR: Good night, Curt.

CURT: Good night, Edgar.

[2]

Same set, but the ceiling lamp is on the verge of going out. Gray morning light and an overcast sky is visible through the windows and the doors at the rear. Heavy seas. The Sentry is on duty as before. Edgar is lying on the chaise lounge, asleep. Curt is sitting in the chair next to him, pale and exhausted.

Alice enters from the left.

ALICE: Is he asleep?

CURT: Yes. Has been ever since the sun was supposed to rise.

ALICE: A bad night?

CURT: He slept off and on. Mostly he talked.

ALICE: About what?

CURT: He argued about religion like a high-school kid and presumed to think that he had solved all the great mysteries of life.

Finally, long about morning, he made a great discovery: the immortality of the soul.

ALICE: For his own everlasting glory!

CURT: Absolutely. I have never in my life met anyone with such a high opinion of himself. "*I* exist; therefore there is a god."

ALICE: Now you see the real Edgar. —Those boots! He would have trampled the earth flat, if he had had his way. With those boots he stomped through life, stepping on everybody's toes and walking all over me. Well, buster, there was a bullet with your number on it.

CURT: He'd be comical if he weren't so tragic. You know, there's a streak of greatness in all that pettiness and small-mindedness. I'll bet you could find something good to say about him if you tried.

ALICE (*sitting down*): Yes, if I were certain he couldn't hear me. He's so stuck on himself; encourage him and he'll never come unglued.

CURT: He can't hear; he's been given morphine.

ALICE: He came from a poor family, you know. Lots of children, and he had to support them, when he was still young, by giving lessons. His father was a louse—a good-for-nothing. So Edgar was denied all the pleasures of a normal adolescence. Had to slave for a bunch of ungrateful kids whom he never put on this earth. I was only a small girl when I first saw him. He was just a young guy who had to go without an overcoat even when it was ten below zero because he couldn't afford one. But his little sisters had duffel coats. I couldn't help but admire him. Even though he was so ugly he made one cringe. Have you ever seen anybody so ugly?

CURT: I don't think so. It can be horrifying at times. Every time I quarreled and broke off with him, I noticed his ugliness. When he wasn't around, the image of him took over, grew into a giant ogre. He literally haunted me.

ALICE: Imagine what it's been like for me! . . . Anyway, his career in the army when he was training as an officer was sheer torture for him. But some rich people helped him financially.

He'll never admit it, though. Everything he's been able to get his hands on he takes as his due. Not a word of thanks.

CURT: I thought we were going to say something nice about him.

ALICE: It can wait until he's dead! —Anyhow, that's all I remember.

CURT: Has he been mean to you? Spiteful?

ALICE: Oh, God! What do you think? . . . Funny. Sometimes he's been so kind and sensitive. —It's when he turns against you, that's when he's absolutely terrifying.

CURT: Why didn't he ever get to be major?

ALICE: Obvious, isn't it? Listen, if he thinks he's Caesar when he's only a captain, who'd be dumb enough to make him a major? —But don't even bring up that subject. He says he never wanted to be top brass. —Did he talk about the children?

CURT: Yes. He longed to see Judith.

ALICE: I thought so. Judith. Do you know Judith? Judith is his second self. He's trained her to bait and badger me. My own daughter . . . and she hit me.

CURT: No! How could she?

ALICE: Quiet! He's stirring. —My God! Suppose he heard me. He's sly; oh, God, he's sly!

CURT: I think he really is waking up.

ALICE: Like a troll, isn't he? Makes me shiver.

Silence.

Edgar stirs, wakes up, raises himself on his elbows, and looks around.

EDGAR: So it's morning. Finally.

CURT: How do you feel now?

EDGAR: Not so hot.

CURT: Do you want the doctor?

EDGAR: No. I want to see Judith. My Judith.

CURT: Don't you think you should be settling your affairs? I mean, before—or in case—anything happens.

EDGAR: What do you mean? What's going to happen?

CURT: I mean what happens to everyone.

EDGAR: Crap! I don't die easy, so get that out of your mind. Don't count your chickens, Alice.

CURT: You should give a thought to your children. And you should make a will so your wife at least will hold on to the furniture.

EDGAR: How can she inherit while I'm still alive?

CURT: It's not a case of that. But if something does happen, she shouldn't end up in the street. This furniture—she's cleaned and dusted and polished this furniture for twenty-five years; she's got a right to hold on to it. Do you want me to call the lawyer in regimental headquarters?

EDGAR: No.

CURT: You're a hard man, Edgar, harder than I thought.

EDGAR: It's coming again! (*He falls back on the chaise lounge, senseless.*)

ALICE (*crossing right*): Somebody's in the kitchen. I have to see—

CURT: Go on. There's not much that can be done here.

Alice exits.

* * *

Edgar comes to.

EDGAR: Well, Curt, how do you plan to set up the quarantine station?

CURT: I'll manage—somehow.

EDGAR: Maybe. But I'm in command on this island, and you'll have to deal with me. Don't you forget it.

CURT: Have you ever seen a quarantine station?

EDGAR: Are you kidding? I knew about them before you were born. A bit of advice: don't put the disinfecting ovens too near the shore.

CURT: I thought the idea was to place them as near the water as possible.

EDGAR: Ha! A lot you know about it. Bacilli thrive on water; it's their element.

CURT: But you need the saltwater and lots of it to wash away the wastes.

EDGAR: Idiot! . . . Anyway, when you get settled in and have a place for yourself, you should bring your children to live with you.

CURT: You don't really think my wife will let them come?

EDGAR: I said "bring." Are you a man or aren't you? It will make a good impression here if people see that you are a caring father and fulfill your responsibilities as head—

CURT: I've never neglected my responsibilities as father!

EDGAR (*raising his voice*): —as head of the family, which you never were!

CURT: I've told you time and again—!

EDGAR (*plunging ahead*): Because the head of the family doesn't leave his children the way you did!

CURT: Charrrge!!

EDGAR: . . . I think of you as a relative, Curt. I'm like an uncle to you, and that makes me feel I have to tell you the truth, even if it hurts. Now don't misunderstand me; it's—

CURT: Aren't you hungry?

EDGAR: As a matter of fact, I am.

CURT: You want something light?

EDGAR: No, something strong.

CURT: That would finish you.

EDGAR: I'm sick; am I supposed to starve, too?

CURT: That's the way it is.

EDGAR: Can't drink; can't smoke. A high price to pay for a little life.

CURT: Death demands its sacrifices; otherwise it doesn't wait.

* * *

Alice enters, carrying some bouquets of flowers and several telegrams and letters.

ALICE: These are for you. (*She throws the flowers on the desk.*)

EDGAR (*flattered; enjoying himself*): For me! . . . Let's see what we've got here!

ALICE: They're only from the sergeants, the corporals, and the regimental band.

EDGAR: Jealousy! Tut, tut, Alice.

ALICE: Don't be ridiculous! Now, if they sent you a prize or a medal—or a laurel wreath—. (*She gestures toward the laurel wreath on the wall.*) —But why talk of things that can never be!

EDGAR: Ha-ha. —Ah, a telegram from the colonel himself—from the Big Brass himself, Alice! Read it, will you, Curt? The colonel is a real gentleman, you know. Even if he is a bit of an idiot. —What's this one? From—? Can't read it. Ah, it's from Judith. . . . Do me a favor and telegraph her and ask her to come with the next boat. —Here's . . . well, well, it's good to have friends who appreciate you. Good people who don't forget a sick man, a man passed over in the promotions; a deserving man, without fear above censure.

ALICE: I don't get it. Are all these nice people congratulating you for being sick?

EDGAR: Bitch!

ALICE (*to Curt*): We once gave a wonderful going-away party here for a doctor. Everybody hated him. So he got his going-away party after he had gone.

EDGAR: Put the bouquets in vases, will you? . . . I'm certainly not credulous, and people—they're just scum. But believe me, this little show of affection is really sincere. By God, it is. No other way of taking it.

ALICE: What an ass!

CURT (*reading one of the telegrams*): Judith says she can't come. The steamship has been delayed because of the storm.

EDGAR: Is that all she says?

CURT: No-o. There's more.

EDGAR: Out with it.

CURT: She says her daddy ought not to drink so much.

EDGAR: Shame on her! One's own child! My dear, sweet daughter. My Judith. My image of heaven.

ALICE: Image of yourself, you mean.

EDGAR: That's life for you. And the best it offers. To hell with it!

ALICE: You're just reaping what you sowed. You taught her to go against me; now she's turned against you. It's enough to make one believe in God!

EDGAR (*to Curt*): What does the colonel have to say?

CURT: He has approved a leave of absence for you, to take effect immediately.

EDGAR: Leave of absence? I never asked for one.

ALICE: I did.

EDGAR: I won't accept it!

ALICE: It's all been arranged and approved.

EDGAR: Not by me, it hasn't!

ALICE: Look at him, Curt! For him regulations don't apply; rules don't exist; directives are not to be obeyed. He's above everything, everybody. The universe was created for his personal enjoyment. The sun and the moon travel the heavens just to carry his praises to the farthest stars. Look at him! A stinking wretch of a captain who never got to be major. A scarecrow who thinks his men are trembling in their boots when they're shaking with laughter. A sniveling coward who is afraid of the dark and believes in barometers. And why all the hullabaloo over this man? For the grand finale when this bag of wind turns into a sack of shit to fertilize the garden! And second-rate shit at that!!

Edgar has been vaingloriously fanning himself with a bouquet of flowers, blithely indifferent to Alice's tirade.

EDGAR: Have you asked Curt to stay for breakfast?

ALICE: No.

EDGAR: All right. Broil two steaks. Chateaubriands will do very nicely. Two of the best.

ALICE: Two?

EDGAR: I'm thinking of having one myself.

ALICE: There are three of us.

EDGAR: You mean, you—? Oh, very well. Three, then.

ALICE: And where am I supposed to get them? Yesterday you invited Curt to supper when there wasn't a crust of bread in the house. He's had to sit up all night, on an empty stomach, without so much as a cup of coffee, because we haven't got any food, and can't buy any because we can't get any more credit!

EDGAR: Oh, dear, she's mad at me because I didn't die—last night.

ALICE: No, I'm mad because you didn't die twenty-five years ago—because you didn't die before I was ever born.

EDGAR (*to Curt*): Listen to her carry on! —This is what happens when you make the marriages, Curt. Wasn't made in heaven, that's certain.

Alice and Curt exchange glances.

EDGAR (*rising and going toward the door*): Enough of this. You can talk all you want. I have my duties to perform. (*Puts on an old-fashioned helmet with crest, buckles his sword around his waist, and puts his army coat on.*)

Alice and Curt try to stop him from going.

EDGAR: Out of my way! (*He leaves.*)

ALICE: Yes, walk out! You always leave when you see you're losing. You turn your back and run away and let your wife cover your retreat. You bigmouth, blowhard bully! All the courage you've ever had came from a bottle of booze. I spit on you!

* * *

CURT: We just sink lower and lower, don't we?

ALICE: You haven't seen anything yet!

CURT: There's worse?

ALICE: Much worse, only I'm ashamed to . . .

CURT: Where is he going now? Where does he find the strength?

ALICE: How the hell do I know?! He's going down to the barracks to thank the NCOs for the flowers. He'll sit down and eat and drink with them. Regale them with gossip about the officers. They've threatened to discharge him for doing that. The officers felt sorry for me and the children. That's all that saved him. And he thinks he stays on because they're afraid of him. The officers' wives, who went out of their way to help us—he hates them and tells lies about them.

CURT: It's funny. I took this job because I thought I might find some peace and quiet by the sea. I didn't know how things were with you.

ALICE: Poor, dear Curt. . . . What am I going to feed you?

CURT: Don't worry about me. I can drop in on the doctor. What about you? Let me do something about it.

ALICE: But don't let him know. He'd kill me.

THE DANCE OF DEATH 611

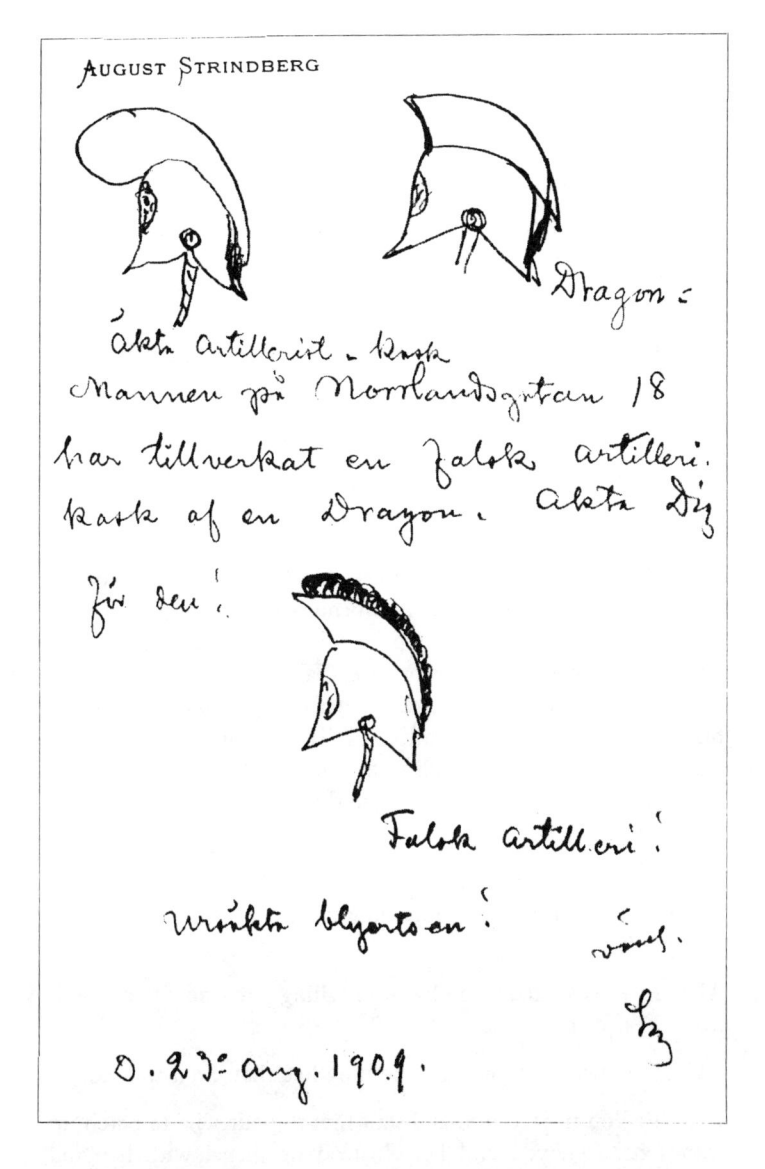

A memo from Strindberg to the director of *The Dance of Death* showing the correct type of old-fashioned helmet worn in the Swedish artillery (upper left). From August Falck, *Fem år med Strindberg [Five Years with Strindberg]* (Stockholm: Wahlström and Widstrand, 1935).

CURT (*looking out the window*): Look at him! He's standing on the platform—right in the wind.

ALICE: I feel sorry for him—for being the way he is.

CURT: I feel sorry for both of you. —What's to be done?

ALICE: I don't know. . . . And we got another big pile of bills. He didn't notice.

CURT: Sometimes it's a blessing not to see.

ALICE (*at the window*): He's opened his coat. He's letting the wind strike his chest. He wants to die.

CURT: I don't believe that. Only a little while ago, when he felt his life slipping away, he clung to me, began to dig into my personal affairs, as if he wanted to creep into my skin and live my life.

ALICE: Of course. He's a vampire. Meddling in other people's business, sucking around others, worming his way into their lives because his own life is an empty shell. And I warn you, Curt, don't ever let him into your private affairs. Never let him get to know your friends. He'll take them from you and make them his. . . . It's like witchcraft. . . . If he got to know your children, they'd soon be calling him uncle. They'd be listening to everything he said, and he'd teach them everything you're dead set against.

CURT: Tell me Alice: at the time of my divorce wasn't he the one who saw to it that my children were taken from me and given to my wife?

ALICE: I guess there's no harm in telling you—now that it's all over. Yes, it was Edgar.

CURT: I always suspected something like that. So it was Edgar.

ALICE: You trusted him and sent him to your wife to patch up things between you and her. Instead he flirted with her and advised her what to do if she wanted to hold on to the children.

CURT: God! . . . God in heaven!

ALICE: Man of a thousand faces, isn't he?

Silence.

CURT: It's strange. Last night—when he thought he might die—he made me promise—that I'd look after his children.

ALICE: You're not thinking of taking your revenge out on my children?

CURT: By keeping my promise? Yes, I'll look after his children.

ALICE: Marvelous! That's the worst revenge you could take. There's nothing he detests so much as magnanimity.

CURT: I would have my revenge. Without taking revenge.

ALICE: I believe in revenge—that's real justice. Nothing pleases me more than seeing a bad man get his punishment.

CURT: Is that all life has taught you?

ALICE: It's the ultimate lesson. If I ever forgave my enemy or loved him, I'd hate myself for being a hypocrite.

CURT: Alice, sometimes it's best to bite your tongue or look the other way. It's called making allowances. We all need it.

ALICE: I don't. I've got nothing to hide, and I've always played fair and square.

CURT: That's a large claim.

ALICE: Not large enough. You don't know what I've suffered undeservedly for the sake of this man, whom I've never loved—

CURT: Why did you marry him?

ALICE: Who knows? . . . Because he took me. Because he seduced me. I don't know. . . . I wanted some sort of social position.

CURT: So you left the theater.

ALICE: The theater—ha!—too bohemian. I wanted respectability. But he cheated me. He pictured a good life for me, a lovely home. What did I get? A pile of unpaid bills. The only gold I saw was the braid on his uniform. And that wasn't gold either. He cheated me.

CURT: Come on, Alice! It's only natural for a young man to have high hopes for the future. If things didn't work out the way he dreamed, you can't blame him. I've disappointed people in the same way, but I don't think of myself as a cheat. —What are you looking at out there?

ALICE: Looking to see if he has fallen in.

CURT: He hasn't?!

ALICE: No, unfortunately. You see: cheated again!

CURT: I'm going to the doctor and the lawyer.

Alice sits down by the window.

ALICE: You do that, Curt. I'll sit here and wait. God knows, I'm good at that.

INTERMISSION

[3]

Same set. Daylight. The Sentry is on duty outside, as before, pacing back and forth. Alice is now seated in the armchair to the right. Her hair is gray.

Curt knocks and enters from the left.

CURT: Hello, Alice.

ALICE: Hello, dear Curt. Sit down.

Curt sits in the armchair to the left.

CURT: The steamer is at the dock now.

ALICE: I know what that means if *he's* on board.

CURT: He is. I could see his helmet shining. . . . What's he been up to in town?

ALICE: That's easy to figure out. He wore his dress uniform. That means he called on the colonel. He put on his white gloves. That means he's been paying social calls.

CURT: Didn't you notice yesterday how quiet he had become? Since he stopped drinking, he's become another person—calm, reserved, considerate.

ALICE: Don't be taken in by that. Sober, he would have been a holy terror. It's lucky for the human race that he took to the bottle. Whiskey made him ridiculous and harmless.

CURT: That's a new one. I hadn't realized that bottled spirits could be moral spirits. Surely you've seen the change in him. After that brush with death he's acquired a kind of dignity. He seems elevated somehow, uplifted. Maybe when he began to have thoughts about immortality, he got a new slant on life, too.

ALICE: Don't kid yourself. He's up to no good. And don't you believe a word he says. He lies like the devil, cooks up plots behind your back—

CURT (*staring at her*): Alice. You look so different. These two nights have made your hair turn gray.

ALICE: No, dear boy. I've been gray a long time. But there's no point in dyeing my hair when my husband is half dead. . . . Twenty-five years in a fortress! —Do you know that these rooms used to be the prison in the old times?

CURT: Prison? Yes, you can almost tell by the walls.

ALICE: And by my skin. Even the children got prison pallor here.

CURT: It's hard to imagine small children laughing and playing within these walls.

ALICE: There wasn't much laughter. And the two that died— they didn't get enough sun.

CURT: What's next, do you suppose?

ALICE: The crucial battle between him and the two of us. I recognized that baleful glance, that flash in his eye, when you read him the telegram from Judith. Of course the lightning was intended to strike her, but, as you know, she lives in a charmed circle. So the lightning struck you.

CURT: And just what does he intend to do with me?

ALICE: Hard to say. He has a genius for nosing out other people's secrets. Didn't you see how all day yesterday he kept worming his way into your quarantine business, leeched on to your life, gobbled up your children. He's a cannibal, a bloodsucker. I know him for what he is. There's nothing left of his own life.

CURT: I see what you mean. He's already crossed over to the other side. His face is phosphorescent, as if he were dissolving. His eyes glimmer like will-o'-wisps over swamps and graves. —I can hear him; he's coming. —Did it ever occur to you that he might be jealous?

ALICE: Forget it! He's too conceited. "Show me the man I should be jealous of!" His very words.

CURT: He's marvelous! Even his failings have merit. —Should I rise and greet him or just sit here?

ALICE: Be rude—otherwise he'll think you're putting on an act. And when he starts telling his stories, go along with him, pretend to believe him. I can translate his lies into the truth. I've got this little dictionary up here. . . . God, something awful is about to happen. I don't know what. —And, Curt! don't lose control. The only advantage I've had over him in all my battles was that I was always cold sober and never lost my head. He always lost his in booze. Ready?

* * *

Edgar enters from the left, wearing his dress uniform, helmet, overcoat, white gloves. He is calm and dignified but looks pale and hollow-eyed. He walks unsteadily across the room, keeping his helmet and coat on, and sits down at the right, far from Curt and Alice. During the following dialogue he keeps his officer's sword between his knees.

EDGAR: Good day! Forgive me for sitting down like this. I'm a little tired.

CURT *and* ALICE (*at the same time*): Hello, Edgar! —Welcome back!

ALICE: How are you feeling?

EDGAR: Fine, fine. A little tired, that's all.

ALICE: What news from the big city?

EDGAR: Not much. It's short but sweet. Stopped in to see the doctor, and he tells me it's nothing serious. I can live for twenty years more, if I take care of myself.

ALICE (*to Curt, sotto voce*): He made that up. (*To Edgar.*) How wonderful, darling!

EDGAR: Yes, isn't it.

>   *Silence, during which Edgar looks at Alice and Curt as if begging them to speak.*
>
>   *Curt is about to say something, but Alice stops him.*

ALICE (*To Curt, sotto voce*): Don't say anything! Let him be the first. He'll show his hand.

EDGAR (*to Alice*): I'm sorry; I didn't hear.

ALICE: I didn't say anything.

EDGAR (*speaking slowly*): Ahem, Curt . . . you know I . . .

ALICE (*to Curt*): You see! He's playing his first card.

EDGAR: . . . you know . . . that I was in town. Yes, of course you know.

>   *Curt nods.*

EDGAR: Yes, in town. And I met a few people. Talked a bit. One was a young cadet—new recruit—(*Drawing it out.*) in . . . the . . . artillery.

>   *Pause. Curt senses trouble.*

And since we don't have many cadets—out here, I mean—I struck a bargain with the colonel and . . . arranged that he—the cadet . . . should . . . be transferred out here. This should come as very good news—especially to you, since the lad in question is—I am happy to inform you—your son!

ALICE (*to Curt*): What did I tell you! A vampire!

CURT: Under ordinary circumstances a father might be pleased by this news of his son. But in my situation I find it extremely painful.

EDGAR: You're upset! I don't understand.

CURT: There's nothing to understand! Just forget about my son!

EDGAR: Well, well, you're serious. How very awkward! You see, the young man has already been ordered to report here, and as of this moment he is under my command.

CURT: Then I shall make him ask for a transfer to another outfit.

EDGAR: You can't. You have no rights over him.

CURT: No rights? I'm his father!

EDGAR: Yes. But the court assigned the rights over him to his mother!

CURT: Then his mother will tell him what to do! And I'll tell her!

EDGAR: That really won't be necessary.

CURT: Good!

EDGAR: Because I've already spoken to her. —It's all settled, you see. (*He smacks his lips contentedly.*)

Curt starts to rise from his chair but falls back.

ALICE (*to Curt*): Does that man deserve to live?

CURT: He *is* a cannibal!

EDGAR: Well, we can put paid to that. (*Peering at Alice and Curt.*) Did you say something?

ALICE: No! Are you hard of hearing?

EDGAR: A little. Why don't you move over here, Alice, so that I can talk just to you?

ALICE: That isn't necessary. Having a witness might be good for both parties.

EDGAR: You may be right. A witness always comes in handy. —Now, have you prepared the will?

Alice hands him a document.

ALICE: It's the standard form. The judge advocate himself drew it up.

EDGAR: With your best interests in mind. (*He reads here and there in the document.*) Good. . . . Good. . . . Good. (*He carefully and deliberately tears it into long strips, which he throws on the floor.*) So much for that! Another matter settled. (*He smacks his lips contentedly.*)

ALICE (*to Curt*): Do you believe this?

CURT: He isn't human!

EDGAR: I have something else to say to you, Alice.

ALICE (*on edge*): Go ahead.

EDGAR (*still speaking calmly*): By reason of your frequently expressed wish to put an end to this unhappy marriage, and by reason of the lack of love you have shown toward your husband and children—and by reason of the debts you have incurred through careless management of the household, I have—only now while I was in the city—applied to the court baron for a divorce.

ALICE: Really? And your reasons?

EDGAR (*still speaking slowly and deliberately*): I just gave them. Apart from those, there are personal ones. Having recently learned that I might live for another twenty years, I have considered the desirability of dissolving this unhappy union and forming a better one. With that in mind, I intend to take as my wife a woman who knows that her husband is to be treated with respect and who will bring with her into the home youth, charm, and—what shall I say?—a little beauty.

Alice takes off her wedding ring and throws it at Edgar.

ALICE: Take it!

Edgar picks up the ring and puts it in his vest pocket.

EDGAR: She threw away her wedding ring. Curt, you're the witness. Please take note.

ALICE (*rising, barely able to control her voice*): And you intend to toss me out and bring another woman into my house?

Edgar smacks his lips and nods.

ALICE: All right! No holds barred. Curt, I'm telling you, as my cousin, that this man is guilty of having attempted to murder me!

CURT: Murder you!

ALICE: Yes! He pushed me into the ocean.

EDGAR: No witnesses!

ALICE: You lie! Judith saw the whole thing!

EDGAR: So what!

ALICE: She can testify to what I said.

EDGAR: No, she cannot! Because she will say that she didn't see anything!

ALICE: You've taught that poor child to lie!

EDGAR: Why would I waste my time? You had already taught her.

ALICE: You've spoken to Judith?

Edgar smacks his lips, and nods.

ALICE: Oh, my God, my God!

EDGAR: The fortress surrenders, the enemy capitulates. The victor grants the vanquished freedom to withdraw and gives them ten minutes notice. (*He puts his watch on the table.*) Ten minutes. According to the timepiece on the table. (*As he stands by the table, he clutches at his heart.*)

ALICE (*moving to his side and holding his arm*): What is it?

EDGAR: I don't know.

ALICE: Can I get you something? Something to drink?

EDGAR: Whiskey? No, I don't want to die. You—! (*He straightens up and shrugs off Alice's hand.*) Don't touch me! —Ten minutes! Or I level the fortress. (*He draws his sword from its scabbard.*) Ten minutes! (*He exits at the rear, holding his sword high.*)

* * *

CURT: I don't believe he's human.

ALICE: He isn't. He's a demon.

CURT: What does he want with my boy?

ALICE: He wants to hold him hostage so he can control you. He wants to isolate you, cut you off from the officers, the doctor, everybody important. . . . Do you know what the people around here call this island? "Little Hell."

CURT: It fits. . . . You know, Alice, you're the first woman I ever felt sorry for. All the others I felt got what they deserved.

ALICE: Don't leave me now, Curt. Don't abandon me. He'll hit me. . . . He's hit me for twenty-five years. Sometimes in the presence of the children. . . . He pushed me into the ocean.

CURT: Yes, hearing that turned me absolutely against him. I came here without any malice in my heart, having put out of my mind all his humiliating treatment of me, his spite. I even forgave him when I learned from you that he had helped my wife get the children. After all, he was sick, dying. But now, when he wants to take my son from me, he's got to go. It's either him or me.

ALICE: Good! No surrender! Blow the fortress sky high. Blow him to smithereens!—even if we go up with it. I've got the dynamite that will do the job.

CURT: I had no evil thoughts when I came here. At first I wanted to run away when I felt how your hatred for him was infecting me. But now I feel called upon to hate this man as I hate evil itself. . . . What do you suggest?

ALICE: I've learned the strategy from the master himself. First, drum up all his enemies; form a league against him.

CURT: I can't get over it! He tracked down my wife just for this. Why didn't the two of them meet thirty years ago? What a pair they would have made. Put the two of them in the ring together and the earth would shake.

ALICE: Well, now they have met—the two soulmates! And now they must be parted. I think I know how to get at him; I've had my suspicions.

CURT: Who is his most dedicated enemy on this island?

ALICE: The supply officer.

CURT: A man to be trusted?

ALICE: Absolutely. And he knows what I—. Well, we both know. . . . He knows what the staff sergeant and Edgar have been up to.

CURT: Up to? Up to what?

ALICE: Lining their own pockets.

CURT: Embezzlement? Oh, no. Leave me out of that. I want nothing to do with it.

ALICE (*laughs sarcastically*): What's the matter? Can't strike the enemy?

CURT: I could at one time. Not now.

ALICE: Why not?

CURT: Because I found out . . . that justice is done—eventually.

ALICE: Have fun while you wait! Wait while your son is taken from you. Wait like I've had to wait. Look at my gray hair. . . . Go ahead, feel it. At least it's thick. . . . He's going to get married again, and I'll be free—to do the same. I'm free. Free! And in ten minutes he'll be sitting down there in a prison cell, down there in the clink—(*She stamps on the floor.*)—down there in the pokey—and I'll dance on his head. I'll dance the Boyar dance. (*Starts to dance, hands on hips, and laughs wildly.*) And hallelujah! I'll play the piano! And God! will he hear it! (*Hammers the piano keys.*) Ho, ho! The prison tower will open wide its gates and the guard with his drawn sword will no longer guard me but him! But him! But him! But'im, but'im, but'im!! (*She imitates the Sentry and makes the sound of a marching band.*) Barum, barum, barum-barum, barum! But him! But him! But'im, but'im, but'im!!

Curt has been staring at her, fascinated and aroused.

CURT: Alice, Alice! You devil!

Alice climbs on a chair and takes down the laurel wreaths.

ALICE: These go with me as my army withdraws. The laurel wreaths of victory! (*Straightening the ribbons on the wreaths.*) And streamers in the air! A little dusty, but forever green. Like me! —I'm not old, am I, Curt?

CURT (*passionately, his eyes flashing*): You *are* a devil!

ALICE: Of course! This is "Little Hell!" —I'm going to fix my hair—(*She undoes her hair and lets it fall about her shoulders.*)—change my dress—in two minutes—we go to the supply officer—two minutes—and then—Bang!—the fortress blows sky high!

CURT (*aroused*): A devil! A devil!

ALICE: You always said so, even when we were children. Remember when we were kids, and we played at getting married? Ha-ha! You were so shy—

CURT (*reproachfully*): Alice!

ALICE: Oh, but you were. It made you irresistible. Bold women like bashful men, that's what they say. And shy men like coarse women. You sure liked me a little then. Didn't you?

CURT: My head's spinning. I don't know where I am.

ALICE: Here, with an actress. An actress. No inhibitions, no prejudices—but a woman all the same—all woman. . . . And now I'm free, free, free! —Turn around. I'm going to change my blouse.

She unbuttons her blouse. Curt rushes to her, embraces her, lifts her high. Kisses her on her neck until she screams. Then he casts her down onto the chaise lounge and runs out the door at left.

[4]

Same set. Evening. Through the windows and glass doors at the rear the Sentry can still be seen, pacing back and forth as before. The laurel wreaths are draped over the arm of one of the chairs. The ceiling lamp is lit.

Soft music covers the break between scenes, continues after the rise of the curtain until Alice's entrance.

Edgar, dressed in his worn fatigue uniform, wearing his riding boots, looking pale and hollow-eyed, his hair streaked with gray, is sitting at the writing desk, playing solitaire. He has his glasses on.

As he moves and shifts the cards, he occasionally gives a slight start, looks up, and listens anxiously.

The solitaire apparently defeats him; he becomes impatient and gathers the cards together. Goes to the window at left, opens it, and throws out the deck of cards. The window remains open, shaking on its hinges.

He goes to the cupboard, opens it, and is frightened by the noise of the window. Looks round to see what is causing it. Takes from the cupboard three dark, square-shaped whiskey decanters. Gives them a long, steady look—and throws them out the window. Takes out several boxes of cigars, sticks his nose in one of them—and throws them all out the window.

Next he removes his glasses, wipes them, and tries looking through them. Throws them out the window. Stumbles his way back through the furniture as if he had trouble seeing, goes to the secretary, and lights the six candles in the candelabrum. Catches sight of the laurel wreaths; picks them up and heads for the window. Changes his mind and goes to the piano. Takes the runner from the top of the piano and carefully wraps the wreaths in the runner. Using common pins he finds on the desk, he fastens the corners of the runner, and places the wreaths on a chair. Walks to the piano and strikes the keys with his fist. Closes the cover, locks it with the little key, and throws the key out the window. Then he lights the candles on the piano. Goes to the étagère, picks up the portrait photo of Alice, studies it, tears it to pieces, and throws the pieces on the floor. Again the window suddenly shakes on its hinges, frightening Edgar.

After he has calmed himself, he takes the pictures of his son and daughter, kisses them quickly, and puts them in his breast pocket. The other pictures he sweeps off the étagère with a stroke of his arm, and kicks them into a pile with his boots.

He goes to the writing table, slumps down in a chair, and clutches his chest. Lights the candles on the desk. Sighs and stares ahead as if seeing unpleasant visions.

He stands up and walks to the secretary, opens the leaf, and takes from one of the compartments a packet of letters tied with a blue ribbon. Throws the packet into the fire in the tile stove. Closes the secretary.

The telegraph sounder clicks once — once only — and is silent. Edgar is deathly frightened. Stands immobile, hand at heart, listening. When there is no further sound from the telegraph, he listens in the direction of the door at the left. Walks over to it, opens it, steps out, and returns a moment later with a cat in his arms. He strokes its back, crosses the room, and exits by the door at the right.

The soft music ceases.

[5]

Alice enters through the glass doors at the rear. She is dressed in outdoor clothes, hat, gloves. Her hair is dark again. Seeing all the candles lit, she stops and looks around in amazement.

Curt enters from the left, tense and nervous.

ALICE: It looks like Christmas Eve.

CURT: Now what?

Alice stretches out her hand for Curt to kiss.

ALICE: Time to thank me.

Curt reluctantly kisses her hand.

ALICE: Six witnesses. Four of them absolutely unshakable. They've made their depositions, and we'll get the news here on the telegraph—smack in the middle of the fortress.

CURT: Really?

ALICE: "Really?" Is that all you can say? You might thank me.

CURT: Why has he lit all these candles?

ALICE: Because he's afraid of the dark, I told you. —Look at that telegraph key. Looks like the handle of a coffee grinder. I'll grind, I'll grind, and the beans will crack like broken teeth being pulled.

CURT: What's he been doing? Look at the room!

ALICE: I'll bet he was thinking about moving. He'll move, all right. Downstairs! (*Taps the floor with her foot.*)

CURT: Steady, Alice! I think the whole thing stinks. We were friends when we were young, and he was often good to me when I was having a rough time of it. I feel sorry for him.

ALICE: And not for me? I never hurt anybody, but for the sake of that monster I had to sacrifice my career!

CURT: What career? When were you a blazing star?

ALICE (*furious*): What the hell are you saying? Do you know who I am? What I've been?

CURT: Easy, take it easy.

ALICE: Just like him—already!

CURT: Already?

> *Alice runs to Curt, hangs on his neck, and kisses him. He takes her arms, pulls them back, and bites her throat. She cries out.*

ALICE: You're biting me!

CURT (*beside himself*): Yes, I want to bite your neck, suck your blood like a panther! There's a wild animal in me and you've let him loose. For years I tried to slay it by living like a monk. I came here thinking I was a bit better than you and Edgar. I'm not. Now I'm the worst. The moment I saw you, really saw you, naked and terrible, I changed. I felt the power of what's evil. What's ugly became beautiful, and what's good grew soft and weak. Come here, Alice. I'm going to suffocate you with my lips and mouth.

> *He kisses her long and passionately. When they separate, she holds out her left hand for him to see.*

ALICE: There's the mark left by the chain that you broke. I was a slave and now I'm free.

CURT: But I'm going to capture you and tie you up.

ALICE: You?

CURT: Yes, me!

ALICE: For a while there I thought you were . . .

CURT: A saint?

ALICE: Well, you spoke about the Fall.

CURT: Did I?

ALICE: I thought you were going to give me a sermon.

CURT: A sermon! We'll be in town within an hour—in our hotel room. I'll give you a sermon!

ALICE: I want to go to the theater tonight. I want to be seen in public. Edgar is the one who suffers the humiliation if I walk out on him, don't you see?

CURT: I see, all right. Prison isn't enough: you want more.

ALICE: That's right! It's not enough. There's got to be shame and humiliation also.

CURT: Crazy world! You're the one who behaves shamefully, and he's the one who has to bear the shame.

ALICE: It is a stupid world, but I didn't make it.

CURT: These prison walls must have absorbed all the crimes of the world. They reek of them. All you have to do is breathe and you get them in your system. Look at you: all you're thinking about is the theater and supper afterward, while I was thinking about my son.

ALICE (*flicking her glove at his mouth*): You fake! Don't give me that crap!

> *Curt raises his hand, about to slap her face. Alice shies back.*

ALICE: Down, boy, down!

CURT: I'm sorry.

ALICE: On your knees!

> *Curt kneels.*

On your face!

> *Curt puts his forehead to the floor.*

Kiss my foot.

> *Curt kisses her shoe.*

And don't you ever dare do that again! —Rise!

> *Curt stands up.*

CURT: God, what's happened to me? Where the hell am I?

ALICE: You know where you are!

CURT (*looking around in horror*): I almost believe that . . . I am in hell!

* * *

> *Edgar enters from the right, looking wretched, supporting himself with a cane.*

EDGAR: Could I talk to Curt? —Alone.

ALICE: What about? Surrendering the fortress?

EDGAR (*sitting down at the worktable*): Curt, would you mind sitting down with me for a minute? Alice, maybe you could give us a few moments—in peace.

ALICE: Now what are you up to? Changing your strategy? (*To Curt.*) Go ahead; sit down.

> *Curt sits down, reluctantly.*

ALICE: Out of the mouths of babes—and old men! —If a telegraph message comes through, give a call.

> *Alice exits to the left.*

* * *

EDGAR (*after a pause, speaks in a very serious tone of voice*): Does it make any sense? An existence like mine—like ours?

CURT: No, no more than mine does.

EDGAR: Then what's the meaning of the whole mess?

CURT: In my better moments I came to believe that the meaning was not to know the meaning, and, while not knowing, going along with it, bending with it.

EDGAR: Bend? Without a fixed point outside myself to hold on to, I can't bend. I'd fall.

CURT: Quite right. But you use mathematics when you aim

your guns. You should be able to find the unknown point when you have several knowns.

EDGAR: I have sought, but—I haven't found.

CURT: You've miscalculated. Try again.

EDGAR: I shall. —Tell me, Curt: where did you acquire your fund of patience and resignation?

CURT: Whatever I had, it's all used up by now. Don't overestimate me.

EDGAR: I suppose you have noticed that for me the art of living has consisted in canceling out what's happened. I mean, crossing out and moving on. Long ago I got myself a big sack. I kept stuffing all my humiliations and frustrations in it, one after the other, and when it was full, I threw it into the sea. . . . I don't believe anybody has suffered so many humiliations as I have. But when I crossed them out and moved past them, they ceased to exist.

CURT: Yes, I have noticed how you make your own world.

EDGAR: How do you think I could have gone on living? How could I have borne it? (*He clutches at his heart.*)

CURT: Are you all right?

EDGAR: No, I'm poorly, poorly. (*Pause.*) The trouble is—there comes a moment when the ability to make my own world, as you put it, vanishes. And in place of that world is reality—naked, ugly reality. Awful! (*His face sags, and he talks like an old man, half-sobbing.*) You see, Curt, my dearest friend—. (*Gets control of himself and speaks in his normal voice.*) Forgive me. Just now when I was in town and saw my doctor—(*With tears in his voice again.*) he said I was a broken man—(*With his normal voice.*) and that I didn't have long to live.

CURT: Is *that* what he said?

EDGAR: That's what he said.

CURT: Then it wasn't true!

EDGAR: What wasn't? —Oh! —No, it wasn't true.

Pause.

CURT: And the rest of it? Wasn't that true either?

EDGAR: What, my dear friend, wasn't true?

CURT: That my son was ordered to report here as cadet.

EDGAR: I never heard that.

CURT: You know, Edgar, your talent for crossing out what you've done is fantastic!

EDGAR: Curt, dear fellow, I don't know what you're talking about.

CURT: You're hopeless, Edgar.

EDGAR: Yes, I guess there isn't much hope left for me.

CURT: Come to think of it, perhaps you haven't tried to shame your dear wife publicly—by applying for a divorce, for instance?

EDGAR: Divorce! Where did you hear that?

CURT (*standing up*): All right, Edgar. Admit it: you've been lying.

EDGAR: Such harsh words—and from my best friend. We all need to make allowances.

CURT: You've come to realize that, have you?

EDGAR (*firmly, with a strong voice*): Yes, I've come to realize that. . . . That's why I ask your forgiveness, Curt. For everything.

CURT: Well, that's frank enough, and straightforward. But there's nothing for me to forgive, Edgar. And I'm not the man you think I am. Not anymore. Certainly not the man to hear your confessions.

EDGAR (*firmly, without whining*): Life played such awful tricks on me. Always setting me back, ever since childhood. And when people were cruel, I got to be cruel also.

> *Curt paces the floor and glances at the telegraph apparatus.*

EDGAR: What are you looking at?

CURT: Can you shut that thing off?

EDGAR: No, not very likely.

CURT (*more and more anxious*): What sort of fellow is this staff sergeant of yours? This Eastberg?

EDGAR: Oh, a good, decent fellow. A little too much interested in money, of course.

CURT: And what about the supply officer?

EDGAR: He and I are sworn enemies; but I can't honestly say he's a bad sort.

> *Curt is looking out the window. In the distance a lantern can be seen, moving and swinging.*

CURT: What are they doing with a lantern out there near the gun battery?

EDGAR: A lantern?

CURT: And some soldiers moving around.

EDGAR: Must be the "bloodhounds." That's what we call them.

CURT: "Bloodhounds"?

EDGAR: The military police. Somebody's got himself in trouble, and they've come to put him in the brig.

CURT: Oh?!

> *Pause.*

EDGAR: Tell me, Curt, now that you've gotten to know her better—what do you think of Alice?

CURT: Hard to say. . . . I guess I really don't understand people at all. She's as much a mystery to me as you are—or as I am, for that matter. I've reached that point in life when my wisdom has crystallized and I can say: I don't know anything; I don't understand anything. . . . However, when something happens, I'm still curious to know why it happened. . . . Why did you push her into the ocean?

EDGAR: I don't know. It just seemed like the thing to do. She was standing on the dock, and it struck me she had to go in.

CURT: No regrets?

EDGAR: None.

CURT: Strange.

EDGAR: Yes, it is. So strange that I don't actually believe I ever did such a thing.

CURT: You must have known that she would get her revenge, sooner or later.

EDGAR: That she has, with a lot left over. For her, that was the thing to do.

CURT: Talk about resignation! What has happened to make you, all of a sudden, so cynical, so resigned?

EDGAR: Since I saw death face-to-face, I've had a different slant on life. . . . Tell me, Curt, if you had to judge between Alice and me, who would you say was right?

CURT: Neither. I have infinite sympathy for both of you. —Maybe a little more for you.

EDGAR: Give me your hand, Curt.

> *Curt extends his right hand and puts his left hand on Edgar's shoulder.*

CURT: Old friend!

* * *

> *Alice enters from the left, carrying a parasol.*

ALICE: Well, well! The old, trusty friends. Isn't that touching? —Did the telegram arrive?

CURT (*coldly*): No.

ALICE: I don't like delays. They make me impatient, and when I get impatient, I give things a push. —Watch this, Curt! I'm going to give him the *coup de grâce*. I'm going to finish him off.

Watch him fall! —First I load the rifle, like this. —I know the manual by heart—that famous manual on hand weapons that didn't even sell five thousand copies. Then I take aim. . . . (*She aims the parasol at Edgar.*) Fire!! (*She pops open the umbrella.*) How's the new wife, Edgar? The young, the beautiful, the nonexistent wife. —You don't know how she feels? What a pity! But I know how my lover feels.

> *She puts her arms around Curt's neck and kisses him. He shoves her away.*

ALICE: Oh, he feels so good. He's just a little shy—still! —You stupid wretch! I never loved you! You were too proud to be jealous. Too blind. You never saw how I pulled the wool over your eyes.

> *Edgar unsheathes his sword and goes after her, swinging his sword but hitting only the furniture.*

ALICE: Help! Help!!

> *Curt does not move.*
> *Edgar falls to the floor, sword in hand.*

EDGAR: Judith! Avenge me, Judith!!

ALICE: Hurray, he's dead! He's dead!

> *Curt sidles up to the rear doors.*
> *Edgar gets to his feet.*

EDGAR: Not—quite—yet! (*He sheathes his sword and goes to sit in the armchair near the worktable.*) Judith! Judith!

> *Alice moves up to Curt.*

ALICE: I'm leaving! With you.

> *Curt repulses her with such force that she falls to her knees.*

CURT: Go to hell! Go back to the abyss you came from! —God! I hope I never see you again! (*He is at the door.*)

EDGAR: Don't leave me, Curt! She'll kill me!

ALICE: Curt, don't abandon me like this! Don't abandon us!

CURT: Goodbye. (*He leaves.*)

* * *

ALICE (*doing a complete about-face*): That sneaky bastard! You call that a friend?!

EDGAR (*gently*): Forgive me, Alice. And come over here. Come quickly!

ALICE (*going to him*): The biggest ninny and worst hypocrite I ever did see! You know, Edgar, at least you're a man.

EDGAR: Alice, listen to me now. . . . I haven't long to live.

ALICE: Oh?

EDGAR: The doctor told me.

ALICE: You mean—everything else was a lie too?

EDGAR: Yes.

ALICE (*frantic*): God! What have I done?

EDGAR: No matter. Whatever it was, it can be put right.

ALICE: Not this! It can never be put right!

EDGAR: Yes, everything can. Just cross it out and move on.

ALICE: No. The telegram! The telegram!

EDGAR: What telegram?

ALICE (*on her knees before Edgar*): We must be damned! Why did this have to happen? I've blown myself sky-high—blown *us* to bits. —Why did you make up those stories? Why did Curt have to come and tempt me? We're lost! —Oh, Edgar, you're a great-souled, generous man. You can forgive, even what's unforgivable.

EDGAR: What's this that can't be forgiven? What haven't I forgiven you?

ALICE: Oh, you're right, Edgar, you're right. But this can never be put right.

EDGAR: I can't even guess what it might be—and I know how fiendish you can be.

ALICE: Oh, if I ever get out of this! If I ever get out of this, Edgar, how I'll care for you, and love you. Oh, Edgar, I'd love you so much!

EDGAR: My ears must be deceiving me. What's going on?

ALICE: No one can help us, can they? No one.

EDGAR: Who do you have in mind?

ALICE (*looking him in the eyes*): I don't know. . . . What will happen to the children?

EDGAR: Have you brought shame and disgrace on them?

ALICE: I can't have! Not me! . . . They'll have to drop out of school. . . . And when they go out into the world, they'll be as lonely as we are, and just as mean. —You never did run into Judith, it's obvious.

EDGAR: No. Cross it out!

The telegraph ticker begins clicking. Alice jumps up.

ALICE (*crying out*): That's it! The end! It's all over. (*To Edgar.*) Don't listen to it!

EDGAR (*calmly*): I won't listen, my darling. Calm yourself.

Alice is by the telegraph apparatus. She stands on tiptoe to look out the window.

ALICE: Don't listen! Don't listen!

EDGAR (*putting his hands over his ears*): I'm not listening, Lisa. Lisa, my little angel, I'm not listening.

Alice kneels with upstretched arms.

ALICE: Oh, God, help us! The "bloodhounds," the hounds of heaven. (*Sobbing violently.*) God in heaven!

> *Her lips move in a silent prayer. The telegraph recorder goes on rapping for a while longer, and a long ticker tape emerges from it. Then all is quiet.*
>
> *Alice gets up, tears off the paper ribbon, and reads it to herself. Then she casts a glance upwards, sighs, and walks over to Edgar. She kisses him on the forehead.*

ALICE: It's over. . . . It was nothing. (*She sits down in the other armchair and cries unrestrainedly into her handkerchief.*)

EDGAR: What are you hiding?

ALICE: Don't ask. Anyway, it's over now.

EDGAR: As you wish, sweetheart.

ALICE: You wouldn't have talked to me like that three days ago. What's come over you?

EDGAR: A change, my darling. When I fell the first time, I went a bit over the other side of the grave. What I saw there I've forgotten, but it left an indelible impression.

ALICE: Of what?

EDGAR: Of hope. The hope of something better.

ALICE: Better?

EDGAR: Yes. That this life was real, was life itself—I've never really believed that. This life is death. Or something even worse.

ALICE: And we are—

EDGAR: We must have been given the job of torturers—torturing each other. So it seems.

ALICE: Have we tortured each other enough?

EDGAR: Yes. I'm inclined to think so. Maybe overdid it a bit: look at the place! (*He looks around the room.*) Isn't it time we tidied things up? And cleaned up this mess?

ALICE (*getting up*): If you think it's possible.

EDGAR (*walks around the room, surveying the damage*): Well, not in one day. Not a chance.

ALICE: Two days, perhaps? Or many days.

EDGAR: Let's hope so. (*Pause. Edgar sits down again.*) So—you didn't get away, did you? Not this time. And you didn't catch me, did you?

> *Alice stands aghast.*

Yes, yes, I know you tried to get me locked up. But—I cross it out! —Well, it's not the worst thing you've tried to do.

> *Alice is still speechless.*

Furthermore, I was never involved in any embezzlement!

ALICE: And so now I'm supposed to be your nurse?

EDGAR: If you want.

ALICE: What else should I do with myself?

EDGAR: I don't know.

ALICE (*sits down apathetically. Looks crushed*): This must be the everlasting fire. Is there no end?

EDGAR: There is, if we have patience. Maybe when death comes, life begins.

ALICE: Would it were so!

> *Pause.*

EDGAR: So you think Curt was a fake and a hypocrite?

ALICE: Of course I do.

EDGAR: I don't believe it. The trouble is that anyone who comes near us becomes like us. Then off they go. Curt was weak, and we were too strong for him. (*Pause.*) Still, it's all so boring nowadays. There was a time when men fought with their bare fists; now they only shake them at each other. . . . Tell you what I do believe, though. In three months I'm pretty certain that you and I will be giving a party. Our silver anniversary. With cousin Curt giving you away – again, like he did twenty-five years ago. And the supply officer will be toastmaster, making pretty speeches, and my staff sergeant will lead the singing: "For they are jolly good fellows. . . . " And if I know my man, the colonel will pop up too. – Uninvited.

Alice laughs.

You think that's funny? What about Adolf's silver anniversary? You know, Adolf in the rangers. His bride of twenty-five years had to wear her wedding ring on this finger – (*He points to his right hand.*) – because Adolf in one of his tender moments had chopped off her left ring finger with his machete.

Alice puts her handkerchief to her mouth to suppress a giggle.

EDGAR: I know. It's enough to make you cry. – Ah, ha, you're laughing. Well, my precious, sometimes we laugh, sometimes we cry. I don't know which is right. . . . I read in the paper the other day about a man. Been divorced seven times. Consequently married seven times. Finally ran away – ninety-eight years old – and remarried his first wife! If that isn't love, what is? . . . Whether life is a serious business or a big joke is something I've never been able to figure out. As jokes go, it's rather sick. Better to take it seriously. Makes it more peaceful and pleasant. . . . However, just when you've made up your mind to be serious, along comes somebody who puts you on. Like Curt. . . . Well, what do you say? A party for our silver anniversary?

Alice is silent.

Oh, come on! Say yes. Sure, they'll laugh at us, but what the hell! We'll laugh with them. Or be very solemn. Whatever we feel like.

ALICE: All right. Why not?

EDGAR (*seriously*): Right. A silver wedding anniversary. (*He stands up.*) Cross out and move on. So—let's move on.

Introduction to *A Dream Play*

The film critic for a leading American newspaper recently said of *A Dream Play* that "it has a cast of fifty, requires sets that are virtually unrealizable, has no coherent story line, and is obsessed with the spectacle of human suffering during the dream that is Life."*

This "unrealizable" play is one of Strindberg's more frequently produced works in Sweden and has had a number of important productions in other European countries. It has been given Reinhardtian treatment with elaborate sets and performed as Grotowskian "poor theatre." It has been staged with projections incorporated in the design, and it has been done with no sets at all — on the radio. Strindberg's own preference was for simple staging. He wanted to "de-materialize" the stage.** In a dream nothing should seem substantial; the sets should be made out of baseless fabric and the characters of the stuff that dreams are made on.

As for actors, *A Dream Play* has been performed with both small casts and huge casts. Significantly, Strindberg did not provide a list of characters. In his preliminary note, he speaks of the characters as dissolving and coalescing, as they do in dreams. The doubling of parts is not an economic desideratum in this play; it is essential to its method. In the ideal production, there would be not fifty actors but two: one man, one woman, who would fragment themselves.

The basis of the critic's mistaken notions about *A Dream Play* is, I suppose, the lack of a "coherent story line." Drama has

* Vincent Canby, *The New York Times*, 21 June 1984.
** See *Strindberg och teater*, ed. August Falck (Stockholm, 1918). German translation of relevant sections in *August Strindberg über Drama und Theater*, ed. Marianne Kesting and Verner Arpe. See also G. M. Bergman, "Strindberg and the Intima Teatern" in *Theatre Research/Recherches Théâtrales*, vol. 9, no. 1 (1967), 14–47.

always meant story and plot. Plot was the most important element in Aristotle's formulation, and character the second most important. In *A Dream Play*, there is no plot to speak of and no characters in the conventional sense, since the figures dissolve into one another.

How can one bring dramatic order and coherence to a plotless and characterless series of incidents and images? One cannot—unless one reexamines the basic nature of dramatic art itself. This is what Strindberg did from 1898 through 1903, his most creative period, when he wrote over twenty-two plays. Those years that saw the birth of a new century also saw the origin of a new form of dramatic art. In seeking to picture the new cosmos that was taking shape in his mind, Strindberg had to create new forms. Similarly, the art of the novel and of painting were to be revolutionized in the first decades of the century. The great innovation in painting followed the realization that in essence a painting was not a representation or imitation of objects but an arrangement of shapes and colors on a canvas. "Remember," said Maurice Denis in 1890, "that a picture—before being a battle horse or a nude woman or some anecdote—is essentially a flat surface covered over with colors in a certain order." Cubism and abstract painting disavowed what was formerly thought absolutely necessary: a recognizable object in a setting of some sort, temporal or spatial. In classic drama the essential elements were plot and character. In *A Dream Play*, Strindberg replaced plot and character with theme and motif. He used the theater as painters like Kandinsky and Pollock were later to use canvas. What *Oedipus Rex* is to Aristotelian drama, and what *Hamlet* is to the drama of character, *A Dream Play* is to the drama of pure form.

Strindberg certainly did not consciously set out to revolutionize dramatic art when he wrote *A Dream Play* in 1901. It grew out of the profound sense of loss that he experienced when his third wife left him. It had a slow genesis, evolving out of a cluster of germinal ideas that Strindberg succeeded in bringing together by treating them as a musician handles motifs and themes. In his preliminary note, Strindberg comments on the musical structure.

To the casual reader, *A Dream Play* may appear to be improvised, a paratactic arrangement of episodes. Actually, like great music, it is worked out with extraordinary skill. It is complex in its details, simple in its themes. There are two principal themes that are varied and repeated: (1) for human beings to live, they must inevitably hurt other human beings; (2) one cannot help feeling sorry for them. Out of this rather banal material, Strindberg created his most compassionate drama, and his most comprehensive. Like a piece of music or a nonrepresentational painting, it allows for all kinds of responses. "Its power of suggestion," writes Maurice Valency in *The Flower and the Castle*, "is enormous, and this is to a considerable degree the result of the intricate scheme of correspondences by means of which the action and its symbols are laced together." In the welter of images and incidents only a few points are fixed and definite. Earthly existence is a dream, a Platonic nonreality; reality exists in the life of the spirit; and the artist who creates dreams is closest to the source of all being.

A Dream Play
(Ett drömspell)

A Note from the Author

Following the example of my previous dream play *To Damascus*, I have in this present dream play sought to imitate the incoherent but ostensibly logical form of our dreams. Anything can happen; everything is possible and probable. Time and space do not exist. Working with some insignificant real events as a background, the imagination spins out its threads of thoughts and weaves them into new patterns—a mixture of memories, experiences, spontaneous ideas, impossibilities, and improvisations.

The characters split, double, multiply, dissolve, condense, float apart, coalesce. But one mind stands over and above them all, the mind of the dreamer; and for him there are no secrets, no inconsistencies, no scruples, no laws. He does not condemn, does not acquit; he only narrates the story. And since the dream is more often painful than cheerful, a tone of melancholy and of sympathy with all living creatures runs through the pitching and swaying narrative. Sleep, which should free the dreamer, often plagues and tortures him instead. But when the pain is most excruciating, the moment of waking comes and reconciles the dreamer to reality, which, however agonizing it may be, is a joy and a pleasure at that moment compared with the painful dream.

The idea that life is a dream* seemed to us in the past to be no more than a poetic dream of Calderon's. But when Shakespeare in *The Tempest* has Prospero say that "we are such stuff as dreams are made on," and when elsewhere this wise Briton, speaking through Macbeth, talks about life as "a tale told by an idiot," we should probably give the matter some more thought.

Whoever during these brief hours follows the sleepwalking author on his wanderings may find a certain similarity between the apparent jumble of a dream and the disordered and mottled

---

* This paragraph and the ones following were written in 1907 in connection with the first staging of the play. They were inserted in the director's copy of the play but not printed at that time. —Trans.

cloth of life, woven by the great World Weaver, who winds the warp of human destinies and then fills the woof using our conflicting aims and changeable passions. Anyone who notes the similarity is surely entitled to think that there may be some substance to it.

As far as the loose, disconnected shape of the play is concerned, that too is only apparent. On closer examination, the composition is seen to be quite firm and solid—a symphony, polyphonic, now and then like a fugue with a constantly recurring main theme, which is repeated in all registers and varied by the more than thirty voices. There are no solos with accompaniments, that is, no big parts, no characters—or rather, no caricatures; no intrigue; no strong curtains demanding applause. The voice parts are subjected to strict musical treatment; and in the sacrificial scene of the finale, all that has happened passes in review, with the themes once again repeated, just as a man's life with all its incidents is said to do at the moment of death. Yet another similarity!

Now it is time to see the play itself—and to hear it. With a little goodwill on your part, the battle is half-won. That is all we ask of you.

Curtain going up!

PROLOGUE*

The backdrop represents banks of clouds resembling shattered slate cliffs with ruins of castles and fortresses.

The constellations Leo, Virgo, and Libra can be seen; in their midst the planet Jupiter is shining brightly.**

Indra's Daughter is standing on the highest cloud.

THE VOICE OF INDRA
(*from above*):
Where are you, my daughter? Where?

INDRA'S DAUGHTER
Here, Father! Here!

THE VOICE OF INDRA
You've gone astray, my child. Be careful;
you're drifting down.
How did you get there?

INDRA'S DAUGHTER
I followed a flash of lightning from the empyrean,
riding on a cloud. But the cloud
sank beneath me, and now I'm drifting down.
Tell me, Indra, my father, what place is this
that I have come to? Why is it so stifling,
so hard to breathe?

THE VOICE OF INDRA
You've left the second world and gone into the third.

---

*This prologue is a later addition to the play. It was written in 1906, in anticipation of the first production of the work, which took place in Stockholm on 17 April 1907.

**Leo, the Lion, is associated with Hercules and stands for man; Virgo, the Virgin, represents woman; Libra is the balance; and Jupiter is God.

649

You've left Sukra,* the morning star, far behind,
and now you've entered the atmosphere of earth.
Regard, my child, the seventh house of the zodiac,
Libra, the Scales, in which the daystar stands
as the year tips toward autumn
and day balances night.

INDRA'S DAUGHTER

The earth, you said? This dark and heavy world
that is lit by the light of the moon?

THE VOICE OF INDRA

Earth is the heaviest, the most leaden
of all the orbs that roam the void.

INDRA'S DAUGHTER

Tell me, doesn't the sun shine there?

THE VOICE OF INDRA

Of course the sun shines there; only not all the time.

INDRA'S DAUGHTER

There's a rift in the cloud. I can see all that's below.

THE VOICE OF INDRA

And what do you see, my child?

INDRA'S DAUGHTER

I see . . . how beautiful it is. . . . Green woods,
blue waters, white peaks, golden fields.

THE VOICE OF INDRA

Yes, beautiful like all Brahma's creations.
But it was still more beautiful once
at the dawning of time. Something happened,
a warping of its orbit—or was it something else?
A revolt, and in its wake
crimes that had to be quelled.

INDRA'S DAUGHTER

Now I can hear sounds from there. . . .
What sort of beings are they who dwell below?

---

*Venus, in Sanskrit.

THE VOICE OF INDRA
Go down and see for yourself.
Far be it from me to malign
the Creator's creatures, but that sound you hear
is the language they speak.

INDRA'S DAUGHTER
It sounds like—. Well, to my ears
it doesn't ring with joy.

THE VOICE OF INDRA
I can well imagine. All their tongues can speak
is the language of complaint. Indeed
those earthly beings are a bickering, badgering,
ungrateful race.

INDRA'S DAUGHTER
Don't say that. I can hear cries of joy,
and shots and roars; see flares bursting.
Bells are ringing, fires blazing,
and voices, thousands upon thousands,
singing the praises of heaven.

Pause.

You judge them too harshly, Father.

THE VOICE OF INDRA
Go down and see. Listen to them.
Then come back up here and tell me
if there is any reason, any grounds
for all their wailing and complaining.

INDRA'S DAUGHTER
Very well. I will go down there.
But you come with me, Father.

THE VOICE OF INDRA
No, I cannot breathe in those depths.

INDRA'S DAUGHTER
The cloud is sinking. The air's so heavy,
I'm suffocating. It isn't air, it's smoke and water.
So heavy, heavy, it's dragging me down, down.

Now I can see it clearly, wobbling and careening. . . .
No, the third world is not the best of worlds.

THE VOICE OF INDRA

The best? Of course not. Neither is it the worst.
Dust they call it, and it rolls round like the others.
That's why those creatures of dust are always dizzy,
lurching between folly and madness.
Don't be afraid, my child. It's only a test.

INDRA'S DAUGHTER

(*on her knees, as the cloud descends*):
I'm sinking.

[1]

The backdrop represents a forest of giant hollyhocks in full bloom — white, pink, purple, violet, sulphur-yellow — and over the top of them can be seen the top of a castle crowned with a dome that resembles a flower bud. Beneath the footings of the castle are scattered stacks of straw covering the manure and litter from the stables. The wings and tormentors, which remain unchanged throughout the play, are stylized wall paintings suggesting rooms, buildings, and landscapes simultaneously.

The Glazier, an elderly man, and Indra's Daughter enter.

DAUGHTER: The castle is still growing up out of the earth — you see how much it's grown since last year.

GLAZIER (*to himself*): I've never seen that castle before in my life — never heard of a castle growing. Oh, well —. (*To the Daughter, with complete conviction.*) Yes, indeed, it's grown two yards. That's because they've manured it good. And if you'll notice, another wing is beginning to sprout over there on the sunny side.

DAUGHTER: It's going to bloom soon, isn't it? It's past midsummer.

GLAZIER: Don't you see that flower bud up there?

DAUGHTER: Oh, yes, yes, I do! (*Claps her hands in joy.*) I wonder, why do flowers grow up from dirt?

GLAZIER (*gently, piously*): They don't like to be in the dirt, so they hurry up into the light as fast as they can—to bloom and die.

DAUGHTER: Who lives in that castle? Do you know?

GLAZIER: I used to know. Can't seem to remember now.

DAUGHTER: I think there's a man imprisoned there. . . . And I'm sure he's waiting for me to come and rescue him.

GLAZIER: Careful. You both might get more than you bargain for.

DAUGHTER: One doesn't haggle over what has to be done! Come on, let's go in!

GLAZIER: All right, all right, let's go.

[2]

They approach the backdrop, which slowly opens up toward the sides.

The stage is now a simple, bare room with a table and a few chairs. An Officer in a very unusual modern uniform is sitting in a chair. He is rocking back and forth and striking the table with his saber.

The Daughter goes over to the Officer and carefully and gently takes the saber from his hands.

DAUGHTER (*as if to a child*): Mustn't do, mustn't do!

OFFICER: Oh, please be nice to me, Agnes; let me keep my saber.

DAUGHTER: No, no! You're chopping the table to pieces! (*To the Glazier.*) You can go down to the harness room and put in the windowpane. I'll meet you later.

The Glazier leaves.

* * *

DAUGHTER: You are a prisoner in your own rooms. I have come to rescue you!

OFFICER: I think I've been expecting this, but I couldn't be sure you'd want to help.

DAUGHTER: It's a strong castle—it's got seven walls—but—well, we'll think of something. . . . Well, do you want to or don't you?

OFFICER: To be perfectly frank, I really don't know. Either way I'll be in trouble. You have to pay for every joy in life with twice its price in sorrow. I hate to sit imprisoned here, but if I bought myself some joy and freedom, I'd pay for it three times over in pain and suffering. —Agnes, I'd just as soon put up with it, as long as I can look at you.

DAUGHTER: What do you see in me?

OFFICER: Beauty personified, the harmony of the universe. There are curves and lines in your form and features that can't be found anywhere else except in the orbits of the planets, in the strings that vibrate with music, in the trembling pulsations of the light. . . . You've come from heaven.

DAUGHTER: So have you.

OFFICER: Then why do I have to take care of horses? Be a stableboy and carry out manure?

DAUGHTER: So that you'll want to get away from it.

OFFICER: I do want to, I do! I want to rise above it. But it's so difficult, so hard.

DAUGHTER: But, don't you see, it's your duty to find your way to the light.

OFFICER: Duty? Doesn't life owe me something?

DAUGHTER: You think life's been unfair to you? Is that what you think?

OFFICER: Yes! Unfair, unjust . . .

* * *

One can now hear voices from behind a partition, which is promptly drawn aside. The Officer and the Daughter look in that direction and then freeze in position, their gestures and expressions frozen, too.

The Mother, looking very ill, is sitting at a table. In front of her is a lighted tallow candle, which she trims and crops now and again with candle snuffers. On the table are piles of new-made shirts and linen, which she is marking with ink and a quill pen. To the left stands a brown wardrobe or clothespress.

The Father hands her a silk shawl.

FATHER (*gently*): You mean you don't want it?

MOTHER: A silk shawl—for me? Oh, dearest, what use can I have for a silk shawl? I'm not long for this world.

FATHER: Do you believe what the doctor says?

MOTHER: Not only what he says. Most of all I believe the voice I hear inside me.

FATHER (*gloomily*): Then it's really serious? . . . And here you are thinking only of the children—first, last, and always.

MOTHER: They were my whole life, my reason for living . . . my joy . . . and my sorrow.

FATHER: Forgive me, Christine. . . . For everything.

MOTHER: For what? You must forgive me, my darling. We've been hard on each other. And why? We don't know. We couldn't help ourselves. . . . Anyway, here are new shirts and linen for the children. You must see to it that they change twice a week. Wednesdays and Sundays. And be sure Louisa gives them their baths, and washes them—all over, you understand. . . . Are you going out?

FATHER: I have to be up at the school—eleven o'clock.

MOTHER: Would you ask Alfred to come in before you leave?

FATHER (*pointing at the Officer*): But, dearest, he's standing right here.

MOTHER: Can you imagine, I'm beginning to lose my sight, too. . . . Yes, yes, it's getting dark. (*She trims the candlewick.*) Alfred, come here.

* * *

The Father goes out straight through the wall, nodding goodbye.

* * *

The Officer goes over to his Mother.

MOTHER: Who is that girl?

OFFICER (*whispering*): Why, that's Agnes.

MOTHER: Oh, really, is that Agnes? Do you know what they're saying? That she's the daughter of the god Indra, and that she asked to come down here on earth to find out what life is really like. —Shh! Not a word!

OFFICER: Yes, indeed, she is a child of the gods.

MOTHER (*aloud*): My dearest Alfred, soon I'll have to leave you and the rest of my children. There's something I want to tell you, something I want you to remember all through life.

OFFICER (*dark and gloomy*): Yes, Mother.

MOTHER: Just one word of advice: don't ever quarrel with God.

OFFICER: I don't understand you, Mother.

MOTHER: You mustn't go around thinking that life has treated you unfairly.

OFFICER: Not even when it has, when I know I've been unjustly accused?

MOTHER: I know, I know. You're thinking of the time you were punished because they said you stole a coin and later it turned up.

OFFICER: That's right. It was unjust. It got me started through life on the wrong foot. Things were never the same.

MOTHER: I see. Now you just go over to that wardrobe and—

OFFICER (*blushing in shame*): You mean you know? You know? That's where—

MOTHER: *The Swiss Family Robinson.* . . . And your—

OFFICER: Please! Don't say any more!

MOTHER: —your brother got punished for having torn it up. But it was *you* who tore it up and hid it.

OFFICER: It's strange. That wardrobe is still standing there after twenty years. We've moved so many times since then, and Mother died ten years ago.

MOTHER: Now, what's that got to do with it? There you go— always asking questions. That's how you destroy the best things in life for yourself. . . . Oh, here's Lina!

* * *

LINA (*entering*): Oh, missis, it's awfully kind of you, and I want to thank you, but I can't go to the christening.

MOTHER: But why not, my child?

LINA: I haven't a thing to wear.

MOTHER: Why, I'll lend you my shawl! —This one.

LINA: Oh, dearest me, I can't take *that*! It wouldn't be right.

MOTHER: I don't understand you. Don't you see, I'll never be going to parties again.

* * *

OFFICER: What will Papa say? He gave it to you. It was a gift.

MOTHER: Oh, what small minds!

* * *

FATHER (*sticking his head in*): Don't tell me you're going to lend my present to a scrubwoman?

MOTHER: Don't say that. . . . I was once a maid, too—remember? . . . Why do you have to hurt the feelings of an innocent girl?

FATHER: Why hurt *my* feelings? I'm your husband.

MOTHER: Oh, I give up! If you're nice to somebody, you're mean to someone else. Help one, hurt another. What a life!

> *She trims and crops the candle until it dies. The stage grows dark, and the partition is drawn back in and conceals the scene.*

* * *

DAUGHTER: Yes, what a life. Poor souls, I feel sorry for them.

OFFICER: Do you really?

DAUGHTER: Yes, life is hard. But love—love conquers everything. You'll see! Come.

> *They move toward the rear of the stage.*

[3]

> *The backdrop is drawn up, and a new backdrop is seen, representing a dirty, brick or stone, peeling party wall. In the middle of the wall is a gate opening onto an alleyway that leads out to a bright green area, in the center of which stands a colossal plant—a blue monkshood (Aconitum). The gate functions as a stage door entrance and to the left of it sits the Stage-Door Keeper—a woman wearing a shawl over her head and shoulders. She is working on a huge bedspread with a pattern of stars. To the right is a billboard, and the Billposter is washing it. Leaning against the wall next to him is a dip net with a green handle. Farther to the right is a door with an air hole in the shape of a cloverleaf. Left of the gate stands a small linden tree with a pitch-black trunk and a few pale green leaves. Next to it is a small, round, cellar window.*

DAUGHTER (*approaching the Stage-Door Keeper*): Haven't you finished that star quilt yet?

STAGE-DOOR KEEPER: of course not, deary! Twenty-six years is no time at all for a job as big as this.

DAUGHTER: Your fiancé never came back?

STAGE-DOOR KEEPER: No. Wasn't his fault, my dear girl. He *had* to leave, *had* to . . . the poor man. Thirty years it's been.

DAUGHTER (*to the Billposter*): She was with the ballet, wasn't she? Here in the opera house?

BILLPOSTER: She was prima ballerina. But when *he* up and left *her*, he took all her dances with him, you might say. . . . She never got any parts after that . . .

DAUGHTER: All they do is complain. At least with their eyes— and their tone of voice . . .

BILLPOSTER: Oh, I don't. Not like I used to—not since I got my dip net and my green fish pot.

DAUGHTER: That makes you happy?

BILLPOSTER: Yes. So happy, I—I—. It was what I dreamed of when I was a boy, and now it's come true. Of course, I'm fifty years old, but—

DAUGHTER: Fifty years for a dip net and a fish pot . . .

BILLPOSTER: Not any fish pot! A *green* one. Green! . . .

* * *

DAUGHTER (*to the Stage-Door Keeper*): Let me have the shawl. I'll sit here for a while and watch the passing parade. You stand behind me and let me know what's going on. (*She puts on the shawl and sits down at the gate.*)

STAGE-DOOR KEEPER: This is the last day of the opera before it's closed for the season. This is when they find out if they got renewed for next year.

DAUGHTER: And those who don't get a place—what about them?

STAGE-DOOR KEEPER: God, I can't bear to see them! I have to cover my face with the shawl, I really do.

DAUGHTER: Those poor people. How awful.

STAGE-DOOR KEEPER: Look, there's one of the girls coming now! . . . She's not one of the lucky ones. Look at her cry.

* * *

A Singer enters from the right and hurries through the gate. She is holding her handkerchief to her eyes. She stands for a moment in the passageway outside the gate, and leans her head against the wall. Then rushes out.

DAUGHTER: Poor souls, I feel so sorry for them.

* * *

STAGE-DOOR KEEPER: Ah, but look at him! Want to see a really happy man? There he is!

* * *

The Officer comes down the alleyway and through the gate. He is wearing a high hat and tails and carrying a bouquet of roses. He is beaming with happiness.

STAGE-DOOR KEEPER: He's going to marry Miss Victoria!

OFFICER (*coming downstage, looks upward, and sings out*): Victoria!

STAGE-DOOR KEEPER: Miss Victoria will be down in just a moment.

OFFICER: Good, good! The carriage is waiting, the table is spread, the champagne's on ice – oh, let me kiss you, ladies! (*He embraces the Daughter and the Stage-Door Keeper. Sings out.*) Victoria!

A WOMAN'S VOICE (*from above, singing out liltingly*): Here I am!

OFFICER (*beginning to wander up and down*): All right, I'll be waiting!

* * *

DAUGHTER: Don't you recognize me?

OFFICER: No, for me there's only one woman in the whole world—Victoria! —For seven years I've walked up and down here, waiting for her. In the morning when the sun reached the chimney tops, and in the evening as night began to fall. . . . Look here in the asphalt; you can see the path worn by true love. Hurrah, hurrah! She's mine, she's all mine! (*Calls out.*) Victoria!

No answer.

Hm, I guess she must be getting dressed. . . . (*To the Billposter.*) I see you've got a dip net. Everybody at the opera is crazy about dip nets—or should I say, about fish. You know why? No voices, that's why. No competition. —How much does a thing like that cost?

BILLPOSTER: Pretty expensive.

OFFICER (*singing out*): Victoria! . . . (*Shakes the linden tree.*) It's blooming again! Look! For the eighth time. . . . (*Singing out.*) Victoria! . . . Now she's combing her bangs. . . . (*To the Daughter.*) Oh, come on now, my good woman, let me go up and fetch my bride!

STAGE-DOOR KEEPER: Sorry, no one's allowed backstage.

OFFICER: Seven years I've been walking and waiting! Seven years! Seven times three hundred and sixty-five makes two thousand five hundred and fifty-five. (*Stops and pokes with his cane at the door with the cloverleaf air hole.*) And I've looked at this door two thousand five hundred and fifty-five times without ever finding out where it leads to. And that cloverleaf hole to let in light—who's in there who needs to have light? Is there anyone in there? Someone live there?

STAGE-DOOR KEEPER: I don't know. I've never seen anyone open that door.

OFFICER: It looks like a door to a pantry I saw when I was four years old and nanny took me out one Sunday afternoon to visit her friends. Out—other families, other maids—but I never got farther than the kitchen—had to sit there and wait between the water barrel and the salt tub—I've seen so many kitchens in my time—and the pantry was always out next to the porch—with round holes bored through it and a cloverleaf. . . . But an opera house can't have a pantry—there's no kitchen! (*Singing out.*) Victoria! . . . Say, she couldn't possibly leave the theater by some other door, could she?

STAGE-DOOR KEEPER: Oh, no, dearie, there's no other way out.

OFFICER: Good, then I can't miss her!

> The Actors and Dancers come pouring out. The Officer looks them all over.

* * *

OFFICER: She's got to come along pretty soon. . . . Madame —that blue flower out there—that monkshood. I remember it from the time I was a child. Can't be the same one, can it? . . . It was at the parsonage, I remember, the minister's house—the garden. I was seven years old. . . . Fold back the top petals— the pistil and stamen look like two doves. We used to do that as children. . . . But this time a bee came—went into the flower. "Got you!" I said. And I pinched the flower together. And the bee stung me. . . . And I cried. . . . Then the minister's wife came and put mud on my finger. . . . Later we had strawberries and cream for dessert at supper. . . . I do believe it's getting dark already. —Where are you off to?

BILLPOSTER: Home. Time for my supper.

OFFICER (*rubbing his eyes*): Supper?! At this time of day? —Say, wait a minute! Do you mind if I make a phone call to "the growing castle"? Take just a minute.

DAUGHTER: Why, what do you have to do?

OFFICER: I have to tell the glazier to put in the storm windows. Winter's almost here, and I'm freezing to death. (*He goes into the Stage-Door Keeper's office.*)

* * *

DAUGHTER: Who is this Victoria he keeps calling for?

STAGE-DOOR KEEPER: His sweetheart. The dearest person in the world to him.

DAUGHTER: I understand. What she may be to us or to anyone else doesn't concern him at all. Whatever he sees in her, that's what she really is.

It grows dark very suddenly.

STAGE-DOOR KEEPER (*lights a lamp*): It's getting dark so early today.

DAUGHTER: For the gods in heaven a year is only a minute.

STAGE-DOOR KEEPER: And for us here on earth a minute can seem like a year . . .

* * *

The Officer returns. He looks rather dusty and dirty. The roses have withered.

OFFICER: Hasn't she come down yet?

STAGE-DOOR KEEPER: No.

OFFICER: She will, she will. I know *she'll* come! (*Walks up and down.*) But it's true, the sensible thing for me to do, I suppose, is to cancel the dinner reservation anyway—since it's already nighttime. . . . Yes—yes, that's what I'll do. (*Goes in to telephone.*)

* * *

STAGE-DOOR KEEPER (*to the Daughter*): I guess I'd better take my shawl back now.

DAUGHTER: No, no this is your time off. I'll do your work for you. . . . I want to learn all about people and this life on earth—I want to find out if it is as hard as they say it is.

STAGE-DOOR KEEPER: You know you can't sleep at this post, don't you? Can't ever sleep—neither day nor night.

DAUGHTER: Not sleep at night?

STAGE-DOOR KEEPER: Well, you can try—with a string from the doorbell tied to your arm. You see, they've got watchmen on duty backstage, and they spell each other every three hours.

DAUGHTER: Forced to stay awake—sounds like torture!

STAGE-DOOR KEEPER: You think so? I know a lot of people who would be glad to have my job. You don't know how they envy me!

DAUGHTER: Envy you! Envy someone who's being tortured?

STAGE-DOOR KEEPER: Well, they do. . . . Darling, I haven't told you the worst part. The worst part isn't slaving all day and staying awake all night, or sitting in the draft, getting cold and damp—it's to have to listen, like I have to, to all their sad stories. All the actors, all the dancers, they all come to me and pour their hearts out. Why do they come to me? I guess it's these wrinkles. What I've suffered is scrawled all over my face, and that's what makes them confide in me. . . . In this shawl, dearie, there's thirty years of suffering, my own and others', all tucked away.

DAUGHTER: It's so heavy—and it stings like nettles . . .

STAGE-DOOR KEEPER: Wear it if you want to, dearie. If it gets too heavy, give a call, and I'll come and relieve you.

DAUGHTER: You run along. If you can bear it, I certainly should be able to.

STAGE-DOOR KEEPER: You be kind to my friends now. Don't let their complaining get you down. (*She disappears down the passageway.*)

> *Complete blackout while the scene changes. The linden tree is stripped bare of all its leaves. The monkshood is virtually dead and withered. And when it grows light again, the green patch seen through the perspective of the alleyway has turned autumn-brown.*
>
> *The Officer enters when the lights come up. Now his hair*

and beard are gray. His clothes are shabby and threadbare. His detachable shirt collar is badly soiled and limp as a rag. The roses have fallen from his bouquet so that nothing is left but a bunch of twigs. He wanders up and down.

OFFICER: No doubt about it. Everything points to the fact that summer is over and autumn is on its way. I can tell from the linden tree—and the monkshood. (*Wanders up and down.*) So what! Autumn is spring for me! That's when the theater opens again. And then she's got to come! —My dear lady, would you mind if I sat down on that chair a few minutes?

DAUGHTER: No, of course not. I can stand for a while.

OFFICER (*sitting down*): If I could grab forty winks, I'd feel better. . . . (*He falls asleep for a moment, then wakes up with a start and begins to pace up and down. Stops in front of the cloverleaf door and pokes at it.*) That door . . . can't get it out of my mind. . . . What's behind it? There's got to be something behind it.

From above one can hear the soft strains of ballet music.

Ah ha! The rehearsals have begun!

The stage is lit up in flashes as if by the revolving lamp in a lighthouse.

What's going on? (*In time with the flashes.*) Light and dark—light and dark!

DAUGHTER: Day and night—day and night! . . . A merciful providence wants to shorten the time you have to wait. The days are flying by, chasing the nights.

The flashes die away, and the light becomes constant. The Billposter enters with his dip net and his paste bucket, paste brush, and the rest of his equipment.

OFFICER: The billposter, with his net. —Make a good catch?

BILLPOSTER: Sure did! It was a hot summer and it dragged on a bit. . . . The net was all right, I guess, but it wasn't exactly what I'd imagined.

OFFICER (*stressing the words*): "Not exactly what I'd imagined." Perfectly put! Nothing is as I imagined it to be. You see, the thought is greater than the deed, finer than the thing itself . . . (*Paces up and down and slaps the rose bouquet against the wall so that the last few petals fall off.*)

BILLPOSTER: You mean to say she hasn't come down yet?

OFFICER: No, not yet. She's on her way, on her way. . . . Say, you don't happen to know what's behind that door, do you?

BILLPOSTER: No, can't say as I do. Never saw that door open.

OFFICER: Well, I think it's about time. I'm going to phone for a locksmith to come and open it. (*Goes in to telephone.*)

The Billposter pastes up a poster and moves out to the right.

DAUGHTER: What was the matter with the dip net?

BILLPOSTER: Matter? Nothing. There wasn't anything really the matter—it just wasn't exactly like I imagined it would be. So the pleasure wasn't all *that* great.

DAUGHTER: How had you imagined it would be?

BILLPOSTER: How had I—? Well, it's hard to say . . .

DAUGHTER: Let me say it. You had imagined it *different* from what it was. It was supposed to be green, but not *that* green!

BILLPOSTER: That's right. It just wasn't the same. You know what it's like, don't you? You really do—and that's why everybody comes to you with their troubles. . . . Maybe you'd listen to me too . . . sometime?

DAUGHTER: Of course I will. . . . Come in here and pour out your heart . . . (*She goes into the Stage-Door Keeper's cage.*)

The Billposter stands outside and talks to her through the window.

* * *

Complete blackout again. When the lights come up, the linden tree is leafy, the monkshood is in full bloom, and the sun is shining on the green place at the end of the alleyway.

The Officer comes in. He is old and completely gray-haired. Clothes ragged and torn, shoes full of holes. Carries the bare twigs of what was once the bouquet of roses. Walks up and down—slowly, like an old man. He studies the poster.

* * *

A Ballet Girl enters from the right.

OFFICER: Has Victoria left?

BALLET GIRL: No, she's still here.

OFFICER: Good, I'll wait. You think she'll be leaving soon?

BALLET GIRL (*earnestly*): I'm sure she will.

OFFICER: Don't run off now or you won't get to see what's behind this door. I've sent for a locksmith.

BALLET GIRL: How exciting! I'd love to see that door opened. That door gets me—and that growing castle. —Do you know the growing castle?

OFFICER: Do I? Who do you think was imprisoned there?

BALLET GIRL: No! Was that you?! —Tell me, why did they have so many horses there?

OFFICER: Because they had all those stalls—why do you think?

BALLET GIRL (*hurt; almost crying*): Oh, I'm so dumb! Why didn't I think of that?

* * *

A Singer from the Chorus enters from the right.

OFFICER: Has Miss Victoria left?

SINGER (*earnestly*): Of course she hasn't left. She never leaves.

OFFICER: That's because she loves me! — Don't go away before the locksmith gets here. He's going to open this door.

SINGER: Really? The door's going to be opened? Hey, that's great! — Excuse me, I want to ask the doorkeeper something.

* * *

The Prompter enters from the right.

OFFICER: Has Miss Victoria left?

PROMPTER: Not as far as I know.

OFFICER: You see! What did I tell you, didn't I say she was waiting for me? — Don't go, don't go, the door's going to be opened.

PROMPTER: What door?

OFFICER: What door? Is there more than one door?

PROMPTER: Oh, that one! The door with the cloverleaf! Don't worry, of course I'll stay for that. — Just have to say a few words to the doorkeeper.

* * *

The Ballet Girl, the Chorus Singer, and the Prompter group themselves beside the Billposter outside the window to the Stage-Door Keeper's cage, and they all take turns talking to the Daughter.

The Glazier enters through the gate.

OFFICER: Are you the locksmith?

GLAZIER: No, he couldn't come; he had company. I'm a glazier and I can handle it just as well.

OFFICER: Of course . . . of course. . . . But do you have your diamond with you?

GLAZIER: Naturally! A glazier without his diamond! What do you take me for?

OFFICER: Never mind, never mind. — All right, let us proceed! (*Claps his hands.*)

Everyone gathers in a circle around the door. Singers from the Chorus in "Die Meistersinger" and Ballet Dancers and Extras from "Aida," both groups in costume, pour onstage from the right.

* * *

OFFICER: Locksmith — or glazier, or whatever you are: do your duty!

The Glazier comes forward with his diamond.

OFFICER: Moments like this recur very seldom in one's life, my good friends, and therefore I urge you strongly to — to — consider carefully what —

* * *

Policemen come forward.

POLICEMAN: In the name of the law I forbid the opening of this door!

OFFICER: Oh, my God, what a lot of fuss and feathers whenever you want to do something new and great! . . . All right, we'll take it to court! We'll get a lawyer. We'll see what the law has to say! They can't stop us! To the lawyer!

[4]

In full view of the audience, the set is changed to the Lawyer's office in the following way. The gate remains standing but now functions as the gate in the office railing, which runs straight across the stage. The Stage-Door Keeper's office or cage remains as the Lawyer's small inner office with his desk, but the opening of the office now faces downstage. The linden tree, stripped of its leaves, serves as a hat tree. The billboard is now a bulletin board covered with government decrees and court decisions. The cloverleaf door now belongs to a filing cabinet.

The Lawyer, dressed in white tie and tails, is sitting at a high desk, completely covered with papers and documents, just to the left inside the gate. His appearance suggests he has experienced indescribable suffering in his life. His face is white as chalk and scarred with deep wrinkles, and the hollows of his face are filled with purple shadows.

He looks hideous, his face reflecting all the crimes and sins his profession has brought him in contact with.

He has two Clerks, one of whom has only one eye, the other only one arm.

The crowd that had gathered for the opening of the door remain in their places, but now they seem to be clients waiting to see the Lawyer, and they appear to have been standing there always.

The Daughter, wearing the shawl, and the Officer are far downstage.

LAWYER (*goes down to the Daughter*): Excuse me, Sister Agnes, but may I have that shawl? I'll hang it in my office until I get a fire going in the stove. Then I'll burn it, and send all the sorrows it contains up in smoke.

DAUGHTER: Not just yet, Brother Axel. First I want to fill it to bursting. Above all, I want to gather up all your pains, all the confessions you've had to take to your heart, of crimes and vices, false arrests, libels, slanders . . .

LAWYER: My dear friend, your shawl wouldn't be nearly large enough. Look at these walls—black with the soot of sin. Look at these legal briefs: one miscarriage of justice after another. Look at *me*! No one comes to me with a smile on his face. They glare at me, bare their teeth, shake their fists. They spew their venom at me, their malice, their envy, their suspicions. Look at my hands—black, and I can never wash them clean. Cracked and bleeding. My clothes have to be cleaned almost every day, they smell so of crime. Sometimes I fumigate the office with sulphur, but it doesn't help. I sleep on a couch in the next room, and all I dream about is crime. Right now I've got a murder case on my hands. That's all right; I can get through that. What's much worse—the worst of all—is divorce. A divorce case is like a cry from the center of the earth, a shriek heard in heaven. Because it goes against nature itself, against the source of all good, against love. And what's the cause of it all? When both parties have filled reams of paper with mutual accusations and finally some dear soul grabs one of them, looks him—or her—straight in the eye, and gently asks, "Come now, what have you really got against your husband—or wife?"—that person will stand there tongue-tied, unable to offer one good explanation. One time—yes, one time all the trouble started over a vegetable salad. Another time, a single wrong word. Most times, nothing at all. But the anguish, the pain! It all falls on me. Look at my face! Look at me. No woman could love me; I look like the worst sort of criminal. Do you think anyone wants me as a friend? No; I'm the man who makes them pay up—either for their debts or their sins. I tell you it's a wretched business. Living, I mean.

DAUGHTER: Poor souls. I feel so sorry for them.

LAWYER: Well you might! What do they live on? They get married on an income of ten thousand a year when they know they need twenty thousand. They borrow, of course, everybody borrows. They scrimp and scrape—live on credit—until the day they die. Who finally pays? Can you tell me that?

DAUGHTER: What of the birds of the air and the lilies of the field? Someone has his eye on them.

LAWYER: Yes. Perhaps He should take His eye off them, come down to earth and take a look at human beings. Then He might have pity for them.

DAUGHTER: Poor souls. I do feel sorry for them.

LAWYER: Who wouldn't? (*To the Officer.*) What can I do for you?

* * *

672   A DREAM PLAY

OFFICER: I just wanted to find out if Miss Victoria has left.

LAWYER: No, she hasn't, I assure you. You can put your mind at ease about that. —Why are you poking at my filing cabinet?

OFFICER: This cloverleaf—it's just like—

LAWYER: Oh, no, no. Oh no.

Church bells begin to ring.

* * *

OFFICER: Is there a funeral today?

LAWYER: No, commencement exercises at the university! I'm just about to receive my degree: Doctor of Laws. —Say, maybe you might like to come along, get a degree and wear a mortarboard.

OFFICER: Yes, why not? Might help to break up the day a bit.

LAWYER: Excellent! Time to get ready to march in the procession. —Hurry and change your clothes!

[5]

The Officer exits. Blackout onstage while the following changes are made. The office railing remains standing, but it now serves as the railing to the choir in a cathedral. The bulletin board becomes a hymn board with numbers of the psalms to be sung. The linden tree/hat tree becomes a candelabrum. The Lawyer's high desk in its niche becomes the dais and lectern for the Dean conferring the degrees. The cloverleaf door now leads to the sacristy of the cathedral.

The Singers from "Die Meistersinger" become Heralds with staffs, and the Extras in "Aida" carry the laurel crowns that are to be given to the degree candidates. The rest of the company are spectators.

The backdrop is pulled up, and the new drop represents immensely high organ pipes; at bottom, the console and the organist's mirror.

Music is heard. The faculties of philosophy, theology, medicine, and law are grouped at the sides of the stage. The rest of the stage is empty for a moment.

The Heralds enter from the right. Following them come the Extras from "Aida," carrying the laurel crowns on their outstretched arms.

Three Doctoral Candidates enter one after the other from the left, are invested, crowned with laurel wreaths, and go out to the right.

The Lawyer comes forward to receive his laurel crown. The Extras turn their backs on him, refusing to give him one. They leave. The Lawyer, shattered, leans against a pillar. Everyone leaves. The Lawyer is left alone.

* * *

The Daughter enters. She is wearing a white veil over her head and shoulders.

DAUGHTER: Do you see? I've washed the shawl. —Why are you standing here? Didn't you get the laurel crown?

LAWYER: No, I wasn't worthy of it.

DAUGHTER: Why on earth not? Because you spoke up for the poor, put in a good word for the criminal, lightened the burden of the guilty, sought to pardon the condemned? . . . What wretched people! They're not angels, are they? Still, I feel sorry for them.

LAWYER: Don't say anything bad about human beings. I'm going to take their case.

DAUGHTER *(leaning against the organ)*: Why do they spit in the face of anyone who tries to help them?

LAWYER: Because they don't know any better.

DAUGHTER: Can't we teach them? Will you help? You and I together!

LAWYER: They don't want to be taught. . . . Oh, if only our grievances could be heard by the gods in heaven—!

DAUGHTER: They shall be heard, they shall reach the highest throne! (*Standing before the organ.*) Do you know what I see in that mirror? — The world — right way round. Because in reality it's backwards.

LAWYER: How did it get turned around?

DAUGHTER: When the copy was made —

LAWYER: How right you are! A copy . . . I'd always suspected it was a bad copy. And when I began to recollect the original image, everything was a disappointment to me. People said I did nothing but complain and that I had bits of the devil's mirror in my eyes* — and so on . . .

DAUGHTER: It's a mad world. Just look at the four faculties of the university. The conservative government pays the salaries of all four of them. Theology, the study of God, which is always being attacked and ridiculed by philosophy, which sets itself up to be the essence of wisdom. And medicine, which is always challenging philosophy and dismissing religion from the learned disciplines and calling it superstition. And yet they all sit together on the University Council which is supposed to teach the youth of the land respect — for the university. It's a madhouse. Heaven help him who first comes to his senses.

LAWYER: The first ones to do so are the theologians. As undergraduates they study philosophy, which teaches them that theology is nonsense. Then they go on to study theology, where they learn that philosophy is nonsense. Fools, aren't they?

DAUGHTER: And the law! Serving everyone — everyone who can afford to have servants!

LAWYER: And the poor judges! — when they try to execute justice, they end up executing people. Justice — so often unjust.

DAUGHTER: What a mess you children of God have made of your earthly lives. Children, little children! . . . Come here. I shall give you a crown — one that becomes you better. (*She places a crown of thorns on his head.*) And I shall play for you! (*She seats herself at the organ and plays a Kyrie. But instead of organ notes human voices well up.*)

* See H. C. Andersen's fairy tale *The Snow Queen*.

VOICES OF CHILDREN: Lord Almighty! Lord Almighty! (*The last note is held.*)

VOICES OF WOMEN: Have mercy on us! (*The last note is held.*)

VOICES OF MEN: Show us thy mercy and deliver us! (*The last note is held.*)

VOICES OF MEN (*basses*): Spare us, oh Lord! Be not angry with your children.

* * *

EVERYONE: Have mercy on us! Listen to our voices! Pity us mortals! . . . Oh, Almighty One, why art thou so far away? . . . From the depths we call to you: mercy, oh Almighty One! Lay not too heavy a burden on thy children! Hear our voices! Hear!

[6]

The stage grows dark. The Daughter rises and approaches the Lawyer. By means of lighting, the organ is transformed into Fingal's Cave. The waves of the sea wash in under the basalt pillars, producing a choir of wind and waves.

LAWYER: Where are we, Agnes?

DAUGHTER: Don't you hear—?

LAWYER: I hear . . . drops . . . falling.

DAUGHTER: Those are tears. . . . People are crying. What else do you hear?

LAWYER: Sighing . . . wailing . . . moaning . . .

DAUGHTER: The complaints of mortals. They reach this far and no farther. Why are they always complaining? Are there no joys in life at all?

LAWYER: Yes, yes! The sweetest thing in life. And the most bitter! Love. A wife and a home. The best of life and the worst.

DAUGHTER: I want to know it. I want to know everything, try everything.

LAWYER: With me?

DAUGHTER: With you. You know where the dangerous corners are, the stumbling blocks. We can avoid them.

LAWYER: I'm a poor man. Haven't a penny.

DAUGHTER: What does that matter, as long as we have each other? A little joy and beauty doesn't cost anything.

LAWYER: What if we don't like the same things? You like what I dislike?

DAUGHTER: We'll have to learn to get along with each other.

LAWYER: Suppose we get bored with each other?

DAUGHTER: A baby will come. We'll be too busy to be bored.

LAWYER: You really want to marry me? Me—a poor and ugly man, cast out, despised by all?

DAUGHTER: Yes. Let us unite our destinies.

LAWYER: If you wish. So be it.

[7]

A very plain and simple room adjacent to the Lawyer's office. To the right, a large four-poster double bed with tester and hangings. A window near it. To the left, a kitchen stove with pots and pans on it. Christine is busy sealing up the inner window of the double window, using strips of paper as weather stripping. In the rear the door to the office stands open; through it can be seen a group of poor clients waiting to see the Lawyer.

CHRISTINE: I'm pasting and sealing. I'm pasting and sealing!

DAUGHTER (*pale and haggard, is sitting at the stove*): You're shutting out all the air. I'm suffocating.

CHRISTINE: Just one little crack left.

DAUGHTER: I've got to have air! Air! I can't breathe.

CHRISTINE: I'm pasting and sealing. I'm pasting and sealing!

LAWYER: That's right, Christine. You're doing fine. Heat's expensive.

DAUGHTER: Oh, I feel as if you were sealing up my mouth.

LAWYER (*standing in the doorway to his office with papers in his hand*): Is the baby asleep?

DAUGHTER: Yes—finally!

LAWYER (*gently*): I'm sorry. It's just that his bawling frightens away my clients.

DAUGHTER (*without harshness*): I don't know what we can do about it, do you?

LAWYER: Nothing.

DAUGHTER: We'll have to get a larger apartment.

LAWYER: With what?

DAUGHTER: Do you mind if I open the window? This stale air is suffocating me.

LAWYER: You'll let all the heat out. You want to sit here and freeze to death?

DAUGHTER: I don't know. It's awful. . . . Maybe at least we could scrub the floor out there?

LAWYER: You're not up to scrubbing any floors now. I'm not either. And Christine's got to go on pasting. She's got to seal up the whole house—every crack—in the ceiling, in the floor, in the walls.

DAUGHTER: I expected to be poor, but I didn't expect to be dirty.

LAWYER: The poor are always relatively dirty.

DAUGHTER: It's worse than I ever dreamed it could be.

LAWYER: We don't have it the worst. There's still food in the pot.

DAUGHTER: Do you call that food?

LAWYER: What's wrong with cabbage? It's cheap—nourishing—tastes good—

DAUGHTER: —If you happen to like cabbage! It makes me sick.

LAWYER: Well, why didn't you say so?

DAUGHTER: Because I want you to be happy. I don't mind giving up something I like for you.

LAWYER: All right, then I have to give up something I like: cabbage. The sacrifices have to be mutual.

DAUGHTER: Then what will we eat? Fish? You hate fish.

LAWYER: It is also expensive.

DAUGHTER: I never imagined it would be like this.

LAWYER (*making a joke of it*): You don't have to imagine any longer—you can see for yourself. . . . What about the baby? It was supposed to be a blessing. It's going to be the death of us.

DAUGHTER: Darling . . . dearest. . . . I'll die in this air, in this room, with nothing to look at but a backyard—with the baby crying for hours on end and never a moment's sleep—with all those people out there, always complaining, quarreling, accusing one another. I can't stand it any longer. I'll die in here.

LAWYER: My poor beautiful flower—without sun, without air . . .

DAUGHTER: And you say some people have got it even worse!

LAWYER: In this part of town I'm envied.

DAUGHTER: I think I could stand anything, if only I could have some beauty in my home.

LAWYER: I know, I know. A flower—a heliotrope—that's what you want! But it costs as much as six quarts of milk or half a bushel of potatoes.

DAUGHTER: I wouldn't mind starving if I could have flowers to look at.

LAWYER: Well, now that you mention it, there is one kind of beauty that doesn't cost anything. And a man with a sense of beauty misses it more than anything else when he can't find it in his home.

DAUGHTER: What's that?

LAWYER: No, you'll get mad.

DAUGHTER: No, I won't! We've agreed not to get mad.

LAWYER: So we have. We can say whatever's on our minds—as long as we don't snap at each other. So far we haven't.

DAUGHTER: And never will.

LAWYER: Never, as far as I'm concerned.

DAUGHTER: All right, now tell me what you were going to say.

LAWYER: All right. When I come into somebody's house, the first thing I look at is the curtains, to see if they're hanging straight. (*He goes over to the window and straightens the curtain.*) If they hang like strings or old rags, I leave—right away. The next thing I look at is the chairs. If they're grouped properly, I stay. (*He adjusts the position of a chair against the wall.*) And then I look at the candles in the candlesticks. If they're crooked, it's a sign the whole house needs straightening. (*He straightens a candle on the chest of drawers.*) There, you see! Now that, my friend, is the kind of beauty that doesn't cost a cent!

DAUGHTER (*lowering her head to her bosom*): You're being snappish!

LAWYER: I am not being snappish!

DAUGHTER: Yes, you are!

LAWYER: Oh, for Christ's sake—!!

DAUGHTER: You see?! Listen to you!

LAWYER: I'm sorry, Agnes . . . but I've suffered just as much from your untidiness as you have from the dirt. And I haven't dared to tidy up things myself, because then you'd think I was reproaching you and you'd get mad. —Oh, what's the use! We'll stop right now. Not a word more. All right?

DAUGHTER: It's awfully hard to be married. It's the hardest thing of all. I guess you have to be an angel.

LAWYER: I guess so.

DAUGHTER: I think I'll begin to hate you after this.

LAWYER: Heaven help us! . . . I tell you what: let's forestall the hate before it comes! I promise I'll never make any more remarks about your housekeeping . . . although it is sheer torture to me.

DAUGHTER: And I'll eat cabbage—although it makes me sick.

LAWYER: Fine! We'll live together and make each other sick. Your pleasure—my pain; and vice versa.

DAUGHTER: We poor souls. I feel sorry for us.

LAWYER: You've come to realize that, have you?

DAUGHTER: Yes. But in the name of God, let's avoid the dangerous corners, since we know exactly where they are.

LAWYER: Let's! After all, we're humane, reasonable, enlightened people. We should be able to make allowances, forget and forgive—

DAUGHTER: —Laugh at the small things—

LAWYER: That's right. If anyone can, we can! . . . You know, I read in *The Times* this morning that—by the way, where is the paper?

DAUGHTER (*abashed*): Which paper?

LAWYER (*snappishly*): Do I get more than one?

DAUGHTER: Smile! And don't bark at me. —I used the paper to start the fire.

LAWYER (*sharply*): Oh, for Christ's sake!

DAUGHTER: Come on now, smile. —I hate that paper. It makes fun of everything that I love and respect.

LAWYER: And that I hate and detest! —Ohhh! (*Throws up his arms, unable to contain himself.*) All right, I'll smile. Grin and bear it. I'll be humane, reasonable, and keep my opinions to myself, and say yes to everything, and be sneaky and hypocritical! . . . So you burned up my paper. . . . How about that! . . . (*He adjusts the bed hangings.*) Look at me! Here I am tidying up again and making you mad. . . . Agnes, the whole thing's impossible.

DAUGHTER: It certainly is.

LAWYER: But we still have to go on with it. Not because of the promises we swore to each other, but because of the child.

DAUGHTER: That's true. For the sake of the child. (*Sighing deeply.*) We have to go on with it . . .

LAWYER: And I've got to go to work. My clients are waiting for me. Listen to them. Growling with impatience to get at one another's throats, tear each other to pieces, force each other to pay penalties and go to jail. . . . Cursed creatures . . .

DAUGHTER: Poor, wretched people. . . . And this pasting, pasting . . . (*She bows her head in silent despair.*)

CHRISTINE: I'm pasting and sealing. I'm pasting and sealing!

The Lawyer stands at the door, nervously twisting the doorknob.

DAUGHTER: Oh, how that doorknob squeals. It's as if you were squeezing my heart . . .

LAWYER: I squeeze, I squeeze . . .

DAUGHTER: Don't! Don't!

LAWYER: I squee–ee–ze . . .

DAUGHTER: No, no!

LAWYER: I–

* * *

OFFICER (*from inside the office, grabbing the doorknob from the other side*): May I come in?

LAWYER (*letting go of the doorknob*): Help yourself! You're a big shot! You've got your doctor's degree!

OFFICER: That's right. The world is at my feet. I can go where I want, do what I want. I've climbed Parnassus, won the laurel crown. Honor, fame, immortality, it's all mine!

LAWYER: And what are you going to live on?

OFFICER: Live on?

LAWYER: Yes. Clothing, housing, food?

OFFICER: Oh, you can always make out, as long as there is someone who loves you and wants you to be happy.

LAWYER: Oh, sure! Sure! . . . Paste away, Christine! Paste until they suffocate! (*He is moving out backward, nodding his head.*)

CHRISTINE: I'm pasting and sealing. I'm pasting and sealing! Until they suffocate!

* * *

OFFICER: Well, are you coming along?

DAUGHTER: Right away! Where are we going?

OFFICER: To Fair Haven! It's summer there, the sun is shining. There's youth and happiness, children and flowers, singing and dancing, picnics and parties!

DAUGHTER: That's where I want to go!

OFFICER: Well, come on!

* * *

LAWYER (*reenters*): Now I shall go back to my first hell. This here was the second hell—and the greatest. The most beautiful was the greatest hell of all. . . . Look, she's been dropping hairpins on the floor again . . . (*He is picking them off the floor.*)

OFFICER: Good Lord! He's found out about the hairpins too.

LAWYER: Too? Of course! There are two prongs, but one hairpin. Two making one. If I straighten it out, it's one single piece. If I bend it, it's two, without ceasing to be one. This means the two are one. But if I break one off—like this—then the two are two. (*He breaks the hairpin and throws away the pieces.*)

OFFICER: Marvelous! He's understood the whole thing! —But before you can break it, the prongs must diverge. If they converge, they stay together.

LAWYER: And if they're parallel, they never meet. It neither breaks nor holds.

OFFICER: The hairpin is absolutely the most nearly perfect of all created things. A straight line that is the same as two parallel lines!

LAWYER: A lock that holds when it's open.

OFFICER: Holds a free band of hair that remains free when it closes.

LAWYER: Like this door! When I close it, I open the way—for you, Agnes! (*He withdraws and closes the door.*)

* * *

DAUGHTER: And now what?

[8]

Scene change. The four-poster with its tester and hangings is transformed into a tent. The stove remains where it was. The backdrop is drawn up. In the foreground to the right are charred hills covered with the red brush and black and white tree stumps remaining after a forest fire; also red pigsties and privies. At the foot of this is an open-air gymnasium for invalids and convalescents where the patients exercise on mechanical contraptions and machines that resemble instruments of torture. To the left in the foreground are some of the open sheds of the quarantine station, housing the boilers, piping systems, and furnaces used in the disinfecting processes. Beyond the foreground is a strait of water. The backdrop represents a beautiful wooded shore lined with docks decorated with flags. White boats, some with sails hoisted, others not, are moored alongside. Between the trees one can catch glimpses of small Italian-style villas, with pavilions, belvederes, and marble statues.

Dressed up like a Moor, the Medical Inspector of the quarantine station is walking along the shore. The Officer goes over and shakes his hand.

OFFICER: Well, I'll be darned, if it isn't old Gabby himself! So this is where you disappeared to!

MEDICAL INSPECTOR: That's right. Here I am!

OFFICER: Is this Fair Haven or isn't it?

MEDICAL INSPECTOR: No, Fair Haven is on the opposite shore. You're in Foul Strand.

OFFICER: Oops! We've come the wrong way.

MEDICAL INSPECTOR: We? —Ah, yes! Aren't you going to introduce me?

OFFICER: Can't. Just wouldn't do. (*Sotto voce.*) She's the daughter of Indra himself!

MEDICAL INSPECTOR: Indra? Don't you mean Varuna himself? —Well, what do you say? Aren't you surprised my face is black?

OFFICER: Dear boy, I'm fifty years old. At that age nothing surprises you. I guessed right away that you were going to a masquerade tonight.

MEDICAL INSPECTOR: Right on the head! Why don't you come along? How about it?

OFFICER: Great idea! This place isn't—. Can't say it attracts me. . . . What sort of people live here, anyway?

MEDICAL INSPECTOR: The sick ones here, the healthy ones over on the other side.

OFFICER: You mean these are all poor people here?

MEDICAL INSPECTOR: Don't be ridiculous! The rich ones here. Look at the fellow on the rack. He's eaten too much *pâté de foie gras*, and drunk so much Burgundy he's got knotted feet.

OFFICER: Knotted?

MEDICAL INSPECTOR: That's right; feet like knotted wood. . . . And that fellow over there lying on the guillotine— he's drunk so much cognac, we've got to straighten out his spine by putting him through the mangle.

OFFICER: Don't like the sound of that!

MEDICAL INSPECTOR: Fact is, on this side everyone's got some sort of problem he wants to hide. Look at the one who's coming now. A real dilly!

> *An elderly Dandy enters in a wheelchair, pushed by an Attendant. Accompanying him is a scrawny, ugly, sixty-year-old Coquette, dressed in the height of fashion. She in turn is accompanied by the "Friend," a man in his early forties.*

OFFICER: Why, there's the Major himself! Went to school with us, didn't he?

MEDICAL INSPECTOR: Yes, that's him: Don Juan! Look at him—he's still in love with that skinny spook at his side. He can't see that she's grown old—that she's ugly, faithless, cruel!

OFFICER: That's real love for you. I never thought that old playboy could ever be so deeply in love, so seriously in love.

MEDICAL INSPECTOR: You do see the bright side of things, I must say.

OFFICER: Well, you see, I've been in love myself. Victoria. . . . Yes, yes, I'm still walking up and down in that corridor waiting for her.

MEDICAL INSPECTOR: Don't tell me you're the stage-door Johnny waiting in the corridor!

OFFICER: That's me.

MEDICAL INSPECTOR: Well, well. Have you got the door open yet?

OFFICER: No, the case is still pending in the courts. The lawyers are fighting it out. . . . Trouble is that the billposter is out fishing with his net, as you might have known, so he's not available to give evidence. . . . And in the meantime, the glazier has put the windowpanes in the castle, which has grown half a story. . . . It's really been a very good year this year. . . . Very warm and humid.

MEDICAL INSPECTOR: You don't know what heat is. I've got heat like nobody else!

OFFICER: How hot does it get in those ovens anyway?

MEDICAL INSPECTOR: When we're disinfecting cholera carriers, we get it up to one hundred forty degrees.

OFFICER: Not another cholera epidemic?

MEDICAL INSPECTOR: Yes, didn't you know?

OFFICER: Of course I knew. My trouble is I keep forgetting what I know.

MEDICAL INSPECTOR: I wish I could forget—at least forget myself. That's why I dress up, go to masquerades, Halloween parties, play charades.

OFFICER: What have you been up to anyway?

MEDICAL INSPECTOR: If I tell you, you'll say I'm bragging. If I don't, you'll call me a hypocrite.

OFFICER: I get it. That's why you painted your face black!

MEDICAL INSPECTOR: That's right. A little blacker than I really am!

OFFICER: Who's that coming this way?

MEDICAL INSPECTOR: That, my friend, is a real live poet. On his way to his mud bath.

The Poet comes in. He is walking with his eyes fixed on the heavens, and he is carrying a bucket of mud.

OFFICER: Mud? Damnation! He should be bathing himself in light and air!

MEDICAL INSPECTOR: Oh, no. He's got his head in the clouds so much of the time, he gets homesick for the mud. Wallowing in the mud makes his skin tough—same as with pigs. After that he doesn't feel the gadflies stinging.

OFFICER: What a strange world! All contradictions!

* * *

POET (*ecstatically*): Out of clay the god Ptah created man on a potter's wheel, a turning lathe—(*Skeptically.*) or what the hell was it? (*Ecstatically.*) Out of clay the sculptor creates his more or less imperishable masterpieces—(*Skeptically.*) or are they only junk? (*Ecstatically.*) Out of clay are created for the world's kitchens and pantries those indispensable vessels known under the generic name of pots, plates, and—(*Skeptically.*) actually, I really don't care what they're called. (*Ecstatically.*) I say to you: lo, here is clay! In its liquid state, it's called mud. —And that's where I come in. (*Calls out.*) Lina!

* * *

Lina enters with a bucket.

POET: Lina, come here and let Agnes have a look at you. She knew you ten years ago, when you were young, happy, and—let's say—pretty. . . . Look at her now! Five kids—and a husband who beats her! Scrimping, slaving, starving! All her beauty faded, all her joy withered, while she was being a good mother and wife—which should have given her an inner satisfaction, a sense of fulfillment that should have found expression in a radiant smile on her face and the glow of contentment in her eyes—

MEDICAL INSPECTOR (*puts his hand over the Poet's mouth*): Shut up, you fool! Shut up!

POET: That's what they all say! And if you shut up, they say, "Speak out, man, speak out!" Crazy people. No rhyme or reason

* * *

DAUGHTER (*moves over to Lina*): What's the matter? I want to know.

LINA: No, I don't dare. They'll punish me. Make things worse for me.

DAUGHTER: Who would be that cruel?

LINA: I don't dare tell you. They'll beat me!

POET: That's the truth! But I can talk—even if this big Moor here knocks my teeth out. —Let me tell you, Agnes, daughter of the gods, about injustice. Do you hear music and dancing up there on the hill? You know who that's for? That's for Lina's sister. She's just come home from the big city. When she was in the big city, she wasn't exactly a good girl, if you know what I mean. But now they've slaughtered the fatted calf for her. And Lina, who stayed at home, has to carry the buckets to feed the pigs!

DAUGHTER: Don't you see? They're happy because the girl was going astray and she found her way back, not because she's come home. What's wrong with that?

POET: Then why not give a party every night for the blameless working girl who never went dancing down the primrose path?

Why not? Where's Lina's party? When she quits work, she has to go to a prayer meeting and be preached at for not being perfect. Is that fair?

DAUGHTER: I don't know. It's hard to say because—because there are always unforeseen circumstances.

POET: That's what the famous caliph realized, too: Harun al-Rashid, Harun the Just sat quietly on his throne, and from up there he could never see how the others had to live way down here. But finally some complaints floated up to his sublime ear. Then one fine day he climbed down from his throne, disguised himself, and took his place with the crowds in the street to learn all about justice in this world.

DAUGHTER: You surely don't take me for Harun the Just, do you?

OFFICER: Let's change the subject. —Look at the new arrivals.

Gliding into the strait from the left comes a white boat shaped like a dragon, with a pale blue, silken sail hoist on a golden arm and a rose-colored pennant flying from a golden masthead. Sitting at the helm with their arms around each other are He and She.

OFFICER: Now just look at that, will you? Look at that! There's real happiness, boundless bliss, the ecstasy of young love!

The stage grows bright.

* * *

HE (*stands up in the boat and sings*):

    Hail to thee, my beautiful bay,
    Where in my green seasons
    I dreamed my golden dreams.
    I've come back to you,
    Not alone as I was then.
    Blue water, blue skies,
    Sparkling bays, shady bowers,

> Greet the girl of my dreams
> My love, my bride,
> My sunshine, my life!

The flags on the docks at Fair Haven dip in salute. White handkerchiefs can be seen waving from the villas and from the shore. An arpeggio of harps and violins ripples across the water.

POET: See how the world is lit up by love. Listen to the music ringing across the water! —Eros!

OFFICER: Why, that's Victoria!

MEDICAL INSPECTOR: Now you've had it!

OFFICER: That's *his* Victoria. I've got my own all to myself. And my Victoria—nobody can see her! She's mine! . . . All right, time to hoist the quarantine flag, and I'll haul in our catch.

The Medical Inspector waves a yellow flag. The Officer tugs on a line that makes the boat head in toward Foul Strand.

OFFICER: Put in! Put in! Come ashore! Come ashore!

He and She suddenly notice the hideous landscape and utter cries of fear and loathing.

MEDICAL INSPECTOR: Yes, I know, it's pretty tough on you, but everyone who comes from infected places has got to go through this station. You've got to be inspected and fumigated.

POET: How can you talk that way, how can you act this way?! They're two people deeply in love. Leave them alone. Let the lovers be. Meddling with true love is a capital crime. . . . Why does everything beautiful have to be dragged down, dragged through the mud?

Ashamed and downcast, He and She come ashore.

HE: What do you want with us? What have we done?

MEDICAL INSPECTOR: Who says you've done anything? You needn't have done anything to have to suffer the little vexations of life.

SHE: Happiness never lasts.

HE: How long do we have to stay here?

MEDICAL INSPECTOR: Forty days and nights.

SHE: I'd rather end it all!

HE: Yes. Live here among charred hills and pigsties? Not a chance!

POET: Wait! Love conquers everything—including sulphur fumes and carbolic acid!

* * *

MEDICAL INSPECTOR (*lights the stove. Blue sulphur fumes rise up*): I'm getting the sulphur going. Now, if you don't mind, please step in.

SHE: But this blue dress will lose its color!

MEDICAL INSPECTOR: And turn white! And those red roses will turn white!

HE: And your cheeks, too. Forty days! Forty nights!

SHE (*to the Officer*): I hope you're satisfied! This is just what you wanted!

OFFICER: No, not at all! —It's true that your happiness was the source of my unhappiness, but—well, it doesn't matter anymore. I've got my degree from the university, and I've got a very good position right across there. . . . Ho, ho, yes, yes, I'm doing all right! . . . And this fall I'll be teaching in a school. . . . Teaching class to the little boys, the same lessons I read all the time I was a child . . . all my youth. . . . And now I'll have to read the same old assignments, the same old lessons over and over again while I pass through middle age. . . . And then through old age . . . the same old assignments. How much is two times two? How many times does two go into four? . . . Until they retire me. . . . Nothing to do but wait for the next meal and the morning paper and the evening paper.

... Until by and by I'm hauled out to the crematory and burned to ashes. ... Don't you have any retired people out here? That's the worst thing, you know — after two times two is four — to start in grade school again after you've been through the university — to ask the same questions over and over again until you die ...

> *A Middle-aged Man walks by with his hands clasped behind his back.*

There goes a retired man, living on his pension, and waiting for his life to trickle out. Probably an army captain who never got to be major. Or a CPA who never quite made it to office manager. Many are called but few are chosen. ... Walking and waiting for his breakfast —

MIDDLE-AGED MAN: No! For my paper. My morning paper!

OFFICER: And he's only fifty-four. He can go on for another twenty years like that, waiting for his meals and his papers. ... It's enough to make you sick.

MIDDLE-AGED MAN: What is there in life that doesn't make you sick? Tell me that, will you? Tell me that.

OFFICER: I wish someone could. ... Now I've got to go and study with little boys — two times two is four — how many times does two go into four? (*He grabs his head in desperation.*) — Oh, Victoria, Victoria! I loved her and wanted her to be the happiest girl in the world. Now she is happy, as happy as she can be. And that makes my heart ache — ache — ache!

* * *

SHE: Do you really think I can be happy when I see how you suffer? How can you think that? Maybe your heart won't ache so much when you see me sitting here like a prisoner for forty days and nights? Maybe you won't suffer so much?

OFFICER: Maybe yes, maybe no. It can't make me happy to see you suffer. Ohhh ...

HE: How do you think I feel? How can I build a happy life out of your agony?

OFFICER: We are poor lost souls—all of us!

EVERYONE (*stretching their arms toward heaven and giving out a cry or shriek like a dissonant chord*): Ohhhh—!

DAUGHTER: Almighty One, listen to them! Life is cruel! Poor lost souls! Take pity on them!

EVERYONE (*as before*): Ohhh—!

[9]

Blackout for a moment while all those onstage either leave or change places. When the lights come up again the shoreline of Foul Strand is in the back and lying in shadow. The strait lies between it and Fair Haven, which is now in the foreground. Both Fair Haven and the strait are brightly lit. To the right, one corner of a ballroom, its windows wide open, can be seen. Couples are dancing within. Standing on an empty box outside the ballroom are three Young Girls, holding one another around the waist and looking in at the dance. On the terrace steps to the casino is a bench on which Ugly Edith is sitting, bareheaded, melancholy-looking, with her hair like a wild mop. In front of her is a grand piano with its lid raised. To the left, a yellow frame house. Outside it two Children, in summer clothes, are playing catch.

Back of the foreground is a pier with white boats tied up and with flags flying from flagpoles. Lying at anchor out in the strait is a white ship of war, square-rigged, gunports open.

But the landscape as a whole suggests winter, with snow on the ground and on the bare trees.

The Daughter and the Officer enter.

DAUGHTER: How wonderful! This is vacation land! Everybody's resting and happy! No work for anybody—parties every day—everybody's dressed in their finest clothes—music and dancing even before lunch! (*To the three Young Girls.*) Why aren't you girls in there dancing?

YOUNG GIRLS: Us?

OFFICER: Don't you see they're chambermaids?

DAUGHTER: Oh, of course! . . . But why is Edith sitting out here? Why isn't she dancing?

Edith hides her face in her hands.

OFFICER: Don't embarrass her! She's been sitting there for three hours and nobody's asked her to dance. (*He goes into the yellow house at the left.*)

DAUGHTER: What a cruel game!

* * *

MOTHER (*in a low-cut dress, comes out and goes over to Edith*): What are you doing out here? Why don't you go in and dance like I told you?

EDITH: Please, Mother! . . . I can't be forward like the other girls, I can't. I know I'm ugly, I know that no one wants to dance with me. Why do you have to remind me of it all the time? (*She begins to play on the piano Johann Sebastian Bach's "Toccata con Fuga," in D Minor, BWV 913.*)

From within the ballroom the waltz can be heard softly at first, then growing louder, as if it were competing with Bach's Toccata. But Edith outplays it, and reduces the waltz to silence. The guests at the ball can be seen in the doorway listening to her play. Everyone on the stage stands entranced by her playing.

Then a Navy Lieutenant grabs Alice, one of the guests at the ball, around the waist, and rushes off with her down to the pier.

NAVY LIEUTENANT: Come on, let's get out of here!

Edith breaks off playing, rises and follows them with her eyes, her face registering her heartache. She remains standing as if turned to stone.

* * *

Now a wall of the yellow frame house is lifted away and we see the interior of a small schoolhouse and three benches with small boys sitting on them. Among them is the Officer, looking troubled and ill at ease. Standing in front of them is the Teacher, wearing glasses, a piece of chalk in one hand and a ruler in the other. He handles the ruler as if threatening punishment.

TEACHER (*to the Officer*): Now, boy, tell me: how much is two times two?

The Officer remains sitting. Searches desperately for the answer.

TEACHER: Stand up when I ask you a question!

OFFICER (*in torment, gets to his feet*): Two . . . times two . . . is—let me see now, it's . . . it's two—two!

TEACHER: I see. I see. You haven't learned your lesson.

OFFICER (*ashamed*): Yes, I have, it's just that . . . well, I know how to do it, but I—I just can't tell you.

TEACHER: Don't try to wiggle out of it! —So you know what it is, but you just can't say it. Well, now, maybe I can help you. (*He grabs the Officer by the hair and shakes him.*) Maybe that will shake it out of you!

OFFICER: My God, this is disgraceful! Disgraceful!

TEACHER: It's disgraceful to see a big boy like you turning into a lazy—

OFFICER (*hurt and stung*): A big boy?! Yes, I am big, much bigger than these boys. I've finished school—(*As if waking up.*) I've got my doctor's degree. What am I doing sitting here? Don't I have my doctorate?

TEACHER: Certainly you do. But you've got to sit here and mature. You've got to mature. —Don't you think that's right?

OFFICER (*his hand on his forehead*): Yes, of course. That's right; you've got to mature. . . . Yes. . . . Two times two—. Two times two—is two! Yes! I shall prove it by means of analogy, the highest form of proof. Follow carefully. One times one is one; therefore two times two is two. What applies to one applies to the other.

TEACHER: Your proof is completely in accord with the laws of logic. But the answer is wrong!

OFFICER: Whatever is in accord with the laws of logic can't be wrong. Let's test it. One goes into one once; therefore two goes into two twice!

TEACHER: Absolutely right according to analogy. But now tell me how much is one times three?

OFFICER: Three!

TEACHER: It therefore follows that two times three is also three!

OFFICER (*pondering*): No, that can't be right. . . . It can't be. . . . Or maybe . . . (*Sits down, looking lost and hopeless.*) I guess I'm not mature yet.

TEACHER: You're not nearly mature enough! Not nearly!

OFFICER: How long will I have to sit here?

TEACHER: How long here? Do you think time and space exist? Suppose time exists. Then you should be able to tell me what time is. All right, what is time?

OFFICER: Time. . . . (*Thinking.*) I can't exactly tell you, but

I know what it is. Ergo, I can know how much two times two is without being able to tell you! Can Teacher tell us what time is?

TEACHER: Of course I can!

ALL THE BOYS: Tell us! Tell us!

TEACHER: Time . . . ? Let me think. (*Stands motionless with his finger alongside his nose.*) While we're talking, time is flying. Therefore time is something that flies while I'm talking!

ONE OF THE BOYS (*stands up*): Teacher, now you're talking, and while Teacher is talking, I'm going to fly from here. Therefore I am time! (*He flees from the classroom.*)

TEACHER: Absolutely correct according to the laws of logic!

OFFICER: Then the laws of logic are crazy. Johnny who flew away can't be time!

TEACHER: That, too, is absolutely correct according to the laws of logic, even though it's crazy.

OFFICER: Then logic is crazy!

TEACHER: It does seem so, doesn't it? But if logic is crazy, then the whole world's crazy. And I'll be damned if I'll sit here and teach these boys how to act crazy! What do you say? If someone will treat me to a drink, we'll go for a swim!

OFFICER: That's a *posterus prius* or the world upside down! You're supposed to take a swim first and a drink after. Stupid old fool!

TEACHER: Don't get arrogant with me, Doctor!

OFFICER: Colonel, if you don't mind! I'm an army officer. And I don't understand why I have to sit here and be scolded and insulted and treated like a schoolboy.

TEACHER (*raising his finger*): We have to mature!

* * *

MEDICAL INSPECTOR (*enters*): We're all under quarantine as of now!

OFFICER: Ah, there you are! Where have you been? Do you

realize this fellow here has been making me sit on this bench with the other boys—and I've got a Ph.D.

MEDICAL INSPECTOR: Really? Why don't you just get up and leave?

OFFICER: Leave! That's a good one! . . . Easier said than done!

TEACHER: You know it, boy! Just you try to leave!

OFFICER (*to the Medical Inspector*): Save me! Hide me from his eyes!

MEDICAL INSPECTOR: Well, come on, never mind! Come and help us dance and make merry. Dance before the plague breaks out! We've got to dance!

OFFICER: Will the warship sail then?

MEDICAL INSPECTOR: That's the first thing! The ship will sail away. What a lot of sobbing and crying there'll be.

OFFICER: Always crying. When the ship comes in and when it puts to sea. . . . Well, let's go!

> *They leave the schoolhouse. The Teacher continues teaching silently.*

* * *

> *The three Young Girls, who were watching the dance through the window, move sadly down to the pier. Edith, who has been standing as if turned to stone at the piano, follows them slowly.*

DAUGHTER (*to the Officer*): You mean there isn't a single happy person in this paradise?

OFFICER: Yes, there is. Two of them. A newlywed couple. Listen to them.

> *The Newlywed Couple enters.*

HUSBAND (*to his Wife*): I'm so happy I want to die.

WIFE: Die because you're happy?

HUSBAND: Yes. "There lives within the very flame of love a kind of wick or snuff that will abate it."* And knowing what's to come turns my love to ashes when it burns most brightly.

WIFE: Then let's die together. Now, before it's too late.

HUSBAND: Die? Why not? I'm afraid of happiness. A mirage, made to lure us on.

They go down toward the sea.

* * *

DAUGHTER (*to the Officer*): What a cruel world! And the poor souls who live in it!

OFFICER: You think so? Look at this man who's coming now. Of all the mortals in this place he's the most envied.

A Blind Man is led in.

He owns every one of these hundred villas. The bays and harbors, the beaches and woods are all his, including the fish in the water, the birds in the air, and the beasts in the woods. All these thousands of people are nothing more than his tenants. The sun rises on his waters and sets on his lands—

DAUGHTER: So? Does he have something to complain about, too?

OFFICER: Yes, and with good reason: he can't see.

MEDICAL INSPECTOR: He's totally blind.

DAUGHTER: The most envied of them all!

OFFICER: He's come to see the warship sail. His son is on board.

* * *

---

* Strindberg does not quote this passage from *Hamlet* (IV, 7) but seems to echo it.

BLIND MAN: I can't see it, but I can hear it. I can hear the claws of the anchor tearing at the mud at the bottom of the sea. Sounds like the hook when it's pulled out of the fish and the heart is ripped out through the throat. . . . My son, my one and only child, is leaving me to travel far from home, to sail the seven seas; and all I can do is follow him in my thoughts. . . . I can hear the anchor chain clanking and scraping. . . . And there's something flapping and snapping like wet sheets on the line whipped by the wind . . . handkerchiefs wet with tears, hm? . . . And I can hear sighing and sobbing and sniffling, like people crying . . . maybe little waves lapping against the hull, maybe the girls on the shore . . . the girls that get left behind . . . with nothing to console them. . . . I once asked a little boy why the sea was salt, and the boy, whose father was away on a long journey, said right away, "The sea is salt because the sailors cry so much." "But why do the sailors cry so much?" I asked. "Because," he said, "they always have to go away from home — and that's why they're always drying their handkerchiefs up on the masthead!" And then I asked him, "But why do people cry when they're sad?" And he said, "That's because they have to wash the glasses of their eyes so they can see better."

> *The warship has gotten under sail and glides away. The Girls on the shore are alternately waving goodbye with their handkerchiefs and drying their tears with them. Suddenly, a signal flag with red, white, and blue stripes* signifying "Yes" is hoisted on a halyard to the yardarm of the foremast. Alice jubilantly waves her answer back with her handkerchief.*

DAUGHTER (*to the Officer*): What does the flag mean?

OFFICER: It means "Yes." It's the lieutenant's way of writing "yes" with the red blood of his heart on the blue cloth of heaven.

DAUGHTER: What does "No" look like?

---

* In the original, a red ball on a white field, which most people today would take for the Japanese flag.

OFFICER: A blue and white checkerboard—tainted blood and anemia.* —Look at Alice! Have you ever seen anyone look so happy?

DAUGHTER: Look at Edith! Have you ever seen anyone look so sad?

BLIND MAN: Coming and going—meeting each other and leaving each other—that's life. I met his mother one day—and then she left me. But at least I had my son with me. Now he's gone!

DAUGHTER: But he'll surely come again!

BLIND MAN: Who are you? I've heard your voice before . . . in my dreams . . . in my youth . . . when summer vacation began . . . when I was a newlywed . . . when my child was born. . . . Every time life smiled on me, I heard that voice, like a softly stirring south wind, like harps from heaven, like the songs I imagine the angels sang the first Christmas . . .

* * *

The Lawyer enters, goes over to the Blind Man, and whispers in his ear.

BLIND MAN: Is that so!

LAWYER: The honest truth! (*He approaches the Daughter.*) You've seen just about everything there is to see, but you haven't experienced the worst thing we've got to live through.

DAUGHTER: The worst! What can that be?

LAWYER: Repeating everything . . . going through it again! Going back to the beginning! . . . Having to learn your lesson all over again! —Come on!

DAUGHTER: Where?

LAWYER: Back to your duties!

---

* A blue flag in the original. The translator has followed the modern International Code of Signals.

DAUGHTER: Duties? What are my duties?

LAWYER: Everything you shy away from. Everything you hate to do and have to do! It means doing without, giving up, denying yourself. It means everything unpleasant, disgusting, and painful.

DAUGHTER: You mean there aren't any pleasant duties?

LAWYER: Yes. After you've done them, they're pleasant.

DAUGHTER: You mean when they don't exist. If duty is everything that's unpleasant, then what's pleasure?

LAWYER: What's pleasant is sin.

DAUGHTER: Sin?

LAWYER: That's right. And sin is something to be punished for. If I have a good time, the next day I have a bad conscience and suffer the torments of hell.

DAUGHTER: Strange!

LAWYER: But true. I wake up in the morning with a headache, and then I have to go through the whole thing again, repeat everything, but in a perverted way. So that all the beauty, fun, and wit of the night before appears, in the light of the morning after, to be ugly, disgusting, and stupid. The good times turn sour; the laughter rings hollow. It's the same with success. Success just sets you up to be knocked down. All the successes I had were the death of me. Because people instinctively hate to see someone get lucky. They think it's unfair that fate should favor any one person, so they try to make things even by switching the dice or changing the rules. Take talent, for instance. A real handicap. If you've got a real gift, you can easily starve to death. —Why are we talking? You've got to go back to your duties! Or else I'll take you to court—county, state, federal, and Supreme Court, if necessary.

DAUGHTER: Go back! To the kitchen stove, with the cabbage stinking up the place, the diapers in the sink—

LAWYER: That's right, my dear! We've got a big wash today— all the handkerchiefs!

DAUGHTER: Oh, no, I can't go through it again!

LAWYER: That's what life is—going through it again and again. —Look at the teacher in there. He got his doctor's degree yesterday, was crowned with the laurel, honored with a ten-gun salute, climbed Parnassus, and got a medal from the king. And today he begins school all over again, asking how much two times two is, and he'll keep on asking until the day he dies. . . . That's how it is. Now come back with me, back to your chores.

DAUGHTER: I'd rather die!

LAWYER: You mean kill yourself? You can't. The game isn't played that way. Suicide is a disgrace—in the first place—so much so that one's corpse is defiled. And in the second place—you'll send yourself to perdition; it's a mortal sin.

DAUGHTER: It isn't easy to be a human being, is it?

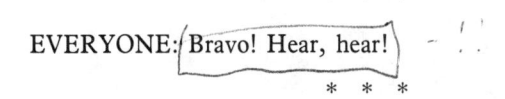

* * *

EVERYONE: Bravo! Hear, hear!

* * *

DAUGHTER: I won't go back with you. I won't sink back and be treated like dirt. I want to rise. I want to rise to the place I first came from. . . . But before I go, I want the door to be opened so that I shall know the secret. I want the door to be opened!

LAWYER: Then you'll have to double back on your tracks, go back the same way you came, and suffer through all the horrors of a trial and lawsuit, the hearings and rehearings, the repetitions and transcriptions, the recapitulations and summations!

DAUGHTER: If that's the way it has to be, very well. But first I want to be alone. I want to go out into the wilderness where I can find myself. We'll see each other soon. (*To the Poet.*) Come along with me.

Distant cries, wails, and moans are heard from the rear.

DAUGHTER: What is that?

LAWYER: The lost souls of Foul Strand.

DAUGHTER: Why are they complaining more than ever now?

LAWYER: Because the sun is shining *here*, because there's music *here*, and dancing *here*, and youth and life *here*. That's why they feel their misery so much more deeply.

DAUGHTER: We must set them free!

LAWYER: Go ahead. Try! Someone once came to set them free. They hanged him on a cross.

DAUGHTER: Who did?

LAWYER: *They* did. All the right-minded, well-meaning people.

DAUGHTER: Who are *they*?

LAWYER: You mean you don't know the right-minded, well-meaning people? You soon will!

DAUGHTER: Were they the ones who turned against you at the university?

LAWYER: Yes.

DAUGHTER: I know them!

[10]

The Riviera.* In the foreground to the left stands a white wall, over the top of which the fruit-laden branches of an orange tree can be seen. In the rear are villas and a casino. On the terrace of the casino are tables with parasols. To the right is a huge pile of coal, and near it two wheelbarrows. In the rear to the right one can catch a glimpse of the blue ocean.

Two Coal Haulers, naked to the waist, their faces, hands, and bodies blackened with coal soot, are sitting, hunched in tired despair, on the wheelbarrows.

The Daughter and the Lawyer enter at the rear.

DAUGHTER: Oh! This is paradise!

FIRST COAL HAULER: This is hell.

---

* In Strindberg's manuscript the Riviera scene has been added as an afterthought.

SECOND COAL HAULER: Hundred twenty in the shade.

FIRST COAL HAULER: Let's go for a swim.

SECOND COAL HAULER: Can't. Police will stop you. No swimming allowed.

FIRST COAL HAULER: What about picking an orange?

SECOND COAL HAULER: Can't. Police will come.

FIRST COAL HAULER: But I can't work in this heat. I've had it! I'm getting out of here.

SECOND COAL HAULER: Can't. Police will stop you. (*Pause.*) Besides, you'd starve to death.

FIRST COAL HAULER: Starve to death? We do most of the work and we get the least to eat. And the rich who don't do nothing get the most.... Wouldn't it be fair to say—without being too blunt about it—something's wrong somewhere? Daughter of the gods, what do you say?

* * *

DAUGHTER: I have no answer.... But tell me, what have you done? Why are you so black? Why do you have to work so hard?

FIRST COAL HAULER: What have we done? We picked the wrong parents—poor and disreputable.... And maybe we got arrested and sentenced a couple of times.

DAUGHTER: Sentenced?

FIRST COAL HAULER: Sure. Some get away with it and some don't. Those who get away with it are sitting up there in the casino eating eight-course dinners—with wine.

DAUGHTER (*to the Lawyer*): Can that be true?

LAWYER: Generally speaking, yes.

DAUGHTER: You mean that everybody at one time or another broke some law and could have been sent to prison?

LAWYER: Yes.

DAUGHTER: Even you?

LAWYER: Even I.

* * *

DAUGHTER: Is it true that the poor folk can't go swimming here?

LAWYER: That's right—not even with their clothes on. Only those who try to drown themselves get away without paying. But don't worry, they have to settle up in court.

DAUGHTER: Why can't they go outside the town, out in the country for a swim?

LAWYER: There isn't any open country; it's all fenced in.

DAUGHTER: I mean way out, where there aren't any fences, where the land is free.

LAWYER: There isn't any free land. It's all owned and occupied.

DAUGHTER: The ocean, the wide-open sea—

LAWYER: Everything! You can't even take a boat out or come ashore without signing a piece of paper and paying money. Neat, isn't it?

DAUGHTER: This is no paradise.

LAWYER: I can promise you that!

DAUGHTER: Why don't the people do something to change things?

LAWYER: They do. But all who want to make the world better end up in prison or in the madhouse.

DAUGHTER: Who puts them in prison?

LAWYER: All the right-thinking, fair-minded—

DAUGHTER: But not the madhouse?

LAWYER: Their own despair puts them there when they realize how hopeless it all is.

DAUGHTER: Hasn't it occurred to anyone that there might be a good reason why things are the way they are?

LAWYER: Yes, as a matter of fact. Everyone who is well-off believes that.

DAUGHTER: Believes that things are best as they are?

* * *

FIRST COAL HAULER: You see in us the foundation of society. If we didn't carry the coal, the kitchen stoves would go out, the rooms you live in would grow cold, the factories would close down. The lights in your streets, your stores, your homes would die. Darkness and cold would fall upon you. Yet we sweat like the damned in hell to carry the black coal. . . . What wilt thou do for us?

LAWYER (*to the Daughter*): Do something for them. . . . (*Pause.*) I realize that complete equality is impossible, but why, why must there be such great inequality?

* * *

A Man and his Wife cross the stage.

WIFE: Are you going to join us for a game of cards?

MAN: No, I've got to take my constitutional. Got to work up an appetite.

* * *

FIRST COAL HAULER: Work up an appetite!!

SECOND COAL HAULER: Work up—!

* * *

Some Children come running in. When they see the coal-blackened workers, they cry and scream in terror.

FIRST COAL HAULER: One look at us and they scream! They scream . . . !

SECOND COAL HAULER: God damn it! It's a sick society. I say it's time to operate on it—with the guillotine!

FIRST COAL HAULER: Damn right! (*He spits in disgust.*)

* * *

LAWYER (*to the Daughter*): Something's wrong. Anyone can see that. People aren't so bad. It's just that—

DAUGHTER: Just what?

LAWYER: The system. The organization.

DAUGHTER (*hides her face and leaves*): It's no paradise!

BOTH COAL HAULERS: No. It's hell.

[11]

Fingal's Cave. Long green waves roll gently into the cavern. In the foreground a red whistling buoy rocks on the waves, but the bell does not sound except when indicated.

The music of the winds. The music of the waves.

The Daughter and the Poet onstage.

POET: Where have you brought me?

DAUGHTER: Far from the murmuring and moaning of human beings—to the outermost edge of the world and the sea—to this grotto we call Indra's Ear. For it is said that here the god of the skies and sovereign of the heavens listens to the pleas and petitions of mortals.

POET: Listens? How?

DAUGHTER: Don't you see that this grotto is built like a seashell? You see it is. Don't you know that your ear is shaped like a seashell? You know it is, but you never thought about it before. (*She picks up a shell from the shore.*) When you were a child, did you never hold a shell to your ear and listen? Listen to the singing of your blood, to the swirling of the thoughts in your brain, to the thousands of tiny little explosions as the wornout threads in the fabric of your body snap and break? . . . If you can hear all that in such a little shell, imagine what you can hear in this great big one!

POET (*listening*): I don't hear anything, except the sighing of the wind . . .

DAUGHTER: Let me help you. I'll be the interpreter. Listen. . . . The lament of the winds. (*Recitative to the accompaniment of soft music.*)

Born in the clouds,
chased by Indra's lightning,
we fled to clayey earth.
The mulch in the fields
sullied our feet.
The dust of the road,
the smoke of the city
we had to endure—
foul smell of crowds,
stale beer, sour wine.
Out to the open sea we swept
to breathe clean air,
to flutter our wings,
to bathe our feet.
Indra, ruler of heaven,
listen to us.
Hear our sighs.
The earth is not clean,
life is not kind.
Man is not evil,
nor is he good.
People live as best they can,
one day at a time.
Living in ashes and dust,
they breed and die.
ashes to ashes, dust to dust.
Feet for plodding
were they given,
not wings for flying.
So the dust covers them.
Is the fault theirs
or yours?

* * *

POET: Once long ago I heard the same—

DAUGHTER: Shhh! The winds are still singing. (*Recitative to the accompaniment of soft music.*)

We are the winds.
It is we who carry

man's complaints.
On autumn nights you heard us
whistling in chimneys,
howling in the stove,
as the autumn rain
cried on the roof.
On winter nights you heard us
whisper in the snow-laden trees.
Out on the storm-swept sea
you heard our whining
in the ropes and sails.
You heard us,
creatures of air,
who learned our songs
in passing through
the lungs of men.
The hospital, the battlefield
taught us what to sing.
Most we learned in the nursery
where the newborn cry,
mewl, and scream
with the pain of coming alive.
We are the winds,
howling, whining,
whistling, wailing.

* * *

POET: I believe that once before—

DAUGHTER: Shh! Now the waves are singing. (*Recitative to the accompaniment of soft music.*)

We are the waves.
We cradle the winds
and lull the winds
to sleep.
Green cradles, wet and salt,
shaped like flames,
flames of water,
slaking, burning,
cleansing, bathing,

spuming, spawning.
We are the waves.
We cradle the winds
and lull the winds
to sleep.

* * *

DAUGHTER: False and faithless waves! Everything on earth that doesn't get burned up gets drowned—in the waves. —Do you see what I mean? Look. (*She points to a scrap heap.*) Look at what the sea has pillaged and plundered and destroyed. . . . All that's left of the sunken ships are these figureheads—and their names. The good ships *Justice, Friendship, The Golden Peace, Hope*—here's all that's left of *Hope*—deceptive *Hope* . . . lee-boards, oarlocks, bailing buckets . . . ! And there's the life buoy. It saved itself and let the souls in distress go down.

POET (*poking around in the scrap heap*): Here's the nameplate of the *Justice*. It must be the same one that sailed from Fair Haven with the Blind Man's son. It must have gone down. And on board was Alice's fiancé, too, the lieutenant Edith loves so hopelessly.

DAUGHTER: Blind Man? Fair Haven? I must have dreamed all that. And Alice's lieutenant, ugly Edith, Foul Strand and the quarantine, sulphur and phenol. Graduation exercises in the cathedral, the lawyer's office, the corridor and Victoria, the growing castle and the officer—it's all a dream I've dreamed.

POET: It's all in a poem I once wrote.

DAUGHTER: Then you know what poetry is.

POET: I know what dreams are. What is poetry?

DAUGHTER: Not reality. Something more than reality. Not dreams, but wide-awake dreams.

POET: And people, innocent earthlings, believe that we poets merely play and pretend and make it all up.

DAUGHTER: And a good thing, too, my friend. Else no one would believe there was any point to living and working, and the world would go to rack and ruin. Everyone would lie on his back and look at the sky. No one would lift a hand to use a plow or rake, pick or shovel.

POET: You admit that, do you? You the daughter of Indra, whose home is the heavens?

DAUGHTER: You're right to reproach me. I've been down here on earth too long and taken too many of your mud baths. My thoughts refuse to take wing. My wings are laden with clay, my feet are heavy with dirt and earth. . . . And, as for myself—(*She lifts her arms up high.*) I'm sinking, sinking. . . . Help me, Father, God of heaven, help me! (*Silence.*) I can no longer hear him. The ether cannot carry the sound of his voice from his lips to the sounding shell of my ear. The silver cord is broken. . . . I am earthbound . . . earthbound.

POET: Do you intend to rise from earth soon?

DAUGHTER: As soon as I have burned away the ashes and dust that cling to me, for not all the water in the world can wash me clean. Why do you ask?

POET: Because I—I have a prayer and a plea—

DAUGHTER: What sort of plea?

POET: A petition on behalf of humanity, addressed to the ruler of the world, and drawn up by a dreamer.

DAUGHTER: And to be conveyed and presented by—?

POET: By Indra's daughter.

DAUGHTER: Can you say the words of your poem?

POET: I can.

DAUGHTER: Then say them.

POET: Better if you did.

DAUGHTER: Where are they?

POET: In my thoughts. And here. (*He hands her a scroll.*)

DAUGHTER: Very well, I shall say them. (*She takes the scroll but recites without looking at it.*)

* * *

DAUGHTER:

"Why are we born in pain,
we human beings? Why
do we hurt our mothers
when we should be giving them
the greatest of joys?
Why do we come crying hither,
why do we greet the light,
wailing in pain and wrath?
Why do we not laugh and smile?
The gift of life should be full of joy.
Why are we, the progeny of angels,
the image of God, born like beasts?
Our souls would have a vesture
other than this of blood and filth.
Must the paragon of created beings
cut his eyeteeth and descend into the flesh?"

You presume too much! The work should praise its creator.* No one has yet solved the riddle of life and being.

"Now the passage through life begins,
over thorns, thistles, sharp stones.
If you find a smooth, well-worn path,
there will soon be detours through the rough.
If flowers will make your journey lighter,
they will cost you more than you can pay.
To make your way you'll have to fight
the crowd and step on someone's toes.
No matter: soon the others will step
on yours to keep the race a close one.
Every joy that comes to you will leave

---

* The Daughter alludes to a saying, "The work praises the master," not uncommon in Swedish, from Ecclesiasticus, an apocryphal book of the Bible. The standard version in English is ineffective: "For the hand of the artificer the work shall be commended."

some poor soul depressed and sadder.
But sorrow breeds no happiness;
all goes one way: from joy to pain,
and the world's cup fills up with sorrow.
So shall it be even when you're dead:
your grave will be the digger's bread."

Is this how you hope to approach
the throne of the Almighty?

POET:

How can a man of earth like me
find words bright enough, pure enough,
light enough to fly from earth?
Child of the gods, will you
render our lament in the tongue
the immortals best comprehend?

DAUGHTER: I will.

POET (*indicating the whistling buoy*): What is that floating there? A buoy?

DAUGHTER: Yes.

POET: It looks like a human lung with the larynx attached.

DAUGHTER: It's the watchman of the sea. When danger lurks, it sings.

POET: I think the sea is rising now. The waves are turning white.

DAUGHTER: I believe you are right!

POET: There's trouble ahead. Do you see what I see? A ship — out beyond the reef.

DAUGHTER: What ship can that be?

POET: It looks to me like the ghost ship.

DAUGHTER: The ghost ship?

POET: *The Flying Dutchman.*

DAUGHTER: Is that the *Dutchman*? . . . Why was he punished so harshly? And why does he never put in to land?

POET: Because he had seven unfaithful wives.

DAUGHTER: Why should he be punished for that?

POET: All the right-thinking people condemned him.

DAUGHTER: Strange world! . . . How can he be freed from his curse?

POET: Freed? Best beware setting anyone free—

DAUGHTER: Why?

POET: Because that—. No, it isn't the *Dutchman*, after all. It's an ordinary ship in distress! —Why doesn't the buoy sound off and warn them? Before it's too late! —Look, the sea is rising, the waves are mounting higher. In a minute we'll be trapped in this cave! —The ship's bells are ringing! Abandon ship! —Won't be long before we can add another figurehead to the pile! —Cry out, buoy! Come on! Do your duty, sentinel of the sea!

> *The whistling buoy sings out with a four-tone chord of a fifth and sixth, the sound resembling foghorns.*

POET: The crew is waving to us for help—but we ourselves are drowning!

DAUGHTER: I thought you wanted to be set free!

POET: Yes, of course I do. But not now! And not in water!

* * *

THE CREW (*singing in four-part harmony*): *Christ Kyrie!*

POET: Now they're calling. And the sea is calling. But no one hears.

THE CREW (*as before*): *Christ Kyrie!*

DAUGHTER: Who is that out there coming toward us?

POET: Walking on water? There's only one who walks on water—certainly not Peter "the rock"; he sank like a stone.

A white glow appears out on the water.

THE CREW: *Christ Kyrie!*

DAUGHTER: Is that he?

POET: Yes, that is He, the Crucified One . . .

DAUGHTER: Why—tell me now, why was he crucified?

POET: Because He wanted to set all men free . . .

DAUGHTER: And who—I have forgotten—who wanted to crucify Him?

POET: All the right-thinking ones.

DAUGHTER: It is a strange world!

POET: The sea is rising. Darkness is falling. The storm rages.

* * *

The Crew screams.

POET: The sailors scream in terror when they see their Saviour. . . . And now . . . they're jumping overboard—afraid of their Redeemer!

The Crew screams again.

POET: Now they're screaming because they're about to die. They scream when they're born and they scream when they die!

The rising waves threaten to drown them in the cave.

DAUGHTER: If I could only be certain that it is a ship —

POET: I see what you mean — I don't think it is. It's a two-story house, with trees around it — and — a telephone communication tower — a tower reaching up to the skies. It's a modern Tower of Babel, sending its wires upward — to let those up there know —

DAUGHTER: You know better than that. Thoughts do not need metal threads to move from place to place. Devout prayers can force their way through all the world. I say it's definitely not a Tower of Babel. If you want to storm the walls of heaven, besiege it with your prayers.

POET: No, it's not a house . . . not a telephone tower. . . . You see what it is?

DAUGHTER: No, what do you see?

POET: I see a plain covered with snow — a drill field. . . . The winter sun is shining behind a church on a hill, and the church tower casts a long shadow on the snow . . . a platoon of soldiers is marching across the field — marching across the tower — up the spire — now they're on the cross — I have a feeling that the first one who steps on the weathercock at the top must die — they're getting closer — the corporal's leading the way. — Ha! a cloud is sweeping over the plain, blotting out the sun, naturally — it's all disappeared — the wet cloud put out the sun's fire. The light of the sun created the dark tower, but the cloud's dark shadow smothered the tower's dark shadow . . .

[12]

While the Poet has been speaking, the set has changed back to the theater corridor.

DAUGHTER (*to the Stage-Door Keeper*): Has the president of the university arrived yet?

STAGE-DOOR KEEPER: No, he hasn't.

DAUGHTER: The deans of the colleges and faculties?

STAGE-DOOR KEEPER: No.

DAUGHTER: Well then, you'd better call them. Right away! Because the door is going to be opened.

STAGE-DOOR KEEPER: Is it really so urgent?

DAUGHTER: Yes, very urgent. A lot of people have come to suspect that the key to the mystery of the universe is kept there. So if you don't mind, call the president and the deans at once.

The Stage-Door Keeper pulls out a whistle and blows on it.

DAUGHTER: And don't forget the glazier and his diamond. Without him there can be no opening of the door.

* * *

The Actors and Dancers come in from the left, as at the beginning of the play.

* * *

OFFICER (*enters from the rear, wearing top hat and tails, carrying a bouquet of roses, radiantly happy*): Victoria!

STAGE-DOOR KEEPER: Miss Victoria will be down in just a moment.

OFFICER: Good, good! The carriage is waiting, the table is spread, the champagne's on ice. Oh, let me kiss you, madame! (*He embraces the Stage-Door Keeper.*) Victoria!

* * *

A WOMAN'S VOICE (*from above, singing out liltingly*): Here I am!

OFFICER (*beginning to pace back and forth*): Very good. I'll be waiting!

* * *

POET: I have a strange feeling I've been through this before.

DAUGHTER: Me too.

POET: Maybe I dreamed it . . . ?

DAUGHTER: Or wrote it in a poem, maybe?

POET: Or wrote it in a poem.

DAUGHTER: Then you know what poetry is.

POET: Then I know what dreams are.

DAUGHTER: And I have the strange feeling that we once stood somewhere else and said these same words.

POET: Then it shouldn't take you long to figure out what reality is.

DAUGHTER: Or dreams!

POET: Or poetry!

* * *

Enter the President of the University, the Dean of the Theological Seminary, the Dean of the Faculty of Philosophy, the Dean of the School of Medicine, and the Dean of the School of Law.

PRESIDENT: You all know what brings us here: the opening of the door. Let me call first upon the Dean of the Theological Seminary. What is your view of the matter?

DEAN OF THEOLOGY: I don't have any views; I believe! —*Credo*—

DEAN OF PHILOSOPHY: I postulate—

DEAN OF MEDICINE: I know—

DEAN OF LAW: I object—until I've seen the evidence and heard the witnesses.

PRESIDENT: Here we go! Quarreling already! . . . Let me begin again. What does the Dean of Theology *believe*?

DEAN OF THEOLOGY: I believe that this door should not be opened. It obviously conceals dangerous truths.

DEAN OF PHILOSOPHY: The truth is never dangerous!

DEAN OF MEDICINE: What is truth?

DEAN OF LAW: Whatever two witnesses testify to.

DEAN OF THEOLOGY: With two false witnesses anything can be proved—by a shyster!

DEAN OF PHILOSOPHY: Truth is wisdom; and wisdom and knowledge constitute philosophy itself. Philosophy is the science of sciences, the knowledge of knowledge; and all other branches of learning are its servants.

DEAN OF MEDICINE: The only science is natural science. Philosophy is not science; it's only empty speculation.

DEAN OF THEOLOGY: Bravo!

DEAN OF PHILOSOPHY (*to Dean of Theology*): Bravo, you say! What do you think you are? You're the archenemy of all knowledge. You're the very antithesis of science. You're ignorance and obscurantism itself—!

DEAN OF MEDICINE: Bravo!

DEAN OF THEOLOGY (*to Dean of Medicine*): Bravo, you say! You of all people! Who can't see farther than the end of your nose in a magnifying glass—you, who don't believe in anything but what your deceptive senses tell you—what your eyes tell you, for example, even though you may be far-sighted or near-sighted; cross-eyed, wall-eyed, or one-eyed; color blind, red-blind, green-blind.

DEAN OF MEDICINE: You blithering idiot!

DEAN OF THEOLOGY: Jackass!

They start fighting.

PRESIDENT: Stop that! Let's not have you birds pecking each other's eyes out.

DEAN OF PHILOSOPHY: Well, if I had to choose between those two—theology and medicine—I would choose—neither!

DEAN OF LAW: And if I sat on the bench and you three were brought before me, I'd sentence—all three of you! You can't agree on a single point, and you never could. . . . Let's get back to business. Mr. President, what is your own view on the opening of this door?

PRESIDENT: My view? I don't have any views. I have simply been appointed by the state to see to it that during our executive meetings you don't tear one another to pieces—while you're educating our youth. Views? Ah, no, indeed, I'm very careful not to have any views. There was a time when I had a few, but they were quickly refuted. Views are always quickly refuted—by those with the opposite views, you understand. . . . And now, perhaps we might proceed to the opening of the door, even at the risk of revealing some dangerous truths?

DEAN OF LAW: What is truth? What is *the* truth?

DEAN OF THEOLOGY: I am the truth, the way, and the life—

DEAN OF PHILOSOPHY: I am knowledge of knowledge—

DEAN OF MEDICINE: I am exact knowledge—

DEAN OF LAW: I object!

They all start to fight.

* * *

DAUGHTER: Aren't you ashamed? You, the teacher of our youth!

DEAN OF LAW: Mr. President! As the representative of the government and as the head of the faculty, you must bring charges against this woman for her remarks. She said we ought to be ashamed. Now that's an insult. And when she referred to us as the teacher of the young, her ironic tone of voice implied that we were incapable. Now that's slander!

DAUGHTER: Heaven help the students!

DEAN OF LAW: Do you hear? She's excusing the students! —That's the same as accusing us. Mr. President, I insist that you prosecute her!

DAUGHTER: Yes, that's right! I accuse you, you as a group, of sowing doubt and breeding skepticism in the minds of our youth.

DEAN OF LAW: Listen to her! There she stands telling the students to have no respect for our authority, and yet she has the gall to accuse us of breeding skepticism! If that isn't a criminal act, what is? I put it to you, all you good, right-thinking people.

* * *

ALL THE RIGHT-THINKING PEOPLE: Yes, yes, absolutely criminal!

DEAN OF LAW: There! All the right-thinking people have condemned you! —Now go in peace and be content with thy gain. Otherwise—!

DAUGHTER: My gain? —Otherwise! Otherwise what??

DEAN OF LAW: Otherwise thou shall be stoned.

POET: Or crucified.

DAUGHTER: Very well, I'll go. —Come with me and I'll give you the answer to the riddle.

POET: What riddle?

DAUGHTER: What did he mean by "my gain"?*

POET: Probably nothing. Just a lot of hot air, as we say. Talking through his hat.

DAUGHTER: But nothing could have hurt me more.

POET: I suppose that's why he said it. That's how people are.

* * *

ALL THE RIGHT-THINKING PEOPLE: Hooray! The door is open!

* * *

PRESIDENT: What lay hidden behind the door?

GLAZIER: I can't see anything.

PRESIDENT: You can't see anything? Well, I can't say I'm surprised—. Learned deans, what lay hidden behind the door?

DEAN OF THEOLOGY: Nothing. That is the key to the riddle of the world. In the beginning God created heaven and earth out of nothing.

---

* The exchange between the Dean of Law and the Daughter evidently reflects the words of Paul, I Timothy 6:1-6, with the Dean turning Paul's admonition against the Daughter.

DEAN OF PHILOSOPHY: Nothing comes of nothing.

DEAN OF MEDICINE: Bosh! Nothing. Period.

DEAN OF LAW: I object to the whole thing. It's a clear case of fraud. I appeal to all the right-thinking people!

DAUGHTER (*to the Poet*): What are the right-thinking people?

POET: I wish I knew. They usually turn out to be a party of one. Today it's me and my side—tomorrow it's you and your side. . . . You get appointed—or rather, you're self-appointed.

* * *

ALL THE RIGHT-THINKING PEOPLE: We've been swindled! Tricked!

PRESIDENT: And who has swindled you?

ALL THE RIGHT-THINKING PEOPLE: She did! The Daughter!

PRESIDENT (*to the Daughter*): Would you be so good as to tell us what you had in mind with this door-opening?

DAUGHTER: No, good people, I won't. "If I tell you, ye will not believe."

DEAN OF MEDICINE: But there's nothing—nothing at all.

DAUGHTER: You say right. But you understand not.

DEAN OF MEDICINE: She's talking nonsense!

EVERYONE: Nonsense! Boo!

DAUGHTER (*to the Poet*): Poor lost souls. I feel sorry for them.

POET: You serious?

DAUGHTER: Always serious.

POET: Do you also feel sorry for the right-thinking people?

DAUGHTER: Perhaps most of all for them.

POET: And what about the four learned faculties?

DAUGHTER: Them too, no less than the others. Four heads on one body, four minds! Who created the monster?

EVERYONE: She's not answering us!

PRESIDENT: Down with her!

DAUGHTER: But I have answered you!

PRESIDENT: Don't you talk back to me!

EVERYONE: Listen to her! She's talking back!

DAUGHTER: Answer or not answer, I can't win. . . . Come with me, you poet and seer, and I shall tell you – somewhere far from here – the answer to the riddle. Somewhere, out in the desert, where no one can hear us, no one see us. Because –

* * *

LAWYER (*coming forward and grabbing the Daughter by the arm*): Have you forgotten your responsibilities?

DAUGHTER: God knows I haven't. But I have more important responsibilities.

LAWYER: What about your child?

DAUGHTER: My child – oh yes! What about her?

LAWYER: Your child is crying for you.

DAUGHTER: My child! How that child ties me down! I feel chained to the earth. . . . And I have this pain in my breast, this feeling of anguish. What is it?

LAWYER: Don't you know?

DAUGHTER: No.

LAWYER: The pangs of conscience.

DAUGHTER: Is that what it is? The pangs of conscience?

LAWYER: That's right. They show up after every duty you neglect, after every pleasure you enjoy, however innocent – if there are any innocent pleasures (which I doubt), and after every harm you do your friends and neighbors.

DAUGHTER: And there's no cure for these pangs, I suppose?

LAWYER: Oh, yes; but only one. You must discharge your duty without a moment's hesitation.

DAUGHTER: You know, you look just like a demon when you say that word "duty." — But what am I supposed to do if I have two duties to discharge?

LAWYER: Simple! First you discharge one, and then the other.

DAUGHTER: The most important one first. — So I leave my child in your care, while I go to discharge my first duty.

LAWYER: But the child needs you; you'll break its heart. Can you bear to know that someone is suffering on account of you?

DAUGHTER: You're turning me against myself. You've broken my heart in two and it's pulling me both ways.

LAWYER: Life is full of little conflicts like that.

DAUGHTER: Oh, how my heart is torn. I don't know which way to turn.

* * *

POET: If you knew how much sorrow and misery I caused by discharging the obligations I owed to my calling in life — notice: my calling, the most important duty of all — you would shun me.

DAUGHTER: Why? What did you do?

POET: My father placed all his hopes in me. I was his only son and he dreamed about how I would carry on the business he had built up. I ran away from business school and my father never got over it. My mother wanted me to study religion, but I didn't have the heart for it. So she disowned me. I had a friend who gave me a helping hand when I was down and out. But my friend had different political views, fought against the causes I spoke for and fought for. I had to cut down my best friend and benefactor in order to be true to myself. Since then I've never known any peace. They call me disloyal, a stinker. And a fat lot of good it does me to hear my conscience tell me, "You did right," because the next moment it's telling me how wrong I was. And that's life for you.

* * *

DAUGHTER: Come with me out into the desert.

LAWYER: Your child! Your child!

DAUGHTER (*indicating all those present*): Here are my children! Taken one by one, they're good and gentle. But put them together and they fight with one another and turn into demons. . . . Goodbye . . .

[13]

> *Outside the castle. Same set as in the first scene of the first act. Only now the ground below the footings is covered with flowers (blue monkshood or aconite). At the very top of the castle, surmounting its tower and lantern, is a chrysanthemum bud ready to burst into bloom. The windows have candles burning in them.*
>
> *The Daughter and the Poet are onstage.*

DAUGHTER: The time has nearly come when with the help of the fire I shall rise and return to the empyrean. This is what you call death, what you approach with fear in your hearts.

POET: Fear of the unknown.

DAUGHTER: Which you really know.

POET: Who knows?

DAUGHTER: Everyone! Why do you not believe your prophets?

POET: Prophets have never been believed. I wonder why? —"If God has spoken, why will men not believe?" His power to persuade must surely be irresistible!

DAUGHTER: Have you always been a skeptic?

POET: No. Many a time I've had absolute faith and certitude, but it always faded away after a while, like a dream upon awakening.

DAUGHTER: It isn't easy to be a human being. I know that.

POET: You have come to realize that, have you, and admit it?

DAUGHTER: Yes.

POET: Tell me something. Was it not Indra who once sent his son here to earth to hear the complaints of mankind?

DAUGHTER: Yes, it was. And how did the people receive him?

POET: What did he do to accomplish his mission? — to answer with a question.

DAUGHTER: To answer with another question: was not the condition of mankind improved as a result of his visit to earth? Tell me truly.

POET: Improved? Yes, a little. Very little! —Now, instead of asking questions, will you solve the riddle?

DAUGHTER: I could. But what good would it do? You wouldn't believe the answer.

POET: You, I will believe. I know who you are.

DAUGHTER: Very well, I shall tell you. . . . At the dawn of time before the sun shone, Brahma, the divine primal potency, went forth and let himself be seduced by Maya, the creative mother of the world, so that he might propagate himself. The divine element thus joined with earthly matter. This was the fall of heaven. Consequently, the world and its inhabitants and life itself are nothing more than phantoms, mirages, images in a dream—

POET: My dream!

DAUGHTER: A dream come true. Now, to free themselves from earthly matter the progeny of Brahma seek deprivation and suffering. There you have suffering as the redeemer. But this yearning for suffering comes into conflict with the craving for pleasure. Which is love. Now do you understand what love is, offering the most sublime joys along with the most profound suffering, sweetest when it is most bitter? Do you understand what woman is? Woman, through whom sin and death entered into life?

POET: I do understand. And the upshot?

DAUGHTER: I don't have to tell you. Constant strife between the anguish of joy and the pleasure of suffering, the torments of remorse and the delights of sensuality.

POET: Strife—is that all we can hope for?

DAUGHTER: The conflict between opposites produces energy, just as fire and water generate steam power.

POET: And peace? And rest?

DAUGHTER: I've said enough. You mustn't ask any more, and I mustn't answer. . . . The altar is decked for the sacrifice. . . . The flowers keep watch, the lights are lit. . . . The funeral wreaths hang in the windows and doors.*

POET: You say that as calmly and coolly as if you didn't know what it means to suffer.

DAUGHTER: Not know? I have suffered all that mortal man suffers but felt it a hundred times more, because my senses are keener.

POET: Tell me what you suffered.

DAUGHTER: You're a poet, but could even you tell me your troubles in words that said it all? Was there ever a time when your words and your thoughts were in perfect harmony? A time when your words soared to the level of your thoughts?

POET: No, you're right. Before my own thoughts I stood deaf and dumb. And when the crowd listened in admiration to my song, it sounded like bawling to me. I guess that's why I always blushed when I heard my praises sung.

DAUGHTER: And yet you expect me to–? Look me in the eye!

POET: I can't. Your gaze is too intense.

DAUGHTER: And so would my words be if I spoke in my own tongue.

POET: At least tell me – before you go – what was the hardest thing to endure – down here?

DAUGHTER: Being, just being. Feeling my sight clouded by these eyes, my hearing muffled by these ears, and my thoughts,

---

* In place of the funeral wreaths, the original has "white sheets in the windows, pine cuttings on the walk" – once customary features at Swedish funerals.

my bright, airy thoughts trapped in the labyrinth of coiled fat. You know what a brain looks like—what crooked ways, what secret passages!

POET: I know. I suppose that's why all the right-thinking people think crooked.

DAUGHTER: Always ready with sarcasm. That's how you all are.

POET: What do you expect?

DAUGHTER: Now I'm going to shake the dust off my feet first—the earth, the clay.) *She takes off her shoes and lays them on the fire.)*

* * *

STAGE-DOOR KEEPER (*enters and lays her shawl on the fire*): Maybe you wouldn't mind if I added my shawl to the fire, would you, deary? (*Exits.*)

OFFICER (*enters*): And I my roses? Nothing left but thorns. (*Exits.*)

BILLPOSTER (*enters*): The posters can go. But my dip net, never! (*Exits.*)

GLAZIER (*enters*): The diamond glass cutter that opened the door! Goodbye! (*Exits.*)

LAWYER (*enters*): The minutes of the great lawsuit concerning the pope's beard or the diminishing water supply in the sources of the Ganges River. (*Exits.*)

MEDICAL INSPECTOR (*enters*): Only a small contribution: the black mask that made me black against my will. (*Exits.*)

VICTORIA (*enters*): My beauty—my sorrow! (*Exits.*)

EDITH (*enters*): My ugliness—my sorrow! (*Exits.*)

BLIND MAN (*enters, sticks his hand into the fire*): I give my hand in place of my eye! (*Exits.*)

> *The old Don Juan enters in his wheelchair, accompanied by the Coquette and the "Friend."*

DON JUAN: Hurry up! Hurry up! Life is short! (*Exits with the others.*)

* * *

POET: I once read that when life nears its end, everything in it comes rushing past in single file. Is this the end?

DAUGHTER: It is for me. Goodbye.

POET: Not even a few parting words?

DAUGHTER: There's nothing I can say. Do you still believe that your words can express our thoughts?

* * *

DEAN OF THEOLOGY (*enters, raging mad*): I've been repudiated by my God, I'm persecuted by the people, disowned by the administration, ridiculed by my colleagues! How can I have faith, how can I believe, when no one else does? How can I fight for a God who does not fight for his own? Junk! That's what it is—junk! (*He throws a book on the fire and leaves.*)

* * *

POET (*snatching the book from the fire*): You know what it is? A martyrology. It lists a martyr for each day of the year.

DAUGHTER: Martyr?

POET: Yes—someone who was tortured and put to death for his beliefs. And why? —Do you think that everyone who is tortured suffers, and that everyone who is put to death feels pain? Doesn't suffering melt our chains and doesn't death set us free?

* * *

CHRISTINE (*enters with her strips of paper and weatherstripping*): I'm going to paste and seal and paste and seal until there's nothing more to paste and seal!

POET: And if heaven itself split wide open, you'd try to paste and seal that too! Go away!

CHRISTINE: Aren't there any inner windows in the castle for me to seal up?

POET: No, there certainly aren't! Not there!

CHRISTINE (*leaving*): Well, then I'm leaving.

* * *

DAUGHTER:

>It's time! Give me your hand, my friend,
>Farewell, you human being, you dreamer,
>you poet, who knows best how to live,
>soaring on wings above the earth,
>swooping down when you feel like it,
>to graze the dust, not to drown in it.
>
>Now when I must leave, how hard it is
>to say goodbye, to bid farewell.
>One longs for all that one has loved,
>regrets all that one has offended.
>Now, now I know what it means to live;
>I feel the pain of being human.
>You miss what you never wanted;
>regret even misdeeds never done.
>You want to leave, you want to stay;
>your heart's drawn and quartered, torn apart
>by conflicting wishes, indecision, doubt.
>
>Goodbye, my friend! Tell your fellow men
>that where I'm going I shall think of them
>and that in your name I shall convey
>their plaints and protests to the throne on high.
>Farewell!

>>*She enters the castle. Music. The rear of the stage is lit up by the burning castle and reveals a wall of human faces, questioning, sorrowful, despairing.*
>>
>>*As the castle burns, the flower bud at the top bursts and blossoms into a huge chrysanthemum.*

Introduction to *The Ghost Sonata*

1906 and 1907 saw a remarkable improvement in Strindberg's theatrical fortunes. *Miss Julie* was performed in Stockholm for the first time, and *A Dream Play* was also staged there for the first time anywhere. Both productions received generally good reviews, and Strindberg followed up these successes by establishing his own theater and writing four plays for it. The man who brought *Miss Julie* to Stockholm was a young actor, August Falck, whose venturesome spirit attracted Strindberg. The two of them determined to open an intimate theater in Stockholm that would be devoted to highbrow drama, classic and modern. The theater they finally got was a small one, seating 161, and with a stage that measured only eighteen by twelve feet. The size of the theater and its lack of technical resources did not dampen Strindberg's spirits. To the theatrical vanguard, heavily realistic stage sets were passé, and theoreticians like Georg Fuchs with his book *Die Schaubühne der Zukunft* and artists like Gordon Craig with his *The Art of the Theatre*, both published in 1905, were opening the way to a simplified symbolic stage that suited Strindberg's artistic purposes. "Retheatricalize the theater" was Fuchs's motto; "dematerialize the stage" was Strindberg's.

The ninety-minute plays (the now successful *Miss Julie* was a ninety-minute play) that Strindberg wrote for his Intimate Theatre were called chamber plays, a term suggesting intimacy, exclusiveness, and a musical treatment. "If you were to ask me," he wrote,

> what the aim of an intimate theater is and what is meant by a chamber play, I would say that in this kind of drama we single out the significant and overriding theme, but within limits. In handling it we avoid all ostentation—all the calculated effects, the bravura roles, the solo numbers for the stars, and the cues for applause. The author rejects all predetermined forms because the theme determines the form.

Hence complete freedom to treat the theme as he will, limited only by the harmony of ideas and a sense of style. [*Öppna brev till Intima teatern.*]

The Ghost Sonata, the third of the chamber plays, is one of Strindberg's most original and startling creations, along with *To Damascus* and *A Dream Play*. Containing many of the forces, impulses, and ideas of the experimental theater of the twentieth century, it defies classification. Ingmar Bergman, who has directed it three times, ranks it among the ten greatest plays of all time.

In saying that theme determines form, Strindberg is not telling us what makes *The Ghost Sonata* such a special play. Theme determines the form of *A Dream Play*, too, but there the freedom with which he handled the theme seems natural because anything can happen in a dream. In *The Ghost Sonata* Strindberg makes theatrical poetry out of everyday reality by magnifying it, x-raying it, so that the familiar and the trivial seem strange, significant, and frightening.

"The earlier dream plays," explains Swedish theater historian Agne Beijer,

> had been set in a visionary, unreal world, where no one expected the same logic and the same scale of values to apply as in everyday life. The chamber plays seek out this everyday world directly and depict it with a naturalism that does not shun the coarsest vulgarities but that simultaneously shatters all the ordinary conceptions of them by distorting the standards by which we measure such things, overstressing the insignificant and italicizing the trivial in order thereby to give them a new import, in other words, to bring the material world we live and work in to the point at which it splits so that through the cracks we can catch glimpses of another world.

In *The Ghost Sonata*, this other world is the world of the spirit, and the action takes place when the spirit is being separated from the physical body. For the visionary Swedenborg, whose theory of correspondences exercised an enormous influence on Strindberg, the physical world was like a mask on the face of the spirit. Remove the mask, remove all that places one in a particular society, all the attributes that go with one's position, and the true person will be revealed. Strindberg provides a vivid demonstration of this unmasking and undressing in the second scene of the play.

At death, of course, the spirit is finally separated from the body. *The Ghost Sonata* represents a journey, signaled by the bells at the beginning, that transports us to the Isle of the Dead and that parallels the emergence of the soul from its physical husk. Visionaries need not take the actual journey. They look at the "real" everyday scene. It breaks up as they look at it and see what lies behind. This mystical, visionary experience constitutes the action of *The Ghost Sonata*.

To elevate the play above the physical, to dematerialize the stage, Strindberg constructs the play along musical lines, as its title intimates. What happens to the characters is less important than what happens to the principal themes, which are announced in the first few moments and developed and varied from episode to episode. Then at the very end, a new kind of music is heard and an even newer kind of theater is created, as Strindberg assembles a montage—before the term had been coined—a collision of elements, of sights and sounds, that together form an artistic unity encompassing the contradictions of life and resolving them in a higher unity.

The Ghost Sonata

Opus Three
of
The Chamber Plays

CHARACTERS

THE OLD MAN, Mr. Hummel
THE STUDENT, Arkenholz
THE MILKMAID, an apparition
THE SUPERINTENDENT's WIFE
THE SUPERINTENDENT
THE DEAD MAN, formerly a consul
THE WOMAN IN BLACK, daughter of The Dead Man and The Superintendent's Wife
THE COLONEL
THE MUMMY, The Colonel's wife
THE YOUNG LADY, The Colonel's daughter, actually The Old Man's daughter
BARON SKANSKORG, engaged to The Woman in Black
JOHANSSON, Hummel's servant
BENGTSSON, The Colonel's manservant
THE FIANCÉE, Hummel's former fiancée, now a white-haired old woman
[THE COOK*]
BEGGARS
A HOUSEMAID

Scene: Stockholm

---

* Not included in Strindberg's list of characters.

[1]

The first two floors of a facade of a new house on a city square. Only the corner of the house is visible, the ground floor terminating in a round room, the second floor in a balcony with a flagpole.

When the curtains are drawn and the windows opened in the round room, one can see a white marble statue of a young woman surrounded by palms and bathed in sunlight. On the windowsill farthest to the left are pots of hyacinths—blue, white, pink.

Hanging on the railing of the balcony on the second story are a blue silk bedspread and two white bed pillows. The windows to the left are covered with white sheets signifying a death in the house. It is a bright Sunday morning.

A green park bench is downstage toward the left.

Downstage right is a drinking fountain with a long-handled drinking cup hanging at its side. To the left a kiosk, plastered with advertisements. A telephone booth is also onstage.

The main entrance to the house is at the left. Through the door can be seen the hall and the staircase with marble steps and balustrade of mahogany and brass. On the sidewalk on both sides of the entryway are tubs with small laurels.

The corner of the house with the round room also faces a side street that runs upstage.

On the first floor to the left of the entryway is a window with a special mirror, quite common in Sweden around the turn of the century, which enables those inside to view the passing scene without sticking their heads out the window.

At the rise of the curtain, the bells of several churches can be heard ringing in the distance.

The double doors in the entryway are wide open. The Woman in Black stands motionless in the doorway.

The Superintendent's Wife is sweeping the vestibule. Having finished that, she polishes the brass on the door and then waters the laurels.

Sitting in a wheelchair near the kiosk is The Old Man, reading a newspaper. He has white hair and beard and is wearing glasses.

The Milkmaid comes in from around the corner, carrying a wire basket filled with bottles. She is wearing a summer dress, with brown shoes, black stockings, and white cap. She takes off her cap and hangs it on the drinking fountain; wipes the sweat from her brow; takes a drink from the cup; washes her hands; arranges her hair, using the water in the fountain as a mirror.

The ringing of a steamship bell is heard, and now and then the silence is broken by the deep notes of the organs in the nearby churches.

After a few moments of silence, and after The Milkmaid has finished arranging her hair, The Student enters from the left. He is unshaven and looks haggard from lack of sleep. He goes directly to the drinking fountain.

Pause.

THE STUDENT: Could I borrow the cup, please?

The Milkmaid hugs the cup to herself.

Aren't you through using it?

The Milkmaid stares at him in terror.

THE OLD MAN (*to himself*): Who on earth is he talking to? —I don't see anyone! —Is he crazy? (*He continues to stare at them in amazement.*)

THE STUDENT: What are you looking at? Do I look so awful? —Well, I haven't slept a wink all night. I suppose you think that I've been out doing the town . . .

> *The Milkmaid still stares at him in terror.*

Think I've been drinking, don't you? —Do I smell like it?

> *The Milkmaid as before.*

I haven't had a chance to shave. . . . Come on, let me have a drink of water. After last night, I think I've earned it. (*Pause.*) Must I tell you the whole story? I've spent the night caring for the injured. I've bound up their wounds. You see, I was there when the house collapsed last night. I was there. . . . Well, that's it.

> *The Milkmaid rinses the cup and offers him a drink of water.*

Thanks!

> *The Milkmaid does not move.*

(*The Student continues, slowly*): I wonder if you would do me a great favor? (*Pause.*) The thing is, my eyes are inflamed, as you can see—but I've had my hands on wounds and on corpses—so I don't want to risk using my hands to wash my eyes. . . . Would you take this clean handkerchief, dip it in that fresh water, and bathe my sore eyes with it? —Would you do that? —Will you be my Good Samaritan?

> *The Milkmaid hesitates for a moment before doing as asked.*

That's very kind of you. And here's something for your trouble—

(*He has taken his wallet out and is about to offer her some money. The Milkmaid makes a gesture of refusal.*) I'm sorry. Forgive me. I'm still in a daze . . .

* * *

THE OLD MAN (*to The Student*): Forgive my speaking to you, but I could not help hearing you say you were in on that terrible accident yesterday evening. I was just sitting here reading about it in the paper.

THE STUDENT: Is it already in the paper?

THE OLD MAN: The whole story! And they've got a picture of you too. But they regret they were unable to obtain the name of the courageous young student . . .

THE STUDENT (*looking at the paper*): So that's me! What do you know!

THE OLD MAN: Who . . . who was that you were talking to just now?

THE STUDENT: Didn't you see?

Pause

THE OLD MAN: I suppose I'm being nosey, but would you do me the honor of giving me your name?

THE STUDENT: Why do you want to know that? I don't care for publicity. First they build you up, then they tear you down. The insult now ranks among the fine arts—and the ranker the finer. Besides I'm not looking for any reward.

THE OLD MAN: Rich, I suppose?

THE STUDENT: Not at all! I haven't got a dime to my name.

THE OLD MAN: It's strange . . . but I can't help thinking that I've heard your voice before. . . . When I was a young man I had a friend who couldn't pronounce window, he always said winder. I've only met one person who said that, and that was him. The other is you, of course. Is it possible that you are related to Arkenholz, the wholesale dealer?

THE STUDENT: He was my father.

THE OLD MAN: Isn't fate strange? Then I saw you when you were a child – under very trying circumstances.

THE STUDENT: I suppose so. I understand I came into the world right in the middle of bankruptcy proceedings.

THE OLD MAN: Exactly!

THE STUDENT: May I ask what your name is?

THE OLD MAN: My name is Hummel.

THE STUDENT: Hummel? Then you're–. Yes, I remember . . .

THE OLD MAN: You've heard my name mentioned in your family?

THE STUDENT: Yes.

THE OLD MAN: And mentioned, perhaps, with a certain antipathy?

The Student remains silent.

I can well imagine! . . . No doubt you heard that I was the man who ruined your father? . . . Everyone who is ruined by stupid speculations comes to realize sooner or later that he was actually ruined by someone he couldn't fool. (*Pause.*) The truth of the matter is that your father fleeced me of seventeen thousand crowns, every cent I had saved up at the time.

THE STUDENT: It's remarkable how the same story can be told in two exactly opposite ways.

THE OLD MAN: Surely you don't think I'm being untruthful?

THE STUDENT: What do you think? My father didn't lie.

THE OLD MAN: That's true, a father never lies. . . . But I too am a father, and consequently . . .

THE STUDENT: What're you getting at?

THE OLD MAN: I saved your father from the worst possible

misery, and he repaid me with all the terrible hatred of a man who feels obliged to be grateful. He taught his family to speak ill of me.

THE STUDENT: Maybe you made him ungrateful. The help you gave him was probably poisoned with unnecessary humiliations.

THE OLD MAN: My dear young man, all help is humiliating.

THE STUDENT: What do you want of me?

THE OLD MAN: Don't worry, I'm not asking for the money back. But if you would render me a few small services, I would consider myself well repaid. You see that I'm a cripple—some say it's my own fault—others blame my parents—personally I blame it all on life itself, with all its traps—in avoiding one you fall right into the next one. Anyway, I can't run up and down stairs—can't even pull bell cords. And so I ask you: help me!

THE STUDENT: What can I do?

THE OLD MAN: Well, first of all you might give my chair a push so that I can read the posters. I want to see what's playing tonight.

THE STUDENT (*pushing the wheelchair*): Don't you have a man who takes care of you?

THE OLD MAN: He's off on an errand. . . . Be right back. . . . Are you a medical student?

THE STUDENT: No, I'm studying languages. But I really don't know what I want to be.

THE OLD MAN: Ah ha! —How are you at mathematics?

THE STUDENT: Fairly good.

THE OLD MAN: Good! Good! —Would you possibly be interested in a job?

THE STUDENT: Sure, why not?

THE OLD MAN: Splendid! (*Reading the posters.*) They're giving *Die Walküre* at the matinee. . . . That means that the colonel will be there with his daughter. And since he always sits on the aisle in the sixth row, I'll put you next to him. . . . You go into that telephone booth over there and order a ticket for seat number eighty-two in the sixth row.

THE STUDENT: An afternoon at the opera!

THE OLD MAN: That's right! Just do as I tell you and you won't regret it. I want to see you happy—rich, respected. Your debut last night as the courageous rescuer is the beginning of your fame. From now on your name is your fortune.

THE STUDENT (*going toward the telephone booth*): All right! Sounds like fun. Let's see what happens.

THE OLD MAN: You're a good sport, aren't you?

THE STUDENT: Suppose so. That's my misfortune.

THE OLD MAN: No more. This will make your fortune.

> *He picks up his newspaper and starts to read. In the meantime The Lady in Black has come out on the sidewalk and is talking with The Superintendent's Wife. The Old Man listens furtively, but the audience hears nothing. The Student returns.*

All set?

THE STUDENT: It's all taken care of.

THE OLD MAN: Take a look at that house.

THE STUDENT: I have already looked at it—very carefully. . . . I went by here yesterday, when the sun was glittering on the panes—and dreaming of all the beauty and luxury there must be in that house, I said to my friend, "Imagine having an apartment there, four flights up, and a beautiful wife, and two pretty kids, and twenty thousand crowns in dividends every year."

THE OLD MAN: Did you now? Did you say that? Well, well! I too am very fond of that house . . .

THE STUDENT: Do you speculate in houses?

THE OLD MAN: Mmm—yes! But not in the way you think . . .

THE STUDENT: Do you know the people who live there?

THE OLD MAN: Every single one. At my age you know everyone, including their fathers and their grandfathers—and you always find you're related to them somehow. I've just turned eighty. . . . But no one knows me, not really. . . . I take a great interest in human destinies . . .

> *The curtains in the round room are drawn up. The Colonel is seen inside, dressed in civilian clothes. After having looked at the thermometer, he moves away from the window and stands in front of the marble statue.*

Look, there's the colonel! You'll sit next to him this afternoon.

THE STUDENT: Is that him—the colonel? I don't understand anything that's going on. It's like a fairy tale.

THE OLD MAN: My whole life, my dear young man, is like a book of fairy tales. But although the stories are different, one thread ties them all together and the same leitmotif recurs constantly.

THE STUDENT: Who is that marble statue in there?

THE OLD MAN: That's his wife, naturally . . .

THE STUDENT: Was she so wonderful? Did he love her so much?

THE OLD MAN: Hmm yes . . . yes, of course . . .

THE STUDENT: Well, tell me!

THE OLD MAN: Come now, you know we can't judge other people. . . . Suppose I were to tell you that she left him, that he beat her, that she came back again and married him again, and that she is sitting in there right now like a mummy, worshiping her own statue. You would think I was crazy.

THE STUDENT: I can't understand it!

THE OLD MAN: That doesn't surprise me! —And over there

we have the hyacinth window. That's where his daughter lives. She's out horseback riding, but she'll be home soon . . .

THE STUDENT: Who's the lady in black talking to the caretaker?

THE OLD MAN: Well, that's a little complicated. But it's connected with the dead man upstairs, there where you see the white sheets.

THE STUDENT: And who was he?

THE OLD MAN: A human being, like the rest of us. The most conspicuous thing about him was his vanity. . . . Now if you were a Sunday child, you would soon see him come out of that very door just to look at the consulate flag at half-mast for himself. Yes, you see, he was a consul. Liked nothing better than coronets and lions, plumed hats and colored ribbons.

THE STUDENT: Sunday child, did you say? I was actually born on a Sunday, so I'm told.

THE OLD MAN: Really! Are you–! I should have guessed it. I could tell by the color of your eyes. . . . But–then you can see . . . what others can't see, haven't you noticed that?

THE STUDENT: I don't know what others see. But sometimes–. Well, there are some things you don't talk about!

THE OLD MAN: I knew it, I knew it! But you can talk to me about it. I understand–things like that . . .

THE STUDENT: Yesterday, for example. . . . I was drawn to that little side street where the house collapsed afterward. . . . I walked down the street and stopped in front of a house that I had never seen before. . . . Then I noticed a crack in the wall. I could hear the floor beams snapping in two. I leaped forward and grabbed up a child that was walking under the wall. . . . The next moment the house collapsed. . . . I escaped–but in my arms–where I thought I had the child–there wasn't anything . . .

THE OLD MAN: Remarkable. Remarkable. . . . I always knew that. . . . But tell me something: why were you making all those gestures just now at the fountain? And why were you talking to yourself?

THE STUDENT: Didn't you see the milkmaid I was talking to?

THE OLD MAN (*in horror*): Milkmaid?!

THE STUDENT: Yes, of course. She handed me the cup.

THE OLD MAN: Indeed? . . . So that's the way it is? . . . Very well, I may not have second sight, but I have other powers . . .

> *A white-haired woman sits down at the window with the mirror.*

Look at the old lady in the window! Do you see her? . . . Good, good! That was my fiancée—once upon a time—sixty years ago. . . . I was twenty. Don't be afraid, she doesn't recognize me. We see each other every day, but it doesn't mean a thing to me—although we once vowed to love each other forever. Forever!

THE STUDENT: How foolish you were in those days! Nowadays we don't tell girls things like that.

THE OLD MAN: Forgive us, young man. We didn't know any better! . . . But can you see that that old woman was once young and beautiful?

THE STUDENT: No, I can't. . . . Well, maybe. I like the way she tilts her head. . . . I can't see her eyes.

> *The Superintendent's Wife comes out carrying a basket of spruce greens, which she strews on the sidewalk, in accordance with Swedish custom at funerals.*

THE OLD MAN: Ah ha, the wife of the superintendent! The lady in black is her daughter by the dead man upstairs. That's why her husband got the job as superintendent. . . . But the lady in black has a lover—very aristocratic and waiting to inherit a fortune. Right now he's in the process of getting a divorce—from his present wife, who is giving him a town house just to get rid of him. The aristocratic lover is the son-in-law of the dead man, and you see his bedclothes being aired on the balcony up there.—Complicated, wouldn't you say?

THE STUDENT: It's damned complicated!

THE OLD MAN: Yes, indeed it is, both on the inside and the outside, although it all looks so simple.

THE STUDENT: But then who is the dead man?

THE OLD MAN: You just asked me and I told you. If you could look around the corner where the service entrance is, you'd see a pack of poor people whom he used to help—when he felt like it.

THE STUDENT: Then I suppose he was a kind and charitable man?

THE OLD MAN: Oh, yes—sometimes.

THE STUDENT: Not always?

THE OLD MAN: No, that's how people are! —Listen, will you give me a little push over there into the sun? I'm so terribly cold. When you never get to move around, the blood congeals. I'm going to die soon, I know that. But before I do, there are a few things I want to take care of. —Feel my hand, just feel how cold I am.

THE STUDENT: My god! It's unbelievable! (*He tries to free his hand, but The Old Man holds on to it.*)

THE OLD MAN: Don't leave me, I beg you—I'm tired, I'm lonely—but it hasn't always been this way, I tell you. —I have an infinitely long life behind me—infinitely long—I've made people unhappy and people have made me unhappy, the one cancels out the other. But before I die, I want to make you happy. . . . Our destinies are tangled together through your father—and other things.

THE STUDENT: Let go, let go of my hand—you are drawing all my strength from me—you're turning my blood to ice—what do you want of me?

THE OLD MAN: Patience. You'll soon see and understand. . . . There she comes—

THE STUDENT: The colonel's daughter?

THE OLD MAN: Yes! *His* daughter! Just look at her! —Have you ever seen such a masterpiece?

THE STUDENT: She looks like the marble statue in there.

THE OLD MAN: She should. That's her mother!

THE STUDENT: Incredibly beautiful! "Thou art fairer than the evening air, clad in the beauty of a thousand stars."

THE OLD MAN: Yes, indeed. "And happy he who on her lips shall press the bridegroom's greeting." —I see you appreciate her beauty. Not everyone recognizes it. . . . Well, then, it is ordained!

* * *

The Young Lady enters from the left dressed in a riding habit like a modern English horsewoman, and, without taking notice of anyone, crosses slowly over to the door of the house. Before entering, she stops and says a few words to The Superintendent's Wife. The Student covers his eyes with his hands.

Are you crying?

THE STUDENT: When I see how far beyond my reach my happiness is, what can I feel but despair?

THE OLD MAN: But I can open doors—and hearts—if only I can find an arm to do my will. Serve me, and you shall be a lord of creation!

THE STUDENT: A devil's bargain? You want me to sell my soul?

THE OLD MAN: Sell nothing! —Don't you understand, all my life I have *taken, taken*! Now I crave to give, to give! But nobody will take what I have to offer. I'm a rich man, very rich—and without any heirs. —Oh, yes, I have a good-for-nothing son who torments the life out of me. . . . You could become my son, become my heir while I'm still alive, enjoy life while I'm here to see it—at least from a distance.

THE STUDENT: What do you want me to do?

THE OLD MAN: First: go an hear *Die Walküre*!

THE STUDENT: That's already been taken care of. What else?

THE GHOST SONATA

THE OLD MAN: This evening you shall be sitting in there—in the round room!

THE STUDENT: How do you expect me to get in?

THE OLD MAN: By way of *Die Walküre*!

THE STUDENT: Why did you pick me for your—your medium? Did you know me before?

THE OLD MAN: Of course, of course! I've had my eye on you for a long time. . . . Ah! Look up there, on the balcony, where the maid is raising the flag to half-mast for the consul—and now she's turning over the bedclothes. . . . Do you see that blue quilt? It was made for two to sleep under, and now it covers only one . . .

>   The *Young Lady*, in a change of clothes, appears at the window to water the hyacinths.

There's my dear little girl. Look at her, just look at her! . . . She's talking to the flowers now. Isn't she just like a blue hyacinth herself? She gives them water to drink, the purest water, and they transform the water into color and perfume. —Here comes the colonel with a newspaper. . . . Now he's pointing to your picture! She's reading about your heroic deed. —It's starting to cloud over. Suppose it starts to rain? I'll be in a pretty mess if Johansson doesn't come back soon.

>   *It grows cloudy and dark. The Old Woman at the window mirror closes her window.*

I see my fiancée is closing up shop. . . . Seventy-nine years. . . . That window mirror is the only mirror she ever uses. That's because she can't see herself in it, only the outside world and from two direction at once. But the world can see her. She doesn't realize that. . . . All the same, not bad-looking for an old woman.

>   *The Dead Man, wrapped in a winding sheet, is seen coming out of the main door.*

THE STUDENT: Oh my god, what—?

THE OLD MAN: What do you see?

THE STUDENT: Don't *you* see? Don't you see, in the doorway, the dead man?

THE OLD MAN: No, I don't see anything. But I'm not surprised. Tell me exactly what—

THE STUDENT: He's stepping out into the street. . . . (*Pauses.*) Now he's turning his head and looking up at the flag.

THE OLD MAN: What did I tell you? Watch, he will count every wreath and read every calling card. I pity whoever is missing!

THE STUDENT: Now he's turning the corner . . .

THE OLD MAN: He's gone to count the poor people at the service entrance. The poor add such a nice touch to an obituary: "Received the blessings of the populace!" Yes, but he won't receive my blessing! —Just between us, he was a big scoundrel.

THE STUDENT: But benevolent.

THE OLD MAN: A benevolent scoundrel. Always thinking of his own magnificent funeral. . . . When he could feel his end was near, he embezzled fifty thousand crowns from the state. . . . Now his daughter is running around with another woman's husband and wondering about the will. . . . The scoundrel can hear every word we're saying. I hope he gets an earful! —Here's Johansson.

Johansson enters from the left.

Report!

Johannson speaks to The Old Man, but the audience cannot hear what he says.

What do you mean, not at home? You're an ass! —What about the telegram? —Not a word! . . . Go on, go on! . . . Six o'clock this evening? That's good! —An extra edition? —With all the details about him? . . . Arkenholz, student . . . born . . . his parents. . . . Splendid! . . . It's beginning to rain, I think. . . . And what did he say? . . . Really, really! – He didn't *want* to? Well, he's going to have to! – Here comes the baron, or whatever he is! – Push me around the corner, Johansson. I want to hear what the poor people are saying. – And Arkenholz! Don't go away. Do you understand? – Well, come on, come on, what are you waiting for!

> *Johansson pushes the wheelchair around the corner.*

* * *

> *The Student has turned to look at The Young Lady, who is loosening the earth in hyacinth pots.*

* * *

> *Dressed in mourning, Baron Skanskorg enters and speaks to The Lady in Black, who has been walking up and down the sidewalk.*

BARON SKANSKORG: What can we do about it? We simply have to wait.

LADY IN BLACK (*intensely*): But I can't wait, don't you understand?

BARON SKANSKORG: Well, if that's the way it is, you'll have to go to the country.

LADY IN BLACK: I don't want to do that!

BARON SKANSKORG: Come over here. Otherwise they'll hear what we're saying.

> *They move over toward the kiosk and continue their conversation unheard by the audience.*

* * *

> *Johansson enters from the right.*

JOHANSSON (*to The Student*): My master asks you not to forget that other matter . . .

THE STUDENT (*warily*): Just a minute—I want to know something first. Tell me, exactly who is Hummel? What is he?

JOHANSSON: What can I say? He's so many things, and he's been everything.

THE STUDENT: Is he in his right mind?

JOHANSSON: Who is? All his life he's been looking for a Sunday child. That's what he says—but he might be making it up . . .

THE STUDENT: What's he after? Money?

JOHANSSON: Power. —All day long he rides around in his chariot like the great god Thor. . . . He keeps his eye on houses, tears them down, opens up streets, builds up city squares. But he also breaks into houses, sneaks in through the windows, ravages human lives, kills his enemies, and forgives nothing and nobody. . . . Can you imagine that that little cripple was once a Don Juan? But no woman would ever stick with him.

THE STUDENT: Sounds inconsistent.

JOHANSSON: Oh, no. You see, he was so sly that he knew how to get the women to leave when he got bored with them. But that was a long time ago. Now he's more like a horse thief at a slave market. He steals people—in more ways than one. . . . He literally stole me out of the hands of the law. I made a little mistake—that's all—and he was the only one who knew about it. But instead of putting me in jail, he made me his slave. I slave for him just for my food—which isn't the best in the world.

THE STUDENT: What's he got up his sleeve? What's he want to do in this house?

JOHANSSON: I wouldn't want to say! I wouldn't even know where to begin!

THE STUDENT: I think I'd better get out while the getting is good.

JOHANSSON: Look at the young lady! She's dropped her bracelet out of the window.

> *The bracelet has fallen off The Young Lady's arm and through the open window. The Student crosses over slowly, picks up the bracelet, and hands it to The Young Lady, who thanks him stiffly. The Student goes back to Johansson.*

I thought you said you were leaving. It isn't as easy as you think once *he* has slipped his net over your head. . . . And he's afraid of nothing between heaven and earth—yes, one thing—or rather one person.

THE STUDENT: I bet I know.

JOHANSSON: How can you know?

THE STUDENT: Just guessing! Could it be . . . he's afraid of a little milkmaid?

JOHANSSON: He turns his head away whenever he sees a milk wagon. . . . Sometimes he talks in his sleep. He must have been in Hamburg once . . .

THE STUDENT: Can I depend on him?

JOHANSSON: You can depend on him—to do anything and everything!

THE STUDENT: What's he up to around the corner?

JOHANSSON: Eavesdropping on the poor. . . . Planting a word here and there, chipping away at one stone at a time—until the whole house falls—metaphorically speaking. Oh yes, I've had an education. And I used to be a bookseller. . . . Are you leaving or staying?

THE STUDENT: I don't like to be ungrateful. This man once saved my father, and all he's asking for now is a little favor in return.

JOHANSSON: What's that?

THE STUDENT: He wants me to go and see *Die Walküre*.

JOHANSSON: That's beyond me. . . . He's always got something up his sleeve. . . . Look at him, he's talking to the policeman. He's always in with the police. He makes use of them, gets them involved in his business, ties them hand and foot with false promises of future possibilities. And all the while, he's pumping them, pumping them. —Mark my words, before the night is over he'll be received in the round room.

THE STUDENT: What does he want in there? What's he got to do with the colonel?

JOHANSSON: I'm not sure, but I've got my ideas. You'll be able to see for yourself when you go there!

THE STUDENT: I'll never get in there . . .

JOHANSSON: That depends on you! Go to *Die Walküre*.

THE STUDENT: Is that the way?

JOHANSSON: If he said so, it is! —Look at him, just look at him! Riding his war chariot, drawn in triumph by the beggars, who don't get a cent for it, just a hint that something might come their way at his funeral!

> *The Old Man enters, standing in his wheelchair, drawn by one of the Beggars and followed by the others.*

THE OLD MAN: Let us hail the noble youth, who risked his own life to save so many in yesterday's disaster! Hail Arkenholz!

> *The Beggars bare their heads but do not cheer. The Young Lady, standing in the window, waves her handkerchief. The Colonel looks at the scene from his window. The Fiancée stands up at her window. The Housemaid on the balcony raises the flag to the top.*

Hail the hero, my fellow citizens! I know indeed it is Sunday, but the ass in the pit and the ears of corn in the field absolve us. And though I may not be a Sunday child, I can see into the future and I can heal the sick. I have even brought a drowned soul back to life. . . . That happened in Hamburg, yes, on a Sunday morning, just like this—

* * *

The Milkmaid enters, seen only by The Student and The Old Man. She stretches her arms above her head like a drowning person and stares fixedly at The Old Man.

* * *

The Old Man sits down and shrivels up in terror.

Get me out of here, Johansson! Quick! — Arkenholz, don't you forget *Die Walküre*!

THE STUDENT: What is all this?

JOHANSSON: We shall see! We shall see!

[2]

In the round room. At the back of the stage a stove of white glazed porcelain, its mantel decorated with a mirror, a pendulum clock, and candelabra. At the right side of the stage a hallway can be seen and through it a view of a green room with mahogany furniture. At the left of the stage stands the statue in the shadow of the palm trees, and with a curtain that can be drawn to conceal it. In the rear wall to the left of the stove is the door to the hyacinth room, where The Young Lady is seen reading. The Colonel's back can be seen in the green room, where he is writing at his desk.

The Colonel's valet, Bengtsson, wearing livery, enters from the hall, accompanied by Johansson, wearing the formal attire of a waiter.

BENGTSSON: Now, Johansson, you'll have to wait on the table while I take care of the coats. Have you done this before?

JOHANSSON: During the day I push that war chariot, as you know, but in the evenings I work as a waiter at receptions. It's always been my dream to get into this house. . . . They're peculiar people, aren't they?

BENGTSSON: Well, yes, I think one might say that they're a little strange.

JOHANSSON: Are we going to have a musicale this evening? Or what is the occasion?

BENGTSSON: Just the ordinary ghost supper, as we call it. They drink tea, without saying a word, or else the colonel talks all by himself. And they chomp their biscuits and crackers all at once and all in unison. They sound like a pack of rats in an attic.

JOHANSSON: Why do you call it the ghost supper?

BENGTSSON: They all look like ghosts. . . . This has been going on for twenty years—always the same people, always saying the same things. Or else keeping silent to avoid being embarrassed.

JOHANSSON: Where's the lady of the house? Isn't she around?

BENGTSSON: Oh, yes. But she's crazy. She keeps herself shut up in a closet because her eyes can't stand the light. She's sitting in there right now. (*He points to a wallpapered door.*)

JOHANSSON: In there?

BENGTSSON: I told you they were a little peculiar.

JOHANSSON: What on earth does she look like?

BENGTSSON: Like a mummy. Do you want to see her? (*He opens the papered door.*) There she sits!

JOHANSSON: Je-sus!

* * *

THE MUMMY (*babbling*): Why do you open the door? Didn't I tell you to keep it closed?

BENGTSSON (*as if talking to a baby*): Ta, ta, ta, ta, ta! —Is little chickadee going to be nice to me? Then little chickadee will get something good! —Pretty Polly!

THE MUMMY (*like a parrot*): Pretty Polly! Are you there, Jacob? Jacob? Cluck, cluck!

THE GHOST SONATA

BENGTSSON: She thinks she's a parrot—and maybe she is. (*To The Mummy.*) Come on, Polly, whistle for us!

The Mummy whistles.

JOHANSSON: I thought I had seen everything, but this tops it all.

BENGTSSON: Well, when a house grows old, it turns moldy and rotten, and when people are together too much and torment each other too long, they go crazy. Take the lady in this house—shut up, Polly! —This mummy has been sitting here for forty years—the same husband, same furniture, same relatives, same friends. . . . (*Closing the door on The Mummy.*) And imagine what's gone on in this house! Even I don't know the whole story. . . . Look at this statue. That's the lady of the house as a young girl!

JOHANSSON: Oh my god! —Is that the mummy?

BENGTSSON: Yes. It's enough to make one cry! But this lady—carried away by her imagination or something—has acquired certain peculiarities, as babbling parrots do. She can't stand cripples, for instance—or sick people. She can't even stand the sight of her own daughter because she's sick.

JOHANSSON: Is that young girl sick?

BENGTSSON: Yes. Didn't you know?

JOHANSSON: No. . . . What about the colonel? Who is he?

BENGTSSON: Wait awhile and you'll see!

JOHANSSON (*looking at the statue*): It's terrifying to realize that—. How old is the lady now?

BENGTSSON: Who knows? But I've heard it said that when she was thirty-five she looked like she was nineteen. —And she convinced the colonel that she was . . . here in this house. . . . Do you know what that black Japanese screen by the couch is for? It's called a death screen, and when somebody's going to die, it's placed around them, same as in a hospital.

JOHANSSON: What a horrible house. . . . That poor student thought that when he entered this house he would be entering paradise.

BENGTSSON: Which student? Oh, yes, of course! The one that's coming here tonight. The colonel and his daughter met him at the opera and were captivated by him. . . . Hm. . . . But let me ask you a couple of questions. Who's your master? The financier in the wheelchair?

JOHANSSON (*nodding*): Yes, that's right. —Is he coming here too?

BENGTSSON: He's not invited.

JOHANSSON: He'll come uninvited—if he has to.

> *The Old Man appears in the hallway dressed in frock coat and high hat. He creeps silently forward on his crutches and eavesdrops on the servants.*

BENGTSSON: I'll bet he's a real mean old one.

JOHANSSON: A perfect specimen!

BENGTSSON: He looks like the devil incarnate!

JOHANSSON: And he's a black magician, I tell you. He can go through locked doors—

* * *

THE OLD MAN (*coming forward and grabbing Johansson by the ear*): Fool! Hold your tongue! (*To Bengtsson.*) Announce me to the colonel.

BENGTSSON: But we're expecting company here.

THE OLD MAN: I know you are! My visit is not unexpected—although undesired.

BENGTSSON: I see. What was the name? Mr. Hummel?

THE OLD MAN: That's right! Precisely!

> *Bengtsson goes down the hall into the green room and closes the door.*

* * *

THE OLD MAN (*to Johansson*): Disappear!

Johansson hesitates.

Vanish!

Johansson vanishes down the hall.

* * *

The Old Man inspects the room. Stops in front of the statue. Much amazed.

THE OLD MAN: Amelia! . . . It is she! . . . Amelia! (*He roams about the room fingering objects. Stops in front of the mirror to adjust his wig. Returns to the statue.*)

THE MUMMY (*from within the closet*): Pretty Polly!

THE OLD MAN (*startled*): What on earth? Sounded like a parrot in the room. But I don't see any.

THE MUMMY: You there, Jacob?

THE OLD MAN: Place is haunted.

THE MUMMY: Jacob!

THE OLD MAN: It's enough to frighten one! . . . So that's the kind of secrets they keep in this house. (*With his back to the closet, he studies a portrait on the wall.*) There he is! —The old colonel himself!

* * *

THE MUMMY (*coming out of the closet, goes up to The Old Man from behind and gives his wig a pull*): Coo, coo, coo! Cuckoo, cuckoo!

THE OLD MAN (*frightened out of his skin*): Oh my God in heaven! —Who are you?

THE MUMMY (*speaking in her normal voice*): Is that you, Jacob?

THE OLD MAN: Yes. My name is Jacob.

THE MUMMY (*movingly*): And my name is Amelia!

THE OLD MAN: Oh no. . . . No, no. . . . Oh my God!

THE MUMMY: Yes, this is how I look! —And that's how I did look once upon a time. Life gives one a great education. Most of my life I've spent in the closet, so that I won't have to see—or be seen. . . . But you, Jacob, what are you looking for here?

THE OLD MAN: My child! Our child!

THE MUMMY: She's sitting in there.

THE OLD MAN: Where?

THE MUMMY: In there, in the hyacinth room.

THE OLD MAN (*looking at The Young Lady*): Yes, there she is! (*Pause.*) And what does her father think of her—I mean, the colonel—your husband?

THE MUMMY: I had a quarrel with him once, and told him everything . . .

THE OLD MAN: And . . . ?

THE MUMMY: He didn't believe me. He said, "That's what all women say when they want to murder their husbands." . . . All the same it was a terrible crime. His whole life has been falsified, including his family tree. When I look at his family record in the peerage, I say to myself she's no better than a runaway servant girl with a false birth certificate, and girls like that are sent to the reformatory.

THE OLD MAN: A lot of people forge their birth certificates. I seem to remember that even you falsified the date of your birth.

THE MUMMY: It was my mother who put me up to it. I'm not to blame for that! . . . And furthermore, you played the biggest part in our crime.

THE OLD MAN: Not true! Your husband started it all when he stole my fiancée from me! I was born unable to forgive until I have punished. I've always looked upon it as an imperative duty. And I still do!

THE MUMMY: What do you expect to find in this house? What do you want here? And how did you get in? – Does your business concern my daughter? Keep your hands off her, I warn you, or you'll die!

THE OLD MAN: I wish her nothing but the best!

THE MUMMY: And you must have consideration for her father, too!

THE OLD MAN: Never!

THE MUMMY: Then you must die. In this room. Behind that screen.

THE OLD MAN: Be that as it may. But I'm a bulldog. I never let go.

THE MUMMY: You want to marry her to that student. Why? He has nothing; he is nothing.

THE OLD MAN: He'll be a rich man, thanks to me.

THE MUMMY: Are you one of the invited guests tonight?

THE OLD MAN: No. I've decided to invite myself to this ghost supper!

THE MUMMY: Do you know who'll be here?

THE OLD MAN: Not entirely.

THE MUMMY: The baron – who lives upstairs, and whose father-in-law was buried this afternoon –

THE OLD MAN: Yes, the baron – who is getting a divorce in order to marry the daughter of the superintendent's wife. The baron – who was once – your lover!

THE MUMMY: And then there'll be your former fiancée – whom my husband seduced . . .

THE OLD MAN: A very select gathering . . .

THE MUMMY: Oh God, why can't we die? If only we could die!

THE OLD MAN: Then why do you keep seeing one another?

THE MUMMY: Our crimes and our secrets and our guilt bind us together! We have split up and gone our separate ways an infinite number of times. But we're always drawn back together again . . .

THE OLD MAN: I believe the colonel is coming.

THE MUMMY: Then I'll go in to Adele. . . . (*Pause.*) Jacob, don't do anything foolish! Be considerate toward him . . .

A pause. She leaves.

* * *

THE COLONEL (*enters, cold and reserved*): Please sit down.

The Old Man takes his time seating himself. A pause. The Colonel stares at him.

Did you write this letter?

THE OLD MAN: I did.

THE COLONEL: And your name is Hummel?

THE OLD MAN: It is.

Pause.

THE COLONEL: Since it's clear that you have bought up all my outstanding promissory notes, it follows that I'm completely at your mercy. Now what do you want?

THE OLD MAN: I want to be paid—in one way or another.

THE COLONEL: In what way?

THE OLD MAN: A very simple way. Don't let's talk about money. Allow me to come and go in your house—as a guest.

THE COLONEL: If that's all it takes to satisfy you—

THE OLD MAN: Thank you!

THE COLONEL: And what else?

THE OLD MAN: Dismiss Bengtsson!

THE COLONEL: Why? Bengtsson is my devoted servant. He's been with me during my whole career. The army awarded him a medal for faithful service. Why should I dismiss him?

THE OLD MAN: I have no doubt he's a very fine man in your eyes. But he's not the man he seems to be!

THE COLONEL: Who is?

THE OLD MAN (*taken aback*): True! —But Bengtsson must go!

THE COLONEL: Are you going to give orders in my house?

THE OLD MAN: Yes! Since I own everything that you can lay your eyes on—furniture, curtains, dinner service, linen . . . and other things . . .

THE COLONEL: What other things?

THE OLD MAN: Everything. I own it all. Everything that you see here is mine!

THE COLONEL: I can't dispute that. But my family honor, my coat of arms, and my good name are things you cannot take from me!

THE OLD MAN: Yes, I can. They don't belong to you. (*Pause.*) You are not a nobleman.

THE COLONEL: I shall give you the opportunity of withdrawing those words!

THE OLD MAN (*producing a piece of paper*): If you will take the trouble to read this extract from the standard book of genealogy, you will see that the family whose name you have assumed has been extinct for over a century.

THE COLONEL (*reading*): Of course I've heard rumors like this before. But it was my father's name before it was mine. . . . (*Reading on.*) I can't deny it. You are quite right. . . . I am not a nobleman! Not even that. . . . Therefore I shall take this signet ring off my hand. —Oh, but of course, excuse me: it belongs to you. There you are.

THE OLD MAN (*putting the ring in his pocket*): Let us continue. —You are not a colonel either!

THE COLONEL: Am I not?

THE OLD MAN: No! You held a temporary commission as a colonel in the American Volunteers, but at the end of the Spanish-American War and the reorganization of the army, all such titles were abolished.

THE COLONEL: Is that true?

THE OLD MAN (*reaching into his pocket*): Do you want to see for yourself?

THE COLONEL: No, it won't be necessary. . . . Who are you? What gives you the right to sit there and strip me naked in this way?

THE OLD MAN: Patience, my good man! And as far as stripping is concerned—do you really want to know who you are?

THE COLONEL: Have you no decency?

THE OLD MAN: Take off that wig of yours and have a look at yourself in the mirror. And while you're at it, take out those false teeth and shave off that moustache and let Bengtsson unlace your metal corset, and then we shall see if a certain valet who shall be nameless won't recognize himself—the cupboard lover who flirted with the maids so he could scrounge in the kitchen.

> *The Colonel reaches for the bell on the table. The Old Man stops him, saying:*

I wouldn't touch that if I were you. If you call Bengtsson I'll order him arrested. . . . I believe your guests are arriving. Now let us be calm and go on playing our old roles for a while longer.

THE COLONEL: Who are you? I've seen your eyes and heard your voice before.

THE OLD MAN: Never mind that. Be silent and do as you're told!

* * *

THE STUDENT (*enters and bows to The Colonel*): How do you do, sir!

THE COLONEL: Welcome to my house, young man! Your heroism at that terrible accident has brought your name to everybody's lips. I deem it an honor to receive you in my house.

THE STUDENT: You're very kind, sir. It's a great honor for me, sir. I've never expected—well, my humble birth—and your illustrious name and your noble birth . . .

THE COLONEL: Mr. Hummel, may I introduce Mr. Arkenholz, who is a student at the university. The ladies are in there, Mr. Arkenholz—if you care to join them. I have a few more things I want to say to Mr. Hummel.

> *The Colonel shows The Student into the hyacinth room, where he remains visible to the audience, engaged in shy conversation with The Young Lady.*

* * *

THE COLONEL: An excellent young man—musical, sings, writes poetry. . . . If it weren't for his birth and social position I certainly wouldn't have anything against—my . . .

THE OLD MAN: Against what?

THE COLONEL: Having my daughter—

THE OLD MAN: *Your* daughter! . . . Apropos of her, why does she always sit in that room?

THE COLONEL: She feels she has to sit in the hyacinth room whenever she's in the house. A peculiarity of hers. . . . Here comes Miss Beatrice von Holsteinkrona. Charming woman. —Very distinguished family, but hasn't a cent to her name. All she's got goes to the nursing home.

THE OLD MAN (*to himself*): My fiancée!

* * *

> *The Fiancée enters, white-haired and giving every appearance of being crazy.*

THE COLONEL: Miss Holsteinkrona—Mr. Hummel.

The Fiancée curtsies and takes a seat.

* * *

Baron Skanskorg enters next—dressed in mourning and with a strange look on his face—and sits down.

THE COLONEL: Baron Skanskorg—

THE OLD MAN (*in an aside, without rising*): A jewel thief, if ever I saw one. (*To The Colonel.*) Now let the mummy in, and the party can begin.

THE COLONEL (*in the doorway to the hyacinth room*): Polly!

* * *

THE MUMMY (*enters*): Coo, coo! Cuckoo, cuckoo!

THE COLONEL: Shall we invite the young people, too?

THE OLD MAN: No! Not the young people! They shall be spared.

They seat themselves in a circle. Silence.

* * *

THE COLONEL: Shall I ring for tea?

THE OLD MAN: Why bother? No one cares for tea. Why play games?

Pause.

THE COLONEL: Then perhaps we should start a conversation?

THE OLD MAN (*slowly, deliberately, and with frequent pauses*): About the weather? Which we know. Ask one another how we're feeling? Which we also know. I prefer silence . . . in which one can hear thoughts and see the past. Silence cannot hide anything—which is more than you can say for words. I read the other day that the differences in languages originated among the primitive savages, who sought to keep their secrets from other tribes. Languages are therefore codes, and he who finds the key can understand all the languages of the world. But that doesn't mean that secrets cannot be discovered without a key. Especially in those cases where paternity must be proved. Legal proof is of course a different matter. Two false witnesses provide complete proof of whatever they agree to say. But in the kind of escapades I have in mind, one doesn't take witnesses along. Nature herself has planted in man a blushing sense of shame, which seeks to hide what should be hidden. But we slip into certain situations without intending to, and chance confronts us with moments of revelation, when the deepest secrets are revealed, the mask is ripped from the imposter and the villain stands exposed . . .

Pause. All look at one another in silence.

Extraordinary, how silent you all are! (*Long silence.*) Take this house, for example. In this estimable house, in this elegant house, where beauty, wealth, and culture are united. . . . (*Long silence.*) All of us sitting here, we know who we are, don't we? . . . I don't have to tell you. . . . And you know me, although you pretend ignorance. . . . Sitting in that room is my daughter, yes mine, you know that too. . . . She had lost all desire to live, without knowing why. . . . She was withering away because of the air in this house, which reeks of crime, deception, and lies of every kind. . . . That is why I had to find a friend for her, a friend from whose very presence she would apprehend the warmth and light radiated by a noble deed. . . . (*Long silence.*) That was my mission in this house. To pull up the weeds, to expose the crimes, to settle the accounts, so that these young people might make a new beginning in this home, which is my gift to them! (*Long silence.*) Listen to the ticking of the clock, like a deathwatch beetle in the wall! Listen to what it's saying: "time's-up, time's-up! . . . " When it strikes—in just a few moments—your time is up. Then you may go—not before.

The clock can be heard preparing to strike the hour.

Hear! The hammer draws back, the wheels whir. It's warning you: "clocks can strike!" —And I can strike too! (*He strikes the table with his crutch.*) Do you understand?

Silence.

* * *

THE MUMMY (*goes over to the clock and stops its pendulum. In her normal voice, speaking purposefully*): But I can stop time in its course. I can wipe out the past, and undo what is done. Not with bribes, not with threats—but through suffering and repentance. (*Approaching The Old Man.*) We are poor miserable creatures, we know that. We have erred, we have transgressed, we, like all the rest. We are not what we seem to be. At bottom we are better than ourselves, since we abhor and detest our misdeeds. But when you, Jacob Hummel, with your false name, come here to sit in judgment over us, that proves that you are more contemptible than we! And you are not the one you seem to be! You are a slave trader, a stealer of souls! You once stole me with false promises. You murdered the consul who was buried today; you strangled him with debts. You have stolen the student and shackled him with an imaginary debt of his father's, who never owed you a penny . . .

> The Old Man has tried to rise and speak but has collapsed in his chair and shriveled up, and, like a dying insect, he shrivels up more and more during the following dialogue.

But there is one dark spot in your life, which I'm not sure about—although I have my suspicions. . . . I think that Bengtsson might help us. (*She rings the bell on the table.*)

THE OLD MAN: No! Not Bengtsson! Not him!

THE MUMMY: Then it is true? He does know! (*She rings again.*)

> The Milkmaid appears in the door to the hall, unseen by all except The Old Man, who shies in terror. The Milkmaid disappears when Bengtsson enters.

Bengtsson, do you know this man?

BENGTSSON: Yes, I know him, and he knows me. Life has its ups and downs, as we all know, and I have been in his service, and once he was in mine. To be exact, he was a sponger in my kitchen for two whole years. Since he had to be out of the house by three o'clock, dinner had to be ready at two, and those in the house had to eat the warmed-up food left by that ox. Even worse, he drank up the pure soup stock and the gravy, which then had to be diluted with water. He sat there like a vampire, sucking all the marrow out of the house, and turned us all into skeletons. And he nearly succeeded in putting us into prison, when we accused the cook of being a thief. . . . Later I met this man in Hamburg under another name. He had become a usurer or bloodsucker. And it was there that he was accused of having lured a young girl out onto the ice in order to drown her, for she was the only witness to a crime that he was afraid would come to light . . .

THE MUMMY (*passes her hand over The Old Man's face*): That is the real you! Now empty your pockets of the notes and the will!

> *Johansson appears in the door to the hall and watches The Old Man intently, knowing that his slavery is coming to an end. The Old Man produces a bundle of papers, which he throws on the table.*
>
> The Mummy strokes The Old Man's back.
>
> Little Polly Parrot
> Sat in the garret,
> Eating toast and tea.

THE OLD MAN (*like a parrot*):

> Polly put the kettle on,
> Polly put the kettle on,
> We'll all have tea.
> Jack and Jill, Jack and Jill!

THE MUMMY: Can—clocks—strike?

THE OLD MAN (*making clucking sounds*): Clocks can strike! (*He imitates a cuckoo clock.*) Coo-coo! Coo-coo! Coo-coo!

THE MUMMY (*opening the jib door to the closet*): Now the clock has struck! Stand up and enter the closet where I have sat for twenty years, crying over our misdeeds. You'll find a rope in there. It can stand for the one you strangled the consul with—for the one you intended to strangle your benefactor with. . . . Go in!

The Old Man goes into the closet. The Mummy closes the door.

THE MUMMY: Bengtsson! Put up the screen. The death screen.

Bengtsson places the screen in front of the door.

It is finished. —May God have mercy on his soul!

ALL: Amen!

Long silence.

* * *

In the hyacinth room, The Young Lady can be seen sitting at a harp on which she accompanies The Student. After a prelude played by The Young Lady, The Student recites.

THE STUDENT:

> I saw the sun
> And from its blaze
> There burst on me
> The deepest truth:
>
> Man reaps as he sows;
> Blessed is he
> Who sows the good.
>
> For deeds done in anger
> Kindness alone
> Can make amends.
>
> Bring cheer to those
> Whom you have hurt,

And kindness reaps
Its own rewards.

The pure in heart
Have none to fear.
The harmless are happy.
The guileless are good.

[3]

A room decorated in a bizarre style, predominantly oriental. A profusion of hyacinths in all colors fills the room. On the porcelain tile stove sits a large Buddha with a bulb of a shallot (allium ascalonicum) *in its lap. The stem of the shallot rises from the bulb and bursts into a spherical cluster of white, starlike flowers. In the rear to the right, a door leads to the round room. The Colonel and The Mummy can be seen in there sitting motionless and silent. A part of the death screen is also visible. To the left in the rear, a door to the pantry and the kitchen. The Student and The Young Lady (Adele) are near a table, she seated at her harp, he standing beside her.*

THE YOUNG LADY: Now you must sing a song to my flowers!

THE STUDENT: Is this the flower of your soul?

THE YOUNG LADY: The one and only! Don't you love the hyacinth?

THE STUDENT: I love it above all other flowers—its stem rising straight and slender, like a young maiden, from the round bulb, which floats on water and sends its white rare roots down into clear, colorless nothingness. I love it for its colors: the snow-white, innocent and pure—the golden yellow, sweet as honey—the shy pink, the ripe red—but above all the blue ones—blue as morning mist, deep-eyed blue, ever-faithful blue. I love them all—more than gold and pearls. Have loved them ever since I was a child, have worshiped them because they possess all the virtues I lack. . . . But still—

THE YOUNG LADY: What?

THE STUDENT: My love is not returned. These beautiful blossoms hate and detest me.

THE YOUNG LADY: How?

THE STUDENT: Their fragrance—as strong and clear as the first winds of spring, sweeping down from the fields of melting snow—confuses my senses—they deafen me, blind me, drive me out of my mind—impale me with their poisonous arrows that stab my heart and set my head afire! . . . Don't you know the story behind that flower?

THE YOUNG LADY: No. Tell me.

THE STUDENT: First you have to interpret it. The bulb is the earth, whether floating on water or buried deep in black humus. Here the stalk shoots up, straight as the axis of the world, and here at its upper end are gathered together the six-pointed star flowers.

THE YOUNG LADY: Above the earth, the stars! How sublime! How did you know that? Where did you discover that?

THE STUDENT: I don't know. Let me think. —In your eyes! . . . So you see, it's an image of the whole cosmos. That's why Buddha sits there with the bulb of the earth in his lap, watching it constantly to see it shoot up and burst forth and be transformed into a heaven. This poor earth shall become a heaven! That is what Buddha is waiting for!

THE YOUNG LADY: Of course! I see that now! —And don't the snowflakes have six points like the hyacinth?

THE STUDENT: Exactly! Then snowflakes are falling stars—

THE YOUNG LADY: And the snowdrop is a snow-star—growing out of the snow.

THE STUDENT: And Sirius, the largest and most beautiful of all the stars in the firmament, golden-red Sirius is the narcissus with its golden-red chalice and its six white rays—

THE YOUNG LADY: Have you seen the shallot burst into bloom?

THE STUDENT: Yes, of course I have! It hides its blossoms

in a ball—a globe just like the celestial globe, strewn with white stars.

THE YOUNG LADY: How heavenly! Wonderful! Whose idea was it?

THE STUDENT: Yours!

THE YOUNG LADY: Yours!

THE STUDENT: Ours. We have given birth to something together. We are wedded . . .

THE YOUNG LADY: No, not yet . . .

THE STUDENT: Why not? What else?

THE YOUNG LADY: Time—testing—patience.

THE STUDENT: Very well! Put me to the test! (*Pause.*) So silent? . . . Why do your parents sit in there, silent, without saying a single word?

THE YOUNG LADY: Because they have nothing to say to each other, since they don't believe what the other says. My father explains it this way: he says, "What good does talking do, we can't pull the wool over our eyes."

THE STUDENT: It makes me sick to hear things like that . . .

THE YOUNG LADY: The cook is coming this way. . . . Look at her, how big and fat she is . . .

THE STUDENT: What does she want?

THE YOUNG LADY: She wants to ask me about dinner. I've been managing the house during my mother's illness.

THE STUDENT: What have we got to do with the kitchen?

THE YOUNG LADY: We have to eat, don't we? . . . Look at her, look at her. I can't bear to . . .

THE STUDENT: Who is that bloated monster?

THE YOUNG LADY: She belongs to the Hummel family of vampires. She's eating us up . . .

THE STUDENT: Why don't you fire her?

THE YOUNG LADY: She won't leave! We can't control her. We got her because of our sins. . . . Don't you see that we're wasting away, withering?

THE STUDENT: Don't you get enough food to eat?

THE YOUNG LADY: We get course after course, but all the strength is gone from the food. She boils the beef until there's nothing left of it and serves us the sinews swimming in water while she herself drinks the stock. And when we have a roast, she cooks all the juice out of it and drinks it and eats the gravy. Everything she touches loses its flavor. It's as if she sucked it up with her very eyes. We get the grounds when she has finished her coffee. She drinks the wine and fills up the bottles with water.

THE STUDENT: Get rid of her!

THE YOUNG LADY: We can't!

THE STUDENT: Why not?

THE YOUNG LADY: We don't know! She won't leave! No one can control her. . . . She has taken all our strength from us.

THE STUDENT: Let me get rid of her for you.

THE YOUNG LADY: Oh, no! I guess this is how it's supposed to be. . . . Here she is! She'll ask me what we're having for dinner—I'll tell her this and that—she'll make objections—and finally we'll have what she says.

THE STUDENT: Then let her decide in the first place!

THE YOUNG LADY: She won't do that.

THE STUDENT: What a strange house! It's haunted, isn't it?

THE YOUNG LADY: Yes. —She's turning back now. She saw you!

* * *

THE COOK (*in the doorway*): Ha, that ain't why! (*Grinning so that all her teeth show.*)

THE STUDENT: Get out!

THE COOK: When I feel like it I will! (*Pause.*) Now I feel like it!

She vanishes.

THE YOUNG LADY: Don't lose your temper. Learn to be patient. She's part of the trials and tribulations we have to go through in this home. And we've got a housemaid, too! Whom we have to clean up after!

THE STUDENT: I can feel myself sinking into the earth! — *Cor in aethere!* — Let's have music!

THE YOUNG LADY: Wait!

THE STUDENT: No! Music now!

THE YOUNG LADY: Patience! — This room is called the testing room. It's beautiful to look at, but it's full of imperfections.

THE STUDENT: I don't believe it. But if it's true, we'll just have to ignore them. It's beautiful, but a little cold. Why don't you start the fire?

THE YOUNG LADY: Because it smokes up the room.

THE STUDENT: Can't you have the chimney cleaned?

THE YOUNG LADY: It doesn't help! . . . Do you see that writing table?

THE STUDENT: What an extraordinarily handsome piece!

THE YOUNG LADY: But it wobbles. Every day I lay a piece of cork under that foot, but the housemaid takes it away when she sweeps, and I have to cut a new piece. The penholder is covered with ink every morning, and so is the inkstand, and I have to clean them up after her, as regularly as the sun goes up. (*Pause.*) What do you hate most to do?

THE STUDENT: To sort the week's wash! (*Grimaces in disgust.*)

THE YOUNG LADY: That's what I have to do! (*Grimacing in disgust.*)

THE STUDENT: What else?

THE YOUNG LADY: To be awakened in the middle of the night, to have to get up and close the banging window—which the housemaid forgot to close.

THE STUDENT: Go on.

THE YOUNG LADY: To climb up on a ladder and fix the damper on the stovepipe after the maid broke off the cord.

THE STUDENT: Go on.

THE YOUNG LADY: To sweep up after her, to dust after her, and to start the fire in the stove after her—all she does is bring in the wood! To adjust the damper, to dry the glasses, to set the table *over* and *over* again, to pull the corks out of the bottles, to open the windows and air the rooms, to make and remake my bed, to rinse the water bottle when it's green with sediment, to buy matches and soap, which we're always out of, to wipe the chimneys and trim the wicks to keep the lamps from smoking—and to keep the lamps from going out, I have to fill them myself when we have company . . .

THE STUDENT: Let's have music!

THE YOUNG LADY: You have to wait! —First comes the drudgery, the drudgery of keeping oneself above the dirt of life.

THE STUDENT: But you're well off. You've got two servants.

THE YOUNG LADY: Doesn't make any difference! Even if we had three! Living is such a nuisance, and I get so tired at times. . . . Imagine, if on top of it all one had a nursery and a baby crib.

THE STUDENT: The dearest of joys!

THE YOUNG LADY: The dearest in more ways than one. . . . Is life really worth so much trouble?

THE STUDENT: I suppose that depends on the reward you expect for all your troubles. . . . There's nothing I wouldn't do to win your hand.

THE YOUNG LADY: Don't say that! You can never have me!

THE STUDENT: Why not?

THE YOUNG LADY: You mustn't ask.

Pause.

THE STUDENT: You dropped your bracelet out the window . . .

THE YOUNG LADY: Because my hand has grown so thin.

Pause. The Cook appears with a Japanese bottle in her hand.

She's the one who's eating me—and all the rest of us.

THE STUDENT: What is she holding in her hand?

THE YOUNG LADY: It's a bottle of coloring matter. It's got letters on it that look like scorpions. It's filled with soy sauce—which takes the place of gravy, which is transformed into soup, which serves as stock for cooking cabbage in, which is used to make mock turtle soup . . .

THE STUDENT: Get out!

THE COOK: You suck the sap from us and we from you. We take the blood and give you back water—with coloring added. This is the coloring! —I'm leaving now, but you won't ever be rid of me.

She leaves.

THE STUDENT: Why was Bengtsson given a medal?

THE YOUNG LADY: Because of his great merits.

THE STUDENT: Has he no faults?

THE YOUNG LADY: Yes, many great ones. But you don't get medals for them.

They smile at each other.

* * *

THE STUDENT: You have a great many secrets in this house.

THE YOUNG LADY: As in all houses. Permit us to keep ours.

Pause.

THE STUDENT: Do you admire frankness?

THE YOUNG LADY: Yes, within moderation.

THE STUDENT: Sometimes there comes over me a crazy desire to say everything I'm thinking. But I know the world would collapse completely if we were completely honest. (*Pause.*) I went to a funeral the other day. . . . In church. . . . Very solemn, very beautiful.

THE YOUNG LADY: Mr. Hummel's funeral?

THE STUDENT: Yes, my false benefactor's. At the head of the coffin stood an old friend of the deceased. He carried the mace. The priest impressed me especially, his dignified manner and his moving words. I cried. We all cried. And afterward we went to a restaurant. . . . And there I learned that the macebearer had been in love with the dead man's son.

The Young Lady looks at him to catch his meaning.

Yes. And the dead man had borrowed money from his son's lover. . . . (*Pause.*) The day after that, they arrest the priest for embezzling church funds! It's a pretty story isn't it?

The Young Lady turns her head away in disgust. Pause.

Do you know what I think of you now?

THE YOUNG LADY: You must not tell me or I'll die!

THE STUDENT: But I must or I'll die!

THE YOUNG LADY: In an asylum they say whatever they feel like.

THE STUDENT: Exactly right! That's where my father ended up—in a madhouse.

THE YOUNG LADY: Was he ill?

THE STUDENT: No, he was quite healthy. But he was crazy! It just came over him. Let me tell you how it happened. . . . Like all of us, he had his circle of acquaintances, whom for convenience' sake he called his friends. Of course they were a pretty sorry bunch of good-for-nothings—like most people. But he had to have some acquaintances, he couldn't just sit alone. Now one doesn't tell a person what one really thinks of him, not in ordinary conversation anyway—and my father didn't either. He knew how false they were. He saw through their deceitfulness right to the bottom of their souls. But he was an intelligent man, brought up to behave properly, and so he was always polite. But one day he gave a big party. It was evening, he was tired after a day's work, and under the strain of forcing himself to hold his tongue half the time and of bullshitting with his guests the other half . . .

The Young Lady glances at him reproachfully.

Well, whatever the reason, at the dinner table he rapped for silence, raised his glass, and began to make a speech. . . . Then something loosed the trigger, and in a long oration he stripped naked every single person there, one after another. Told them of all their deceits. And at the end, exhausted, he sat down right in the middle of the table and told them all to go straight to hell!

The Young Lady moans.

I was there and heard it all. I'll never forget what happened afterward. . . . Father and Mother began to fight, the guests rushed for the door—and my father was taken off to the madhouse, where he died! (*Pause.*) If you keep silent too long, things begin to rot. Stagnant, stinking pools begin to form. That's what's happening in this house. Something's rotting here. And I thought it was paradise when I saw you come in here for the first time. . . . It was a Sunday morning, and I stood looking into these rooms. I saw a colonel who wasn't a colonel. I had a magnanimous benefactor who turned out to be a bandit and had to hang himself. I saw a mummy who wasn't one, and a maiden who—speaking of which, where can one find virginity? Where is beauty to be found? In nature, and in my mind when it's all dressed up in its

Sunday clothes. Where do honor and faith exist? In fairy tales and plays for children. Where can you find anything that fulfills its promise? Only in one's imagination! . . . Now your flowers have poisoned me, and I have passed the poison back. I begged you to become my wife in my home. We played and we sang. We created poetry together. And then came the cook. . . . *Sursum corda!* Try just once again to pluck fire and brightness from the golden harp! Please try! I beg you, I implore you on my knees! . . . Very well. Then I shall do it myself. (*He takes the harp, but no sound comes from the strings.*) It is silent and deaf. Tell me, why are beautiful flowers so poisonous, and the most beautiful the most deadly? Why? The whole creation, all of life, is cursed and damned. . . . Why would you not become my bride? Because you are sick, infected at the very core of life. . . . Now I can feel that vampire in the kitchen beginning to suck the blood from me. She must be one of those lamias that suck the blood of suckling babes. It's always in the kitchen that the children are nipped in the bud. And if not there, then in the bedroom. . . . There are poisons that seal the eyes and poisons that open them. I must have been born with the latter kind in my veins, because I cannot see what is ugly as beautiful and I cannot call what is evil good. I cannot. They say that Christ harrowed hell. What they really meant was that He descended to earth, to this madhouse, jailhouse, charnel house. And the inmates crucified Him when He tried to free them. But the robber they let go. Robbers always win sympathy. . . . Woe! Woe to all of us! Saviour of the World, save us! We are perishing!

> *The Young Lady has collapsed during this speech. She is obviously dying. She rings the bell. Bengtsson enters.*

THE YOUNG LADY: Bring the screen. Quickly! I'm dying.

> *Bengtsson returns with the screen, opens it, and places it in front of The Young Lady.*

THE STUDENT: Your redeemer is coming! Welcome, pale and gentle one. . . . And you, my darling, you beautiful, innocent, lost soul who suffers for no fault of your own, sleep, sleep a dreamless sleep. And when you wake again . . . may you be greeted by a sun that doesn't scorch, in a home without dust, by friends without faults, and by a love without flaw. . . . Buddha, wise and gentle Buddha, sitting there waiting for a heaven to grow out of the earth, grant us the purity of will and the patience to endure our tribulations that hope will not come to shame.

The harp strings begin to move and hum. Pure white light pours into the room.

I saw the sun
And from its blaze
There burst on me
The deepest truth:

Man reaps as he sows;
Blessed is he
Who sows the good.

For deeds done in anger
Kindness alone
Can make amends.

Bring cheer to those
Whom you have hurt,
And kindness reaps
Its own rewards.

The pure in heart
Have none to fear.
The harmless are happy.
The guileless are good.

A moaning is heard from behind the screen.

You poor little child! Child of this world of illusion and guilt and suffering and death—this world of eternal change and disappointment and never-ending pain! May the Lord of Heaven have mercy on you as you journey forth . . .

The room vanishes. In the distance Boecklin's The Island of the Dead *appears. Music—soft, pleasant, and melancholy—is heard coming from the island.*

CURTAIN

Introduction
to
The Pelican

"Life is such a web of lies, errors, misunderstandings, of debts due and owing, that a closing of the books is impossible" [*En blå bok*].

That was how Strindberg summed up the human condition when he was in a forgiving and compassionate mood. Because our lives are intricately ensnarled and entangled with one anothers', everyone is guilty of some cruelty or offense. This state of affairs is represented in the first scene of *The Ghost Sonata*. All too often, however, Strindberg was quick to sit in judgment on individuals who did not measure up to his standards and to presume that he could separate the strands in the web of guilt. In *The Dance of Death*, he had condemned his brother-in-law for his materialistic beliefs, castigated him for his self-centeredness, and monumentalized his conceit and intellectual arrogance. When Hugo Philp died in 1906, Strindberg regretted what he had done. In *The Pelican*, the fourth of the chamber plays, Strindberg tried to set the record straight by showing the other side of the man. The dead man haunts the play just as he haunted Strindberg's conscience.

But that is only the starting point for another moral inquiry and only incidental to a drama in which Strindberg once again studies the web of guilt. At the center of the web, he finds the vampire cook of *The Ghost Sonata*. She is seen to be the mother, the terrible mother who deprives her children of spiritual nourishment, who gives them mustard instead of milk. Then, as the picture becomes clearer, the mother in her turn is seen to be a somnambulist, like the hyacinth girl. In Swedenborg's metapsychology, somnambulists were those people, perhaps the majority of humankind, who live the lives of beasts, acting from the will, the senses, the instincts, "while the understanding sleeps." Strindberg's first title for this play was "The Sleepwalkers." Unintentionally and unconsciously, the sleepwalking mother has ruined the lives of her children. But there were sleepwalkers in her life, too, which was warped and twisted when she was a child. Is she more to be blamed than her children?

Unlike *The Ghost Sonata*, with its quietly magical ending, a musical invocation to death the liberator, *The Pelican* ends with an explosion of destructive energy. Death comes not so much as a release from daily tribulations and unavoidable guilt, or as a diminishment of spiritual energy in accordance with some principle of moral entropy, but as a violent stab at justice, a willful act of annihilation, both absurd and necessary, that blots out the heavens and causes the moral universe to collapse into a primeval state of innocence.

The Pelican

*Opus Four
of
The Chamber Plays*

CHARACTERS

THE MOTHER, Elise, a widow
THE SON, Frederick, a law student
THE DAUGHTER, Gerda
THE SON-IN-LAW, Axel, married to Gerda
MARGARET, the cook

[1]

A living room. A door in the rear wall to the dining room. To the right, at an angle, a door to the balcony. A secretary-bookcase; a writing table; a chaise longue with a woolen purple-red lap rug; a rocking chair. The Mother enters, dressed in mourning; sits listlessly in an armchair. Listens agitatedly. Beyond the room Chopin's "Fantaisie Impromptu," Oeuvre Posthume, opus 66, is being played. Margaret, the cook, enters from the rear.

THE MOTHER: Would you mind closing the door?

MARGARET: Are you sitting here alone?

THE MOTHER: Would you mind closing the door? —Who's playing the piano?

MARGARET: Such awful weather tonight, windy and rainy . . .

THE MOTHER: Would you mind closing the door? I can't stand the smell of flowers and disinfectants.

MARGARET: Don't blame me. I told you to have him taken to the cemetery as quickly as possible.

THE MOTHER: It was the children who wanted the funeral at home, not I.

MARGARET: Well, why on earth do you stay in this place? Why don't you all move?

THE MOTHER: The landlord won't let us move. We're all stuck here. (*Pause.*) Why did you take the slipcover off the red chaise longue?

MARGARET: I had to have it cleaned. (*Pause.*) I know you can't help being reminded that your husband drew his last breath on that sofa, but all you have to do is take away the sofa—

THE MOTHER: I'm not allowed to touch a thing until the inventory has been taken. I sit here like a prisoner. . . . And I can't endure being in the other rooms.

MARGARET: Now what's the matter with them?

THE MOTHER: Memories—all unpleasant. —And that horrible smell. . . . Is that my son playing?

MARGARET: Yes. He doesn't like it in here, I can tell you. Can't sit still. And he's always hungry. Says he's never had a full stomach in his life.

THE MOTHER: He was weak from the day he was born.

MARGARET: A bottle baby needs rich, good food after it's been weaned.

THE MOTHER (*sharply*): Really! Didn't I give him everything he wanted?

MARGARET: Not exactly: You always shopped for the cheapest and poorest food. Sending a child off to school on a cup of chicory coffee and a slice of bread—imagine!

THE MOTHER: The children have never complained.

MARGARET: Not to you, oh, no, they wouldn't dare. But when they grew up, how often didn't they come out to me in the kitchen—

THE MOTHER: We've always had limited means—

MARGARET: Come now! I read in the paper how your husband some years paid taxes on twenty thousand crowns.

THE MOTHER: It all went, I don't know where.

MARGARET: Yes, yes, of course. But look at the children. Look at Miss Gerda—twenty years old and she hasn't filled out yet.

THE MOTHER: What are you trying to say?

MARGARET: All right, never mind. (*Pause.*) Don't you want me to put some logs in the stove? It's cold in here.

THE MOTHER: No, thank you. We can't afford to burn up our money.

MARGARET: But Frederick is frozen to his bones. He has to go outside to get warm—or else play the piano.

THE MOTHER: He's always been cold.

MARGARET: I wonder why?

THE MOTHER: That's enough, Margaret! . . . (*Pause.*) Do you hear someone walking out there?

MARGARET: No, there's no one.

THE MOTHER: I suppose you think I'm afraid of ghosts?

MARGARET: I'm sure I wouldn't know. . . . But one thing I do know: I'm not staying here any longer than I can help it. I first came to this house as if I had been condemned to watch over the children. I wanted to get away when I saw how the servants were mistreated, but I couldn't—or I wasn't allowed to—I don't know which. But now that Miss Gerda is married, I feel that I've done my duty, and soon the doors will open for me and I'll be free. But not quite yet . . .

THE MOTHER: I don't understand a word you're saying. The whole world knows how much I have sacrificed for my children, how I have taken care of this house and never neglected my duties. You're the only one who accuses me. But don't think that bothers me for a moment. You're free to leave whenever you want to. When my daughter and her husband move into this apartment, I don't intend to keep any servants.

MARGARET: I wish you the best of luck. Children aren't grateful by nature. They don't care to see their mothers-in-law moving in unless they bring money with them.

THE MOTHER: Don't you worry yourself about me, Margaret. I'll pay for my keep, and help about the house too. Besides, my son-in-law isn't like other sons-in-law.

MARGARET: That one! Ha!

THE MOTHER: He isn't! He doesn't treat me like a mother-in-law. He treats me like a sister, like a friend . . .

> *Margaret grimaces.*

What are you smirking about? Oh, I know what you're thinking. But I happen to like my son-in-law; there's no law against that, and he's very likeable. . . . Of course, my husband didn't like him. He was envious, I might even say jealous. (*Laughs quietly.*) Flattering, don't you think, even if I'm not so young anymore. —What did you say?

MARGARET: Nothing. I thought I heard someone. . . . It must have been Frederick. He's the only one who coughs. Let me light the fire.

THE MOTHER: No, it isn't necessary!

MARGARET: Listen to me. I have been frozen to the marrow of my bones in this house; I've starved; and I haven't complained. But at least you can give me a bed, a decent bed. I'm old and I'm tired—

THE MOTHER: Fine time to ask, when you're all set to leave!

MARGARET: That's true, I almost forgot. But for the sake of your own self-respect, burn up my bedclothes where people have lain and died, so you won't have to be ashamed when the next maid comes—if any ever will.

THE MOTHER: Don't worry. No one will.

MARGARET: But if anyone should, I can tell you she won't stay. I've seen fifty maids come and go.

THE MOTHER: Because they were unreliable and disreputable. That's what you all are.

MARGARET: Thank you! How kind of you! . . . But your time is coming. Just wait. Everyone gets his turn. Soon it will be yours.

THE MOTHER: Don't you ever stop? I'll soon have had enough of you.

MARGARET: Yes, soon. Very soon. Sooner than you think!

She leaves.

* * *

The Son enters with a book in his hand, coughing. He has a slight stammer.

THE MOTHER: Would you mind closing the door?

THE SON: Give me one good reason.

THE MOTHER: Is that any way to answer me? —What do you want?

THE SON: Do you mind if I sit in here and read? It's too cold in my room.

THE MOTHER: Oh, you're always cold, you are.

THE SON: When you sit still, you feel it more, if it is cold. (*Pause. He pretends to read at first.*) Is the inventory finished yet?

THE MOTHER: Why do you ask that? Can't you wait until after the mourning is over? Or perhaps you don't mourn the loss of your father?

THE SON: Yes—but—well, he's better off. And I envy him the peace he found, the peace he finally found. But that doesn't prevent me from being concerned and worried about my own position. I have to know whether I can get through my exams without having to borrow money.

THE MOTHER: Your father didn't leave anything, you know that—except debts, I suppose.

THE SON: But the business must be worth something?

THE MOTHER: There isn't any business if there isn't any stock or goods. Can't you understand that?

THE SON (*pondering a moment*): But the company, the name, the clientele—?

THE MOTHER: You can't sell a clientele.

A pause.

THE SON: I've heard you can!

THE MOTHER: Have you been to see a lawyer? (*Pause.*) So that's the way you mourn your father?

THE SON: No, it isn't. —But one thing at a time, you know. . . . Where's my sister and my new brother-in-law?

THE MOTHER: They got back from their honeymoon this morning—. Got themselves a room in a boardinghouse.

THE SON: Where they can at least eat their fill!

THE MOTHER: Always harping on that! Anything wrong with the food you get here?

THE SON: Oh no, Mother! Of course not.

THE MOTHER: Tell me something. Recently, when I had to live separated from him for a time, you and your father were alone here—didn't he ever talk about his business?

THE SON (*engrossed in his book*): No, I can't remember anything special.

THE MOTHER: Then how do you explain why he didn't leave anything behind him when he was making twenty thousand crowns the last few years?

THE SON: I don't know anything about Father's business. He said the house cost a lot. And then he bought all this new furniture recently.

THE MOTHER: Is that what he told you? Do you think he was in debt?

THE SON: I don't know. He had been, but he got out.

THE MOTHER: Then where did the money disappear to? Didn't he make a will? He hated me, that's it. More than once he said he'd cut me off without a cent. I wonder if he could have hidden his savings somewhere? (*Pause.*) Is someone out there?

THE SON: I don't hear anything.

THE MOTHER: All this business about the funeral and the money has made me a little nervous the last couple of days. . . . By the way, you know you'll have to see about getting a room in town before Gerda and her husband move in here.

THE SON: Yes, I know.

THE MOTHER: You don't like him, do you?

THE SON: We don't have much in common.

THE MOTHER: Well, he's a fine boy and very capable. You should force yourself to like him. Might do you good.

THE SON: He doesn't like me. And besides, he was very unkind to Father.

THE MOTHER: And whose fault was that?

THE SON: Father wasn't unkind—

THE MOTHER: Oh, no?

THE SON: I think you're right, there is someone out there!

THE MOTHER: Turn on a couple of lights. But only a couple!

The Son turns on the electric lights. A pause.

Why don't you take your father's portrait into your room? That one on the wall.

THE SON: Why do you want me to?

THE MOTHER: I don't like it. The eyes look so evil.

THE SON: I don't think so.

THE MOTHER: Then take it. If you like it so much, you can have it.

THE SON (*taking the portrait down*): Yes, I just might do that.

A pause.

THE MOTHER: I'm expecting Axel and Gerda at any moment. Do you want to meet them?

THE SON: No, thanks. I'm going to my room. —But I could use a little fire in the stove.

THE MOTHER: We can't afford to burn up our money.

THE SON: I've heard that for twenty years. But we've always been able to afford idiotic trips abroad so you could brag about them. And to eat in restaurants where the check came to a hundred crowns, which is just about the price of four cords of birchwood. Four cords of wood for one lunch!

THE MOTHER: Nonsense!

THE SON: There have been a lot of crazy things going on here, but it's all over now. Except for a final settling of accounts—

THE MOTHER: What do you mean?

THE SON: I mean the inventory, and other things . . .

THE MOTHER: What other things?

THE SON: The debts, the unfinished business . . .

THE MOTHER: Oh.

THE SON: In the meantime, I hope you don't mind if I buy myself some warm clothes?

THE MOTHER: How can you ask that now? It's about time you began thinking about earning something for yourself.

THE SON: When I pass my exams, I—

THE MOTHER: Until you do, you'll have to borrow as everyone else does.

THE SON: Who would lend me anything?

THE MOTHER: Your father's friends.

THE SON: He didn't have any friends. A man who thinks for himself can't afford to have friends—because having friends means belonging to a mutual admiration society.

THE MOTHER: Aren't you the wise one! You must have learned that from your father.

THE SON: He wasn't stupid—although he did some foolish things once in a while.

THE MOTHER: Not really! . . . Tell me, when are you going to get married?

THE SON: Never. Running an escort service for bachelors—being a legalized pimp for some tramp—handing yourself over on a silver platter to be carved up by your best friend—I mean your worst enemy—I'm not that stupid!

THE MOTHER: What *are* you saying? —Oh, go to your room. I've had enough of you for today. You must have been drinking.

THE SON: I have to—a little—all the time. To stop coughing, and to feel a little less hungry.

THE MOTHER: Complaining about the food again?

THE SON: Oh, no, no complaints. Only it's so light, it tastes like air!

THE MOTHER (*stung*): Get out!

THE SON: Or else it's got so much salt and pepper in it, eating it only makes you hungrier. It's like spiced air.

THE MOTHER: You are drunk! Get out of here!

THE SON: Yes, I'm going. . . . There was something I was going to say. . . . But it can wait. . . . Yes. (*He leaves.*)

* * *

> The Mother, restless, paces the floor. Looks through the drawers in the table.

* * *

> The Son-in-Law enters hastily.

THE MOTHER (*greeting him warmly*): At last! You're really here, Axel! I've been longing to see you. But where's Gerda?

THE SON-IN-LAW: She's coming. Well, how are you? Tell me all about yourself.

THE MOTHER: No, you sit down and let me ask the questions first. I haven't seen you since the wedding. —What are you doing back home so soon? You were going to be gone for eight days, and it's only three days since you left.

THE SON-IN-LAW: Oh, it got to be tiresome, you know, after we had talked ourselves out. Being alone together got to be oppressive. And we were so used to having you around, we missed you very much.

THE MOTHER: That's kind of you, Axel. Well, I suppose we three have stuck together through thick and thin, and I believe I can say I have been of some use, don't you think?

THE SON-IN-LAW: Gerda's only a child. She doesn't know how to live. She's prejudiced, and stubborn—like a fanatic sometimes.

THE MOTHER: I know, I know. But tell me, what did you think of the wedding?

THE SON-IN-LAW: It was perfect, absolutely perfect! And my poems, how did you like my poems?

THE MOTHER: The ones you wrote to me, you mean? I don't suppose a mother-in-law ever got such poems on her daughter's wedding day. . . . You recall the one about the pelican that gives its own blood to its young ones? You know, I cried, I really—

THE SON-IN-LAW: Not for long, you didn't. You danced with me, remember? Our dance. Gerda was almost jealous of you.

THE MOTHER: It wouldn't be the first time. She wanted me to come dressed in black—for proper mourning, she said. But I didn't pay any attention to her. Why should I obey my own children?

THE SON-IN-LAW: Don't pay any attention to Gerda. She's crazy sometimes. I only have to look at a woman—

THE MOTHER: What's this? Doesn't she keep you happy?

THE SON-IN-LAW: Happy? How do you mean?

THE MOTHER: It sounds as if you've been quarreling already.

THE SON-IN-LAW: Already? We haven't done anything else since we were engaged. . . . And now I had to tell her I'll have to leave her for a while, since I'm a reserve officer. —You know, it's funny, but I think she likes me less in civvies.

THE MOTHER: Then why not wear your uniform? I have to admit, I hardly recognize you as a civilian. You're a completely different person.

THE SON-IN-LAW: I'm not supposed to wear my uniform except on duty and on parade days.

THE MOTHER: Why not?

THE SON-IN-LAW: Regulations.

THE MOTHER: It's a shame about Gerda in any case. She got engaged to a lieutenant, and she married a bookkeeper.

THE SON-IN-LAW: What do you expect me to do? I have to live. And speaking of that, what have you found out about the business?

THE MOTHER: Quite honestly, nothing much. But I'm beginning to wonder about Frederick.

THE SON-IN-LAW: Wonder what?

THE MOTHER: He talked so strangely just now.

THE SON-IN-LAW: That sheepshead!

THE MOTHER: I've heard that sheep are rather crafty. And I just wonder if there might not be a will or some savings lying around somewhere—

THE SON-IN-LAW: Have you looked?

THE MOTHER: I've searched all his things.

THE SON-IN-LAW: The boy's?

THE MOTHER: Yes, of course. And I look through his wastepaper basket all the time. He writes letters which he tears up—

THE SON-IN-LAW: You're wasting your time. Haven't you looked through the old man's desk?

THE MOTHER: Well, naturally!

THE SON-IN-LAW: I mean carefully. All the drawers?

THE MOTHER: Every one.

THE SON-IN-LAW: But there are always secret drawers in secretaries.

THE MOTHER: I hadn't thought of that.

THE SON-IN-LAW: Then let's take a good look at it.

THE MOTHER: No, you mustn't touch it! It's been sealed by the inventory people.

THE SON-IN-LAW: Can't you get around the seal?

THE MOTHER: No! I don't see how you can.

THE SON-IN-LAW: Yes, you can, if you loosen the boards in the back. Secret drawers are always in the back.

THE MOTHER: You would have to have tools for that.

THE SON-IN-LAW: Not necessarily; it could be managed without.

THE MOTHER: But Gerda mustn't know anything—

THE SON-IN-LAW: Of course not. She'd only go and squeal to her dear brother.

THE MOTHER (*closing the doors*): Let me close the doors just to be safe.

THE SON-IN-LAW (*examining the back of the secretary*): Look, someone has already been in here—the whole back is loose—I can put my whole hand in—

THE MOTHER: It's the boy, he's done it. I told you—I suspected him—.... Hurry, someone's coming.

THE SON-IN-LAW: I can feel some papers in there—

THE MOTHER: Hurry, I can hear someone coming.

THE SON-IN-LAW: A big envelope—

THE MOTHER: Gerda's coming! Give me the papers—quick!

THE SON-IN-LAW (*giving The Mother a large envelope, which she hides*): Take it! Hide it!

* * *

Someone tries to open the door; then there is knocking.

THE SON-IN-LAW: You stupid—! You locked the door. We're caught!

THE MOTHER: Quiet!

THE SON-IN-LAW: You idiot! —Open it! —Or else I will! —Get out of the way! (*He opens the door.*)

THE DAUGHTER (*enters, looking out of sorts*): Why did you lock yourselves in?

THE MOTHER: Aren't you even going to say hello first, my dear child? I haven't seen you since the wedding. Did you have a nice trip? Now tell me all about it. And don't look so gloomy.

THE DAUGHTER (*sits down in a chair, looking dejected*): Why did you lock the door?

THE MOTHER: Because it keeps opening by itself, and I get so tired of nagging at everybody to close it. . . . Now we've got to think about the furniture for your apartment. You're going to live here, aren't you?

THE DAUGHTER: I guess we have to. It doesn't make much difference to me. What do you say, Axel?

THE SON-IN-LAW: I think this will be fine. And your mother won't have it bad at all, since we all get along so well . . .

THE DAUGHTER: Why, where is Mother going to stay?

THE MOTHER: Right here. I'll only have to move in a bed.

THE SON-IN-LAW: Come now, dear, you don't plan on having a bed in the living room?

THE DAUGHTER (*thinking she is being spoken to*): Are you asking me?

THE SON-IN-LAW: No, I—was—asking your mother. . . . But we can arrange that later. We have to help one another out now, and we can live on what Mother will be paying us.

THE DAUGHTER (*brightening*): And she can help me with the housekeeping—

THE MOTHER: Of course, dear child. Only don't ask me to wash the dishes. You know how I hate that.

THE DAUGHTER: Don't be silly! Everything will be all right, as long as I can have my husband to myself. I don't want anybody so much as looking at him. That's what they were doing at that hotel. So we cut the honeymoon short. If anybody tried to take him from me, I'd kill her! I mean it.

THE MOTHER: I think we had better start rearranging the furniture.

THE SON-IN-LAW (*holding The Mother's eyes with his*): Good idea! And Gerda, you can begin in here—

THE DAUGHTER: Why me? I don't like to be left alone in here. I won't feel right until we've moved in completely.

THE SON-IN-LAW: All right, if you're afraid of the dark, then let's all go together.

All three leave.

* * *

The stage remains empty for a while. The wind is blowing outside. One can hear it rattling the windows and howling in the stove. Papers from the writing table fly around the room; a potted palm on the console trembles crazily; a photograph falls from the wall. The voice of The Son is heard: "Mama!" *Shortly thereafter:* "Close the window!" *A pause. The rocking chair begins to rock. The Mother enters, wild with rage, reading a paper that she holds in her hand.*

THE MOTHER (*sees the rocking chair*): What—! The rocking chair—it's moving!

THE SON-IN-LAW (*coming in after her*): What is it? What does it say? For God's sake, let me read it! Is it the will?

THE MOTHER: Close the door before we're blown away! I have to open a window, I can't stand this smell. No, it wasn't the will. It was a letter to the boy, filled with lies about me—and you!

THE SON-IN-LAW: Give it to me!

THE MOTHER: No, it would only poison your mind. I'm going to tear it up. Thank heavens it didn't fall into the boy's hands! (*She tears up the letter and throws it into the stove.*) He rises from his grave and you can't shut him up. He's not dead! I tell you I could never stay here. He wrote that I murdered him. I didn't! He died of a stroke; the doctor certified it. But that isn't all he wrote. Lies, all of it lies! He says I ruined him!—Listen to me, Axel! You must see to it that we leave this apartment at once. I can't stand it here. Promise me!—Look at the chair rocking!

THE SON-IN-LAW: It's the draft from the hall.

THE MOTHER: We have to get away from here! Promise me!

THE SON-IN-LAW: I can't promise that. I've been counting on the inheritance. You hinted at something like that, otherwise I wouldn't have gotten married. Now we have to take things as they are. You can consider me from now on as a swindled son-in-law—and bankrupt! We have to stick together now in order to live. We'll have to pinch pennies, and you'll have to help us.

THE MOTHER: Are you suggesting I'm to be employed as a maid in my own house? Oh, no. Oh, no, you don't!

THE SON-IN-LAW: Necessity knows no—

THE MOTHER: You're contemptible!

THE SON-IN-LAW: Listen, you old—

THE MOTHER: Be a maid to you!

THE SON-IN-LAW: It'll give you a chance to see how your maids have had it, freezing and starving. At least you won't have to do that.

THE MOTHER: I have my annuity—

THE SON-IN-LAW: That wouldn't get you a spare room in an attic! But here it will take care of the rent *if* we take it easy and don't live it up. And if you don't take it easy, I'm leaving.

THE MOTHER: Leave Gerda! You have never loved her—

THE SON-IN-LAW: You know better than I. You tore her out of my heart and my mind, pushed her aside everywhere—except in the bedroom; that was hers at least. And if a baby comes, you'll take that away from her, too. She doesn't know anything yet, doesn't understand anything. But she's going to stop walking in her sleep pretty soon. And when she opens her eyes, watch out!

THE MOTHER: Axel, you know we have to stick together! We mustn't part. I could never live alone. I'll go along with whatever you say. But not the chaise longue—

THE SON-IN-LAW: The chaise longue stays! I don't want to spoil the place by having a bedroom in here. That's final!

THE MOTHER: But let me have another one then—

THE SON-IN-LAW: We can't afford it. That one's pretty enough.

THE MOTHER: My God, it looks like a gory butcher's block!

THE SON-IN-LAW: Oh, shut up. Listen, if you don't want it this way, there's always a lonely room in some attic, and handouts from the church, and the nursing home.

THE MOTHER: All right, you win.

THE SON-IN-LAW: Now you're being sensible.

A pause.

THE MOTHER: But can you imagine that he wrote to his son that he was murdered?

THE SON-IN-LAW: There's more than one way of committing murder. And your way has the advantage of not coming under the law.

THE MOTHER: You mean *our* way. You were in it me. You teased and tormented him and drove him to

THE SON-IN-LAW: He was getting in my way. What did you expect me to do?

THE MOTHER: The only thing I reproach you with is that you lured me away from home. I'll never forget that evening, the first evening in your home, when we sat at that beautiful dinner table, and we could hear those horrible cries from the garden below. They sounded as if they came from the prison or from the madhouse. Do you remember? It was him walking in the garden in the darkness and the rain, crying out in anguish for his lost wife and children.

THE SON-IN-LAW: Why talk about that now? You don't even know if it was him.

THE MOTHER: It said so in his letter!

THE SON-IN-LAW: What does that have to do with us? He was no angel.

THE MOTHER: No, he wasn't. But he had some human feelings, sometimes. More than you, I might say—

THE SON-IN-LAW: Changing sides, are you?

THE MOTHER: Now don't get mad. We have to learn to get along with each other.

THE SON-IN-LAW: Yes, we have to. Like cell mates in a prison.

Hoarse cries from within.

THE MOTHER: What's that? Do you hear? It must be him . . .

THE SON-IN-LAW (*brutally*): Which him?

The Mother listens.

Who is it? . . . The boy! He's been drinking again.

THE MOTHER: Frederick? Oh, yes, of course. But for a moment it sounded just like—like *him*. I thought—. I can't stand much more of this. What's the matter with him?

THE SON-IN-LAW: Go and see! He's probably stinking drunk!

THE MOTHER: That's no way to talk! He's my son in any case.

THE SON-IN-LAW: In every case, yours! (*Taking out his watch.*)

THE MOTHER: Why are you looking at your watch? Aren't you going to stay for supper?

THE SON-IN-LAW: No, thanks. I don't like weak tea and I never touch rancid fish—or pudding. Besides, I have to go to a meeting.

THE MOTHER: What kind of a meeting?

THE SON-IN-LAW: Business that doesn't concern you. Don't tell me you intend to start behaving like a mother-in-law?

THE MOTHER: And do you intend to leave your wife the first night you move into your new home?

THE SON-IN-LAW: Now that's another thing that doesn't concern you.

THE MOTHER: I begin to see what lies ahead for me—and my children. The masks are coming off, aren't they?

THE SON-IN-LAW: That's right. They're coming off.

[2]

Same set. The "Berceuse" from Godard's Jocelyn *is being played within. The Daughter is sitting at the desk.*

A long pause.

THE SON (*enters*): Are you alone?

THE DAUGHTER: Yes. Mama is in the kitchen.

THE SON: Well, where's Axel?

THE DAUGHTER: Oh, he's at some kind of meeting. . . . Sit down and talk to me, Frederick. Keep me company.

THE SON (*sits down*): I don't think we've really spoken to each other before. We always avoided each other. Never had anything in common.

THE DAUGHTER: You were always on Father's side, and I was always on Mother's.

THE SON: Maybe that will change now. Did you really know Father?

THE DAUGHTER: What a strange question. But it's true I only saw him through Mother's eyes.

THE SON: But couldn't you see how fond he was of you?

THE DAUGHTER: Then why did he want me to break off my engagement?

THE SON: Because he saw that your fiancé would never give you the kind of support you need in life.

THE DAUGHTER: And that's what he was punished for — when Mama went away and left him.

THE SON: Wasn't it your boyfriend who talked her into leaving?

THE DAUGHTER: Yes, he and I together! I wanted Father to know how it feels to be separated from the one you love, as he tried to separate me.

THE SON: So you simply shortened his life, you know that. Believe me, he only wanted you to be happy.

THE DAUGHTER: You were with him. — What did he say? How did he take it?

THE SON: I wouldn't know the words to describe his misery.

THE DAUGHTER: What did he say about Mama?

THE SON: Nothing. . . . But after all that I've seen, I'm never going to marry! (*Pause.*) Are *you* happy, Gerda?

THE DAUGHTER: Oh, yes! When you catch the man you've had your eye on, you're happy.

THE SON: Why did he leave you tonight—your first night at home?

THE DAUGHTER: Business. He had to go to a meeting.

THE SON: At a restaurant?

THE DAUGHTER: What do you mean? How do you know?

THE SON: I thought you knew!

THE DAUGHTER (*crying into her handkerchief*): Oh, my God! My God!

THE SON: I'm sorry, I didn't mean to hurt you.

THE DAUGHTER: But you did! So deeply! Oh, I wish I could die!

THE SON: Why did you come back from your honeymoon so soon?

THE DAUGHTER: He was worried about his business. He wanted to see Mama. He hates to be away from her—

They look at each other.

THE SON: I see. (*Pause.*) How was your trip otherwise? Pleasant?

THE DAUGHTER: Oh, yes!

THE SON: My poor Gerda!

THE DAUGHTER: What do you mean?

THE SON: Well, you know Mother's curiosity. She can use a telephone like nobody else.

THE DAUGHTER: I don't understand. Has she been spying?

THE SON: Hasn't she always? She's probably behind one of those doors right now listening to us.

THE DAUGHTER: You always think the worst of Mama.

THE SON: And you always think the best! Why is that? You know what she's like—

THE DAUGHTER: No, I don't! And I don't want to.

THE SON: That's something else—you don't want to know. You probably have your reasons.

THE DAUGHTER: Sh! I know I'm walking in my sleep, I know I am. But I don't want anyone to wake me up. I couldn't live if they did.

THE SON: Don't you think we're all walking in our sleep? Listen, I study law, as you know, and I'm always reading the transcripts of famous trials, cases involving great criminals. And, you know, they can't explain how it happened. They thought they were doing the right thing right up to the moment they got caught. Then they woke up. If they weren't dreaming, at least they must have been sleeping.

THE DAUGHTER: Let me sleep. I know I shall have to wake up sometime, but please let it be a long time from now. Oh how many things there are I don't exactly know but have an inkling of! Do you remember as a child—? They called you evil if you spoke the plain truth. "You're so evil-minded," they always said to me when I told them that something ugly was ugly. So I learned to hold my tongue. Then they began to tell me what a pleasant disposition I had. So then I learned to say things I didn't mean at all. And then I was ready to make my debut.

THE SON: It's best to overlook your neighbor's faults and weaknesses, no doubt of that. But the first thing you know you're flattering and fawning and playing up to people. It's hard to know what to do. But sometimes it's your duty to speak out.

THE DAUGHTER: No, please!

THE SON: All right. I'll be quiet.

Pause.

THE DAUGHTER: No, I'd rather have you talking. But not about what you're thinking! I can hear your thoughts in the silence. When people get together they talk, talk, talk, all the time, just to hide their thoughts. To forget, to benumb themselves. They want to hear all the latest, of course, about the others. But their own affairs they keep concealed.

THE SON: Poor little Gerda!

THE DAUGHTER: Do you know what hurts more than anything in the world? (*Pause.*) To find that everything you've dreamed of really amounts to nothing.

THE SON: That's the truth.

THE DAUGHTER: I'm freezing. Can't we have a little fire?

THE SON: Are you cold, too?

THE DAUGHTER: I've always been cold and hungry.

THE SON: You too! What a strange house! But if I went out and got some wood, what a scene there would be! She wouldn't get over it for a week.

THE DAUGHTER: Maybe a fire has already been laid. Mama sometimes used to lay a fire just to make fools of us.

THE SON (*goes over to the tile stove and opens it*): Well! There actually are a few sticks laid here. (*Pause.*) What on earth is this? A letter, all torn up. Good for starting the fire—

THE DAUGHTER: Frederick, don't light the fire. It would only start a quarrel that would go on forever. Come and sit down, and let's talk some more. Please!

> *The Son crosses over and sits down, putting the torn letter on the table next to him. A pause.*

Do you know why Father hated my husband as he did?

THE SON: Yes. Your Axel came and took away his daughter and his wife and left him sitting all alone. And then the old man noticed that the rest of you were eating better food than he was. You shut yourselves up in the parlor, played music, read books—and always the kind that he didn't like. He was shut out and eaten out of his own home. And so finally he took to hanging around the bars.

THE DAUGHTER: We didn't know what we were doing. . . . Poor Father! It's good to have parents whom everybody respects, with reputations above reproach. I guess we have a lot to be thankful for. . . . Do you remember their silver wedding anniversary? And the wonderful speeches everybody made?

THE SON: I remember. And I thought what a cheap sideshow it was, with everybody celebrating the happy couple who had lived together like cat and dog.

THE DAUGHTER: Frederick!

THE SON: I can't help it. You know as well as I how they lived. Don't you remember the time Mama wanted to jump out the window and we had to hold her back?

THE DAUGHTER: Please, Frederick!

THE SON: I'm sure there were reasons that we don't know about. . . . And when they were separated and I had to watch over the old man, he seemed to want to say something, many times, but the words never got past his lips. . . . I still dream of him sometimes . . .

THE DAUGHTER: I do too. And when I see him in my dreams, he's thirty years old. He looks at me in a friendly way, hinting at something. I don't know quite what. Sometimes Mama is along. But he's not angry with her. Because he always held her dear. Even up to the last, in spite of everything. You remember how beautifully he spoke to her on their silver anniversary, thanking her *in spite of everything*.

THE SON: In spite of everything! That's saying a lot, and yet not enough.

THE DAUGHTER: But it was beautiful! And she did have many merits. She was a good housekeeper.

THE SON: Ah, but was she? That's the question!

THE DAUGHTER: What do you mean?

THE SON: Now look how they stick together! Just so much as mention housekeeping and you're on the same team. What is it? A secret lodge, the Mafia? Even if I ask my dear old friend

Margaret anything about the household finances—if I ask her for instance why you can never get a full meal here, then she, who is always willing to talk your ears off, she shuts up! Shuts up and gets mad! Can you explain that?

THE DAUGHTER (*curtly*): No.

THE SON: It isn't hard to see that you belong to the secret lodge too!

THE DAUGHTER: What on earth do you mean? I don't understand.

THE SON: Sometimes I believe that Father must have fallen a victim to the Mafia, which he probably uncovered.

THE DAUGHTER: Sometimes you talk just like an idiot.

THE SON: I remember Father sometimes used to mention the Mafia as a joke, but toward the end he kept silent.

THE DAUGHTER: It's awful how cold it is here, cold as a tomb.

THE SON: Then let's light the fire, whatever the consequences. (*He picks up the torn letter, absentmindedly. Something catches his eye and he begins to read.*) What is this? (*Pause.*) "To my son!" In Father's handwriting! (*Pause.*) It's to me! (*He reads. He half falls into a chair and continues reading to himself.*)

THE DAUGHTER: What are you reading? What is it?

THE SON: It's awful! (*Pause.*) I can't believe it!

THE DAUGHTER: Tell me, what is it?

> *A pause.*

THE SON: No, it's too much. . . . (*To The Daughter.*) It's a letter from my dead father, written to me. (*Reading on.*) Now I'm beginning to wake up.

> *He throws himself on the chaise longue and writhes in agony. Puts the letter in his pocket. The Daughter kneels beside him.*

THE PELICAN

THE DAUGHTER: What is it, Frederick? Tell me what it is. Frederick, Frederick. Are you ill? Say something, Frederick! Speak to me!

THE SON (*sitting up*): I don't want to live any longer.

THE DAUGHTER: Tell me what it is, Frederick.

THE SON: It's unbelievable. (*He recovers himself and stands up.*)

THE DAUGHTER: Perhaps it's not true.

THE SON (*bristling*): Oh, yes it is! He wouldn't spread lies from his grave.

THE DAUGHTER: He let his imagination get the better of him. He was sick. He didn't know what he was saying.

THE SON: The Mafia! Well, let me tell you! You just listen!

THE DAUGHTER: I think I know it all already. But I won't believe it anyway!

THE SON: I know you don't want to! But here's how it is, all the same. The dear mother who gave us life was nothing but a thief!

THE DAUGHTER: No!

THE SON: She stole from the housekeeping money, she forged bills, she bought the poorest stuff for the highest prices, she had her meals in the kitchen in the morning and let us have what was left over, thinned out and warmed up, she skimmed the cream off the milk—that's why we're poor, miserable children, always sick and hungry. She stole the money for the wood and let us freeze. And when Father found out about her, he warned her, and she promised to be better. But she went right back to her old tricks and even came up with two new ones—Worcestershire sauce and cayenne pepper!

THE DAUGHTER: I don't believe a word of it!

THE SON: The Mafia! —But that isn't the worst, Gerda! Oh, no! That contemptible person who is now your dear husband has never loved you, Gerda. He loves your mother!

THE DAUGHTER: No! No!

THE SON: When Father found out, and when your boyfriend borrowed money from your mother – our mother – he tried to pull a fast one by proposing marriage to you! That's the general idea, you can fill in the details for yourself.

The Daughter cries into her handkerchief.

THE DAUGHTER: I knew this all along – but I didn't want to. I closed my mind to it because it was too awful.

THE SON: What are you going to do now to salvage what's left of your pride?

THE DAUGHTER: Go away.

THE SON: Where?

THE DAUGHTER: I don't know.

THE SON: So you'll stay and see how things develop.

THE DAUGHTER: You can't raise your hand against your own mother. She's like something sacred.

THE SON: Like hell she is!

THE DAUGHTER: Don't talk like that!

THE SON: She's as sly as a fox, but so much in love with herself she can't see farther than her nose.

THE DAUGHTER: Let's run away.

THE SON: Where to? No, we'll stay right here until her darling boy drives her out of the house. – Shh! I think lover-boy is coming home. – Listen, Gerda! Now we two are going to form a secret order of our own. I'll give you the word, our password: "He struck you on your wedding night."

THE DAUGHTER: Yes, remind me of that often, Frederick! Otherwise I'll forget. I want so much to forget.

THE SON: It's all over for us Gerda. No one to believe in, nothing to have faith in. . . . Impossible to forget. . . . Let's live to redeem ourselves, and the memory of Father.

THE DAUGHTER: And see justice done!

THE SON: Justice? You mean revenge!

* * *

The Son-in-Law enters.

THE DAUGHTER (*feigning*): Why, good evening, Axel! Did you have a good time at your meeting? Did they give you anything good?

THE SON-IN-LAW: It was put off.

THE DAUGHTER: You were put out, did you say?

THE SON-IN-LAW: It was put off, I said!

THE DAUGHTER: Oh. —Tell me, are you going to take care of things around the house tonight?

THE SON-IN-LAW: You're in such a good mood tonight, Gerda. Frederick must be delightful company.

THE DAUGHER: Oh, he is. We've been playing secret societies.

THE SON-IN-LAW: You shouldn't play such games. They're dangerous.

THE SON: Then we can play Mafia instead! Or vendetta!

THE SON-IN-LAW (*uneasily*): What are you talking about? What's been going on here? Are you keeping secrets?

THE DAUGHTER: You're not going to tell us your secrets, are you? Maybe you don't have any secrets?

THE SON-IN-LAW: What happened here tonight? Has someone been here?

THE SON: Gerda and I were holding a séance, and we were visited by a departed spirit.

THE SON-IN-LAW: All right, cut the games! You're too cute, the two of you. —But I must say it is very becoming, Gerda, to see you smiling. You're usually so sullen. (*He starts to pat her cheek, but she pulls away.*) Are you afraid of me?

THE DAUGHTER (*stops acting*): Not at all. I may look afraid, but you're wrong. Some gestures speak more plainly than looks do. And if neither the way I act nor the way I look tell you what I'm really feeling, what I say won't tell you anything either.

> *Astonished, The Son-in-Law fumbles at a bookshelf. The Son rises from the rocking chair, which continues to rock until The Mother enters.*

THE SON: Here comes Mother with her oatmeal.

THE SON-IN-LAW: Is it—?

* * *

> *The Mother enters, sees the chair rocking, starts back in fear, but controls herself.*

THE MOTHER: I've made something for supper. Anyone interested?

THE SON-IN-LAW: No thanks. What is it? Oatmeal? Give it to the dogs. Bran meal? Put it on your boils.

THE MOTHER: I can't help it. We have to economize.

THE SON-IN-LAW: Not with twenty thousand a year you don't.

THE SON: You do if you lend it to those who don't pay it back!

THE SON-IN-LAW: What are you talking about? Are you nuts?

THE SON: Maybe I have been.

THE MOTHER: Are you coming or not?

THE DAUGHTER: Come, let's go and eat! Don't look so glum. Come with me and you shall have steaks, sandwiches, whatever your hearts desire.

THE MOTHER: Where will they get them? From you?

THE DAUGHTER: Yes, from me! It's my house!

THE MOTHER: Listen to her! Found your tongue, have you?

THE DAUGHTER (*gesturing toward the door*): Gentlemen, if you please!

THE SON-IN-LAW (*to The Mother*): What the hell's going on?

THE MOTHER: I think I smell a rat!

THE SON-IN-LAW: I think you're right!

THE DAUGHTER: Come, gentlemen!

They all start to leave.

THE MOTHER (*to The Son-in-Law*): Didn't you see the chair rocking? *His* chair rocking?

THE SON-IN-LAW: No, I didn't. I saw something else!

[3]

Same set. A waltz, "Il me disait" by Ferrari, is being played on the piano offstage. The Daughter is sitting, reading a book.

THE MOTHER (*coming in*): Do you recognize it?

THE DAUGHTER: The waltz? Of course.

THE MOTHER: Your wedding waltz. I danced it all night long.

THE DAUGHTER: You? —Where is Axel?

THE MOTHER: How should I know?

THE DAUGHTER: It's like that, is it? Have you quarreled already?

A pause. They exchange glances.

THE MOTHER: What are you reading, my child?

THE DAUGHTER: The cookbook. Can you tell me why it doesn't say how long you're supposed to cook anything?

THE MOTHER (*evasively*): It varies so much, you see. It's a matter of taste. Some like it one way, some another.

THE DAUGHTER: I don't understand that. Food should be served freshly cooked; otherwise it's only warmed-up food, which means spoiled. Yesterday, for example, you roasted a small game bird for three hours. The first hour the whole apartment was filled with a wonderful gamey smell. Then it became quiet in the kitchen. And when the food was finally served all the aroma was gone and it tasted like air. How do you explain that?

THE MOTHER (*embarrassed*): I don't understand at all.

THE DAUGHTER: Then tell me what happened to the sauce and the gravy. Where did that disappear to? Who ate that up?

THE MOTHER: I have no idea what you're talking about.

THE DAUGHTER: I've been asking myself some questions lately, and now I know a lot about a great many things.

THE MOTHER (*turning on her sharply*): I know you do. But you can't teach me anything I don't already know. I could show you a thing or two about housekeeping —

THE DAUGHTER: Like using Worcestershire sauce and cayenne pepper? —I know that one already. And preparing for friends dishes you know they don't like so there will be plenty left over for the next day. And inviting people in when you see the pantry is filled with leftovers — oh, I know all those tricks, so from now on I'm going to be in charge here!

THE MOTHER (*furious*): You mean I'm going to be your maid?

THE DAUGHTER: I, yours; and you, mine. We'll help each other. —Here comes Axel.

* * *

THE SON-IN-LAW (*enters with a heavy cane in his hand*): Well, how do you like the chaise longue?

THE MOTHER: All right, I guess.

THE SON-IN-LAW (*threateningly*): You mean you don't like it? What's the matter with it?

THE MOTHER: I think I understand.

THE SON-IN-LAW: Good for you! And while I think of it,

since Gerda and I never get enough to eat in this house, we intend to eat by ourselves from now on.

THE MOTHER: And what about me?

THE SON-IN-LAW: Why, you're as big as a barrel. You don't need much. In fact, you should reduce a little bit for your health's sake, as we've had to do. —And listen, while I'm thinking of it, you go out for a moment, Gerda; and in the meantime, Mother can start a big warm fire in the stove for us.

THE MOTHER (*trembling with rage*): There's wood there—

THE SON-IN-LAW: Oh, but just a few sticks. Now I want you to go out and get some more. Fill up the whole stove.

THE MOTHER (*hesitating*): Do you want to burn up money?

THE SON-IN-LAW: No, but wood doesn't do us any good unless we do burn it, now does it? Get going! March!

The Mother hesitates.

One. Two . . . three! (*Strikes the table with his cane.*)

THE MOTHER: I don't think there's any wood left.

THE SON-IN-LAW: Either you're lying or you've stolen the money. A whole cord was ordered the day before yesterday!

THE MOTHER: Now I see what you're really like.

THE SON-IN-LAW (*sitting in the rocking chair*): You would have seen that long ago, if your age and experience hadn't taken advantage of my youth and innocence. Snap to it! The wood— or—else—(*Raises his cane.*)

The Mother goes out. Returns shortly with the wood.

Now let's have a real fire. Nothing halfway. One, two, three!

THE MOTHER: How much you're like the old man now, sitting in his rocking chair!

THE SON-IN-LAW: Light it!

THE MOTHER (*controlling her rage*): I will, I will.

THE SON-IN-LAW: Now you stay here and keep your eye on the fire, while we go into the dining room and eat.

THE MOTHER: And what am I supposed to eat?

THE SON-IN-LAW: The oatmeal Gerda put out for you in the kitchen.

THE MOTHER: With blue skim milk?

THE SON-IN-LAW: Why not? You devoured all the cream. It's only fitting. And just!

THE MOTHER (*hollowly, dully*): I'm leaving here. I'm getting out.

THE SON-IN-LAW: You can't. I'll lock you in.

THE MOTHER (*whispering*): Then I'll throw myself out the window!

THE SON-IN-LAW: As you wish! You should have done that long ago. You would have spared the lives of four people. —Now light it. Blow on it! That's better. Now you sit right there until we come back.

He leaves.

* * *

A pause. The Mother stops the chair from rocking; listens at the door; and then she takes some of the wood from the stove and hides it under the chaise longue. The Son enters, somewhat drunk. The Mother is startled.

THE MOTHER: Is it you?

THE SON (*sitting in the rocking chair*): Yes, just me.

THE MOTHER: How do you feel?

THE SON: Terrible. I won't last much longer.

THE MOTHER: That's just your imagination. —Don't rock like that! —Look at me, I've reached a certain—well, respectable age—although I've worked and slaved and done my duty to my children and my home. Now haven't I?

THE SON: Ha! Like the pelican, which does not give its heart's blood. The zoology books say it's all a lie.

THE MOTHER: If you've anything to complain about, out with it!

THE SON: Listen, Mother, if I were sober, I couldn't answer you honestly because I wouldn't have the nerve. But now I'm going to tell you that I have read Father's letter, the one you stole and threw into the stove.

THE MOTHER: Letter? What do you mean, what letter?

THE SON: Always lying! I remember when you first taught me how to lie. I was hardly old enough to talk. Remember?

THE MOTHER: No, I don't remember anything of the kind! —Stop rocking!

THE SON: Not remember the first time you told lies about me? When I was little? I had hidden myself under the piano, when one of my aunts came to call on you. You sat and lied to her for three hours straight, and I had to listen to it all.

THE MOTHER: That's a lie!

THE SON: Do you want to know why I'm so utterly worthless? Because I was never breast-fed. All I got was a nursemaid with a glass bottle. And when I was a little older, she took me along with her to her sister, who was a prostitute. And there I got to see all the most secret, most intimate scenes, the kind that children are ordinarily treated to only by dog owners on the street in the spring and fall. When I told you about it—I was only four years old—when I told you what I had seen in that house of sin, you said it was a lie, and you struck me for lying, but I was telling the truth. This encouraged the nursemaid—she thought you approved—so she initiated me—at the age of five—into all the secrets. Five years old. (*He starts to cry.*) And then I began to get cold and hungry, like Father and the rest of us. I never knew until today that you stole the housekeeping money and the wood money. —Look at me, pelican. Look at Gerda, with her flat chest.

How you murdered my father you know as well as I do—how you dragged him down to the depths of despair, a crime that isn't punishable by law. And how you murdered my sister you know better than anyone. But now she knows it too!

THE MOTHER: Stop rocking, will you! —What does she know?

THE SON: What you know and what I can't bring myself to say. (*Sobbing.*) It's terrible that I've said what I have. But I had to. When I sober up, I'll kill myself. I can feel it. That's why I keep on drinking. I don't dare sober up.

THE MOTHER: Tell me some more lies.

THE SON: Father once said in anger that you were the greatest fraud ever perpetrated by nature. He said that you didn't learn to talk like other children; you learned to lie from the first word. He said that you always shirked your duties. Parties came first: I remember when Gerda was virtually dying, you went off that evening to see an operetta. I remember your very words: "Life is sad enough without making it any sadder." And that summer, for three whole months, when you were in Paris with Father, going to parties while the family was going into debt, Gerda and I had to live shut up with two maids in this apartment. And in our parents' bedroom a fireman made himself at home with the housemaid, and the marriage bed rocked to their lovemaking.

THE MOTHER: Why haven't you told me this before?

THE SON: You have forgotten that I did tell you, just as you have forgotten that I was whipped for tattling—or lying, to use your other word for it. As soon as you heard an honest word, you called it a lie.

THE MOTHER (*paces the room like a caged tiger*): I've never heard a son say such things to his own mother!

THE SON: Yes, isn't it strange? Entirely contrary to nature. Don't tell me. But it had to come out sometime. You went about as if you were asleep. And no one could wake you up, so you couldn't change your ways. Father said that even if they stretched you on the rack, no one could make you admit a simple fault or confess you ever told a lie.

THE MOTHER: Father! Father! Do you think he was so perfect?

THE SON: He had great failings, but not in his relations with his wife and children. —And there are other secrets in your marriage that I have guessed, suspected, but never wanted to admit even to myself. Secrets that Father took with him to his grave—partly!

THE MOTHER: Have you said all you're going to say?

THE SON: Yes. I'm going out for a drink. . . . I could never pass my exams. I could never be a lawyer. I don't believe in the legal system. The laws must have been passed by thieves and murderers for the benefit of criminals. One truthful witness proves nothing, but two false witnesses is proof positive. At noon I've got a clear-cut case; at twelve-thirty I've lost it. One slip of the pen, one missing marginal comment, can put a blameless man behind bars. If I take pity on some scamp, he sues *me* for defamation of character. I tell you my contempt for life, humanity, society, and myself is so boundless, I wouldn't raise my little finger to go on living. (*Goes toward the door.*)

THE MOTHER: Don't go!

THE SON: Afraid of the dark?

THE MOTHER: I'm a little nervous.

THE SON: That follows.

THE MOTHER: That chair drives me insane. It always sounded like two knives being whetted when he rocked in it . . . and hacked at my heart.

THE SON: Don't tell me you have one!

THE MOTHER: Don't go! I can't stay here. Axel is so cruel!

THE SON: I thought so too until recently. Now I believe he's only the victim of your vicious tendencies—the young man who was seduced.

THE MOTHER: You must keep very bad company!

THE SON: Bad company? What other kind have I ever kept!

THE MOTHER: Please don't go!

THE SON: What good can I do here? I would only torture you to death with my talk.

THE MOTHER: Please don't go!

THE SON: Are you waking up?

THE MOTHER: Yes, I'm waking up. As if out of a deep, deep sleep. It's terrifying! Why couldn't someone wake me before?

THE SON: Since no one could, I guess it was impossible. And if it was impossible, then you weren't responsible.

THE MOTHER: Yes, that's true! That's true!

THE SON: I suppose it couldn't possibly be any other way.

THE MOTHER (*kissing his hand servilely*): Yes, yes. Tell me more!

THE SON: I can't, I can't. —Yes, one thing more: I beg you, don't stay here. You would only make the bad worse.

THE MOTHER: You are right. I shall go—away from here!

THE SON: Poor Mother!

THE MOTHER: Do you take pity on me?

THE SON (*crying*): Yes, of course I do! How many times haven't I said of you, "Her heart is so black, I feel sorry for her!"

THE MOTHER: Thank you, Frederick, thank you. —Go now.

THE SON: It's hopeless, isn't it?

THE MOTHER: Yes, there's no hope at all.

THE SON: That's right. . . . No hope at all! (*He leaves.*)

* * *

A pause. The Mother alone. Stands with her arms crossed over her bosom a long time. Then she goes to the window, opens it, and looks down. Moves back into the room and prepares to leap out the window. But changes her mind when she hears three knocks on the door at the rear.

THE MOTHER: Who is it? What was that? (*She closes the window.*) Come in.

The rear door opens.

Is someone there?

The Son can be heard bawling within the apartment.

It's him—in the garden! Isn't he dead? What shall I do? Where can I go?

She hides behind the secretary. The wind begins to blow as before; the papers fly around.

Close the window, Frederick!

A flowerpot is blown down.

Close the window! I'm freezing to death and the fire is dying in the stove!

She lights all the electric lights and closes the door, which is immediately blown open again. The chair rocks in the wind. She goes around and around the room, finally throwing herself headlong on the chaise longue, burying her face in the pillows.

* * *

"Il me disait" is played within. The Mother lies as before on the chaise longue, her face hidden. The Daughter enters, with the oatmeal on a tray. She sets it down. She turns off all the electric lights except one.

THE MOTHER (*awakens and sits up*): Don't turn off the lights!

THE DAUGHTER: We have to economize.

THE MOTHER: You came back soon.

THE DAUGHTER: Yes, he didn't think it very amusing when you weren't around.

THE MOTHER: Well, thank you!

THE DAUGHTER: Here's your supper.

THE MOTHER: I'm not hungry.

THE DAUGHTER: Oh, but you are hungry, you just won't eat oatmeal.

THE MOTHER: Yes, I do—sometimes.

THE DAUGHTER: No, never! But I don't care about that. This is for every time you smirked and smiled as you tortured us with your oatmeal. You reveled in our suffering. You cooked the same slop for the dogs in the backyard.

THE MOTHER: I can't eat blue milk. It gives me chills.

THE DAUGHTER: You always skimmed the cream for your morning coffee! Now help yourself! (*She serves the oatmeal on a small table.*) Eat! I want to watch you!

THE MOTHER: I cannot!

THE DAUGHTER (*bends down and takes some of the wood from under the chaise longue*): If you don't eat, I'll show Axel you've been stealing wood.

THE MOTHER: Axel loves my company—he won't hurt me. Do you remember how he danced with me? *"Il me disait!"* There it is! (*She hums the second refrain, which is now being played.*)

THE DAUGHTER: How can you have the nerve to remind me of that outrage!

THE MOTHER: He sent me a bouquet of flowers, with a card.

THE DAUGHTER: That's enough!

THE MOTHER: Shall I tell you what the card said? I know it by heart. . . . "In Ginnistan. Ginnistan is the Persian Garden of Paradise, where the fairest peris live on fragrances. And peris are genii or spirits, so created that the longer they live, the younger they grow . . . "

THE DAUGHTER: Oh, my God, do you think you're a peri?!

THE MOTHER: Yes. He said I was. And your Uncle Victor has proposed to me. What would you say if I got married again?

THE DAUGHTER: Poor Mother! You're still asleep, as we all were. But will you never wake up? Don't you see how everybody laughs at you? Don't you understand it when Axel insults you?

THE MOTHER: Insults me? I have always found him to be more polite to me than to you.

THE DAUGHTER: Even when he raised his cane against you?

THE MOTHER: Against me? That was against you, my dear child!

THE DAUGHTER: Mama, Mama, have you gone out of your mind?

THE MOTHER: He missed me this evening. We have so much to talk about. He's the only one who understands me. And you're only a child, after all . . .

THE DAUGHTER (*taking The Mother by the shoulders and skaking her*): For God's sake, wake up!

THE MOTHER: You're not full-grown yet, not mature. But I'm your mother, I've nourished you with my life's blood.

THE DAUGHTER: No, you gave me a bottle and stuck a rubber in my mouth. I had to go to the cupboard and steal. But there was nothing there except stale rye bread, which I ate with mustard. And when that burned my throat, I cooled it with vinegar. The vinegar bottle and the bread box – that was the pantry for me!

THE MOTHER: You see! Even as a child you were stealing! Oh, how nice! And you're not even ashamed to tell me about it! What kind of children have I sacrificed myself for?

THE DAUGHTER (*crying*): I could forgive you for everything but not for taking my life from me, never. Yes, he was my life, because with him I first began to live.

THE MOTHER: Can I help it if he preferred me? He probably found me – how shall I say? – more amiable. He had much better taste than your father, who didn't appreciate me until he had rivals, and then —

There are three knocks on the door.

Who is that knocking?

THE DAUGHTER: Don't you dare say anything unkind about Father! I don't think my life will be long enough for me to make up for what I did to him. But you shall have to pay for it — for setting me up against him. Do you remember when I was still a very small child how you taught me to say ugly, insinuating things to him that I didn't understand? He had sense enough not to punish me for rubbing salt into his wounds because he knew who had put him up to it. Do you remember how you taught me to lie to him? I would tell him I needed money for schoolbooks, and when we had wormed the money out of him, we split it. How can I ever forget all the lies in the past? Isn't there some drug that wipes out memories without snuffing out life? If only I had the strength to escape. But I'm like Frederick. We're weak, helpless sacrifices — your sacrifices. You with your heart of stone, you couldn't suffer for your own sins!

THE MOTHER: And what do you suppose my childhood was like? Have you any idea what an ugly home I had, what evil things I learned there? It's all inherited —. From whom? From generation to generation. From the first parents, it says in children's books, and that seems to make sense. So don't blame me, and I won't blame my parents, who won't blame theirs, and so on and on. Besides, it's just as horrible in all families, except that outsiders don't get to see it.

THE DAUGHTER: If that's true, I don't care to live. And if I'm forced to, I'd prefer to walk deaf and blind through this miserable existence, hoping for a better life to come . . .

THE MOTHER: You're too sensitive, too delicate, my dear child. When you have a baby, there will be other things to think about.

THE DAUGHTER: I'll never have any children.

THE MOTHER: How do you know?

THE DAUGHTER: The doctor has told me.

THE MOTHER: He's mistaken.

THE DAUGHTER: There you go making up lies again! —I'm sterile, stunted. Don't you understand? I, like Frederick! —I don't want to go on living.

THE MOTHER: Oh, how you talk!

THE DAUGHTER: If I could only do the cruel things I want to do, you—you wouldn't exist anymore! Why should it be so difficult to be cruel? When I lift my hand against you, I only hurt myself!

> *The music stops suddenly. The Son is heard bawling within.*

THE MOTHER: He's been drinking again!

THE DAUGHTER: What else can he do? Poor Frederick!

* * *

THE SON (*enters, noticeably drunker*): There's . . . smoke . . . I think . . . coming from—the kitchen . . .

THE MOTHER: What? . . . Smoke?

THE SON: I—think—I think there's—a fire!

THE MOTHER: A fire? What are you saying?

THE SON: I—I think—I think it's all on fire! The whole house!

THE MOTHER (*rushes to the rear of the stage and opens the door. The bright red glow of fire confronts her*): Fire! —How can we get out?! —I don't want to burn! —I don't want to burn! (*She rushes around in distraction.*)

THE DAUGHTER (*taking her brother in her arms*): Frederick! Run, the fire is on top of us! Run!

THE SON: I haven't the strength.

THE DAUGHTER: Escape, Frederick! You must!

THE SON: Where to? . . . No, I don't care to.

THE MOTHER: I'd rather go through the window! (*She opens the balcony door and throws herself out.*)

THE DAUGHTER: Oh, God in heaven, help us!

THE SON: It was the only way!

THE DAUGHTER: You did this!

THE SON: Yes, what could I do? —There was no other way. —Was there any other? Was there?

THE DAUGHTER: No. Everything had to burn up, otherwise we could never get out of here. Hold me in your arms, Frederick, hold me tight, dear brother! I'm happier than I've ever been before. It's getting light, poor Mama, who was so mean, so mean . . .

THE SON: Dear sister, poor Mama, do you feel how warm it is, how wonderful, I'm no longer cold, listen to it crackling out there, everything old is burning up, everything old and mean and evil and ugly . . .

THE DAUGHTER: Hold me close, dear brother, we're going to be burned, we'll smother in smoke, doesn't it smell good? That's the palm plants burning and Papa's laurel wreath from the university—now the linen closet is burning, smell the lavender, and now, now the roses! Dear little brother! Don't be afraid, it's soon over, dearest, dearest, don't fall, poor Mama! who was so mean! Hold me tighter, squeeze me, as Papa used to say! It's like Christmas, when we got to eat in the kitchen, dipping into all the pots, the only day we got to eat our fill, as Papa used to say. Smell, oh, smell, it's perfume, it's the cupboard burning, with the tea and the coffee, and all the spices, and the cinnamon, and the cloves . . .

THE SON (*in ecstasy*): Is it summer? The clover's in bloom, summer vacation is beginning. Remember when we ran down to the steamboats and clapped their sides, fresh with paint and waiting for us, how happy Papa was then, this is really living, he said, and we threw away our schoolbooks! This is how it should always be, he said. It was he who was the pelican, he picked himself clean for us, he always had baggy pants and dirty collars, while we went around like little aristocrats. . . . Gerda, hurry up! Come on, will you, the boat bells are ringing, and Mama's sitting in the salon, no she's not here, poor Mama! She's not with us, did we leave her on the shore? Where is she? I don't see her anywhere. It's no fun without Mama. There she comes! —Now it's summer again!

> *A pause. The door at the rear opens. The glow is a strong, vivid red. The Son and The Daughter sink to the floor.*

CURTAIN

Strindberg's Plays

Strindberg's Plays

Fritänkaren (The Freethinker), 1869*
Hermione, 1869–70
I Rom (In Rome), 1870
Den fredlöse (The Outlaw), 1871
Mäster Olof (Master Olof), prose version, summer 1872
Mäster Olof, in verse, 1875–76. Epilogue probably written 1877
Anno fyrtioåtta (1848), 1876–77
Gillets hemlighet (The Secret of the Guild), 1879–80
Lycko-Pers resa (The Travels of Lucky Peter), 1882
Herr Bengts hustru (Sir Bengt's Wife), summer 1882
Marodörer (Marauders), 1886. Revised in collaboration with Axel Lundegård as *Kamraterna (Comrades)*, 1887
Fadren (The Father), January–February 1887
Fröken Julie (Miss Julie), summer 1888
Fordringsägare (Creditors), summer 1888
Den starkare (The Stronger), December 1888–January 1889
Paria (Pariah), January 1889
Hemsöborna (The People of Hemsö), January–February 1889. Adapted by Strindberg from his novel of the same name.
Samum (Simoom), February–March 1889
Himmelrikets nycklar (Keys to the Kingdom of Heaven), autumn 1891–February 1892
Första varningen (The First Warning), February–March 1892
Debet och kredit (Debit and Credit), February–March 1892
Inför döden (Facing Death), March–April 1892
Moderskärlek (A Mother's Love), April–May 1892
Leka med elden (Playing with Fire), August–September, 1892
Bandet (The Bond), August–September 1892
Till Damaskus, Part I *(To Damascus)*, January–March 1898
Till Damaskus, Part II, summer 1898
Advent, November–December 1898
Brott och brott (Crimes and Crimes), January–February 1899

*Dates correspond to year of composition.

Folkungasagan (Saga of the Folkungs), January–April 1899
Gustav Vasa, April–June 1899
Erik XIV, summer 1899
Gustav Adolf, September 1899–March 1900
Midsommar (Midsummer), summer 1900
Kaspers fet-tisdag (Punch's Shrove Tuesday), September 1900
Påsk (Easter), autumn 1900
Dödsdansen, Part I *(The Dance of Death)*, October 1900
Dödsdansen, Part II, December 1900
Kronbruden (The Bridal Crown), August 1900–January 1901
Svanevit (Swanwhite), February–March 1901
Karl XII (Charles XII), spring 1901
Till Damaskus, Part III, February–September 1901
Engelbrekt, August–September 1901
Kristina (Queen Christina), September 1901
Ett drömspel (A Dream Play), September–November 1901
Gustav III, February–March 1902
Holländarn (The Flying Dutchman), not completed, July 1902
Näktergalen i Wittenberg (The Nightingale in Wittenberg), August–September 1903
Genom öknar till arvland, eller Moses (Through the Wilderness to the Land of Their Fathers, or Moses), September 1903
Hellas, eller Sokrates (Hellas, or Socrates), October 1903
Lammet och vilddjuret, eller Kristus (The Lion and the Lamb, or Christ), October–November 1903
Oväder (Storm Weather), January–February 1907
Brända tomten (The Burned House), February 1907
Spöksonaten (The Ghost Sonata), February–March 1907
Toten-Insel (The Isle of the Dead), a fragment, April 1907
Pelikanen (The Pelican), May–June 1907
Siste riddaren (The Last Knight), August 1908
Abu Cassems tofflor (Abu Cassem's Slippers), August–September 1908
Riksföreståndaren (The Regent), September 1908
Bjälbo-Jarlen (The Earl of Bjälbo), autumn 1908
Svarta handsken (The Black Glove), November–December 1908
Stora landsvägen (The Highway), spring 1909

Selected Readings

Selected Readings

SURVEYS OF THE LIFE AND WORKS

Campbell, G. A. *Strindberg*. London, 1933.
Gustafson, Alrik. *A History of Swedish Literature*. Minneapolis, 1961.
Johnson, Walter. *August Strindberg*. Boston, 1978.
Lagercrantz, Olof. *August Strindberg*. Translated by Anselm Hollo. New York, 1984.
Lamm, Martin. *August Strindberg*. Translated and edited by Harry G. Carlson. New York, 1971.
Lind-af-Hageby, L. *August Strindberg*. London, n.d.
McGill, V. J. *August Strindberg, the Bedeviled Viking*. New York, 1930.
Meyer, Michael. *Strindberg*. New York, 1985.
Mortensen, Brita M. E. and Downs, Brian W. *Strindberg: An Introduction*. Cambridge, 1949.
Ollén, Gunnar. *August Strindberg*. Translated by Peter Tirner. New York, 1972.
Sprigge, Elizabeth. *The Strange Life of August Strindberg*. New York, 1949.
Steene, Birgitta. *August Strindberg: An Introduction to His Major Works*. Atlantic Highlands, N.J., 1982. (A revised edition of *The Greatest Fire: A Study of August Strindberg*. Carbondale, 1973.)
Uddgren, Gustaf. *Strindberg the Man*. Translated by Axel Johan Uppvall. Boston, 1920.

ON STRINDBERG'S DRAMATIC WORKS

Bentley, Eric. *The Playwright as Thinker*. New York, 1946. Paperback edition, revised: New York, 1955.
Blackwell, Marilyn Johns, editor. *Structures of Influence: A Comparative Approach to August Strindberg*. Chapel Hill, 1981.
Brustein, Robert. *The Theatre of Revolt*. Boston, 1964.
Carlson, Harry G. *Strindberg and the Poetry of Myth*. Berkeley, 1982.
Huneker, James. *Iconoclasts: A Book of Dramatists*. New York, 1905.
Reinert, Otto, editor. *Strindberg: A Collection of Critical Essays*. Englewood Cliffs, N.J., 1971.
Smedmark, Carl Reinhold, editor. *Essays on Strindberg*. Stockholm, 1966.
Sprinchorn, Evert. *Strindberg as Dramatist*. New Haven, 1982.
Törnqvist, Egil. *Strindbergian Drama*. Atlantic Highlands, N.J., 1982.
Valency, Maurice. *The Flower and the Castle*. New York, 1963.
Ward, John. *The Social and Religious Plays of Strindberg*. London, 1980.
Williams, Raymond. *The Drama from Ibsen to Eliot*. London, 1953.

SPECIALIZED STUDIES

Andersson, Hans. *Strindberg's Master Olof and Shakespeare*. Uppsala, 1952.
Bergman, G. M. "Strindberg and the Intima Teatern," *Theatre Research/ Recherches Théâtrales*, vol. 9, no. 1 (1967), pp. 14–47.
Berman, Greta. "Strindberg: Painter, Critic, Modernist," *Gazette des Beaux-Arts*, vol. 86 (1975), pp. 113–22.
Borland, Harold H. *Nietzsche's Influence on Swedish Literature with Special Reference to Strindberg, Ola Hansson, Heidenstam and Fröding*. Göteborg, 1956.
Brandell, Gunnar. *Strindberg in Inferno*. Translated by Barry Jacobs. Cambridge, Mass., 1974.
Bulman, Joan. *Strindberg and Shakespeare*. London, 1933.
Dahlström, Carl Enoch William Leonard. *Strindberg's Dramatic Expressionism*. Ann Arbor, 1930.
Dittmar, Reidar. *Eros and Psyche: Strindberg and Munch in the 1890s*. Ann Arbor, 1982.
Johannesson, Eric O. *The Novels of August Strindberg*. Berkeley, 1968.
Johnson, Walter. *Strindberg and the Historical Drama*. Seattle, 1963.
Kauffman, George B. "August Strindberg's Chemical and Alchemical Studies," *Journal of Chemical Education*, vol. 60, no. 7 (July 1983), pp. 584–90.
Madsen, Børge Gedsø. *Strindberg's Naturalistic Theatre: Its Relation to French Naturalism*. Seattle, 1962.
Marker, Frederick J. and Marker, Lise-Lone. *The Scandinavian Theatre*. Oxford, 1975.
Meidal, Björn. *Från profet till folktribun. Strindberg och Strindbergsfejden 1910-12*. Stockholm, 1982. (English summary, pp. 390–403). On Strindberg's last years.
Palmblad, Harry V. E. *Strindberg's Conception of History*. New York, 1927.
Sprinchorn, Evert. "Strindberg and the Psychiatrists," *Literature and Psychology*, vol. 14, nos. 3-4 (1964), pp. 128–37. (Comment and reply by Theodore Lidz and Harry Bergholz in the following issue.)
Sprinchorn, Evert. Introduction to Strindberg, *Inferno, Alone, and Other Writings*. New York, 1968.
Stockenström, Göran. *Ismael i öknen. Strindberg som mystiker*. Uppsala, 1972. (English summary pp. 451–82.) On the religious and mystical thought in the post-Inferno works.
Uhl, Frida. *Marriage with Genius*. London, 1937. On Strindberg's second marriage.

FURTHER READING

Bryer, Jackson R. "Strindberg 1951-1962: A Bibliography," *Modern Drama*, vol. 5, no. 3 (December 1962), pp. 269–75.
Gustafson, Alrik. Bibliographical guide in his *History of Swedish Literature*, pp. 601–9.

Lindström, Göran. "Strindberg Studies 1915–1962," *Scandinavica*, vol. 2, no. 1 (May 1963), pp. 27–50.

Steene, Birgitta. "August Strindberg in America, 1963–1979: A Bibliographical Assessment," in *Structures of Influence. A Comparative Approach to August Strindberg*, edited by Marilyn Johns Blackwell, pp. 256–75.

Evert Sprinchorn, professor of drama at Vassar College, is the author of *Strindberg as Dramatist*, editor and co-translator of Strindberg's *Chamber Plays* (revised edition, Minnesota, 1981), and translator of several of the dramatist's autobiographical works. He has also edited Ibsen's letters and Wagner's writings on music and drama.